THE TRIPLE

TANTRA

THE TRIPLE
TANTRA

by

Panchen Ngawang Choedak

translated and annotated by

Lama Choedak Rinpoche

Foreword by

H.H. Sakya Trizin

GORUM PUBLICATIONS

Canberra, Australia 2018

Published in Australia in 2018 by
Gorum Publications
Sakya Losal Choe Dzong
Tibetan Buddhist Society of Canberra
PO Box 3430 Manuka,

Canberra, ACT 2603
Australia

Website: www.sakya.com.au
Email: mail@sakya.com.au

Lamdre: the essence of the elegant teachings of the Triple Tantra, translated and annotated by Lama Choedak Rinpoche

First Edition: Printed 1997 by Gorum Publications

Reformatted and redesigned in 2018.

ISBN 0 9587085 1 7

1. Lam-'bras (Sa-skya-pa) 2. Vajrayana I. Yuthok, Lama Choedak

BQ7672.Y88 1997   294.3'44

ISBN 0 9587085 1 7

TABLE OF CONTENTS

PART TWO

THE ESSENCE OF THE ELEGANT TEACHINGS
OF THE THREE TANTRAS

SECTION ONE: MEDITATING ON THE VIEW THROUGH
THE CAUSE TANTRA

ABBREVIATIONS

BA	Blue Annals
BEFS	Biography of Eighty-Four Saints
BHB	Bu-ston's History of Buddhism
BL	Buddha's Lions
BLG	Blossoming Lotus Grove: A Lamdre History
CSP	Catursiti-siddha-pravrtti
CWGMS	The Collected Works of the Great Masters of Sakya
CWJT	The Collected Works of Jo-nang Taranatha
DHM	The Dynastic History of Magadha
EFS	Eighty-Four Siddhas
EMRGS	The Essential Moon's Rays For Generation Stage
FGSD	The Flourish of the Great Secret Doctrine: A Lamdre History
FHWT	Five Historical Works of Taranatha
FS	The Feast For Scholars: A History of Buddhism
GGAL	The Golden Garland Annals of Lineages
HBG	History of Buddhism In Gujarat
HIG	Hagiography of The Indian Guru [Virupa]
HMSIL	The History of Medieval School of Indian Logic
HRPDBI	History of Rise, Progress and Downfall of Buddhism in India
HS	Hagiography of Saroruha
HST	History of Sakya Tradition
HT	Hevajra Tantra
IBE	An Introduction to Buddhist Esotericism
IPLS	Indian Pandits in the Land of Snow
ISRD	Illuminating Sun's Rays of the Doctrine: A Lamdre History

ITB	Indo-Tibetan Buddhism
LLM	The Lives and the Legends of the Mahāsiddhas
LMT	The Life of Marpa The Translator
NU	The Nalanda University
OCES	The Ocean of Collected Elegant Sayings: A Lamdre History
OWB	The Ocean of Wondrous Biographies: A Lamdre History
PHT	Political History of Tibet
PPCT	Power-Places of Central Tibet
PTC	Pad-ma dkar-po's Tibetan Chronicle
SIL	The Seven Instruction Lineages
SIL. tr.	The Seven Instruction Lineages Translated
SLLS	Sakya Lam 'bras Literature Series (31 Vols.)
SPS	Satapitaka Series
TCTC	Tohoku Catalogue of Tibetan Canons
TED	Tibetan English Dictionary (Das, Sarat Candra)
THB	Taranatha's History of Buddhism
TITSR	A Treasure of Instructions and Techniques for Spiritual Realizations [gdams ngag mdzod]
TLK	Taranath's Life of Krishnacarya
WV	The Wondrous Vision: A Lamdre History
YCTI	On Yuan Chwang's Travels in India

His Holiness
Sakya Trizin
HEAD OF THE SAKYAPA ORDER
OF TIBETAN BUDDHISM

FOREWORD BY H.H SAKYA TRIZIN

Amongst many esoteric teachings introduced in the Land of Snows, Lamdre is a very vast and profound teaching, being the quintessence of all the pith instructions of Buddhadharma. The greatest luminary of Lamdre teachings is Mahasiddha Virupa, who is the crown of the eighty-four Mahasiddhas of Vajrayana Buddhism in ancient India. After enjoying the heart teachings directly from Vajranairatmya, Virupa transmitted the sacred Lamdre teachings which have remained as a complete whispered lineage for a long time.

When the sacred Lamdre teachings eventually came to the great Sachen Kunga Nyingpo, who was already the repository of an ocean of pith instructions, Lamdre with its eleven great qualities was accorded with great respect as the wish-fulfilling jewel among all the instructions he had held.

There have been a great number of masters who have authored important exegeses on the Lamdre teachings. One of the outstanding masters of Lamdre instructions is Panchen Ngawang Choedak, whose succinct and concise manual on Lamdre enjoyed the widest currency at all important seats of Lamdre transmissions.

It is my fervent belief that the present English translation of Panchen Ngawang Choedak's Triple Tantra (rgyud gsum) will go a long way to greatly benefit many sincere practitioners of this tradition and will foster the growth of the precious teachings of Lamdre. I rejoice in the commendable undertaking of Lama Choedak and those who helped him in making this translation a fulfilled reality.

With sincere prayers,

His Holiness Sakya Trizin
31 March 1997

ACKNOWLEDGEMENTS

I would like to thank a number of people for their support and encouragement. Firstly, I would like to dedicate this work to His Eminence Chogye Trichen Rinpoche, His Holiness Sakya Trizin and His Eminence Ludhing Khen Rinpoche who bestowed the Lamdre teachings upon me and nurtured me with their infinite compassion and wisdom. I must express my particular appreciation to His Holiness Sakya Trizin, whose original suggestion gave me the inspiration to undertake the project, and from whom I have received both the common and uncommon Lamdre on five occasions; to H. E. Chogye Trichen Rinpoche for everything I am blessed with and from whom I have received the comprehensive and experiential instructions (myong 'khrid) on Lamdre Lobshe; to Mr. Joseph Ling, Mr. Lim Chan Kwang and Mr. Tan How Chee of Sarawak, who are the main sponsors of this translation as well as all those generous contributors whose names are listed with the dedication at the end of this book; to Dr. Geoffrey Samuel, who kindly read the whole translation and gave me constructive suggestions and improved my original outline; to Ken Gardiner, Merril Cook, Jenny Chen, Kunga Chozin (Natasha Dyer), Pauline Westwood, Ron Foster and Brooke Mills (Ngawang Rabten) who gave their generous time to proofread the translation; to Sara Hogwood who provided technical assistance in the lay out of the book; to Alan Mogridge and his associates from Goanna Print for their efficient and professional service; to my students at Sakya Losal Choe Dzong and Rongton Buddhist Training College in Canberra for their loyalty and devotion; to my parents and family members for understanding the sharp twists of my life's journey and finally to my three gorgeous children, Sherab, Emma and Jigme for their understanding and love.

PREFACE

It was twenty years ago when I first heard the teachings on the Three Tantras. At that time, I was more attracted to the contents of the Three Visions, as I had been thoroughly steeped in Shantideva's classical work *Bodhisattvacaryavatara*. The heart rinsing teachings of the Bodhisattva path were my solace whenever I felt myself becoming submerged in the ocean of self-inflicted sufferings that we call samsara. However, a series of events was in the process of unfolding which would lead to my increasing involvement with the Three Tantras. This translation of Ngawang Choedak's Three Tantras is the culmination of those events.

The late Dampa Rinpoche Ngawang Lodro Nyingpo (1876-1952)[1] once predicted that in the near future when the Buddhist doctrine faced great obstacles, His Eminence Chogye Trichen Rinpoche would establish a three-year retreat training centre (lam-'bras sgrub-grva) which would revitalise the precious Lamdre teachings. After completing the construction of the Tibetan monastery[2] in Lumbini, the birth-place of Sakyamuni Buddha, H. E. Chogye Trichen Rinpoche was pondering one day over the question of how to make the best use of this monastery. It was then he recalled Dampa Rinpoche's prediction. He decided to act on this, and accordingly scheduled a retreat to begin in November 1976. The retreat was sponsored by His Holiness the Fourteenth Dalai Lama Tenzin Gyatsho, who like the Fifth Dalai Lama (1617-1682) took a special interest in the uncommon Lamdre Lobshe. He would subsequently receive the Lamdre teachings himself from H. E. Chogye Trichen Rinpoche.

I was one of only five fortunate Sakya monks selected for the first three and half years of this retreat. It was a rigorous course of training based on the uncommon Lamdre teachings, under the tutelage of His Eminence Chogye Trichen Rinpoche. The venue was the Tibetan monastery in Lumbini where I received my monastic training. Of the five monks selected from several Sakyapa monasteries in India and Nepal, Venerable Drakpa Gyaltshen from Tsedhong monastery died during the retreat itself, and Venerable Lekdrup Gyatsho suffered a nervous breakdown. He was to die a few years afterwards. I was one of only three survivors, probably because my practice was insufficiently developed. We were the first group of Sakyapa monks to undergo such a structured and rigorous training regime under the supervision of Rinpoche, who is among the shining gems of Tibetan Buddhism today. Since that first retreat, Rinpoche has led two other groups of Sakyapa monks on similar Lamdre retreats in Bodh Nath.

The main topic of our meditation was the Three Tantras, in association with the generation and completion stage practices taught in the Hevajra Tantra. This included all the common and uncommon preliminary practices of the Vajrayana teachings. The main Three Tantra texts that we used in the retreat were those by Jamyang Khyentse Wangchuk (1524-1564) and Mangtho Ludrup Gyatsho (1523-1594), the sun and moon-like disciples of Tsharchen Losal Gyatsho (1502-1567). I also had the opportunity to conduct a comparative study of some five works on the Three Tantras including the one by Panchen Ngawang Choedak (1571-1641) which is translated in this book. I have three hundred pages of notes taken from Rinpoche's commentary on various Lamdre instructions. Although we meditated as thoroughly as possible on each topic covered before moving onto the next, three and half years was not long enough to thoroughly master all the instructions contained in the Three Tantras. Nevertheless, that retreat had a profound effect on the course of my life. It is beyond the scope of the present work to dwell on this. However, it should be said that this work is in many ways a manifestation of the blessings which I continue to receive from the precious Lamdre teachings.

I did not undertake any serious textual study of Ngorchen Konchok Lhundrup (1497-1547) and Panchen Ngawang Choedak's works on the Three Tantras until 1987, when H. H. Sakya Trizin asked me to conduct revision classes for foreign students attending the Lamdre teachings at Sakya College. When I became aware of the dire shortage of literature on the Lamdre teachings in the English language, I took pity on the foreign students who had come all the way from far lands to attend. They were, of course, very fortunate in being able to receive instruction in the English language directly from the mouth of His Holiness Sakya Trizin. However, ideally, they should have had access to some printed back-up material. With this in mind, I quickly extracted the outline[3] from Ngawang Choedak's work on the Three Tantras, and translated it into English, together with some associated Lamdre prayers. Later on, when His Holiness Sakya Trizin visited Australia and gave Lamdre teachings in 1988, I was again able to assist by offering revision classes and conducted meditation sessions.

In 1989 I moved to Canberra, where I worked on my sub-thesis, which was entitled *The Origin of Lamdre Tradition in India,* while at the same time trying to master the elements of Sanskrit, the sacred language of the former Tibetan translators. I also pursued an academic discipline in Buddhist Studies. A year later, His Holiness Sakya Trizin sent me a copy of notes on the Three Tantras which had been prepared by one of his British student who had attended the Lamdre at Sakya College. The notes were accompanied by a request to translate Ngawang Choedak's text into English. Although I was honoured to receive this request, I did not know how I would manage to find the time or the resources to undertake a project of such magnitude.

In 1991, I was asked to translate for His Eminence Ludhing Khen Rinpoche who was to give common Lamdre Tshogshe at the Sakya Centre in Ipoh, Malaysia. If I had declined, the event would have had to be postponed indefinitely. I agreed to the request, leaving aside the things I was working on in Australia. I found it very inspiring to see many faithful Malaysian Chinese students attending the precious Lamdre teachings, trying to follow the teachings through English and Mandarin translation. It was then that I saw the urgency of translating the Three Tantras into English. However, owing to other pressing commitments, the task has taken me longer than I would have wished. In finally completing this work, I am grateful to have been able to fulfill at least one wish of my teachers, His Holiness Sakya Trizin and His Eminence Chogye Trichen Rinpoche. I gained the inspiration to actually commence the work after praying at dawn on the full-moon in May 1992, recalling the selfless sacrifice made by former Tibetan Lotsawas and Indian Panditas to establish the sacred Dharma in the Land of Snows. That prayer session and the accompanying meditation on Bodhicitta was the impetus which enabled me to undertake this task. I hope the outcome will be a contribution, however small, toward a more widespread appreciation of the Dharma.

My first step was to write to some Lamdre students to ask for financial assistance. Most of the people I contacted responded promptly and kindly. This gave me the encouragement and support I needed. Without the kindness and generosity of many Dharma friends in Malaysia and Hong Kong, and the support and assistance of members of Sakya Losal Choe Dzong in Canberra and from other individuals whose names appear at the end of this book, I would not have been able to accomplish this work. Certain material needs had to be met. My ever faltering Bodhicitta alone would not have sufficed.

The present work is the result of several years of humble effort dedicated solely to contributing to the growth of the precious Lamdre teachings for the benefit of all sentient beings. I invite readers to rejoice in the generosity of the sponsors who made this translation a reality. Above all, the credit for producing this work really goes to His Eminence Chogye Trichen Rinpoche, my supreme Vajra Master. Without the constant inspiration of his character as an example to me, I would not have become worthy to receive these teachings, let alone produce this translation. If there is any merit involved, it is his, not mine. This work, despite my own inadequacies, is an extension of Rinpoche's infinite compassion, wisdom and enlightened activities.

Because of the very nature of Tantric teachings, I would have been reluctant to publish materials such as this several years ago. However, having witnessed the confusion and misunderstanding that has grown up around Buddhist Tantric teachings over the years due to a paucity of authentic translation I have reached the conclusion that it is better to make these works widely available. It should be mentioned that the present text is not light reading material on the Buddhist Tantra. I have met scholars in the field of comparative religion who were left more confused than enlightened after reading Alex Wayman's translation of Khedrup Je's (1385-1438) work on the Buddhist Tantra.[4] But after a period of careful study, their comprehension greatly improved.

Reading a general work on the theory of the Buddhist Tantra is different from hearing the oral transmission of exclusive teachings such as Lamdre from a lineage holder. Overseas students who have attended Lamdre teachings have felt the life, warmth and continuity of the lineage in a way which contrasts markedly with the sort of dry academic analysis of religious ideas carried out in the sterile environment of an academic classroom. As H. H. Sakya Trizin once said to me, it is necessary to see 'both the virtue and non-virtue' of publishing a work such as this. In weighing up the balance, I have opted for the pragmatic view of H. H. the Dalai Lama, who writes:

> *Especially nowadays, secret mantra has become a topic of interest, but merely as an object of inquiry. From the point of view of a practitioner, it seems to have become an object of entertainment and to have arrived at the point where one cannot know whether it will help or harm. Many of the*

secrets have been disseminated; many lectures are explaining
Tantra, and books are being translated. Even though secret
mantra is to be achieved in hiding, many books have
appeared that are mixture of truth and falsity.[5]

The proliferation of treatises on the Buddhist Tantra and the
fruitless effort of trying to distinguish between false and true
doctrines of Tantra was an obsession of Khedrup Je and other like-
minded Tibetan scholars. If 'secret mantra' is really achieved better
'in hiding', how does one go about obtaining the knowledge? An
over-emphasis on secrecy can pose greater problems than any
alleged damage which may result from dissemination. It is the
Tibetan dialecticians who included esoteric Tantric subjects in the
literary debates, when some may say that they should simply have
done the practice in hiding. We are now faced with a fait accompli.
There were remarkable masters who are said to have unearthed
hidden texts and treasures from the rocks and mountains of Tibet.
Nowadays, similar texts are reprinted in offset printing factories
for worldwide distribution, since the assumed incarnations of
those past great masters are not repeating the legendary free
production process carried out by their predecessors.

As no secret Tantric texts in the English language are being
revealed from the bowels of the Grand Canyon or from the surface
of Uluru (Ayers Rock) by whisky drinking Tibetan teachers in
imitation of past siddhas, we need translations of the texts for the
benefit of new adherents. The argument against publishing based
on the requirement for secrecy seems difficult to sustain when we
witness hundreds of non-Tibetans tuning in to FM radio stations
for the explanation of initiations. While attendance at initiations is
being actively encouraged nowadays, few teachers are prepared to
provide written materials, for fear of criticism. We live in a time
when the Kalachakra initiation is given almost annually, and the
Tibetan government in exile in Dharamsala communicates events
by way of special media releases. Attendances at events rival

sporting Grand Finals and the success of such events unfortunately seems to be measured by some in terms of the criteria adopted in this modern age, that is by the number attending rather than by the number of disciples who sincerely adopt these practices. Furthermore, skilled Tibetan monks have visited many world centres making precious coloured sand mandalas. The monks, mainly from Gyuto and Namgyel monastery exhibit their 'works of art' at major art galleries and museums around the world in the name of culture and art. As they chant in their remarkably deep voices, display the spectacular sacred Tantric dance costumes at ordinary dance theatres and set up their portable card-board shrines, I have been among those Tibetans concerned about the appropriateness of such theatrical demonstrations of Vajrayana rites and rituals. One becomes naturally concerned about how this public viewing of the sacred sand mandalas, previously only seen by initiates during initiation ceremonies, is going to help to maintain the perpetuation of the 'accomplishment of secret mantra in hiding' from the point of the view of the orthodox Tibetan tradition. Are we going to see the birth of yet another 'new reformed tradition' in the twentieth century?

These days while faithful disciples may be barred from witnessing the master performing the initiation, TV crews of CNN and BBC may be seen rushing inside the initiation halls with great urgency to air an interview so that the non-practitioners may see in their living rooms what is taking place, ostensibly in hiding, during Vajrayana initiation rites. When we take into account the glittering display of Vajrayana performances to mass audiences today, it is difficult to imagine that this fire-fly like translation of the Three Tantras would in any way delay the achievements of those who know how to accomplish secret mantra in hiding.

For sincere students with a firm faith in Vajrayana teachings and practices, this is an indispensable book to read, study and use as a guide to practice. However, I do not suggest that any self-proclaimed Vajrayanist do any of the non-preliminary practices without first receiving the Hevajra initiation and the Lamdre teachings. There are many missing tips not included in the text, which must be filled in by an experienced Lamdre teacher. Although distribution is not restricted, readers should bear in mind that this is not a book intended for light entertainment. One or two readings of the text will supply only a basic introduction. To develop one's Lamdre practice, one must sit at the feet of a Lamdre master and receive appropriate instructions, step by step. There is no scope in Lamdre for sudden mastery based on merely reading a text. This work will be of most benefit to those who truly understand the basic teachings of Buddhism, have an appreciation of the Vajrayana path and have received or are preparing to receive the Lamdre teachings from a qualified master.

A factor in my decision to publish this translation was the knowledge that the entire Lamdre is already available in the Tibetan language to all who may wish to read it. That being the case, it would appear discriminatory to restrict access by non-Tibetan speaking readers. Furthermore, there is ample precedent for taking the line of propagation rather than exclusivity. Sachen Kunga Nyingpo dealt with this problem eight hundred years ago when he produced his eleven commentaries on the subject.

In order to place the teachings into historical context, I have included three chapters about the origin of Lamdre in India and its introduction into Tibet. The English translation of Panchen Ngawang Choedak's Three Tantras is based on the 1983 edition of *Sakya Lamdre Literature Series*, which was published in New Delhi by the Sakya Centre in Dehra Dun. As there were not many scribal errors in this edition, it was unnecessary to locate any other edition of the text. I must admit, also, that I have not come across another redaction, other than the one from the Derge which was the original of the New Delhi edition. A few scribal errors and some doubtful terms in the text have been corrected on the basis of Ngorchen Konchok Lhundrup's Triple Tantra and other associated manuals.

Lama Choedak Rinpoche
Sakya Losal Choe Dzong, Canberra
18 April 1997

PREFACE TO THE REDESIGNED EDITION

A WAY FORWARD TO TRANSLATE LAMDRE TEXTS

Sakya Losal Choe Dzong first sponsored this translation of Panchen Ngawang Choedak's Triple Tantra in 1997 in preparation for the precious Lamdre Lobshe Teachings given by H. H. Sakya Gongma Trichen at Vajradhara Gompa in Kyogle, Australia. Many things have happened since then. This second edition of the book was prepared in urgent necessity to coincide with the precious Lamdre Lobshe being given by both His Holiness Kyabgon Gongma Trichen Rinpoche and Holiness Kyabgon Gongma Trizin Rinpoche in the Earth Dog year in New York, USA.

Six-hundred people are estimated to receive these sacred empowerments at this transmission given entirely in English. This shows the West has been a fertile ground for Dharma, and it is hungry for more. Due to hard work and the making of much good karmic merits, we were able to make the changes needed to present this re-edition for you.

Ever since its initial distribution by Groum Publications in 1997, this book has remained in demand especially when Lamdre is given in the West. Due to the unknowable causes and conditions, the book has been out of print for some years. Admittedly, I have remained committed to teaching and leading retreats in Australia and upholding weekly classes and annual retreats teaching Tibetan language and translation. As such my time has been limited. Despite this my passion for translation remains unshakable.

Many people thanked at the end of the 1997 Acknowledgements have passed away. We take time to remember and thank Joseph Ling from Kuching and Ken Gardiner from Canberra in particular. I rejoice the merit all had throughout each of their lives. Thanks naturally continue to those currently living, for without their help in the interdependence of this work, this very important text would remain unavailable in English.

With Phil Cooper's help to relocate the master copy of this text, Kath has been working very diligently to make the necessary edits and style changes needed to re-publish the book. More recently with the help of Joseph, Jampal and the team at SIBA combined with the swiftness of Tara's enlightened activities at the 21 Tara Retreat, the book is in this form, including a new cover. As we have never paid for any editors, designers or publishers but had a strong and viable community base of volunteers to complete this work, I am very proud of this redesign. I again thank everyone involved.

In the old days, Lamdre teachings were given as the inaugural teachings of a newly established monastery belonging to the Sakya Order of Tibetan Buddhism. Lamdre is only given by few genuine Sakya lineage holders on very important occasions. Lamdre is the most complete path containing the essence of both sutra and tantra. The Sakya lineage has kept the pure lineage by bestowing major empowerment to no more than twenty-five initiates at one time. Giving Lamdre in such a way deeply respects and honours the authentic enlightened lineage. As each set of two ears *really* hear the secret reading transmission of 31 volumes of Sakya Lamdre Literature, there is blessing not just for those human ears, but throughout the cosmos.

As many know, the rain-like nectar of Lamdre teachings are equally only profound as they are inaccessible for the new initiate. When any anuttara yoga transmission of any of the major Buddhist schools are given, we are connecting an entry to liberation for sentient beings, dawning a new horizon of every recipient. Many eyes become wide open and study and practice of this unique turning of the wheel continues. When anyone practices these teachings, both they and the linage thrive. This is as true both inside my homeland Tibet or in a spare room in Canberra.

There is a very special distinction between the lineage and the students. The power of the Lamdre teachings lies in recipients vowing a sacred oath to perform the tantric liturgy, *Hevajra Sadhana* every day. Without the vital bond of continuity of Sadhana, the literal meaning of Tantra is broken. This bond is proving challenging for many as the Sadhana was written many centuries ago and is very wordy, complex and esoteric. The struggle to maintain this samaya is something we need to address by supporting our fellow sangha, both lay and ordained. The rate of those who have lapsed doing their Sadhana seems to me to be many that I speak with, often sharing they are daunted to try it again. To remedy this doubt and encourage people to 'get back on the horse', knowledge about the Sadhana is needed. Such study increases pliancy, which reinforces pragmatic faith, which increases diligence for practice and study of the Dharma.

This proves that Lamdre teachings must be supported by clear informative teachings. Beings can only study the unspeakable truths using texts written in a language they understand. I rejoice that the Traditional teaching method is maintained and urge it to remain strong for the benefit of sentient beings. However, without the resources that support the teachings being understood, sentient beings remain unable to maintain the Tantric transmission. This is true of all beings of the six realms, not just humans.

As these teachings are truly profound, and we have the karmically blessed life to be communicating though these words, please realise English translations are desperately needed. I have done draft translations of some important Lamdre texts but much more work needs to be done. I need moral support from all well-wishers. People who wish to volunteer or sponsor the translation and publication of any Lamdre texts, please do not hesitate to contact me. There are at least eight large volumes that are entirely biographies of Lamdre lineage masters that remain untranslated. I have finished translating one such volume containing Mahasiddha Virupa's biography and this is included in this book as an example of the quality and detail contained in other volumes. As you enjoy the richness of those chapters, you must realise that only with your help will more become readable.

Some of the current translation works in progress include Tsharchen's Rays of the Sun, a famous commentary of Hevajra Sadhana and Lama Ngaklo Rinpoche's Sakya Ngondro Manual. But without further help mainly from professional proof readers, editors and translators they will not continue the melody of Dharma. There is the complete list of all the Lamdre texts at the back of this book. I request and implore everyone including each of the Sakya centres to appoint someone to coordinate to find sponsors, raise funds and help translation projects to realise their crucial objectives. Think globally but act locally. It is an important project that every Sakya centre and Dharma community must prioritise.

In short, this is an appeal to all readers of this book: You, reading this, have the power to help. You must believe it to be true, due to karma and merits of being empowered to practice this sacred Lamdre. Although I remain content with the efforts of the many I meet I feel like there is no time to lose. Lamdre is given almost once every year somewhere in the world, so a consolidated initiative to translate the texts that transmit the living pulse of these peerless teachings is desperately needed. It is simple: the ever increasing English Lamdre transmissions must be matched by texts that practitioners can study, debate, and most importantly aid in experiencing true Dharma.

The great merit of simply translating one text is as vast as it is crucially important. I believe the translation and publication of authentic Dharma books is much greater merit than doing a puja to remove obstacles of one's individual life as translation *spreads* the Dharma for the benefit of all sentient beings. The Sakya lineage used to pride itself on being the lineage of four translators. Unfortunately, this currently seems to be part of glory of ancient history.

May be the sponsorship of translation of Lamdre texts be among the list of things recommended from performing divination! May all devotees realise the importance of translation!

Lama Choedak Rinpoche
SAKYA LAMDRE TRANSLATION PROJECT
Canberra, Vaisakha Purnima 2018

TRANSLATOR'S INTRODUCTION

1. PROLOGUE

The Khon family, who head the Sakya tradition to this day, was a dominant force during the two periods of dramatic growth and development of Buddhism in Tibet. These periods are known respectively as the Early [seventh to tenth century] and Later [post tenth century] Spread of Buddhism (bstan pa phyi dar). This family also paved the way for Buddhism to take seed and flourish in neighbouring countries such as Mongolia. The Khon family's contribution began during the early period of the Tibetan empire at the time when the Sakyapa lineage was founded over 920 years ago. During the Early Spread of Buddhism, the family were great upholders of the Nyingmapa tradition. Khon Palpoche[6] was a minister of the renowned Tibetan King Trisong Detsen. His third son Khon Lui Wangpo was one of the famous group of seven Tibetans who were the first to be ordained as Buddhist monks.

Another major pioneer who figured more specifically in the history and development of Lamdre was not a member of the Khon family. This was the remarkable Tibetan pilgrim, Siddha and Tantric savant known as 'Drogmi Lotsawa Shakya Yeshe' (993-1074). He was the first Tibetan to carry the Lamdre teachings to Tibet. Drogmi was a towering figure in his time. He is regarded as one of the three most influential teachers involved in the Later Spread of Buddhism. Because of his great contribution to the dissemination and development of Lamdre teachings, Drogmi would probably be regarded as the founder of the Sakya lineage had he been born into the Khon family. To set Drogmi's achievements in their historical context, he taught Sanskrit to the renowned translator Marpa (1012-1096), undisputed founder of the Kagyupa lineage. With respect to the development of Lamdre,

1

the Sakyapa lineage is more indebted to Drogmi than to any other Tibetan teacher.

Lamdre, which means 'the path including its result,' is the system of esoteric Tantric Buddhist teachings transmitted by Mahasiddha Virupa[7] in India during the seventh century. Virupa wrote the original text on Lamdre,[8] based on the *Hevajra Tantra*, the highest of all classes of Tantra. He passed it on to his disciples Dombi Heruka and Krishnacarin. These highly esoteric teachings remained largely secret. They were handed down through an oral tradition and imparted only to exceptionally faithful and intelligent disciples. Traditionally a future disciple capable of carrying on the transmission was predicted by the lineage holder's preceptor. Thus, Lamdre was transmitted from teacher to single disciple in what is known in Vajrayana as 'the Sole lineage' (chig brgyud) tradition. After it was brought to Tibet during the mid-10th century by Pandita Gayadhara and Drogmi Lotsawa Shakya Yeshe, Lamdre became the central teaching and practice of the Sakyapa School. The Sakyapas later established the first legitimate priest rulership in Tibet. Such was their influence that they managed to convert the Mongol emperor Kublai Khan to Buddhism. Today, 1400 years after the formulation of the teachings in India, the Sakya school continues to uphold Lamdre as its principal practice.

2. The Impact of the Lamdre Tradition on the History of Tibet

Drogmi introduced Lamdre to Tibet during the eleventh century. The total secrecy surrounding the lineage prior to its firm establishment in Tibet was to play a significant part in setting the scene for the Later Spread of Buddhism. The introduction of Lamdre to Tibet not only re-established the Dharma, it helped to develop Buddhism into a powerful medium for conducting socio-political relations with neighbouring countries. This occurred at a time when the old Tibetan kingdom had collapsed into warring principalities and the prevailing religious climate was one of revivalism in reaction to King Lang Darma's persecution of the Dharma. Various religious schools attracted large numbers of followers, and petty Tibetan rulers were sponsoring young monks to study in India. Drogmi and Lochen Rinchen Sangpo (958-1055) were among these. They were later to become foremost among contemporary Tibetan masters. In order to fully understand the importance to Tibetan Buddhism of the tradition which originated in India, it is necessary to look at some key political, diplomatic and religious changes which occurred in Tibet largely through the influence of Lamdre adherents.

The introduction of Lamdre and its propagation within Tibet mark the beginning of the Later Spread of Buddhism. Drogmi, who was one of the three outstanding Tibetan translators, played a leading role. He was also the teacher of the other two, Marpa and Goe Lotsawa.[9] Some sixty canonical works which he translated are preserved in the Tibetan Buddhist Canon, a fact which indicates how crucial his literary contribution was to the spread of the Dharma. His translations included the *Hevajra Tantra*, which is the source of the Lamdre teachings. It was these teachings with their coloured sand Mandala initiation rites which played so great a role in the conversion of Emperor Kublai Khan (1216-1294). Close study of both the Hevajra Tantra and the Lamdre teachings is indispensable for anyone aspiring to research the history of Buddhism in Mongolia, China, Tibet and other countries in the Himalayan region.

One of Drogmi's principal disciples was Khon Konchog Gyalpo (1034-1102), a member of the much blessed Khon family who founded the famous Sakya monastery in 1073. Countless Tibetan scholars, including the first Tibetan to receive the prestigious and envied title 'Pandit,' were trained in this monastery. Due to the spiritual fame and honour of Sakya Pandita Kunga Gyaltshen (1182-1251), the Mongol prince Godan (K'uo-tan) became his devotee. This was in 1244. The famous 'Priest and Patron Relationship' (*mchod yon zung 'brel*) between the Manchu

Emperors and the Dalai Lamas began and continued right up to 1911. It then ended abruptly with the overthrow of the Ch'ing Dynasty.[10] Sakya Pandita's nephew, Phagpa (1235-1280), whose full name is Drogon Choegyal Phagpa Lodro Gyaltshen, gave the Hevajra initiation to Kublai Khan, his queens and some twenty ministers in 1253 at the palace of Hutu. After being initiated into the Hevajra Mandala, the Emperor offered the whole of Tibet to Phagpa in thanksgiving. Phagpa thus became the first Lama priest king of Tibet. From then on Tibet was ruled by Buddhist priests up to the rulership by the Dalai Lamas. Subsequently, whichever Buddhist order exercised political power in Tibet was always an adherent of the Lamdre tradition and adopted the style of rule modelled by Phagpa.

The weakening position of the Mongol rulers contributed to a shift of power from the Sakya hierarchy to the Tibetan aristocrat Tai Situpa Changchup Gyaltshen (1302-1364). In spite of this, the religious rulers of Tibet continued to practice Lamdre.[11] The strict traditional guidelines which limited the Hevajra initiation to twenty-five disciples at a time continued in force. Despite the fluctuating fortunes of the Sakyapas, the Lamdre teachings continued to be practiced by the greatest lineage masters of every Tibetan tradition throughout the ensuing centuries. The Great Fifth Dalai Lama, the first to rule Tibet, was a pupil of the renowned Lamdre master Gonpo Sonam Chogden.[12] The First Karmapa, Dusum Khyenpa (1110-1193) received Lamdre from Khampa Aseng, a disciple of Sachen Kunga Nyingpo (1092-1158). The omniscient Bu-ston Rinchen Drub (1290-1364), founder of the Bu tradition, received all the Lamdre teaching from Lama Dampa Sonam Gyaltshen (1312-1375) and Tishi Kunga Lodro (1296-1327).[13] It was Lama Dampa Sonam Gyaltshen who imparted the teachings to the illustrious Nyingmapa teacher Longchen Rabjam (1308-1363).[14] Dolpuba Sherab Gyaltshen (1292-1361) and Choeku Oser of the Jonangpa tradition also based their study on Sakyapa philosophy in general and the works of Sakya Pandita in particular. Tsongkhapa Losang Drakpa (1357-1419), founder of the Gelugpa tradition, was a student of Rendawa Shonu Lodro (1349-1412) and Sazang Mati Panchen (1294-1376), both of whom were Sakyapa masters. Gyaltshab Je and Khedrup Gelek Palsang (1385-1438), two of Tsongkhapa's chief pupils, were both originally Sakyapa scholars. It was these early upholders of the Lamdre tradition who gained and established genuine religious rulership and propagated the doctrine extensively throughout Tibet.

When the teachings came down to the priest kings of Tibet, otherwise known as the 'Five Former Sakya Masters' (sakya gong ma nam-nga) they lost some of their exclusivity and secrecy. Hence, they became more accessible to lay people. However, despite wider accessibility and the fact that the tradition had been so closely associated with religious power and dominance in the social and political affairs of Tibet, their essential purity was maintained. Two major Lamdre traditions developed: common *Tshogshe* and uncommon *Lobshe*.[15] The three sub-traditions of the Sakya Order, namely Sakya, Ngorpa and Tsharpa are each directly linked with the development of common and uncommon Lamdre traditions.[16] Most of the finest Tibetan scholars and masters have been Lamdre practitioners. Included amongst them is the present 14th Dalai Lama, who privately received the Lamdre Lobshe transmission from His Eminence Chogye Trichen Rinpoche in 1991.

3. THE ROLE OF HISTORY IN TIBETAN RELIGIOUS TRADITIONS

Owing to the paucity of written history on the origin of Buddhist Tantra, there has been much doubt and controversy surrounding the subject. We should remember that the difficulty of separating historical fact from legend is common to the study of all religious history and hagiography. It is by no means unique to the Tantric tradition. From the standpoint of Tibetan Buddhist teachings, an important indicator of validity is their traceability to an Indian source. The Vajrayana lineages originated with the Indian Mahasiddhas and Panditas. These great masters inspired and influenced many in their time, contributing greatly to the propagation of the Dharma. The Indian siddhas and the great Tibetan masters, who were canonised by being included in the official list of lineage Gurus, were not only very important historical figures in their own right, but also played a crucial role as exemplars of the teachings and practices. Although canonisation elevates the status of a man or a woman to that of a siddha or great master, not all great masters were ever listed formally. Siddhahood or lineage masterhood in Tantric Buddhism is not achieved through heroic circumstances resulting in death, as with martyrdom in Christianity. It is achieved through total devotion to the Guru and relentless effort in the practices prescribed by the teacher. The lives of these teachers display an extraordinary variety of human personalities and dispositions. Unlike biographies written by contemporaries and near-contemporaries, the hagiographies of Buddhist Tantric masters were kept as oral history within the tradition for long periods before they were committed to writing.

Hagiographical works known as 'Namthar' (rnam thar) honour the virtues of the teacher. They were used to evoke enthusiastic feelings and rekindle the vitality of hitherto lethargic and discouraged aspirants. Since it is considered meritorious to do so, the names of past masters are memorised and recited in the daily prayers of practitioners. They are invoked frequently to bestow blessings on the minds of the faithful. Their name Mantras used to be inscribed on rocks and on clothes and given away as amulets. Lama Dampa Sonam Gyaltshen explains the importance of studying hagiography in the following line:

The history of the lineage Gurus should be studied for the purpose of knowing the traceability of its origin and to cultivate faith. [17]

Hagiography reveals the inner spiritual drama of faith, conflict, transformation and realisation. Outer crises and changes depicted in biographies are only perceived interpretations of inner, subtle mental experiences, whether religious or otherwise. In the Vajrayana traditions, a great deal of importance is accorded to the history of the lineage masters. Their histories are seen as a means of evoking inspiration and encouragement amongst practitioners and fostering a deep connection between them and the teachings and instructions. A faithful disciple must feel a strong connection with the master and his teachings. A close look at the lives of the masters is a simple and direct technique for producing inner transformation. Those who have understood the lives of these masters will not only respect them deeply but will emulate their example.

Narrative histories, on the other hand, bear witness to people's beliefs. They are evidence of what people think about past spiritual masters and their lives. Students of these narratives will be aware that accounts of a past master's life are not edited in order to highlight miracles and gloss over less attractive character traits. The life stories of siddhas are not intended to draw a distinction between 'the man' and 'the siddha,' but to show the true value of a life when it is lived to the full. They are spiritual teachings of great power, which speak for themselves. To censor them would defeat the whole purpose. Irrespective of the existence of 'historical evidence,' these stories are recounted repeatedly, and devotees believe them to be true. They have thus become 'historical facts' in themselves, which continue to shape people's lives. This is what gives power and continuity to ancient traditions. The main 'historical evidence' relating to these traditions is the presence of that 'living spirit' which illuminates the hearts of practitioners down to the present day. There is no justification for changing these stories or disparaging them, unless of course one were to discover real proof to the contrary. Even then, many religious adherents might well be unimpressed. Spiritual truths contain universal, heart-level knowledge. They transcend the relative and fragmentary facts of the scientific rationalists.

The present work does not pretend to adhere to the purely verifiable historical accounts of the origin of Lamdre and its founding fathers. To the extent that this approach requires justification, it is asserted that 'pure history' is too young to fathom the crucial role of oral history, hagiography, myth and legend in forming ancient Buddhist traditions. Furthermore, 'pure history' is a recent imposition of western scholarship. Because of this modern western bias, many of the realities of the history, customs and beliefs of the peoples of other races and civilisations tend to be overlooked. The fact is that there remains a healthy living tradition which accords great significance to its oral history and hagiography. Its present reality is a product of those oral roots. To have any credibility in the field at all, scientific historical analysis of such traditions must treat the oral narratives as objective data in themselves, irrespective of their scientific 'verifiability'.

In summary, Lamdre represents a Tantric Buddhist tradition which has consistently emphasised the role of practice through faith, loyalty, enthusiasm, patience and dedication. The very existence of Tibetan Buddhism and its flowering in recent years can be traced back to the renaissance of Buddhism in Tibet in the 10th century. This is the time when the Lamdre masters of Tibet truly established Dharma rule. There were very few Tibetan Buddhist masters who were not blessed by the teachings and transmissions of the Sakyapa Lamdre masters. Their very lives were a demonstration of the efficacy of the teachings when practiced faithfully

4. THE SCOPE AND TYPOLOGY OF THE LAMDRE NAMTHAR HAGIOLOGY

The considerable influence of the early Lamdre masters on the Later Spread of Buddhism together with the establishment of Buddhist priest rulership in Tibet give an indication of the important role played by the hagiographies of the Lamdre lineage masters. A general survey and examination of Lamdre hagiography reveals the literary sources of this tradition. A close look at the hagiography of the Guru, and the role of hagiography in training disciples and perpetuating the lineage is indispensable for an understanding of the Lamdre tradition.

The Lamdre teaching itself is the principal subject matter of the present work. It comprises Part II. Part I provides historical background, drawing largely on a work entitled *The Origin of Lamdre in India.* This work includes accounts of the lives of the Indian Mahasiddhas and of Drogmi Lotsawa Shakya Yeshe and his Indian teacher and collaborator Gayadhara. It was originally produced as part of a sub-thesis which I submitted in partial fulfilment of the Degree of Bachelor of Letters at the Australian National University in 1990. It examines the authenticity and traceability of the Lamdre tradition by providing biographical information on some of its leading lineage masters. It also lists their monumental works, which form such a large and significant segment of the Tibetan Buddhist Canon. Although it has not always been possible to verify the dating with absolute accuracy, these accounts of the lives and works of the siddhas nevertheless constitute significant historical evidence in support of their existence. The material includes important and hitherto little-known hagiographical episodes in the lives of Virupa and his successors. The compilation of such information is not an easy task. This is due to factors such as the deliberate suppression of early Lamdre history, the anti-historical tone of much of the material and the traditional secrecy which surrounded the lineage for so long.

The first chapter includes study, collation and analysis of all the available data on the life of Virupa, who is known as the first human teacher of Lamdre. The main theme of this chapter is the identity of Dharmapala, the famous abbot of Nalanda Monastery who later became known as Mahasiddha Virupa. Most historical works fail to make any link between Dharmapala and Virupa. Far less do they accept the fact that they are one and the same person. Taranatha cautiously denies any link between them in his *'Taranatha's History of Buddhism,'* although he fails to provide any convincing justification for his stance. The present writer challenges Taranatha's view and asserts that Dharmapala and Virupa are in fact the same person. This position is based largely on material contained in previously unrevealed Lamdre hagiographical literature. It is my hope that through making this material more widely available, it will stimulate other scholars to take a fresh look at Dharmapala and his place within the Tibetan Buddhist tradition. Some Tibetan writers have alleged that the Sakyapa philosophical viewpoint belongs to the Yogachara school rather than the Prasanghika Madyamika. They base this assertion on the philosophical viewpoint expressed by Dharmapala in his commentary on Aryadeva's *'Catushataka.'* In doing so, they assume that Dharmapala maintained the Yogachara view even after attaining the stage of a Bodhisattva on the sixth bhumi as Virupa. But I argue that it is absurd to claim that a sixth bhumi Bodhisattva would continue to cling to a philosophical viewpoint he had held prior to attaining enlightenment. Although there is no real basis to the allegation that Virupa belongs to the Yogachara School,[18] the very fact that it was made at all indicates unquestioning acceptance that Dharmapala and Virupa were in fact one and the same person, a position which supports my own stance.

The second chapter contains an analysis of the meaning of discipleship and describes how various disciples became successors to Virupa. The sharp distinction advocated in the traditional Lamdre view between 'superior' and 'unintelligent' or 'sudden' and 'gradual' disciples is examined. There is an attempt to interpret the symbolic and religious meaning of what happened during the encounters between Virupa and Dombi Heruka. The question of the correct identity of Dombi Heruka has been addressed, but the identity of Krishnacarin has not been examined in great detail. The third chapter focuses on the life of Drogmi Lotsawa and Pandita Gayadhara and gives an account of the introduction of Lamdre to Tibet.

A brief reading of the ten volumes of Lamdre hagiographical literature is sufficient to demonstrate the importance played by this hagiography in the spiritual life of past masters. There is insufficient space here to study the typology of all Lamdre hagiographies. This section is limited to covering the hagiography of Virupa. The geographical components of the biography discussed in this study are rather loose. However, owing to the subsequent sanctification of the places where he studied, taught and died, some precise data is available. For example, Nalanda where Virupa was an abbot, Sovanatha, where he transformed into a stone image after subduing the Tirthikas (heretics), and the river Ganges, where he met Dombi Heruka are all mentioned. Disciples are advised to go on pilgrimage to those sacred places to cultivate a stronger and closer spiritual connection with the master.

The time factor plays a significant role in Lamdre Hagiology. Lamdre hagiographers are unanimous in claiming that Virupa made his first appearance in India 1020 years after the Mahaparinirvana of the Buddha.[19] Just as saints' feast days are observed in some Christian traditions, the anniversary of Virupa's Enlightenment is celebrated by performing Ganacakra[20] food offerings. Although the accounts mention his approximate age when he left Nalanda, there is no time reference available for when he passed away. A striking feature of Virupa's hagiography is that, in common with all of the Mahasiddhas, he was a strong individual who made his own way on the spiritual path despite the many obstacles he faced. While the accounts of his life certainly glorify his admirable spiritual power, they do not balk at describing the idiosyncrasies of his personality. Without reservation they relate his forceful approach in subduing and subjugating Tirthikas. They give a forthright account of his impatience when he became discouraged with his Vajrayana practice. They recount how he threw his prayer beads into the latrine after waking from a disturbing dream. Details of his abbotship of the monastery in Nalanda are included along with his visits to brothels. Such frank inclusions suggest that the hagiographers were not selective in presenting their material. There is every indication of an attempt to present the master's life in its entirety. Such uncompromising frankness, while enhancing the credibility of the material, deliberately challenges the disciple's faith and trust.

Nevertheless, despite their openness and objectivity these hagiographies, in common with all religious hagiographies, contain narratives of miraculous events designed to edify and encourage the faithful and to rally the spirits of hitherto lukewarm or discouraged practitioners. There are special ceremonies in which disciples receive transmissions of the biographies. The anniversaries of the masters are widely celebrated. Their statues and paintings are enshrined, and their altars constantly re-stocked with fresh offerings. Special commemoration halls are dedicated to them. Monastic institutions are named after them. Contemporary masters or intelligent and disciplined monks are often selected as possible reincarnations[21] of celebrated and canonised lineage masters. The continuing existence of a tradition such as Lamdre is regarded as being among the unobstructed Enlightened Activities ('phrin las) and compassion of the master. Hence the lives of past masters have continually operated to maintain the tradition not only by inspiring the faithful but also by attracting new adherents. The concept of Trikaya or three bodies in Mahayana, together with the institution of Tulku [sprul ku], both operate to maintain hagiography as a living tradition and to foster the uninterrupted flow of spiritual blessings which are the real grandeur of Tibetan Buddhism.

5. SOURCES OF THE LAMDRE HAGIOLOGY

Buddhist scholars and historians writing from within a traditional monastic environment produced a great many biographies known as 'namthar.' Although modern scholars[22] believe that these are largely devoid of historical significance, they are in fact the most important sources for research into Tibetan Buddhist historiography available today. 'Namthar' were written in praise of a master's charismatic qualities, religious glory and spiritual achievements. They were a means of paying a last tribute to a deceased master. They generally followed a fairly standard format. The word 'namthar' itself means 'complete liberation.' As the name suggests, there is a belief that one may attain complete liberation merely by reading one of these biographies. At the very least, they provide examples to be emulated by the faithful. Although Lamdre historical works belong to this category, our sources dealing with Lamdre masters are known as 'Lamdre Khogphub.'

These sources may be categorised into two divisions: *primary* and *secondary*. The *primary sources* are the traditional Lamdre hagiographies which deal exclusively with the history of Lamdre. The earliest of these was written in the 12th century. The *secondary sources* are well known Tibetan historical works which discuss Lamdre and its early Indian masters. Although many of the Lamdre teachings remained in the form of oral transmission until the 12th century, selections containing biographical details of the early masters began to appear soon after the first commentaries on Lamdre were written. Although Sachen Kunga Nyingpo did not write a history of Lamdre as such, Jetsun Drakpa Gyaltshen (1147-1216) wrote the most important Lamdre hagiography, *'Hagiography of Indian Gurus.'*[23] Much of our knowledge of Virupa's life derives from this text. Lama Dampa Sonam Gyaltshen's *'Wondrous Vision'*[24] is perhaps the most comprehensive historical work on the Lamdre tradition. This is part of his *'Black Annals.'* This work also discusses the general history of Buddhism in Tibet in some detail. Jamgon Ame-shab Kunga Sonam (1537-1601)[25] wrote a lengthy Lamdre history entitled *'Ocean of Collected Elegant Sayings'*[26] and also a versified Lamdre history, *'Gratifier of the Readers,'* which appeared in 1556 when he was only twenty years old. Jamyang Khyentse Wangchuk's (1524-1568) history entitled *'Flourishing of the Great Secret Doctrine'*[27] has been consulted extensively during the course of this study. It contains partially secret hagiographical notes of early masters unreported in other works. Hagiographies comprise a third of the entire body of Lamdre literature. On the whole, there are few major discrepancies amongst the contents of these works. Where discrepancies do exist, I have attempted to point these out.

The secondary sources include the biographies of the Eighty-Four Siddhas[28] found in the *Tengyur* as well as famous Tibetan historical works. Goe Lotsawa Shonu Pal's (*1392*-1481) monumental work the *'Blue Annals'* includes a significant chapter on the flowering of Lamdre in Tibet[29] which I found most useful. Other prominent Tibetan historians whose works touch briefly on Lamdre history include Pawo Tsuklag Trengwa (1504-1566)[30] and the Fourth Drukpa Pema Karpo (1527-1592).[31] I have also consulted the sections dealing with the siddhas, Panditas and scholars associated with the Lamdre tradition in Taranatha's (1575-1634) impressive *History of Buddhism in India.*[32] This work is an exceptional contribution to the study of medieval Buddhist India. In spite of his silence on the subject of Lamdre itself, Taranatha provides brief and striking comments on Virupa, Dombi Heruka and Krishnacarin which to some extent challenge the Lamdre version. The *'Seven Instruction Lineage'*[33] is also ascribed to Taranatha, but I have some reservations about this. Nevertheless, regardless of its authorship, this work is a valuable tool for establishing the connection between different Tantric lineages and constructing succession lists of masters and disciples.

6. THE BUDDHIST TANTRAS IN THE SCRIPTURES

All Buddhist schools concur in dividing the earliest Buddhist scriptures into three collections, known as 'tripitaka' or 'three baskets.' Sutrapitaka, compiled by Ananda,[34] contains the collection of Sutras. These consist chiefly of discourses by the Buddha. Abhidharmapitaka, compiled by Mahakashypa[35] contains the collections of Buddhist metaphysics dealing with systems of the universe, cosmology and Buddhist psychology. Vinayapitaka, compiled by Upali[36] contains moral codes for various categories of ordained members of the monastic community and the laity. In addition to constituting the richest source of information on the way in which vows were formulated to suit prevailing social conditions, Vinaya also contains all the legends about the Shakya clan and stories about the past lives of the Buddha and others. From the Vajrayana viewpoint, the Mahayana Sutras and the Tantras were compiled by the three Bodhisattvas[37] and form part of the Buddhist scriptures. Some scholars identify a fourth collection which they have named 'Collection of Vidyadhara Mantrapitaka' (rig pa 'dzin pa sngags kyi sde snod) containing all the Tantras. However, others argue that the Buddhist Tantras are included in the three basic collections, so that there is no need to relegate these to a separate 'pitaka.'

The Tibetan Buddhist canon uses a different classification. Canonical works in Tibetan belong to either *Kagyur* or *Tengyur*. *Kagyur* contains 'words of the Buddha,' while Tengyur contains 'exegetical works' by Indian scholars. The Sutras, Vinaya, Abhidharma, root Tantras, Continuation Tantras and Commentary Tantras are to be found in the *Kagyur*. The exegetical works by Indian Pandits are found in the *Tengyur*. Native Tibetan works are excluded from the canon. They are to be found amongst the collected works of individual scholars.

Buddhist Tantric writings generally distinguish four classes of Tantra. These are Action Tantra (Kriya), Performance Tantra, (Carya), Union Tantra (Yoga) and Highest Yoga Tantra (Anuttarayoga). Hevajra Tantra belongs to the last of these. It is claimed by some modern scholars that because the Tantras came to light much later than the Sutras, they must have been composed by later writers. In order to bolster up the sometimes surprisingly late dating of the Tantras, these scholars have found it necessary to separate various masters into several discrete individuals, who in some cases are said to have existed at different times. Thus, we are told that there were three Nagarjunas, two Aryadevas, two Candrakirtis etc. Given the meticulous care with which Buddhist scholars collect and preserve the teachings and traditions, it would seem highly implausible for them to have been unaware of the existence of these multiple editions of great masters. Of course, one reason for the confusion in the minds of some scholars is the fact that there are works on a variety of disciplines appearing under the name of a single author. Hence some scholars insist on referring to 'alchemist Nagarjuna,' 'Tantric Nagarjuna' and 'philosopher Nagarjuna.' But in fact, we know that some Indian scholars wrote treatises on medicine and philosophy in addition to works on Buddhist tantra. We must remember that in former times knowledge was not fragmented into myriad specialised areas as it is today. Just as in former times the Italian Leonardo da Vinci wrote on many different topics ranging from the circulation of the blood to aviation, while producing poetry and practicing as a painter, so Indian scholars of ancient and medieval times also mastered many branches of knowledge. We should perhaps remind ourselves that the masters who brought the Tantras to light were not secular scholars competing against each other for recognition. These were individuals of great spiritual attainment. They were men of the highest integrity, not mere opportunist's intent on inscribing their names on the title pages of these works. Those who have studied their biographies would realise this.

Individual Tantras are dated from the time when they were revealed to a number of suitable disciples by specifically realised Pandits and Siddhas who were themselves prophesied by the Buddha. Originally all the Buddhist Tantras were taught by the Buddha just as the Sutras were taught both in this world and in other realms. It is important to remember that one of the many qualities of a fully enlightened being is the ability to manifest at different places and teach simultaneously on different topics. The Buddha may also have manifested as the interlocutor, the narrator or even as the audience. There are Sutras such as the one Buddha taught to his mother in the realm of the Trayastrimsha heaven. As with the Sutras, Buddhist Tantras begin with the phrase "Thus I have heard at one time, ..." which is an indication that they were taught by the Buddha to particular disciples at a particular place and time. After the great demise of the Buddha, Ananda was requested to give discourses on the teachings. He inserted this phrase at the introduction of each Sutra and concluded with a standard paragraph describing how everyone present rejoiced and praised the Lord. Amongst the discourses given by Ananda were some on Sutras which he had last heard from the Buddha thirty-five or more years previously. The Sutras were certainly not written down immediately after being revealed by particular Arhats or Bodhisattvas. Some were deliberately concealed for hundreds of years to be revealed later on.[38] Likewise many Tantras were recorded centuries after the time of Buddha. In the Buddhist tradition, such delays do not preclude authenticity, nor do they argue for authorship by those who merely revealed them.

It is sometimes difficult for western scholars to accept the great feats of memorisation required to uphold an oral tradition. But we should recall that many disciples of the Buddha who were assigned to reveal teachings had already attained Arhatship and had acquired the art of 'non-forgetfulness.' The 'practice of memorisation' and the tradition of the esoteric whispered lineage prevailed in the Buddhist tradition for a long time even after the recording of the Sutras began. Even today in the Tibetan tradition there are novices who memorise three or four volumes of Sutras and Tantras before they reach the age of eighteen. There are a number of monasteries where monks unable to chant certain Sutras or Tantras by heart are forbidden to take part in the ceremonies. Although such feats of memorisation are uncommon in modern western education, they nevertheless persist amongst Tibetan monks to this day.

We should remember that even though Ananda, Upali and Mahakashyapa gave discourses on Sutra, Vinaya and Abhidharma respectively, they are not regarded as the authors of those scriptures. Or are they? So why then should Saroruha be regarded as the author of the *Hevajra Tantra* or a certain 'Tantric Nagarjuna' the author of *Guhyasamaja Tantra*? The compiler of *Hevajra Tantra* was Vajragarbha. Saroruha was not even the compiler let alone the author of the Tantra. He became an important commentator on *Hevajra Tantra*, but it does not follow that he was its author. His commentary on the Tantra along with many others [39] is to be found in the Tengyur section of the Tibetan canon, while the *Hevajra Tantra* itself is found in the Kagyur. Bu-ston Rinchen Drub (1290-1364), who was responsible for the edition of the Tibetan Buddhist canon, had special reasons for classifying the Buddhist scriptures the way he did. He carefully compiled the whole Tibetan Buddhist canon into Kagyur and Tengyur to avoid possible fabrication by incompetent scholars in the future. If the narrator of a Sutra or a Tantra explains the time and place where the Lord Buddha taught to Bhikshus, kings, Arhats, Bodhisattvas and others who were present, surely we can infer that the teaching was not written either by the narrator or by the compiler. There is no need to question the identity of the person who taught the Sutras or the Tantras when the evidence clearly appears in the relevant texts.

Classical Buddhist texts were compiled in such a way as to ensure future generations of students would take the time to read and understand them in their entirety, before dissecting them into superfluous editorial classifications. Much of the so-called 'scholarly confusion' has arisen because of the craving of ambitious scholars who attempt to uncover dry facts at the expense of pursuing true knowledge. Their enthusiasm might be better utilised by taking a break from accumulating facts for a while and spending some time learning traditional practices. I do not say this flippantly. Real knowledge of Buddhism is experiential. While intellectual knowledge is a necessary component of studying Buddhism, it is only a component. Unless scholars learn to balance this by practice, they risk losing their bearings and floundering upon a sea of irrelevancies.

Although a scientific methodology with its roots in the physical sciences has something to offer students of Buddhist history, we must take care not to push it beyond its limitations. To illustrate this with an analogy, we would not expect a chemical analysis of the paints used on the Mona Lisa to unravel the mystery of the painting's appeal and shed light on the genius of Leonardo. It may, however, add to our store of knowledge about the composition of the paints used by artists of Renaissance Italy, if that interests us. Even if 'modern' scholars solve their self-imposed problem of dating Buddhist Tantras and identifying their authors to their own satisfaction, who will benefit? Temporarily, perhaps, the scholars. But their findings will be toppled in a few years by a new generation of scholars. As for Buddhist cultures, they have maintained their traditional religious traditions throughout millennia, and they are as fresh and relevant today as they were over two thousand years ago. It is difficult to see how they will derive any benefit from research issuing from scholarly confusion and scepticism which furthermore applies techniques often quite foreign and unsuited to an understanding of a spiritual tradition.

There are two basic reasons why practicing Buddhists are unlikely to be very excited by scientific discoveries about their early sacred history. One is that unlike many western religious traditions, adherence to Buddhism does not rely heavily on beliefs about specific events which occurred in the past. As I mentioned earlier, the practice of Buddhism is largely experiential. Buddhists place great emphasis on trying out the teachings for themselves, rather than blindly following instructions handed down over many centuries. Of course, practices which prove efficacious and remain useful to this day will continue to be treasured and utilised. But Buddha himself advised his disciples to put his teachings to the test. Given their freedom from the past, discoveries concerning details of early Buddhist history may seem irrelevant to many. The second reason, which is linked to the first, concerns the Buddhist view of the nature of reality. This is quite different from the scientific western viewpoint. The modern scientific perspective takes as its basis a material world. There is an assumption that the continuing process of amassing data from this material world will teach us about the operations of our universe, and that our state of knowledge will continue to expand and cumulate with each new discovery. Buddhists on the other hand, see the material world as nothing more than the creation of our own deluded perceptions. That being the case, material discoveries cannot lead to ultimate truth. If all beliefs held by ordinary people are deluded, then ultimately there are no right or wrong beliefs for them to hold about the material world. In a sense, there is nothing either to prove or to refute. Beliefs are therefore relative rather than absolute. As spiritual progress in Buddhism is achieved through modifying behaviour, training the mind and developing wisdom, 'beliefs' are useful only to the extent that they help us to make progress on the path. Beliefs which are unhelpful, although 'scientifically verifiable' may be happily discarded by the spiritual seeker once they have served their purpose.

Still on the topic of means of verification, there are many safeguards within the traditional framework of Buddhist scholarship to protect the integrity of the teachings and guard against accepting spurious works and those of doubtful authenticity. For example, there are certain basic criteria to which all teachings of the Buddha must adhere. These apply equally to works in the Buddhist canon and to exegetical works. They are designed to safeguard against any possibility of spurious claims.

Firstly, a person who professes to be Buddhist must take refuge in the Three Jewels and accept the four seals of the Buddha's words. The four seals are:

1. All phenomena are by nature suffering;
2. All compounded phenomena are impermanent;
3. All things have no self; and
4. Nirvana is peace.

In addition, any legitimate teaching found in the Buddhist canon must show that:

1. It was taught by the Buddha;
2. It was compiled by a recognised Arhat, Bodhisattva or Siddha;
3. It must be a well-known and accepted work amongst Buddhist scholars, and widely discussed amongst the Buddhist Panditas;
4. It must have been translated from a classical Buddhist language such as Sanskrit, Pali, Tibetan or Chinese by eminent translators into the language in which the teaching is preserved; and
5. The translator(s) must be competent in the Buddhist philosophy and related languages and should have worked in collaboration with another competent scholar.

There has never been any suggestion on the part of Buddhist scholars that those who cannot understand Buddhist Tantras should accept them as legitimate teachings of the Buddha simply because the works have Sanskrit titles attached to them along with the names of recognised translators and collaborators. The contents of the work must also echo the four seals in general and harmlessness and helpfulness to other living beings in particular. The works must show how specific methodology, discussed according to the vehicle, puts those ideas into practice without contradicting fundamental Buddhist teachings. It follows that one must be a practicing Buddhist with experiential knowledge in order to make informed judgments. I would like to reassure any Tantric practitioners who have been discouraged by the sometimes-disparaging remarks of non-practitioners. Such comments, however well meaning and sincerely offered, are put forward by those who are not really in a position to make informed judgments about the highly sacred, esoteric path of Tantra. To use another analogy, imagine some scientists were to select a thousand ordinary people at random and ask them to practice composing music for the piano for eight hours a day over ten years. They would be given no teaching by any music master, just unlimited access to sheet music and books on musical theory. They would be allowed to write papers and talk amongst themselves. If at the end of the ten years, none of these people had managed to produce a single piano concerto of genius, would this prove Chopin did not exist after all, or that others who received proper instruction might not reach similar heights?

There are those who confuse Buddhist tantra with Hindu tantra. It would be foolish to deny the existence of any connection between Buddhist and Hindu Tantras. The Buddha was brought up in a Brahmanic culture and was well versed in Vedantic teachings before he renounced the world and became the Buddha. One can clearly see the influence of some of the Vedic rituals even in the Theravadin ordination ceremonies just as much as in the Vajrayana rites and rituals. It is important to remember that Buddha skilfully integrated prevailing social norms and religious customs into his teachings without in any way compromising his unique message. It would be a disservice to Buddhism to totally reject Hinduism and overlook its valuable contributions to Buddhist culture. But claims that Vajrayana Buddhism is a branch of Hinduism are ill-informed and have been refuted in detail by other writers. India is the birth place of Buddhism, and there are certainly superficial similarities. When it comes to practices such as tantra, one must understand that these practices are esoteric and deal with subtle levels of energy. Esoteric streams are to be found in the methodologies of many ancient religions, including Taoism and Hinduism amongst others. It is the framework in which these techniques are used and the uses to which they are put which distinguish them from each other. A monkey and a man cannot be distinguished easily from a distance. One must conduct a closer examination to tell them apart. It is always unwise to base judgments on superficial appearances. Take the example of two people who are using the technique of meditation. Even when we approach closer, they may still look as though they are doing exactly the same thing. They may be sitting in exactly the same posture. But that may be all they have in common. One may be watching his breath, or simply trying to relax or even going over his shopping list. The other may have reached the very highest levels of meditative absorption.

7. THE HEVAJRA TANTRA AND ITS COMMENTARIAL WORKS

In order to understand the origin of the Lamdre tradition in India, it is important to examine the origin of the Hevajra Tantra and its commentaries. It is said that in the distant past, at a time when the Form and Desire realms were ruled respectively by Brahma and Maheshvara, all living beings had been manipulated into indulging in the three defilements (greed, hatred and ignorance) and were thus led onto the wrong path. In order to subdue these mundane gods and to establish living beings on the right path, the Sambhogakaya Heruka assumed the appropriate manifestations and taught both root and commentary Tantras. After having subdued these two worldly gods, the Fully Enlightened One assumed the Nirmanakaya form of Heruka and taught the 700,000-verse Long Form Shri Hevajra Tantra, 500,000 verses of Realisation Tantra, the Uncommon Explanatory Dakini Vajrapañjara Tantra, Samputa and the commentary Tantras common to other classes of Tantra. Once again, the historical Shakyamuni Buddha assumed the form of Heruka and taught the Hevajra Tantra[40] which contains 23 chapters and 750 verses. The compiler of Hevajra Tantra was Vajragarbha.

Tshar-chen Losal Gyatsho (1502-1566) cites twelve main Indian siddha masters who wrote commentaries on the Hevajra Tantra. These are: Vajragarbha,[41] Naropa,[42] Krishnacarin,[43] Bhavapa,[44] Tamkadasa,[45] Padmapa,[46] Durjayacandra,[47] Shantipa,[48] Samayavajra,[49] Pad-myug,[50] Kamadhenu[51] and Dharmakirti.[52]

There were six main commentarial traditions (bshad srol drug) of the *Hevajra Tantra* which were handed down from the Indian Mahasiddhas. These are directly connected with the origin of the Nine-fold Paths.[53] They are:

1. Saroruha's tradition;
2. Durjayacandra's tradition;
3. Northern Gate-Keeper Pandita Shantipa's tradition;
4. Shantabhadra's tradition;[54]
5. Kashmiri Nyendrak Sangpo's tradition;[55] and
6. Adipati Maitripa's tradition.[56]

Numerous Hevajra traditions reached Tibet, from Marpa to Ngok Choku Dorje, in addition to traditions following Rapa Choerab, Chalse Lotsawa, Tumton Lodro Drakpa and Ram Dingmapa, following Naropa's,[57] lineage. The main Hevajra tradition concerned with Lamdre was brought to Tibet by Drogmi Lotsawa and probably also by Goe Khugpa Lhaytse.[58] Drogmi received the transmission from Gelong Pawo Dorje (Viravajra) which followed the lineage that came from Durjayacandra. He also received the transmission from Gayadhara who followed the lineage from Krishnacarin. Although there were many other Tibetan commentaries on the *Hevajra Tantra*, the seven famous works kept in the Sakyapa tradition are:

1. Word by Word Explanation (tshig 'grel) [59] by Lama Ngaripa Salway Nyingpo;
2. Commentary on Difficult Points (dka' gnad);
3. Commentary on Perfect Purity (dag ldan) [60] by Jetsun Drakpa Gyaltshen;
4. General Explanation of all the Tantras (rgyud sde spyi rnam) [61] by Lopon Sonam Tsemo;
5. mngon rtogs ljon shing [62] by Jetsun Drakpa Gyaltshen;
6. Rays of Sun [63] by Lopon Sonam Tsemo; and
7. Commentary on Difficult Points (dka' gnad) [64] by Sachen Kunga Nyingpo.

There are many other commentaries on *Hevajra Tantra* by Tibetan masters. We do not have space to list here. These do not include the whispered lineage's pith instructions (man ngag), passed down from one master to a single disciple, e.g. Virupa to Dombi Heruka. Because the Tantra was initially transmitted through whispered lineage, there were no instructional manuals or books on Lamdre until the late 11th century. A disciple was not permitted to give teachings to others or to write about the teachings without special permission from his teacher. However, fearing that people in a degenerate time might not be able to keep the whispered lineage correctly, Sachen Kunga Nyingpo wrote 'exegetical works' after having fulfilled the requirement of eighteen years dedicated practice which had been imposed upon him by his teacher.[65] Sachen wrote approximately twenty instructions based on the *Vajra Verses* which became the main instructional guidelines for

Lamdre. Eleven of these are considered very important. Although there are different schools of thought about which exactly are the eleven commentaries, the following list is according to Dagchen Lodro Gyaltshen (1444-1495). They are all named after students for whose sake they were written:

1. *"Thondu-ma (don bsdus ma)"* [also known as 'Asengma'] was written at the request of Khampa Aseng. It is probably the shortest and the first of all the works;

2. *'Shujay-ma (zhu byas ma)'* was written at the request of Zhujey Ngodrup;[66]

3. *'Lokya-ma (klog skya ma)'* was written at the request of Logkya Choedak of Gyerphu region; [67]

4. *'Yumdon-ma (yum don ma)'* was written at the request of his senior consort; [68]

5. *'Saydon-ma (sras don ma)'* compilation of numerous difficult points on *Vajra Verses* was written for his two sons Jetsun Drakpa Gyaltshen and Sonam Tsemo.[69] It was compiled and edited by his disciple Tsuktor Gyalpo, who is also known as Sonam Dorje;

6. *'Da-gyal-ma (zla rgyal ma)'* was written at the request of Bodhisattva Dawa Gyaltshen; [70]

7. *'Zangri-ma (bzang ri ma'* was written at the request of Geshe Zangri Phukpa;

8. *'Gatheng-ma (sga theng ma)'* was originally a set of notes prepared by Khampa Gatheng on the basis of Sachen's teachings. It was later corrected and edited by Sachen himself;[71]

9. *'Mangkhar-ma (mang mkhar ma)'* was written for his female disciple Mangchung;

10. *'Hahu-ma (ha hu ma)'* was written for a female disciple whose meditative realization of a dog made her say 'Hahu Hahu;'.[72]

11. 'Nyak-ma (gñags ma)' was written for Geshe Zhirawa Wangchuk Pal.

Except for 'Asengma' which was especially written by Sachen himself, all the rest are believed to be revised and corrected versions of notes prepared by his disciples from Sachen's oral teachings. Since then many works have been written and most of the transmissions are still preserved in scriptures as well as in practice.

8. THE MEANING OF LAMDRE

The term 'Lamdre' (path and result) can best be understood from the point of view of its secret philosophical meaning. *Lam* means 'path' and *dre* (*'bras)* means 'result' in Tibetan. Lamdre is about a path including its result and its cause. This also implies the cause including its path and its result and result including its cause and its path. This principle of wholeness nullifies duality. The notion of 'Path Including its Result' emphasises neither disassociating the path from the result nor the result from its cause. Central to the Tantric philosophy is the importance of annihilating the conceptual dichotomy which exists between conventional opposites. Hence the term Lamdre contains a philosophical and scientific explanation of reality both at its operational or relative level and also at the ultimate level.

Just as a faultless seed can germinate if provided with the right conditions, a faithful disciple can achieve enlightenment if he meets the circumstantial conditions of the pith instructions. The *path* includes its *cause* since it is only by following the *path* (meditation) that the actual purifiable stains (defilements) which constitute the *cause* can be recognised. It is our own particular defilements (*cause*) which we need to remedy through meditation (*path*). The *path* includes its *result* since the *result* is achievable only through practice of the *path*. It is only for the purpose of obtaining the *result* that one practises the *path*. The *result* includes the *cause* since the *result* is nothing other than the transformed aspect of its *cause*. The realisation of the *result* simply uncovers the unseen side of the *cause* and dispels the misconception that they were ever different. Just as gold paint transforms the black colour of iron into gold without completely abandoning the base metal, negativities will gradually be transformed into their natural qualities without the need to annihilate the causes.

In short, since nothing exists inherently outside the mere perceptions of one's mind, all concepts manifest according to the state of the mind itself, which is ultimately free of activities. In spite of the distinct, adventitious and conditional reflections of the mind, notions such as good and bad, path and result do not exist as they may appear to our conscious or conceptual mind. What appears to our conceptual mind does not conform to reality. For example, objects such as a chamber pot, an ear-ring and an image of the Buddha, all made out of copper, will be seen as dirty, beautiful or venerable respectively according to the way we conceive of them and label them. But in spite of their different conventional appearances, functions and usages, the substance 'copper' has not become better or worse, whatever use we make of it. Similarly, there is no difference between the true and basic nature of the mind of a beginner, an advanced practitioner and a Fully Enlightened One. The difference is only in the perception, conditioned as it is by the deluded mind. It is by purifying the apparent impurities on the path that the causal Buddha, previously unrecognised due to the presence of adventitious obscurations, emerges as 'Resultant Buddha' once he recognises the self. In order to develop enlightened experiences, one must recognise the expedient method of embarking on the correct path. The expedient method is called *upadesha* or 'pith instructions.' In order to receive the instructions from a qualified Guru, one must first be initiated into the Path by receiving *abhisheka*.

9. THE THREE TANTRAS

Part II of this book contains a translation of the Tibetan text of *Three Tantras* by Panchen Ngawang Choedak (1572-1641). Teachings on the *Three Tantras* (rgyud gsum) are usually given only during Lamdre teachings which are always conducted by prominent Lamdre lineage masters of the Sakyapa tradition. The text *Three Tantras* is the backbone of the Lamdre teachings, drawn from the *Hevajra Tantra*. The concept of the *Three Tantras* is not unique to the Lamdre system. It is the basic formula which explains all of the teachings of the Vajrayana tradition. Ground (gzhi), path (lam) and result ('bras-bu) are the three components of Vajrayana. There are however, a number of factors which distinguish Lamdre from other Vajrayana teachings. One of the most important of these is its comprehensive, graduated methodology.

No Sanskrit equivalent of the term 'Lamdre' appears to have been used in the *Hevajra Tantra* on which the Lamdre teachings are based. It is clear, however, that the term gained currency some time after the passing away of Virupa and his disciples. From one point of view, terms such as 'Lamdre' (lam 'bras), the Path including its Result and 'Lamrim' (lam rim), the Stages of the Path are so broad that they could be used for any complete form of teaching which includes a path leading to a result. Nevertheless, within Tibetan Buddhism, the terms Lamdre and the *Three Tantras* are synonymous with Hevajra Tantra and Sakyapa lineage. The *Three Tantras* are a basic formula for the entire path leading to the ultimate liberation. It may be used with any of the four classes of Tantra which contain ground, path and result. They may be explained as follows:

A. The Basis of All Cause Tantra, the Non-Differentiation of Samsara and Nirvana

In discussing the *Three Tantras* we also look at their relationship to the *Three Visions* or *Three Appearances*. In the Lamdre system, instructions associated with the common vehicles are found in the section on the *Three Visions*, while the secret Mantra teachings of the Vajrayana are to be found in the *Three Tantras*. From one point of view, there would be no difficulty in including all the teachings on the *Three Tantras* within the *Three Visions*, as all the realisations of the views and final accomplishments of the Four Initiations belong to the vision of experience as well as to pure vision. The instructions on the *Three Visions* focus primarily on the nature of subjective Samsara and on ways to enter the path to enlightenment if Samsara is to be renounced and eliminated. The notion that conventional Samsaric appearances are 'impure vision' or reflections of a deluded mind leads us to examine more closely the nature of mind and why it perceives in that way. There is discussion on the need to cultivate virtuous causes in order to attain Enlightenment by following the Bodhisattva's way of life. This opens the possibility of purifying the impure vision. The notion that Samsara and Nirvana, in common with all dualities, are mere reflections of the mind introduces the path of non-abandonment and transformation. As long as there is duality, the self will see a gulf between itself and its objects. This veil which hinders the self from seeing the truth and the oneness of all things is called 'impure vision.' The intrinsic purity of the self which experiences the impure vision is based on the continuity of mindstream which flows from one moment to another.

The word 'Tantra' simply means 'continuity of one's mindstream.' The fundamental base of all this is the mind. There is nothing whatsoever which does not include the mind. No dualities such as good and bad, one and many, Samsara and Nirvana exist inherently. They are mere imputation and false imagination

(Parikalpita) of the mind. When one examines the nature of mind, it has no colour, no shape, no form and no locality. It is simply the state of being or self-nature (svabhava) unadulterated by concepts and ideas. Like the sky, mind is clear, spacious and empty. As soon as one analyses the clarity of the mind and its spacious presence, one discovers that mind is empty. It cannot be verbalised, nor can it be conceptualised.

Because of their failure to realise the nature of their own mind, beings have clung to objects as real and permanent. Those very manifestations of the unrealised nature of the mind are conventionally labelled 'objective reality.' What appears to be an existent reality 'in appearance only' is erroneously grasped to be true and real, just as a man frightened in the dark by a striped rope mistakes it for a snake. Until he realises the way in which causes and conditions arise interdependently, and that he has himself projected the image of a snake onto the emptiness of a rope, the frightened man will remain afraid. He remains under the influence of dependence (Paratantra). Whereas were he to take his torch and examine the supposed snake at close quarters, he would understand dependent arising, cease to grasp at his self-created image of the snake and simultaneously be released from fear. The realisation that snake nature is absent from the rope reveals that the rope is empty of snake at all times. This discovery calls into question the very nature of the rope, and by extension, the validity of all labelled phenomena. The fact that the rope can manifest alternately as snake and then rope, according to the man's level of knowledge, indicates its lack of inherent existence. Once one realises this, one is released from grasping onto phenomena. This sense of freedom is known as 'complete perfection' (Parinispanna).

Until a sentient being realises the lack of inherent existence of the self and all phenomena and while it continues to grasp objects as though they were real and permanent, the being's mindstream will continue throughout countless rebirths. The mind is the underlying cause of all (Alaya hetutantra). To ordinary beings, it appears difficult to discover and know the true nature of the mind. Whatever one's circumstances, whether one is experiencing happiness or misery, heat or cold, the intrinsic nature of the mind maintains its everlasting attributes of clarity and emptiness. This is called the 'Embryo of the Tathagata' in Mahayana terminology. Habits of mental grasping accumulate projections of the unrealised self onto the outside world. This process relies on the medium of the gross physical body and its sense organs. All sensory objects become the property of the relevant senses which grasp onto them as inexorably as a moth is drawn towards a lighted lamp. The unrealised self is reflected in all objects, forms, sounds, smells, touch and thought. The cause of all perceptions and experiences is the failure to realise the *Alaya consciousness*. The relative appearances of the various realms of existence experienced by an ordinary sentient being who has failed to realise the nature of his mind are known as 'impure appearance' or vision of the Karma. It is this grasping onto the impure appearances as real which creates the habit energy. This in turn is imprinted onto the consciousness. The *Lankavatara Sutra* states:

> *Varieties of habit-energy growing out of error are united with the mind; they are perceived by the ignorant as objects externally existent; and the essence of the mind (cittasya dharmata) is not perceived.*[73]

Those who realise the lack of true existence of all appearances and meditate on the true nature of their mind will undergo deep meditative experiences which will totally alter appearances and their impact. This is called the 'vision of experience'.

B. The Body Method Tantra in Association with the Four Initiations to Introduce the True Nature of One's Mind and See the 'All-Encompassing Truth.'

Vajrayana makes skilful use of the human physical body as a medium for achieving enlightenment. The unrealised self can relate best to his own forms, feelings, volition, perceptions and states of consciousness. These are the five aggregates, known also as *skandas*. Although still unrecognised as such, they are by nature the *five Tathagatas*. As they are the natural extension of the unrealised *Alaya consciousness*, the five aggregates communicate with the external world through the medium of the five sense organs. The way in which sense objects manifest and impact on the mental consciousness is largely determined by the *five defilements* (greed, hatred, ignorance, jealousy and pride). The intrinsic nature of the five defilements is in reality the *five transcendental wisdoms*. In this way the self which fails to know its own true nature will project an entire world around it. Every mental event when not watched calmly will extend its horizon to exaggerate the mere mind-created appearance into something 'real' and 'permanent.' What a person perceives and experiences becomes his individual *Mandala* (dkyl 'khor). He is the centre (dkyil) of the universe. Everything else is his circumference ('khor). He is the creator of all.

All dualities dissolve instantly when the naked mind's aspects of clarity and emptiness are permitted to surface. However, as long as the mind continues under the influence of its adventitious habitual tendencies and Karmic defilements, impure appearances will be mistaken as real and beings will be controlled and manipulated by their own projections, like a worm which ties itself up in its own saliva.

The Lamdre tradition identifies four factors within the human body which are instrumental in portraying the 'circumference.' These four factors are:

body vein mandala	(lus rtsa'i dkyil 'khor, Skt. kayanadimandala);
vein letter mandala	(rtsa yi ge'i dkyil 'khor, Skt. nadyaksharamandala);
element nectar mandala	(khams bdud rtsi'i dkyil 'khor, Skt. dhatvamrtamandala); and
essence air mandala	(snying po rlung gi dkyil 'khor, Skt. hrdyavayumandala).

The physical body creates chemistry which varies according to the person's state of mind. By radiating its aura, the body then communicates this state of being to the outside world. We have many thousands of veins or nadis in our body. These serve as channels for both the vital air and the elements which determine our impressions and experiences. *Rasana* and *Lalana* are the veins of both Samsara and Nirvana, happiness and unhappiness as well as all dichotomies. They are located in the form of subtle letters at different parts or psychic centres of the body. The central channel, known as *Avadhuti*, is a neutral vein. An ordinary person's mental waves, controlled by his dualistic thoughts, do not flow through this vein.

Subtle white and red elements circulate through the *Rasana* and *Lalana*. These perpetually display the appearance of duality. Movements in the *vital air mandala* determine to which vein letters and locations the element nectars flow, and the mode and frequency of this flow. The movements of the *vital airs* are produced by our *thoughts*. When a person is in an angry state of mind, for example, the forceful vital air movements direct the flow of the elements towards the appropriate vein letter which is located at specified points within the *body vein mandala*. An angry person sees all things around him as hostile. His habitual impatience and aversion induce him to react by rejecting and resisting. An emotionally charged state of mind causes an increase in the blood circulation. An irresistible energy within seems to take control of the psycho-physical experience.

A quiet state of mind, free from gross dualities will make less use of the two dualistic veins. A being may thus experience balance and harmony. Owing to individual Karma and defilements, beings develop *habit energies* which operate to direct the flow of energy in a habitual pattern to the same locations and centres of the body time after time. The energy follows a well-worn path. It is the path of least resistance. This is why our habitual patterns seem so powerful. It requires great effort for an ordinary being to divert the energy flow from these paths, or a fundamental shift in consciousness which activates new thoughts and renders the old pathways irrelevant. In this way the mechanism does not even get the chance to build up momentum. In order to introduce a major change to the way individuals perceive and experience their world, the *four body mandalas* need to be purified or reactivated. This is accomplished through receiving the *four initiations*, on each of the body mandalas.

C. The Procedure of the Ceremony of the Hevajra Cause Initiation

The *Three Tantras* forms the greatest part of the Vajrayana section of the Lamdre teachings. It is given only to disciples who have received the Hevajra Cause Initiation. This conforms to the statement in the *Three Tantras* that the view of 'Non-Differentiation between Samsara and Nirvana,' the subject matter of the *Basis of All Cause Tantra,* may be taught only to those who have received the Hevajra Cause Initiation. Hence in the Sakyapa Lamdre tradition, no high teachings on 'Mahamudra,' 'Dzogchen' or 'Non-Differentiation between Samsara and Nirvana' are given outside the format of complete Lamdre teachings.

A student must firstly be ripened by the blessings of initiation before receiving pith instructions on the view. The initiation must be received from a well-known and qualified lineage master, not from anyone who holds a title of 'Lama' or 'Rinpoche.' Eminent teachers such as Sakya Pandita have remarked that the introduction of teachings on the nature of the mind to unripened students is the doctrine of the heretics. Prior to receiving the Hevajra Cause initiation, students attend ten to fifteen days of teaching sessions and guided meditation on the *Three Visions* (snang gsum). At the conclusion of these teachings, the Bodhisattva Vow (sems bskyed chen-mo) is conferred. Then the Hevajra Cause Initiation is imparted.

The Lamdre teaching is timed[74] so that the Bodhisattva Vow can be conferred on a full-moon day or some other auspicious day such as the anniversary of an eminent Lamdre lineage master. At the formal request of the students, the Guru accepts them as his disciples (slob ma rjes 'dzin) and instructs them to engage in virtue. Then the Vajra master performs a supplementary retreat (kha gso'i bsnyen pa) which usually takes several days, before conferring the Hevajra Cause Initiation. During this teaching break, would-be initiates are asked to accumulate merit by performing Refuge, prostrations, Vajrasattva, Mandala offerings and Guru Yoga to make themselves worthy of receiving the initiation and the esoteric teachings on the *Three Tantras*. As the teachings on these practices are to be found in the *Three Tantras* at Part II, I do not need to elaborate on them here. There are occasions when teachings on the *Three Tantras* may be given outside Lamdre, but only to students who have received the Hevajra Cause Initiation. Certain Sections of the *Three Tantras* are restricted to people who have received the Hevajra Path Initiation. This is conferred only upon students who have received the Hevajra Cause Initiation and who undertake to do the daily *Hevajra Sadhana* with body Mandala.

The Hevajra Cause Initiation takes two days. The Vajra master officiates at the ceremony in accordance with the rites and rituals prescribed in the Tantra. Both the Vajra master and the disciples should understand and possess the qualities required by a Vajracharya (diamond master) and Vajrachela (diamond disciple). Vajrachelas must possess strong faith in the Vajrayana path and must have reached a certain level of maturity through teachings on the Mahayana and common teachings. On the first day of the initiation, known as 'preparation day (sta-gon),' the Vajracharya must perform four to five hours of sanctification *ceremony* (sgrub-bshags) before conducting the actual preparation ceremony with the disciples. A number of ritual monks assist him in preparing the various ritual objects. When the sanctification ceremony is over, students are asked to rinse their mouths. They then enter the initiation hall, perform three prostrations and take their seats. An assistant then distributes rice and grains from a tray at the centre of which is a mandala plate. He collects some rice back from the disciples, returning it to the tray which he will use to offer the Mandala on behalf of all the disciples. The Vajra master begins the ceremony with a short introduction to Tantra and the importance of initiation in the secret Mantrayana. Speaking briefly on the good fortune of the students, he then explains the following fourteen preparatory rituals:

1. Physical behaviour: Disciples should do three prostrations before taking their seats, rinse their mouths and sit respectfully with clasped hands.
2. Development of Renunciation: The Vajra master explains the importance of generating a strong sense of renunciation from the shortcomings of Samsara and encourages the disciples to cultivate an altruistic motivation to benefit other sentient beings as the main purpose of receiving the initiation.
3. Inner Initiation: A brief inner initiation (nang-dbang) will be performed so that the Vajra master does not transgress his vows by disclosing the secrets to the

uninitiated. It also prepares the disciples to receive secret teachings.

4. Special Request: The disciples make a special request to the teacher to bestow the Vajrayana vows and pledges as well as Refuge and Bodhicitta.75

5. Encouragement: Calling the disciples 'my children' the Vajra master encourages them by explaining briefly the efficacy of Vajrayana path.

6. Purification: In order to cultivate the enlightenment thought and to make themselves worthy of receiving the necessary Pratimoksha, Bodhisattva and Vajrayana vows the disciples repeat the Seven-fold Prayer.

7. Protection: The Vajra master performs rites of protecting and blessing the disciples' body, speech and mind into the nature of the deity's three Vajras. He performs this by touching their forehead, throat and heart with holy water blessed during the preparation.

8. Receiving Offerings: The Vajra master then makes the eight offerings to the disciples whose three doors (body, speech and mind) have already been blessed into deities and instructs them from then on to enjoy all sensory perceptions without attachment.

9. Tooth-Stick Examination: The disciples are asked to throw a tooth-stick onto a drawing of an eight-petalled lotus on a square white cloth spread in front of the Vajra master so he may examine the signs of siddhis they are likely to attain on the path. As brushing one's teeth washes away the impurities of the body, throwing the tooth-stick prepares the disciple to receive the vase initiation which will be given on the disciple's body vein Mandala.

10. Drinking Holy Water: The Vajra master gives the disciples holy water to drink. This is poured from a conch-shell into their palms in order to purify their

defilement of speech. This makes preparation for the secret initiation which will be given on one's vein letter Mandala.

11. Protection Cord: A red string is folded thrice with three knots. The string is blessed by the Vajra master, and then given to each of the disciples, who tie them onto their upper arms to protect their subtle elements and as a preparation for the transcendental wisdom initiation which will be given on one's element nectar Mandala.

12. Kusha Grass: One long and one short tuft of Kusha grass is given to each disciple. These are to be placed under their pillows and mattresses that night in order to free their minds from conceptualisation during sleep and to enable them to have clear dreams without disturbance. This prepares for the fourth initiation which will be given on one's essence air Mandala.

13. Dharma Discourse: The Vajra master gives a succinct discourse on the preciousness of the Dharma and the rarity of obtaining a human rebirth which provides all the freedoms and endowments to practice Dharma. This is done in order to evoke a strong feeling of delight and joy in the minds of the disciples. He announces that disciples who have taken part in the preparatory rituals will be admitted into the supreme Hevajra Mandala the next day.

14. Observation of Dreams: The Vajra master instructs the disciples to go to bed in the posture in which the Lord passed away and asks them to observe the general significance of dreams they might have during the night. He reiterates that they should neither become attached to good dreams nor fear bad ones, since all phenomena and perceptions are just dreams and illusions.

On the second day, which is the day of the main initiation (dngos gzhi), the Vajra master blesses all the initiation objects by performing the Hevajra Sadhana and Hevajra self-initiation. He blesses the painted cloth or coloured sand Mandala, the Vajra and the other initiation objects. I will give a brief summary of the initiation procedures.

D. Admission to the Mandala

The initiation will be given on the basis of either a coloured sand or a painted cloth Mandala. The first part of the initiation begins with a request to be admitted into the Mandala and repetition of the vows of the five Tathagatas. Before being admitted, the disciples are each given a red blindfold to bind around the forehead. This signifies that the disciples have not yet entered the Hevajra Mandala. They are given flowers to hold, because it is inappropriate to see the deities in the Mandala while empty-handed.

The Vajra master pronounces various injunctions with regard to the harm which will befall disciples if they disclose the secrets of Vajrayana to the uninitiated. He describes the benefits accrued in keeping them secret. In order to sow the seed of enlightenment, he performs the rites of the descent of transcendental wisdom (ye shes pa dbabs pa) which introduces the disciple to the intrinsic nature of the mind. This is to awaken the Basis of All Cause Tantra (Alaya Hetutantra). On this occasion disciples with firm faith and devotion may experience from one to three signs of the descent of the transcendental wisdom. During the admission into the Mandala, the Vajra master removes the blindfold and the disciples offer their flowers to the Mandala. At this point the Vajra master returns the blindfold and the flower to each disciple and tells each of them to which Tathagata family he belongs.[76] This is followed by a description of the indwelling deities and the whole symbolism associated with the resident deities and residence Mandala.

E. Main Bestowal of Initiation

Following admission into the Mandala, the main bestowal of the initiation is divided into four sections: *Vase Initiation, Secret Initiation, Transcendental Wisdom* and the *Fourth Initiation*. The *Vase Initiation* is sub-divided into two sections: Vajra disciple and Vajra master's initiations. The Vajra disciple's Vase Initiation consists of the *Initiation of the Six Tathagatas* which is given in order to purify the aggregates and defilements by means of the initiating objects. I will tabulate them accordingly:

Initiation	Defilement	Aggregate	Object	Wisdom	Family
water	hatred	consciousness	vase	mirror-like	Akshobhya
crown	pride	feeling	crown	equanimity	Ratnasambhava
vajra	passion	perception	vajra	discrimination	Amitabha
bell	jealousy	volition	bell	accomplishment	Amoghasiddhi
name	ignorance	form	nil	dharmadhatu	Vairocana
behaviour	grasping	nil	vajra	dharmata	Vajrasattva

After receiving all the initiations of the six Tathagatas, disciples receive the vows of the respective Tathagatas which they recited at the commencement of the initiation. Some Tibetan scholars have argued that the three-fold repetition of the vows of the five Tathagatas in itself constitutes initiation. In other words, they question the need for the Tathagatas' initiations. It will suffice for me to say that this viewpoint has been refuted by past masters. The Vajra master's initiation, which is referred to as the 'irreversible initiation,' is bestowed by giving the three Samayas of body, speech and mind in conjunction with Vajra, bell and mudra. The oral transmission of the Mantra is also given at this time. Disciples are asked to make undertakings as to the number of

Mantras they will recite each day. This is followed by several additional initiations to empower disciples to benefit other sentient beings by preaching the Dharma. The efficacy of the disciples is tested in a symbolic exercise during which disciples express the way they would benefit other living beings. The procedures of the last three initiations will not be discussed here. Before each of these three initiations one ties on the blindfold. It is removed at the conclusion of each initiation.

F. Mahamudra Result Tantra

The bestowal of the Hevajra Cause Initiation involves direct progression from Cause Tantra to Path Tantra. This facilitates the realisation of Result Tantra. The disciple who practises the Hevajra Sadhana every day, provided he also understands the Triple Tantra teachings, will be able to undertake all the relevant practices included in the vase initiation and may subsequently attain six bhumis either in this life, at death or in the intermediate state.

It is said that a person with the least intelligence will attain enlightenment in sixteen lifetimes provided he does not transgress his vows. The mediocre person who maintains his daily Sadhana practice will attain liberation in less than six lifetimes, a person of the highest intelligence in this lifetime, at death or in the intermediate state. The generation stage, which is the path (lam) of the vase initiation must be practised before one may realise the view (lta ba) and its final accomplishment (grub mtha'). As an aid to this realisation, one should apply the instructions on dream yoga, (rmi lam gri rnal 'byor). This is an extremely powerful practice. Dream yoga, when properly applied, enables practitioners to transform their sleep into meditation. Sleep is then no longer seen as a hindrance to meditation.

In case practitioners may be unable to attain realisation in this lifetime, they are given instruction on *Dakama* ('da' ka ma)[77] of the

Vase Initiation, which can be actualised at the time of death. Conventionally this is known as '*Phowa*', the practice of ejecting and merging one's consciousness into the heart of the Guru at the moment of death. Those who are successful in performing this will not experience *Bardo* (intermediate state) but may choose to assume an incarnation in the world for the benefit of other beings.

For those who may not realise accomplishment at the time of death through the Dakama practice, instructions on the intermediate state (bar do) are given. According to Buddhist Tantric teachings, deceased beings remain in the *Bardo* state for between three and forty-nine days before finding a new rebirth. The death rituals performed for the deceased help him to understand and accept his own death. It is then easier for the deceased to find a new rebirth to release him from the misery of Bardo.

Following this, similar practices are given for the three later initiations (dbang gong ma gsum) which are largely to do with the stages of completion practices. Each of the three initiations also has its own set of path, view, and final accomplishment. In the Sakyapa tradition, both Hevajra Cause and Hevajra Path initiations are limited to twenty-five students or fewer. There must always be an odd number. The Hevajra Result Initiation is said to be given when one attains enlightenment in the Akanishta Heaven by Vajradhara and the complete initiation deities in their Sambhogakaya aspect.

The complete teachings of the *Three Tantras* are delivered in stages so as to prepare students for the Hevajra Cause and Path initiations. The instructions on Cause Tantra and related instructions on the Vase Initiation are given straight after the disciples receive the Hevajra Cause Initiation (rgyu dbang). Before giving the instructions on the last three initiations, the Path Initiation (lam dbang) is bestowed on the basis of the Vajra master's inner body Mandala. During the Path initiation, the Vajra master repeats most of the initiations he has given during the

Cause initiation and introduces the disciples to the intrinsic nature of the veins, droplets, letters and elements in their subtle bodies. This confers the authority to practice the path of the completion stage practices which are the subject matter of the instructions contained in the last three initiations.

G. Overview of Lamdre Literature

Lamdre texts are meditational and practical manuals used by hundreds of ecclesiastics and lay practitioners of the Sakya tradition. Lamdre is a sacred and secret path which has been trodden by many great masters. It is the sole path to Enlightenment for many faithful students. Those who are fortunate enough to own a set of Lamdre texts should treat them as objects of the highest value. They should take them with them wherever they go. Thus, these texts are known as 'non-detachable' (bral spangs), because they must always remain with the practitioners. Works on Lamdre contain sacred oral history, hagiographies of the lineage masters, instructions on esoteric meditation practices of the Hevajra Sadhana, numerous commentaries on Hevajra Tantra, and related liturgies on rites and rituals of the Tantra. Traditionally these texts are accessible only to faithful and fortunate initiates, who are allowed to touch, possess, read, contemplate and practice them.

What follows is a brief account of the origin of the selective accumulation of Lamdre works written by scholars and Yogins during a period that spanned from the 7th to the 20th century. The entire body of Lamdre literature may be divided into six main divisions:

I. Expositions on Hevajra Tantra (gzhung bshad)

In addition to the expositions written by Lamdre masters, there are numerous Indian expositions called 'gzhung bshad' or 'rnam 'grel' (or simply 'grel pa) on Hevajra Tantra included in the Tibetan

Buddhist canon. 'Gzhung bshad' expositions are pre-13th century commentaries on Hevajra and associated Tantras. The eleven works by Sachen are known as 'rnam 'grel' (pronounced 'Namdrel') meaning commentary on Virupa's *Vajra Verses*. Many of these Indian and Tibetan commentaries are widely consulted both within and outside the Lamdre tradition. We have already identified the seven highly regarded commentaries on Hevajra Tantra by the Sakya lineage.

II. Classical Lamdre Manuscripts (lam 'bras glegs bam)

In spite of the abundance of authoritative commentarial works on the Root Hevajra Tantra, it is still beyond the comprehension of ordinary students. The classical Lamdre manuscripts (lam 'bras glegs bam) are pre-15th century scriptures extracted from both those expositions and from oral instructions compiled and edited by eminent Sakya masters as an aid to students. Their titles were derived from the respective colours of the pieces of cloth used to wrap the practice manuals. Prior to the 13th century, notes on the secret oral teachings were passed down from master to disciple and circulated as manuscripts. It was not until the 13th century when carving and production of xylographic blocks began in Tibet, that selected works were compiled, edited and included amongst the collected works of the five founding masters of Sakya (sa skya gong ma lnga). The earliest Tibetan Lamdre authors (as distinct from Virupa and other Indian authors) were Sachen Kunga Nyingpo (1092-1158) and his sons Sonam Tsemo (1142-1182) and Jetsun Drakpa Gyaltshen (1147-1216). Their works were published exclusively as part of their collected works (bka' 'bum). Later on, the works on Lamdre by Sakya Pandita Kunga Gyaltshen (1182-1251/52) and his nephew Drogon Choegyal Phakpa (1235-1280) were also published as integral sections within their collected works. In spite of this inclusion of the Lamdre commentaries by the Five Masters in their collected works, the existence of Lamdre literature did not become generally known until the emergence of separate editions of extracted Lamdre work(s) wrapped in different coloured cloths.

There are, however, many works on Lamdre in the *bka' 'bum* (collected works) of Sakya masters which are not included in these editions. The high reputation of Sakyapa scholarship from the 13th to the 16th century together with the glorification of many of its individual scholars and Yogins led to a high degree of support and patronage for the compilation of *'Collected Works'* [bka' 'bum]. However, the secrecy surrounding the esoteric contents of Lamdre texts precluded their inclusion in printed compilations. There were self-imposed restrictions on the disclosure of Tantric instructions in almost every tradition at that time. For instance, Zhangton Choebar instructed Sachen not to write or even talk about Lamdre practice for eighteen years. It was only after this period had elapsed that Sachen began to teach and write. Out of his eleven commentaries, which were in fact commentaries to the same root text [gzhung rtsa ba rdo rje tshig rkang], *lam 'bras gñags ma*, was the last. Because of its concise nature, it was compiled together with notes. These were sealed and locked in a wooden trunk. Although originally known as *'sag shubs ma,'* a name derived from the word for *'wooden trunk,'* its actual name is *'gñags ma'* since it was given to Ngak Zhirawa Wangchuk Pal. He is not to be confused with Nyak Nyingpo Gyaltshen, a disciple of Tshogom Kung Pal.

According to Ngorchen, since Jetsun Drakpa Gyaltshen located, selected, compiled and wrapped this and other instructions on Lamdre in a yellow cloth, it became known as 'Lamdre Yellow Annals' [lam 'bras pod ser ma].[78] As can be seen, this particular work received three different names within one generation, much to the confusion of the historians of Lamdre literature. One can imagine how the discrepancies in identification of the eleven commentaries would have arisen. Another important Lamdre author is Mar Chokyi Gyalpo who was a close disciple of Sapan. He wrote *'gzhung bshad dmar ma'* on the basis of instructions given by Sapan. This work became known as *'Lamdre Red Annals'* (lam 'bras pod dmar). In his introduction, he states that *'lam 'bras gñags ma'* was used as a principal reference by Sapan when he delivered his teachings on Lamdre.

The first systematic and comprehensive Lamdre treatise *'Lamdre Black Annals'* [lam 'bras pod nag] was based on *Lamdre Yellow and Red Annals*. It was written by Lama Dampa Sonam Gyaltshen (1312-1375), who also sponsored the first edition of the collected works of the five masters as a tribute at the funeral observance of his deceased teacher Palden Senge. His treatise was so named because it was wrapped in a dark iron-coloured cloth. There are a number of other works on Lamdre written by disciples of Drogmi and the five masters which are not listed in this edition.

III. Hagiography of the Lineage Masters (bla ma brgyud pa'i rnam thar)

The hagiographies of Lamdre lineage masters cover one third of the entire Lamdre literature. The earliest of these is the life of Virupa by Jetsun Drakpa Gyaltshen.

IV. Treatises on Common Lamdre Teachings (lam 'bras tshogs bshad)

The sixteenth century saw the emergence of a galaxy of Lamdre masters and scholars. Apart from the already mentioned Lamdre works named after the different colours of the volumes, there are other works found in the collected works of numerous masters which may have been carved earlier. However, there is no evidence of other Lamdre texts being printed at this stage. Within this edition of the Sakya Lamdre Literature Series, the works are divided into *Lamdre Lobshe* and *Lamdre Tshogshe*. Prior to the

15th century, the literature did not distinguish between the *Lobshe* and *Tshogshe* lineages, nor is there any evidence of the existence of the two lineages. The two-lineage system may have developed from a practice of Muchen Konchog Gylatshen (1388-1469), who gave pith instructions to Dagchen Lodro Gyaltshen (1444-1479) in privacy. These instructions were given infrequently and restricted to a small number of advanced disciples who were making experiential progress (myong 'khrid). They were given as the teacher's experiential advice (man ngag). The common lineage however, allowed for a larger group of students. It was given annually at Ngor monastery in Tibet, under the title of *Tshogshe* (tshogs bshad). Hence Dagchen Lodro Gyaltshen, who has also written numerous works, is regarded as the first promulgator of both of these lineages. Subsequently his disciples and grand-disciples, who followed the two distinct lineages made a vast liturgical contribution to their development. The texts of the two lineages are distinguished more in their respective style and language than in their actual contents. *Lobshe* manuals are straight-forward instructions written in the warm colloquial language of Upper Tsang. *Tshogshe* manuals tend to use rather classical and scholastic Tibetan and include numerous quotations from Sutras and Tantras.

A prolific Sakya author named Ngorchen Konchog Lhundrup (1497-1547) wrote some scholastic treatises on the *Three Visions* and the *Three Tantras*. These texts simplified the task of many later Lamdre masters, who often read directly from them in their teaching sessions. Consequently, these works developed into the classical Lamdre *Tshogshe* manual of Sakya and Ngor monasteries. His works are very widely read. My introduction to Lamdre literature was this author's *Beautiful Ornament of Three Visions* (snang gsum mdzes rgyan) which I first read in 1970, and which is freely available in translation today. Later works by Jamgon Amezhab Kunga Sonam (1537-1601) and Panchen Ngawang

Choedak (1572-1651) became alternative or supplementary to the manuals by Ngorchen in the *Tshogshe* tradition.

V.   *Manuals on Uncommon Lamdre Teachings (lam 'bras slob bshad)*

The uncommon Lamdre lineage was transmitted through Doringpa Kunpangpa Chenpo (1449-1524) to Gorum Kunga Lekpa then from both of these masters to Tsharchen. It remained solely an oral teaching until Jamyang Khyentse Wangchuk (1524-1568) and Mangthos Ludrup Gyatsho (1523-1594), who became respectively the sun and moon-like disciples of Tsharchen Losal Gyatsho (1502-1567). These two eminent masters took notes on the basis of instructions from Tsharchen. These developed into two complete sets of Lamdre Lobshe manuals which were endorsed by Tsharchen himself. In 1904 Jamyang Loter Wangpo (1847-1914) courageously undertook and sponsored the task of preparing xylographic blocks of a seventeen-volume text of *Lamdre Lobshe*. He persevered in this task despite opposition from others who feared that the printing and disclosure of the secret teachings might displease the Dharma protectors. He largely ignored their opposition. He wrote a synthesis of two Lamdre Lobshe manuals by Jamyang Khyentse Wangchuk and Mangthoe Ludrup Gyatsho which dispelled doubts and clarified certain apparent contradictions between these two works which had been raised by other scholars. Without his tireless effort and noble example in sponsoring, editing and publishing many important Sakya works e.g. *sgrub thabs kun btus* including *lam 'bras slob bshad*, the edition of the complete collection of Lamdre in thirty-one volumes would not have materialised. This was the first time common and uncommon texts were printed together. Prior to this time, printing of the *Lobshe* texts had been resisted owing to voluntary censorship on the part of the lineage masters.

VI. *Liturgy on Initiation Rites, Mandala Rituals and Hevajra Sadhana (dbang dang dkyil chog sgrub thabs skor)*

Lamdre liturgies are perhaps the most widely used works by Lamdre practitioners. Many of the Mandala rites, manuals on Hevajra initiation and Sadhanas are memorised by all monks of the Sakya lineage. They are all native Tibetan works. Although there are some Sadhanas written by Indian Siddhas found in the *Kagyur*, they have all been replaced by more concise native Tibetan editions, such as the *Hevajra Sadhana* by Muchen Konchog Gyaltshen. The bibliography of the complete Lamdre works prepared according to the *Sakya Lamdre Literature Series* edition published by Sakya Centre in Dehra Dun gives some indication of the richness of the literature in this lineage.

H. Panchen Ngawang Choedak (1572-1641)

In order to provide a spiritual and historical setting for *The Three Tantras*, I will briefly discuss the author's religious training, including the transmissions and instructions he received and the teacher disciple relationships he formed. The author of the text of *The Three Tantras* herein translated is Panchen Ngawang Choedak. His name is often abbreviated to Panchen Ngagchoe. He was born in 1572 a few miles from Sakya in central Tibet, son of a celebrated physician named Drungtsho Phuntsok. He received novice vows from Chen-nga Konchok Gyatsho at Thubten Yanpachen monastery. This teacher gave his own ninety-five-year-old teacher's name to Ngawang Choedak. He studied Abhidharma, Pramana, Madhyamika, Vinaya and Prajnaparamita with Je Wangchuk Palzang. By the age of eighteen he had become a bright scholar. It was at Sakya where he gained extraordinary confidence in his study after his excellent performance in the examination on *Pramanayuktaniddhi*, Sakya Pandita's famous treatise on Buddhist logic. He then embarked on a debating tour of Ngamring, Gadhen and other major monastic institutions. In the process, he became famous as a man of great skill and learning. At Mangkhar, seat of Lamdre teachings in Tibet, he received the complete *Lamdre Lobshe* instructions and affiliated initiations from Mangtho Ludrup Gyatsho (1523-1594) who became one of his main teachers. At the age of twenty-nine he helped to establish a newly designed system of eleven teaching methods which accommodated the needs of students from China, Uighur and Mongolia studying at the Ngamring College.

In 1601 at Ngamring College he started writing his famous exposition on Vinaya. He was highly respected by Chokyi Wangchuk, Shamarpa VI (1584-1635) who was one of his favourite teachers. At Dhar Drangmoche monastery, the seat of Tsharchen Losal Gyatsho (1502-1566) [79] he received many initiations and instructions on Sakya Dharmapalas and protectors from the great master Ngakchang Sonam Choephel (1527-1603).[80] At the age of thirty he received Lamdre teachings according to the Ngorpa tradition from Palyon Zangpo, Abbot of Tanak Thubten monastery. He also received his Bhikhu ordination from this abbot. At the age of thirty-five he was enthroned at Samdrup Gonsar monastery. In addition to looking after this monastery, he saw to the welfare of several other institutions. During this time, he received some instructions of the Niguma tradition from Jonang Taranatha (1575-1634). At the age of thirty-nine he was appointed to the throne of Rabjampa Thukje Palzang at Thubten Yanpachen monastery, a position which he occupied for six years.

Panchen Ngawang Choedak's abbotship at Thubten Yanpachen was of great benefit to the Dharma activities of many surrounding Sakyapa monasteries in U-Tsang province, including Nyenyo Jagoeshong, Choekhor Lhunpo and Yaga Choedhing. After retiring from the abbotship of Thubten Yangpachen, he dedicated more time to practice. He remained in retreats on Cakrasamvara, Hevajra and Yamantaka. The *Hevajra Tantra, Sancayagatha*[81] and the *Five*

Treatises of Maitreyanathv [82] were included among his daily recitation of Sutra and Tantra in addition to his Sadhana commitments. He gave both *Lamdre Lobshe* and *Lamdre Tshogshe* teachings over a dozen times at Samdrup Gonsar, Labdrang Dzong, Thubten Gephel monastery and Tanak. He ordained hundreds of novices and Bhikhus. He also gave many whispered lineage teachings on major and minor Mahakala practices as well as Vajrayogini, the Three Red Deities [83] and Six Teachings of Nigu to Dagchen Kunga Sonam Lhundrup, [84] then the holder of the Sakya throne. He received the oral transmission of the *Collected Works of the Founding Fathers of the Sakyapa Order* and initiations of Amoghapasha, Amitayus and wrathful Red Padmasambhava from Dagchen Rinpoche. It was Dagchen Rinpoche who convened an important conference at Sakya which was jointly conducted by Panchen Ngawang Choedak and Jamyang Shakya Tenzin, then abbot of Serdhokchen monastery, seat of Panchen Shakya Chogdhen (1428-1507).

Ngawang Choedak received many important initiations and teachings from Wangchuk Rabten (1559-1636) of Dhar Drangmoche monastery. He is reputed to have made 100, 000 circumambulations of Lhasa, the sacred city and 100, 000 circumambulations of a sacred image of Jetsun Drakpa Gyaltshen in Sakya. He visited Tanak Thubten monastery, seat of Gorampa Sonam Senge (1429-1489) and gave numerous teachings at the request of Tanak Khenpo Choe Namgyal and Ngawang Tenpe Dorje. He gave the Vajramala (Dorje Trengwa) initiation to Gonpo Sonam Chogden.[85] He took over the throne of Dhar Drangmoche, where he spent the last two years of his life. During this period, he made plans for the restoration of the monastery. He died peacefully in deep meditation at the age of seventy in 1641. Several relics and bone pieces clearly marked with the images of Vajrayogini, Vajrabhairava and two armed Heruka were discovered in the ashes of his cremated body.

Ngawang Choedak can be best remembered as a remarkable master of Buddhist philosophy and a pillar of both *Lamdre Lobshe* and *Lamdre Tshogshe* lineages. Despite his achievements, he did not enjoy the privileges of recognition as an incarnate Lama or birth into a hereditary lineage. Although his works on Lamdre are included within the *Lamdre Tshogshe*, his contribution to *Lamdre Lobshe* is of paramount importance as indicated by his death on Tsharchen's throne. He is probably best known outside Sakya circles for his extensive exposition on Vinaya. The following list of his works is indicative of the breadth of his knowledge and the invaluable contribution he made to Sakyapa scholarship and its literature.

I. Works by Panchen Ngawang Choedak

1. An exclusive commentary on Sakya Pandita's Pramana.
2. An exposition on Prajnaparamita *'Illuminating the thoughts of the Omniscient.'*
3. A thesis on turning the Wheel of the Dharma *'The Torch of Sacred Words.'*
4. An exposition on Madhyamikavatara *'Essential Clarifier of the Excellent Vehicle.'*
5. A commentary on Sakya Pandita's *'Distinctions of the Three Vows.'*
6. An exposition on Vinaya *'Sun's Rays of the Sage's Teaching.'*
7. An exposition on Abhidharmakosa *'Clarifier of knowable objects.'*
8. A commentary on Uttaratantra.
9. A commentary on Nagarjuna's *Suhrllekha.*
10. A thesis on Debates between the Sautantrika and Vaibhashika Madhyamika doctrine.
11. A synopsis of Sakya Pandita's *Entrance to the Wise.*

12. A commentary on the *Hevajra Tantra.*
13. History of *Guhysamaja Tantra.*
14. Refuting the charges laid against *Lamdre Lobshe.*
15. Replying to Questions on Lamdre.
16. History of Mahakala.
17. Numerous biographies and eulogies of eminent teachers.
18. Initiation rites on Pancakrama.
19. A History of Lamdre.
20. An interlinear commentary on *Vajra Verses* of Virupa.
21. An exposition on Vajrabhairava stage of Generation.
22. Questions regarding Cakrasamvara practices.

J.   The Text

The full title of the work herein translated is: 'The Essence of the Elegant Teaching of the Main Stages of Instructions on The Three Tantras' (gsung ngag dngos gzhi'i khrid rim rgyud gsum snying po'i legs bshad). It is found in the Lamdre Tshogshe Volume Ra (25) of the 31-volume edition of the Sakya Lamdre Literature Series (SLLS), published by Sakya Centre in 1983. It is printed in the traditional Pecha form containing 110 folios (ff. 389-399) copied by a team of monk calligraphers from the original manuscript preserved in the private library of the Most Venerable Ludhing Khen Rinpoche of Ngor monastery in Dehra Dun. This work was written in 1623 when the author was fifty-one years old. It is by no means Ngawang Choedak's best known work.

The language he uses in his Lamdre work is very distinct Tsangpa colloquial dialect. This clearly indicates the spoken language used in the whispered Lamdre teachings. He carefully avoids using quotations or the flowery and poetic style we find in his philosophical works. His fundamental outline of the text does not always correspond to his sub-headings and their actual explanations. As he mentions in his colophon, his work on the Three Tantras is a concise version of Ngorchen Konchog Lhundrup's (1497-1557) monumental work. His writings on Lamdre [86] became more frequently incorporated into Lamdre Tshogshe teaching manuals, gradually replacing the use of the otherwise comprehensive Lamdre works of Ngorchen Konchog Lhundrup. Although his is a complete manual with its own collection of Lamdre history, it contains hardly anything not found in earlier works. Later Lamdre expounders seem to have appreciated his works greatly, probably because they are both concise and complete. In consequence the work has gained great currency, especially for use in Lamdre Tshogshe teachings. With his infinite wisdom and compassion, he would have seen the need for such a manual at a time when beings are not so blessed with ample time to attend long Lamdre teachings.

It is hoped that this translation will help English speaking adherents of the wonderful lineage of the Palden Sakyapas to taste the sweet ambrosia of the Lamdre teachings and benefit all sentient beings!

Lama Choedak Rinpoche
Canberra, Australia
18 April 1997

PART ONE

THE ORIGIN OF THE LAMDRE TRADITION IN INDIA

by

Lama Choedak Rinpoche

THE TRIPLE TANTRA

1

THE LIFE OF MAHASIDDHA VIRUPA

Virupa was born a crown prince, the son of King Suvarnacakra (*gser-gyi 'khor-lo*) of the city of Vesasa[87] in eastern India. The court astrologers predicted at his birth that he would develop tremendous spiritual powers and would illuminate the teachings. He was given the name Rupyacakra (dngul-gyi 'khor-lo). As a young child, he entered the famous monastery of Somapura in North Bengal where he received novice ordination from the abbot Vinitadeva[88] and the Acharya Jayakirti.[89] He mastered all the five major sciences and became a great scholar of both Buddhist and non-Buddhist doctrines. It was here that he built a stone temple in which he installed holy images of the Buddha. He established a tradition of making regular offerings to cleanse the misdeeds of his deceased parents. When the temple was complete, he offered a big celebratory feast to the whole monastic community and dedicated the merits.

Having concluded his studies there, he left for Nalanda where the Dharma was firmly established. There he received Bhikhu ordination from the abbot Dharmamitra[90] also known as Jayadeva[91] of Nalanda University.[92] He was given the name Shri Dharmapala.[93] He continued his study under the tutorship of his abbot who was very pleased with him and gave him many private teachings on Vajrayana practices in general and on Chakrasamvara Tantra in particular. The abbot left instructions in his will that Shri Dharmapala should be appointed his successor and asked the monastic officials to show equal respect and honour to his successor as they had always shown to him. When Dharmamitra passed away, Dharmapala was accordingly appointed abbot of Nalanda. He supervised his predecessor's grand funeral ceremony and arranged to have the entire remains of the abbot transformed into relics which he carefully distributed amongst the various kings, patrons and monks.

Dharmapala practised Chakrasamvara diligently every night according to the secret instructions he had received from his abbot. His days were devoted to teaching and composition. Although he gave teachings on both Theravadin and Mahayana texts, he devoted most of his own time and energy to the esoteric practices of Vajrayana. He continued to practice Chakrasamvara wholeheartedly year after year. However, at the age of seventy[94] despite so many years of faithful practice, Dharmapala was yet to experience any signs of spiritual attainment. He also had to contend with all his old diseases which plagued his body and his mind. He was saddened and frightened by the constant harm caused by Yakshas[95] and evil-spirits. To add to his general state of discouragement and frustration, he had been having the most frightful nightmares. In one of these dreams he saw a huge fire burning at the lower end of a valley and a flood arising from the upper end. He saw hail-storms, glaciers, icicles and icebergs falling from the sky. He saw his Guru, Yidam and spiritual friends hanging upside down, or with their faces torn apart, noses cut-off, eyes gouged out and dripping with blood.[96]

Not surprisingly, Dharmapala interpreted these dreams as bad omens. He concluded that he must lack the karmic connection to attain realisation through the path of Vajrayana in that lifetime. He decided to give up his Vajrayana practices completely. Accordingly, on the night of the 22nd day of the fourth lunar month he relinquished his practice of Deity Yoga and threw his prayer beads into the latrine.

These dreams were actually indications that Dharmapala was about to achieve a major spiritual realisation through his Tantric practices. But he had no way of knowing this at the time, so he completely misread the signs. He was unaware that he had already perfected the Path of Accumulation,[97] the Path of Preparation[98] and was about to attain the Path of Seeing.[99] At that time his vital energy and his mind had merged in the *ksa* and *ma* syllables below the Navel Cakra.[100] This had caused the symbolism which appeared so terrifying in his dreams. He failed to recognise the signs of what was happening to him because his abbot had died before imparting the complete pith instructions. These would have explained the drastic changes occurring in the subtle energy flows within his psychic body and clarified the dream experience.

Shri Dharmapala decided that from then on, he would devote his entire time to teaching, writing and other duties for the Sangha (monastic community) instead of spending many hours a day on Deity Yoga meditation practice. However, on that very night he dreamed that the Goddess Nairatmya appeared before him in the form of a beautiful blue woman wearing heavenly silk garments, and spoke to him thus:

> *"O noble son, it is not good that you should behave in this manner when you are about to attain the Siddhi. Although all the Buddhas have non-discriminatory compassion, I am the deity with whom you have strong Karmic affinity and I shall bless you to quickly attain Siddhi. Go and retrieve your prayer beads, wash them with scented water, confess your misdeeds and resume your practice properly."* [101]

Then she disappeared. Dharmapala awoke feeling a mixture of regret and joy. He followed her instructions, resuming his practice early that morning. Subsequently the Mandala of the Nirmanakaya aspect of the Fifteen Goddesses of Nairatmya appeared before him and gave him the four complete initiations. He thereupon attained the Path of Seeing of the First Bhumi.[102] He now realised the true significance of his dreams. The rough dreams and visions of Yakshas were the interdependent manifestations of his mind and vital energies merging into the *ksa* and *ma* syllables below the navel Cakra. This was caused by the untying of the vein knots which brought about the First Merging of Elements [103] and signs of the vital energies of Candali heat.[104] The unconventional experiences which appeared to his conceptual mind resulted from the re-adaptation process between the veins and the mind. As a sign of the intermediate Merging of Elements[105] the Candali fire blazes upward and causes the Bodhicitta nectar to flow upward. Such an interdependent manifestation of internal events would be experienced conceptually by the Yogi as a blazing fire from the bottom of the valley and a flood coming from the upper part of the valley. The forceful circulation of subtle droplets in many minor veins was reflected in the dreams about hail-storms, and the icebergs falling from the sky. The Third and Final Merging of the Elements[106] revealed the bare face of flawless transcendental wisdom. This has the effect of dissolving all attachment to ordinary appearances. These interdependent manifestations were reflected in his dreams as the torn faces of his Guru and Yidams. He came to realise that all those signs had been direct meditative experiences related to the three sequential mergings of the subtle elements within his body.

Through the timely appearance and guidance of Vajranairatmya, Shri Dharmapala had finally attained realisation. From then on, he reached a higher Bhumi each day until in the early morning of the 29th of the same month he attained the sixth Bhumi. He was now a great Bodhisattva dwelling on the sixth Bhumi. His receipt of the four complete initiations[107] confirmed that the continuous flow of the empowerment had not ceased. The attainment of the six Bhumis[108] was confirmation that the lineage of the blessings was unbroken. His failure to recognise previous signs of attainment and his misinterpretation of these signs as bad omens confirmed that he had not received certain pith instructions.

This enabled him to realise that the order of the instructions was not wrong. In consequence, Dharmapala's devotion to the teachings was restored and redoubled. He became confident that he would definitely attain the realisation of a Fully Enlightened One, as did the Buddha. In this way he was blessed with the Four Whispered Lineages, which came to be known as the *Instruction of the Four Whispered Lineages.*

Out of gratitude to his Guru and Yidams, Shri Dharmapala asked his companions to prepare Ganachakra feast offerings. Meat and wine were included amongst the requisite offering substances. The other monks became apprehensive when they saw the meat and alcohol being taken into their abbot's quarters. Some of them eavesdropped at his door at night. Depending on the level of purity or impurity of their respective minds, they each saw different things going on in his room. Some saw the abbot surrounded by fifteen women, others saw only eight. Some saw him surrounded by fifteen lamps, while others could see only eight of them. These nocturnal sightings aroused considerable suspicion within the monastic community. However, the monks dared not speak out for he was their abbot, and his reputation in the wider world was not just untarnished, it was brilliant, like the sun.

In the meantime, Shri Dharmapala had already decided that, in order to avoid any possibility of disparagement to the doctrine which might arise from misunderstandings about his behaviour, he should without delay confess his wickedness. Accordingly, he left his room and went before the Buddha image. Removing his Dharma robes and setting down his begging bowl, he declared, "Ame Virupa" which means "I am wicked." Next, he went off and adorned his head with flowers and leaves which he took from florists. He snatched radishes from vegetable shops, stuffing some into his mouth and others beneath his armpits. He began frequenting wine bars and brothels. His behaviour caused a scandal and it was not long before the monastic gong was beaten, signalling his dismissal from the monastery for violation of the monastic code of conduct.   Virupa responded by singing joyously.[109]

In order to benefit the Buddhadharma and also to rekindle the faith of those who had lost their faith in him, he had admitted his wickedness. After his dismissal he adopted the name 'Virupa'. He became very famous under this new name and his ordination name 'Dharmapala' was virtually forgotten. Hence very few scholars or historians, apart from the Lamdre historians of the Sakyapa tradition,[110] realise that it was the famous abbot Dharmapala who later became Virupa.

Virupa set off for Varanasi. When he reached the river Ganges, he spoke the following words:

> I am wicked, so let me pass without touching you, as you are believed to be pure. I do not want to pollute you.

Even as he spoke the waters of the Ganges parted and there appeared before him a dry white path. He walked along the path singing joyously. Some monks had followed him as far as the river. When they saw this amazing feat, they realised that Virupa had already attained the siddhis. They begged their dismissed abbot for forgiveness and requested that he return to the monastery. Virupa forgave them but declined to return.

He wandered through the forests of Varanasi for a long time. Some sources say this went on for six years, others say six months. Because of his nakedness, his complexion turned bluish and he became frightful to behold. Peasants who saw him reported his presence to the king. Some thought he was a Hindu Yogi, while others suspected he was a Buddhist Yogi. The king of Varanasi, Govindachandala was a staunch devotee and patron of Hindu Yogis. He wanted to offer comfort to the wanderer should he prove to be a Hindu but feared the man might bring harm to his citizens if he turned out to be a Buddhist. Accordingly, he ordered his ministers to investigate the Yogi. However, the ministers could find no clue to his identity. The king then ordered that this mysterious Yogi be brought to the palace so that he could examine him personally. On the way, Virupa indiscriminately devoured many worms, pigeons and butterflies which he then vomited up and resurrected. The king's men labelled him 'wicked.' He told them that he had no idea how he should behave since they labelled him 'wicked' whether he devoured worms or resurrected them. Virupa was finally brought before the king. The king asked him many questions, but Virupa answered not a single word. Then the king said:

> *Since this Yogi has neither any of the qualities of Vishnu nor any noticeable signs of a Hindu Yogi, chain up his limbs and throw him into the river. He must be a Buddhist Yogi.*

The ministers had Virupa thrown into the river exactly as the king had commanded. However, before the ministers returned, the magical Virupa had already reappeared and was standing before the king. This process was repeated many times until finally the king became convinced that the Yogi knew a magical spell to control the water element. The king then ordered all the butchers of the city to stab the Yogi. But their knives and axes became blunt as if they had been striking rock and failed to inflict even the slightest injury. Next the king's men dug a deep ditch. They buried Virupa and poured molten iron and bronze over his body. Then they dumped soil on top and let many elephants trample over it. Even after all this, he appeared before the king unharmed. At this point, the king developed great faith in Virupa's spiritual power and confessed his misdeeds. Subsequently Virupa converted all the citizens of Varanasi to the Vajrayana path.

After that he left for the south to subdue Bhimesara. On his way he asked a boatman to ferry him across the Ganges. The man declined to do so unless he would pay a fee. Virupa told the boatman that he would offer him whatever would make him happy.[111] He asked the boatman, "Do you want this river to be large or small?" "Sometimes I like this river large, at other times I like it small," the boatman replied. Promising to give him the river itself as payment, Virupa reversed the flow of the Ganges by pointing at it with a threatening gesture.[112] The river almost deluged nearby houses and lands. The inhabitants became alarmed that their property would be destroyed. Knowing that this was due to the power of the Yogi, king Calabhadra and the villagers requested Virupa to return the water to its normal channel. They offered him all kinds of inducements, including gold, silver, cattle, grain and flowers. In response, Virupa burst into song. With a snap of his fingers he restored the river to its normal channel. He gave all the offerings he received to the boatman. The man refused the gifts. Instead, he touched Virupa's feet and asked to be accepted as a disciple. The boatman, who later became known as Dombi Heruka, is said to have been a fortunate disciple with ripened Karma suited to liberation by way of the 'sudden path.'[113] Virupa accepted the boatman as his pupil and the two set of for the south, leaving the villagers to collect the abandoned offerings.

The pair reached Daksinipata[114] near Bhimesara and entered the house of a wine-seller named Kamarupasiddhi.[115] They asked for some wine and the wine-seller responded by asking whether they could pay for it. Virupa replied, "Serve me until I am satisfied, then I will pay whatever you want."[116] The wine seller, who was highly sceptical, asked, "But when will you pay?" Virupa drew a line on the floor with his dagger and said, "I will settle the bill when the shadow of this house reaches this line." The wine seller served the two men but Virupa used magical powers to restrain the 'day star' from moving along its usual course. He demanded more and more wine and drank until the tavern was dry. Much time passed but the shadow of the house got no closer to the line. The tavern-keeper was obliged to import wine from the taverns of eighteen great cities to fulfil her part of the bargain.

Although to the amazement of all the tavern-keepers, Virupa drank more than five hundred elephant loads of wine, there was no indication that his thirst was quenched. In the meantime, the town of Daksinipata was plagued with continual daylight and everyone lost track of time. All the inhabitants were exhausted, crops withered in the fields, lakes and rivers began to shrink and no one had any idea of the order in which events had occurred. Unaware of Virupa's magical powers, the king ordered his ministers to investigate what was stopping the sun. When he found out that all this was due to the power of the Yogi, the king requested Virupa to let the sun resume its course. Finally, Virupa assented, on condition that the king agree to settle his bill. Then he released the sun. By then it was mid-night of the third day after he had stopped the sun.

Virupa became known as one who had not only parted the waters of the Ganges on two occasions but had also halted the sun in its course for three days. His fame spread far and wide. Meanwhile he continued his journey to subdue Bhimesara in the south and to find Krishnacarin, a future disciple who it is said was a suitable candidate for the 'gradual path.' Bhimesara was ruled by a Hindu king named Narapati[117] who was a devotee of five hundred Yogis with plaited hair.[118] They worshipped at a massive Shivalinga and at an image of Mahadeva which had been installed by a previous king named Bhayasena.[119] They sacrificed tens of thousands of buffaloes and goats every year. Virupa arrived among them and wrote many eulogies to the Shivalinga in Sanskrit. The king was greatly impressed with his scholarship. He asked him to become the leader of the five hundred Yogis, an offer which Virupa found difficult to refuse.

During the regular worshipping ceremonies, the Yogis bowed down to the image of Mahadeva and made flower offerings. While this was going on, Virupa would pull out a volume of the Prajñaparamita text which he kept tucked in his hair and pay homage to it. He never bowed to the image of Mahadeva. The Yogis became suspicious and reported this behaviour to the king. Instead of paying heed to their allegations, the king accused the Yogis of jealousy. "He is such a great scholar and master of the

Vedas. It is impossible that such a man does not pay homage to Mahadeva, the king of the gods. You must be jealous of him," the king replied. However, the Yogis kept on reporting Virupa's behaviour until at last the king decided he must observe the truth himself by attending one of these ceremonies personally. When he did, Virupa paid his homage to the Prajñaparamita text as usual. The king was amazed. He addressed Virupa, saying, "Why are you not bowing down to the image of Mahadeva?" "Why should I?" replied Virupa. "He cannot bear my homage." The king then said, "There is no one more powerful than he in the whole desire realm.[120] Why do you say he cannot bear your homage? You must show your respect." "Since I have no choice but to do what the sinful king demands of me, you must forgive me," Virupa said to the image. As soon as he placed his hands together to pay homage and said, "Namo Buddhaya" (I pay homage to the Buddha), one third of the gigantic image cracked to pieces. When he said, "Namo Dharmaya" ([I pay homage to the Dharma), two thirds of the image cracked and when he said, "Namo Sanghaya" (I pay homage to the Sangha), the entire figure crumbled into pieces and fell to the ground.[121]

The king was shocked. With a mixture of fear and faith, he requested Virupa to restore the statue. Thereupon Virupa instantly restored it and placed upon it a black stone image of the Great Compassionate One, Avalokiteshvara.[122] He then said to the king, "The statue will remain intact so long as no one removes the image of Mahakarunika. Should anyone remove this, the statue will instantly crumble to bits." Then he left. Amongst the five hundred Yogis was one who was dissatisfied with the behaviour of the Tirthikas (heretics). Having witnessed Virupa's wondrous qualities he developed deep devotion to him and became his disciple. This was Krishnacharin of the East who, although never previously a follower of the Buddhadharma, now decided to enter the path.

Virupa and his two disciples, Dombi Heruka and Krishnacharin, wandered further into the south to a district ruled by devout Brahmins. They reached a place where there was a huge image of Shiva, which stood one hundred and twenty feet high. It had been built by King Jomgi. It was known as 'Tambrapratima.' It had three faces, six hands and was made of bronze. This shrine attracted hundreds of devotees who sacrificed thousands of animals in order to offer meat and blood. As the trio pushed their way into the crowded gathering at the worshipping ceremony, someone was heard to say, "There is no room for you inside. Wait outside and we will give you your share of the feast." Ignoring this, Virupa entered forcibly and commanded, "If there is no room, it is you who should get out of this place." So, saying, he kicked the statue. The figure followed him, taking seven wobbly steps outside the shrine before crashing down on its face. The terrified devotees then requested Virupa not to take the image away but to leave it behind. Virupa threatened to remove it unless they gave up animal sacrifices. He said that he would leave it behind on condition that they agree to make only vegetarian offerings in future, and vow never to sacrifice any more animals. The devotees agreed and vowed as Virupa had commanded.

In this way all who had heard the name of Virupa placed a Buddhist image on top of their Hindu images, for fear that Virupa might come and destroy them. The very name of Virupa, Baleshvara, the Lord of Power or Yogeshvara, the Lord of the Yogis, brought great benefit to limitless living beings. When Virupa saw an image of Goddess Tara placed on top of a Hindu image, he circumambulated the image which turned her face towards him as he walked. This became known as the 'Turning Face [Image of] Tara.'

1. SUBJUGATION OF THE GODDESS CHANDIKA

Virupa and his companions continued traveling south. They arrived at a place where there was a self-arisen image of Goddess Chandika, named Sahajadevi which was worshipped by many Hindu Yoginis. This shrine had a Trishula (a three-pointed ritual knife) which of its own accord without any human intervention would pierce through the neck of pilgrims, killing them as soon as they entered the shrine. The Yoginis would then make offerings of flesh and blood to the image. Virupa knew about this and had come purposely to subdue it. He instructed his two companions to remain outside and perform special breathing meditation. The Yoginis were delighted to see Virupa and asked him to bring his two companions inside with him. Virupa said that they could invite them in themselves, if they wished. The Yoginis went and asked the pair to enter. But neither of them replied. The Yoginis felt the stomachs of the two meditating disciples. Excrement emerged from wherever they touched. The Yoginis concluded that the two were already dead and rotten, so left them undisturbed. Virupa had seen the Trishula knives ready for slaughter and moved very fast as he entered the shrine. He clapped his hands and the knives were instantly pulverised. Immediately the image started jumping towards him. Virupa smacked the head, which then slumped down onto its shoulders. All the Yoginis began vomiting blood and fainting as they saw this unexpected tragedy befall their god. "Aren't you Buddhists meant to be kind and compassionate to other living beings? Please do not do this to us," said the Yoginis when they recovered. "It is due to compassion that I am doing this," replied Virupa.

He placed a small votive stupa on top of the image and admitted all the Yoginis to the practice of Buddhadharma. At this time, the boatman Dombi Heruka, who had been with Virupa since the second parting of the Ganges was blessed to attain the realisation of a Bodhisattva at the level of the sixth Bhumi. Virupa then sent him to Rada province in eastern India to subdue an evil Hindu king named Dehara, who had a palace named Kangkana. Mounted on a pregnant tiger and brandishing a deadly snake bridle and whip, Mahasiddha Dombi Heruka subdued the king and his subjects. They were all admitted into the path of Vajrayana.[123]

Meanwhile, Virupa and Krishnacharin travelled to Devikota in south eastern India where an Upasaka named 'Iron-legged,' sometimes also identified as the teacher of Acharya Maitreyagupta, had an image of Khasarpani which he had imported from the Potala realm. Virupa paid homage to Khasarpani and made an offering of all the activities in which he had been involved from the time of his ordination up to the defeat of Sahajadevi. The Great Compassionate One said:

> O! Noble son! You have the magical power to pulverise even Mount Sumeru. Nevertheless, there are varieties of sentient beings whose karmic propensities are inconceivable, so you should cultivate great compassion to the Tirthikas instead of frightening them.[124]

Virupa replied, saying, "There is a place called Sovanatha in the west where thousands of animals are sacrificed every year. I must first of all go there to subdue it. After that I shall do as the Great Compassionate One has ordered." The Great Compassionate One advised Virupa to subdue them without force using skilful means. As Virupa and Krishnacharin journeyed towards the west to subdue Sovanatha, the god had discovered Virupa's intention by means of his contaminated clairvoyance.[125] Sovanatha disguised himself as a pure Brahmin and when he met the two travellers on the road, he asked them knowingly, "Where are you two Yogis going?" "We are going to subdue Sovanatha," Virupa replied, also knowingly. "If you are a kind and compassionate Buddhist, why do you have to subdue him?" asked the disguised Sovanatha. "That is the very reason why I need to subdue him," Virupa replied. "He is not there now. He has gone to Purvavideha,[126] the eastern continent," Sovanatha advised. "I will also go there as I must subdue him come what may. Wherever he has gone, whether to one of the four continents or to the realm of the Brahmas, I must go there and subdue him," said Virupa. Hearing this Sovanatha became very afraid and admitted, "I am Sovanatha." He revealed his ordinary manifestation and requested Virupa not to subdue him forcefully. Virupa replied, "In that case you must establish Sangha communities and build Buddhist monasteries. On top of their doors, draw my image and make regular offerings. You can first make rice flour and vegetarian food offerings to the Triple Gem, then to me and finally to yourself if there is any left over. If you abandon the sacrifice of animals and replace that practice with the offerings I have described, I will let you remain there. If you fail to do this, I will reduce everything to dust."[127]

Sovanatha happily vowed to do all of these things. He requested Virupa to remain in the world until the sun and moon ceased to exist and Virupa agreed. In a dream Sovanatha revealed to King Candradeva of Tishala in western India that the King must see to the accomplishment of all the promises he had made to Virupa. If the King should fail to fulfil all of Sovanatha's vows within three months, his kingdom would be conquered. Seeing this in the dream, the frightened king hurriedly arranged to give effect to all the promises. Accordingly, the king built a monastery about a half day's journey from Sovanatha in the region of Gujarat,[128] in beautiful surroundings with luxuriant shrubs, waterfalls and flower-filled meadows. About a hundred monks were settled there. He forbade the slaughter of goats and buffaloes and made it illegal to kill or harm any animal. With mixed feelings of excitement and curiosity, the king offered a grand reception to Virupa whose power could frighten even Mahadeva.

By this time, Virupa had given the *Vajra Verses* to his disciple Krishnacharin, who had not yet gained realisation equal to that attained by Virupa and blessed him with this level of realisation. He then asked Krishnacharin to fulfil three main tasks:[129]

1. To subdue an evil Hindu king in eastern India;

2. To accept Acharya Damarupa as his disciple and to pass on the whispered lineage knowledge to him; and

3. To bring out the five scriptures of *Vajra Verses* from Uddiyana in the west.

2. MYSTERIOUS PASSING AWAY

There are two versions of Virupa's passing away. Some say he dissolved into a stone image, others say he became a stone image. The image's right hand was in the gesture of holding the sun while the left, in the gesture of granting supreme realisation, was holding a container of gold paint[130] capable of transmuting all base metals into gold. The gold paint was said to be the size of a medium sized arura[131] fruit. There are several legends about this stone statue.[132] It is said that:

1. One who approaches the image respectfully, even a small child, can reach high enough to place flower garlands around its neck;

2. One who approaches disrespectfully, even the tallest person, cannot reach high enough to place anything on the image;

3. In front of the image is a stone skull-cup which never overfills even if one pours hundreds and thousands of jars of wine into it ;

4. There is a dumb boy believed to be an emanation of Vajrapani in front of the image;

5. There is a manifestation of Vajra Varahi in front of the image which appears alternately as a leperess or a dumb girl.

It is said that, at the request of a Brahmin, Virupa (who had transformed into a stone image) gave the stone paint to a Brahmin, who subsequently made a lot of gold. When the local king,[133] heard this news, he tried to rob the Brahmin. The Brahmin hurriedly returned the gold paint stone to the hand of the image and said to the king, "Since it is not mine, I cannot give it to you. I have returned it to the hand of the owner. You can go and get it from his hand if you want it."[134] The statue closed its fist and did not give the stone to the king. The king, frustrated in his greedy endeavour, ordered his men to cut off the hand of the image. However, the man who attempted to do so vomited blood and died immediately.[135] Following this incident the local people became afraid that the stone image might bring them harm. They consequently enshrined the statue in gold which they obtained by pushing wires through the fingers. This became a most sacred shrine where both non-Buddhists and Buddhists would come to worship. It became known as Punyahara,[136] the robber of merits to the non-Buddhists and Shri Balanatha,[137] the glorious master of Power to the Buddhists. The Hindu god Kumara Karttika[138] was bound by oath to maintain the offerings to the sacred image. This shrine of Sovanatha [139] is said to be situated in the Saurastra district of the modern Gujarat state in western India.

3. THE DATING OF VIRUPA

Aryadeva is said to have been a disciple of Nagarjuna in the latter part of Nagarjuna's life. Virupa is said to have been a disciple of Aryadeva. The Chinese Buddhist Canon holds that it was an oral tradition among the Lamas that prior to his expulsion from Nalanda, Virupa wrote a commentary on Aryadeva's *Catusataka*.[140] It is also stated in numerous historical Lamdre texts that Virupa was a disciple of Asanga. Asanga lived 900 years after the Mahaparinirvana of the Buddha to one hundred and fifty years of age. Shantaraksita, who came in the 8th century, is said to have been a disciple of Virupa.

According to Lamdre sources, Virupa came to the world approximately 1020 years after the Mahaparinirvana, which is about 476 AD. This is 80 to 100 years too early to be accurate since he was in his late seventies when he left Nalanda and met Dombi Heruka. Notwithstanding the difficulty in determining the exact lifespan of Virupa (who made at least three appearances in this world) it is important to attempt to date his first appearance with the relatively limited data available. It is estimated that the meeting between Virupa and Dombi Heruka occurred between 630 and 635 AD soon after Virupa left Nalanda. This suggests that Virupa was born around 565-570 AD. He would have lived until early in the 8th century, as he was also a teacher of Santaraksita. This was his first appearance. He came for the second time as the Yogi Siropa. In that life, he subdued Nyimacharka,[141] a wild elephant which destroyed trees, villages and cities in central India. According to Taranatha in the work attributed to him entitled the Seven Instruction Lineages, Virupa's third appearance took place in the bed room of an Iranian king:

> At a later time, in the eastern land of Gora, a king of Iran
> awoke to find a Yogin beside his bed-head. The Yogin was
> thrown into the river time after time only to return on each
> occasion. He was thrown into fire but he did not burn. When
> he was struck by various weapons, they shattered into pieces
> instead of hurting him. He was forced to drink six khals[142] of
> poison and was guarded by many people a whole day and
> night. Having witnessed that the Acharya's health and
> complexion became even more splendid, they knew he had
> attained the Siddhi, and they asked him who he was. "I am
> Virupa," he said. There also he gave instructions to some
> fortunate people, whose mere utterance of the oath out of
> their reverence to him, caused many of them to attain the
> ordinary siddhis. During his stay of approximately four
> months in Bhangala,[143] he made himself available to all,
> personally seeing anyone who wished to approach him.
> Thereafter (I) do not know where he disappeared to,
> although it is about this time he went to China. Virupa is

reputed to have appeared on earth on three occasions and all three have been discussed.[144]

The Lamdre sources are not clear about his third appearance. Some say he came specifically to re-subdue Bhimesara in the south, while others believe that he is yet to come. It is said that Acharya Dharmakirti, King Ashoka and Yogisvara Virupa are the three most remarkable beings who propagated the teachings respectively through debate, military power and magical power. As H. E. Chogay Trichen Rinpoche concludes in his book:

> *In summary, just as no-one has paralleled logician Dharmakirti's ability to uphold the teaching through skill in debate, nor King Ashoka's ability to uphold the teachings through power, Virupa's ability to uphold the Dharma through magical power is unequalled.*[145]

4. THE IDENTITY OF VIRUPA

A large part of Virupa's story concerns his demonstration of magical powers after he attained Siddhi. The Lamdre hagiography lists all Virupa's names, whereas other texts such as Caturasiti-siddha-pravrtti[146] fail to do so. The problem of the historical identification of Dharmapala has resulted from this inconsistency in the sources. Since he had more than two or three names, it is difficult to solve the problem unless we know when his childhood and ordination names ceased to be used and when he became a siddha and adopted different names. Merely counting him as one of the eighty-four Mahasiddhas and narrating a few magical and legendary accounts is insufficient for a full historical understanding of his life. One must bear in mind that he was not known as Virupa until his late seventies, at which time he was expelled from Nalanda monastery. We must ask who expelled him and who succeeded him.

Dharmapala was originally a Pandita of the Yogacara Cittamatrin school, a viewpoint which is reflected in his commentary on Aryadeva's *Catursataka*. However, when he attained the Path of Seeing (the First Bhumi of enlightenment), it is argued by Lamdre scholars that he must already have gone beyond this earlier view and realised the Prasanghika Madhyamika view of emptiness. Virupa himself wrote about this realisation in the following Doha:

> *Having uprooted oneself from self-grasping, one is victorious over the troops of evil; Owing to the self-disintegration of the grasping onto objects, one is entirely liberated from Samsara and Nirvana.*[147]

Unaware that Shri Dharmapala had become the siddha known as Virupa late in life, many scholars dealing with his life have failed to identify him with the Mahasiddha. Dharmapala's family background is referred to in the records of Chinese travellers and he appears as the abbot of Nalanda in Vidyabhusana's work[148] (although the author claims to have based his version of the story on the Chinese traveller's records). What is important, however, is that Hsüan Tsang refers to 'a mountain monastery' where Dharmapala was admitted after he left home. The Lamdre sources confirm that it was the Somapura monastery in the south where Dharmapala was first admitted before he went to Nalanda. Scholars who rely entirely on the Chinese sources do not seem to understand the significance of who it was who ordained Dharmapala and gave him that name. This is an instance where we should not undervalue the traditional oral histories of Lamdre which were passed down from generation to generation. According to Taranatha, Shri Dharmapala took ordination from Acharya Dharmadasa, a name which might easily be a mistranslation of Dharmamitra, who ordained Dharmapala according to the Lamdre sources. Since Taranatha has little to say about Dharmadasa it is not clear whether he was a Pandita of

Nalanda or not[149] and his identity remains in doubt. It is plausible that there might have been more than one Pandita of Nalanda with the name Dharmapala. However, the much talked about Dharmapala of the Chinese travellers and the Dharmapala referred to by Taranatha was in fact Shri Dharmapala, who later became known as Virupa.

What became of abbot Dharmapala if he did not become siddha Virupa? There is an important and often overlooked reason for contemporary silence on this subject. At the time, the monks who had regarded Dharmapala as one of the great luminaries of Nalanda would have been reluctant to advertise the fact that he had become Virupa, particularly to students in the cloistered atmosphere of the monastery. We should remember that Virupa's reputation as a Mahasiddha was not yet established. Attitudes towards his transformation were, to say the least, ambivalent and this is particularly so within the monastic community. It is clear that the monks of Nalanda disapproved of his Carya practices of Tantric realisation and this was the reason they expelled him when he adopted the name 'Virupa.' Virupa's refusal to return to the monastery later on when requested to do so by the monks who witnessed the parting of the river, may well have contributed to their reticence on the subject of his eventual whereabouts.

There appears to be no record in the Lamdre histories about who assumed the abbotship of Nalanda after him. Neither is there information about his main disciples in Nalanda. This is curious, considering that he taught there until he reached the age of seventy. It is not plausible that such a renowned scholar and abbot of prestigious Nalanda had no successors. Praises to Virupa by Sachen and Sakya Pandita indicate that he had hundreds and thousands of Sthavira disciples. Historically his behavioural change and the vast differences between his activities as abbot and as a Siddha may have created a division amongst his followers which widened the gap of misunderstanding.

Virupa's two main Tantric disciples, Dombi Heruka and Krishnacharin appear not to have known who succeeded their teacher at Nalanda. We know, of course, that neither Dombi Heruka nor Krishnacharin became Pandita of Nalanda. Lamdre histories lack details of Virupa's earlier life and his Sutra and philosophical disciples. It is possible that Shilabhadra, who was Hsüan Tsang's preceptor, may have been Dharmapala's successor. Vidyabhusana[150] places him at Nalanda in 635 AD. However, Sarat Candra Das, who lists the names of several teachers of Hsüan Tsang, does not mention Shilabhadra.[151]

Vinitadeva and Dharmamitra are described in the Lamdre histories as Dharmapala's teachers at Nalanda. Jayadeva is said to be another name for Dharmamitra, a name he may possibly have received after defeating Tirthikas. It is likely that it was Dharmamitra who gave Virupa the name 'Dharmapala' since the abbot traditionally gives part of his name to the disciple during Bhiksu ordination. Taranatha argues that although Virupa is also known as Shri Dharmapala, he is not be confused with the Sthavira Dharmapala, who was abbot of Nalanda.[152] Hence Taranatha not only identifies two separate individuals, but also regards them as contemporaneous.[153] Taranatha shows no indication of knowing about the Lamdre records on Virupa, nor does he appear to remember that he had elsewhere mentioned the expulsion of Virupa from Nalanda by the monks [154] He states, "While studying in the monastery of Nalanda, he once went to Devikotta." Taranatha's assumption that Virupa travelled back and forth between Devikotta and Nalanda proves that he was unaware of Acharya Dharmapala's dismissal from Nalanda. Since there is no record to prove that he returned to Nalanda after the dismissal, Virupa's trips between Devikotta and Nalanda are unlikely to have occurred after his expulsion. If, as is claimed, the *Seven Instruction Lineage* was in fact written by Taranatha ten years before he wrote the *History of Buddhism*, he would not have contradicted what he had written in his earlier work. Could it be that the author of the

Seven Instruction Lineage was a later Jonangpa scholar passing his or her work off as being that of Taranatha himself?[155]

The absence of any reference to Dharmapala's dismissal in either the Chinese sources or Taranatha's *History of Buddhism* lends support to the view that Dharmapala and Virupa were two separate entities. The author of the *Seven Instruction Lineage* must have learned about Dharmapala's dismissal somehow, probably from the Lamdre sources. There is no indication in his *History of Buddhism*, that Taranatha had even heard of Virupa's ordination name Dharmapala. There is no reason, of course, to suspect deliberate suppression on the part of Taranatha, as might be the case with Shilabhadra and his followers. It appears that Taranatha simply knew nothing about it. Taranatha does not omit mention of Shilabhadra as a scholar of Nalanda, but he does not name him as successor to Acharya Dharmapala. It is interesting that Taranatha makes mention of the short duration of Dharmapala's period as abbot. However, he fails to offer any reason for this. According to him, Jayadeva became the Upadhyaya of Nalanda after Dharmapala.[156] Since he mentions Jayadeva as Shantideva's and Virupa's teacher, Taranatha's Dharmapala is not Shilabhadra's teacher. Although Taranatha deserves some credit for identifying Jayadeva, I personally believe it is a mistake to say that "Jayadeva became the Upadhyaya of Nalanda after Dharmapala." It is apparent that the name 'Dharmapala' was more popular than the name 'Virupa' in the annals of non-Tantric Buddhist masters.

The uncertainty as to whether Dharmapala was dead or had merely retired[157] when Hsüan Tsang arrived, suggests the possibility of a 'conspiracy of silence' by the monastic community, and particularly by his orthodox disciple, Shilabhadra. Why would Shilabhadra not tell Hsüan Tsang what had happened to his teacher, Dharmapala, if he had succeeded him? It is unlikely that Hsüan Tsang would have failed to describe the passing away of his grand-teacher if he had known the details, when he went to such great pains to describe every single monument he encountered and even made notes of the number of families he saw in a town as he travelled. On the other hand, why would Shilabhadra not mention the details of his teacher's death or retirement?

We should recall that the Nalanda monks, Shilabhadra among them, had failed to persuade Dharmapala to return to their monastery. Shilabhadra was an elderly and some might say ambitious Pandita by the time he met Hsüan Tsang. It would be logical for him to have kept silent on the subject of his teacher's later life. To reveal what happened may have brought discredit not only to Nalanda but to himself by possibly impugning the reputation of the man who had been his teacher. At the very least, such a story would have fomented controversy and possibly doubt amongst foreign students. If Shilabhadra lived up to his name, it seems likely that he was a monk of upright moral conduct. It is likely that he was amongst those who failed to understand Dharmapala's unorthodox behaviour or realise that he had attained Siddhi. He may well have been foremost of those who expelled Dharmapala. He had little to gain from either side by drawing attention to his earlier relationship with Dharmapala. To those who disapproved of the former abbot's transformation, he might appear somehow tainted by his close acquaintance. To those who were supporters of the Tantric master Virupa he would have appeared as disloyal, if not personally at least by association. He would also appear to have lacked discernment for not understanding that Virupa had realised Siddhi. The word "retired" has a better connotation than "expelled" and is thus a more skilful choice of words. But there is no evidence that the concept of retirement existed in those days. It appears more likely that Dharmapala's tenure as abbot was expunged from the records, so to speak.

Since the Chinese travellers failed to report anything about Jayadeva in their travel records, Sankalia (a contemporary Indian scholar) appears puzzled to find Taranatha's reference to him.[158] Taranatha appears to be correct in mentioning the existence of a teacher named Jayadeva. This is corroborated in the Lamdre sources. However, one would have thought it unlikely that Jayadeva was Dharmapala's successor because he was in fact one of his teachers. There is the possibility that, if Jayadeva was still alive, he assumed some of Dharmapala's teaching duties after the latter was expelled. In which case Taranatha may have been correct in his assertion that Jayadeva succeeded Dharmapala. This would indicate that Jayadeva was not another name for Dharmamitra as stated in the Lamdre sources, but that they were two different teachers of Dharmapala. Taranatha adds further confusion when he writes, 'He preached the doctrine at Vajrasana for over forty years and succeeded Shri Candrakirti as the Upadhyaya of Shri Nalanda.'[159]

It is clear that Dharmapala was one of the most influential abbots of Nalanda. The disagreement about who succeeded him may have derived from a narrow assumption that there was only one abbot or upadhyaya in a great monastic institution like Nalanda. Judging from the number of Panditas responsible for teaching in other institutions like Vikramalasila, it stands to reason that Nalanda would have had many assistant abbots or Panditas under one main abbot. If this were so, all of the suggested successors may have held similar positions.

Perhaps there are several reasons why the Lamdre sources have remained silent regarding Dharmapala's successor in Nalanda. Firstly, Lamdre was an exclusively esoteric lineage of Vajrayana Buddhism. This being the case, there would have been little interest in discussing non-esoteric matters within the literature. Furthermore, it is unlikely that the enlightened Virupa would have had any interest in recounting mundane details of his earlier life to his Tantric successors. Secondly, Dharmapala never returned to Nalanda after his eviction. The assistant abbots probably tried to magnify their own importance after the expulsion of their abbot, rather than focusing attention on him. Thirdly, the successors at Nalanda had to keep the matter secret, since they had failed to recognise the signs of his enlightenment until after the expulsion, and then failed to persuade him to return. They had the added motivation of avoiding scandal, confusion and misunderstanding amongst new students, particularly foreigners like Hsüan Tsang. They would not have foreseen the problem of future historical confusion. In the same way, the Lamdre hagiographers have recounted the barest details which have come down to us through the centuries. Ngorchen sums up the story in these words:

> *Formerly, when he was the abbot of Nalanda, he had*
> *countless disciples who were mainly ripened though the*
> *Paramitayana. After his attainment of Siddhi he only had two*
> *disciples who were ripened through Mantrayana: (1) The*
> *boatman who followed him, Mahasiddha Dombi Heruka and*
> *(2) One Yogin, from Bimehasa [Bhimesara] country, one of*
> *the five hundred hair-plaited [Yogins], Acharya Krishnapa.*
> *(This is said since there was no one else who held the lineage*
> *of teaching and meditation beside these two. In addition,*
> *there were an inconceivable number of people within both*
> *Buddhist and non-Buddhist circles who made spiritual*
> *contact [with him] due to his immense spiritual power.)*[160]

2

THE SUCCESSORS OF VIRUPA IN INDIA

The traditions of Lamdre transmission draw a clear distinction between two types of disciple.[161] Dombi Heruka and Krishnacharin were the two most outstanding disciples of Virupa. They are described as the two 'model disciples,' each having different predispositions and intelligence. Each received teachings in a way which suited his background and level of understanding. Accordingly, each of them had a particular, distinctive spiritual impact on the Lamdre lineage, which has also been interpreted in different ways. The present chapter investigates the identity and the lives of these two siddhas in conjunction with a discussion of the theory of two types of successors.

1. LIFE OF DOMBI HERUKA ACCORDING TO TENGYUR

Until now Dombi Heruka[162] has been portrayed as a boatman at the time of meeting Virupa. Abhayadatta, however, states that he was the King of Magadha and tells an entirely different story. A translation of Abhayadatta's version of Dombipa's biography follows:

> *This is the story of Guru Dombipa: In the kingdom of*
> *Magadha, there was a king who attained Siddhi from*
> *Hevajra. Since he had been initiated by the Guru Virupa and*

*had been granted the instructions, he practised their
meaning. Although he regarded his subjects in the way a
father regards his only son, the people did not know that their
king had entered the door of the Dharma. Nevertheless, in
view of the natural loving-kindness he showed to each of
them, all the people unanimously declared: "This king is
indeed a religious man." One day, the king said to his
minister: "In our country thieves and robbers are plundering
people's property, and because of the people's insignificant
merit, there is an increasing number who are ravaged by fear
and poverty. In order to protect the land from fear and
poverty, cast a large bell and hang it on the trunk of a large
tree. When anyone experiences harm or suffers from poverty,
let him strike the bell. But do not allow those who do not
witness these sufferings to strike it." The minister did as he
was commanded, and consequently fear and poverty were
brought to an end in Magadha. Sometime later, a group of
low-caste entertainers came to the capital. They made
offerings of songs and dances to the king and remained there.
One had a twelve-year-old daughter who, untainted by
worldly impurity was very pretty and attractive to the eye.
She had a lovely face and a good complexion. She was
endowed with all the qualities of a padmavati. So the king
said to the low-caste entertainer, "Will you give this daughter
of yours to me?" The father replied, "Your majesty is a great
king, ruling the kingdom of Magadha which has 800,000
cities. Because of your royal wealth, you have nothing to
worry about. We are of low caste, disparaged and shunned
by all other classes of people. It is improper for you to make
such a request." Whereupon the king took the girl by force
and gave her father gold equal to the weight of her body. She
became the king's consort, without any one knowing her
background. However, after twelve years had passed, the
people discovered where she had come from. Soon it became*

known to everyone throughout Magadha that "the king consorts with a low-caste woman." So the king relinquished his kingdom and gave it to his son (by his queen, not by the low-caste woman) and (to the regency of) others. Having done this, he went into the forest with his low-caste mistress and practised there for twelve years.

In the meantime, the fortunes of the land were diminishing by degrees. The prince and his subjects, who were unable to hold the country together, held an urgent meeting. There they passed a resolution to search for the former king and request him to rule the kingdom once again. A group of people went to seek him in the forest where he was residing. There they saw him sitting at the base of a tree, while the girl had gone to fetch water. She stepped out on a lotus leaf on the surface of the lake and, without sinking, drew water from a depth of fifteen fathoms. She then served it to the king. The amazed men returned home and reported what they had seen to the populace. The people then sent an invitation to the king to call him back to the throne.

The king and his consort came riding out from the forest on a pregnant tigress, using a poisonous snake as a whip. The people were astonished and said, "Surely if you rule the country everything will prosper? Please take the kingdom." But the king replied, "Since I am of low-caste, it is improper for me to rule the kingdom. However, since it does not matter whether caste is good or bad after death; burn us in the fire, and when we are born again from it, I will do as you have asked." So the people burned the two, the king and consort, in a fire of Goshirsa sandal-wood. Due to an excessive amount of wood, the fire remained alight even after a week. The people caught a glimpse of the couple transformed into Hevajra and consort, in a self-produced body, shining like dew upon a fully blossomed lotus. Seeing this, the people of Magadha

*developed great faith, and the king became known as the
Master Dombipa, or 'He of the Low-caste Dombis.'
The king then spoke to his ministers and to all his subjects in
the following terms, "If you are able to do as I have done, I will
rule the kingdom. If you are unable to do this, I will not rule."
All of the people were taken completely by surprise, and
replied, "How could we do what you have done?" At this the
king declared, "In ruling this kingdom, there is little benefit
and much fault; rather, I will rule a kingdom of Dharma."
Having said this, he departed and went to the realm of the
Dakas for the sake of sentient beings. Here ends the story of
Guru Dombipa.'.[163]*

2. WAS DOMBI HERUKA A KING OR A BOATMAN?

This story raises a number of difficulties. Firstly, it raises the
problem of establishing the king's correct identity. The genealogy
of Maghada contains no record of a king named Dombi. However,
if we accept for the moment the possibility that Dombi Heruka may
have been a king at some stage, perhaps under another name, this
does not necessarily preclude him from having been a boatman
later on. He may have become a boatman after he left his kingdom
along with his consort. Secondly, if Dombi Heruka had already
been a Tantric practitioner while king and had special miraculous
powers to alleviate his people's fear and poverty, surely his
subjects would not have denounced him for taking the low-caste
girl as his consort. Even if he had a teacher other than Virupa, this
story does not indicate how and when the meeting between him
and his teacher took place. It would be most unlikely for
Krishnacharin to have been his teacher before he met Virupa, since
Krishnacharin became Virupa's disciple after Dombi Heruka
according to the Lamdre sources. Although there is no evidence to
support this, it is possible that he had a teacher other than

Krishnacharin before meeting Virupa. This view is not, however, supported by Lamdre sources.

Another problem with this version and also with the account by Taranatha is that in neither case is there any mention of Dombi being a boatman when he met Virupa, a fact which the Lamdre version regards as crucially important for the development of the Guru disciple relationship between them. The failure to explain where and how Dombi met Virupa is one of the major drawbacks of the version of events recounted above. This confusion is quite apart from the question of whether Dombi was a king or a boatman when he met Virupa.

There are problems with the theory that he may have been a king and then became a boatman and Virupa's disciple. If Dombi was really denounced by his people merely for taking a low-caste woman as his consort, it is hard to believe that this would have happened to a king who displayed miraculous powers to alleviate poverty, even if he had another teacher before meeting Virupa. Furthermore, taking a girl of padmavati class as Tantric consort is a usual practice of a highly realised master in the Tantric tradition. If the king had already realised such heights, he would not have needed to seek a teacher even if he was disguised as a boatman after attaining Siddhi. On the other hand, if Virupa had met Dombi Heruka when he was ruler of Magadha, before the latter demonstrated his miracle powers and took the consort, there may be reasons why he should have appeared to Virupa as a boatman at other times. While Dombi is well known as the boatman in Tibetan religious histories, Taranatha rejects this and claims that he was in fact a king. He writes:

> Although the Acharya is known as a boatman in Tibet, he in fact was a king of Tripura in the East.[164]

The fact that Taranatha acknowledges Dombi Heruka was known as a boatman in Tibet must cast doubt on the theory that he was a king, either of Tripur or of Magadha. Since there was no indication of any surviving royal lineage of Dombi Heruka in India around Taranatha's time in the 17th century, nor around the time of Abhayadatta in the 12th century, the oral Lamdre tradition holding Dombi Heruka to be a boatman appears to be the more plausible version. This is all the more so given that the Lamdre tradition has maintained the transmission of his teachings unbroken to this day.

According to Taranatha, Dombi Heruka attained Siddhi ten years after Virupa.[165] If this statement is true, Dombi Heruka could not have attained Siddhi before meeting Virupa, even if he had been a Tantric practitioner under another teacher. Virupa left Nalanda monastery soon after his attainment of Siddhi and his meeting with Dombi Heruka occurred after this. Lamdre sources clearly show that when Virupa first met Dombi Heruka, the latter was a boatman. Although other versions disagree, they fail to provide evidence for the theory that Dombi Heruka was or had been a king. Unfortunately, in his *History of Buddhism in India*, Taranatha fails to mention whether Dombi was a boatman or a king at the time of his meeting with Virupa. The eminent historian, Pawo Tsuklak Trengwa, although he says very little about Dombi Heruka, agrees with the Lamdre view that he was a boatman who followed Virupa and became his disciple.[166]

The Lamdre sources say that after having blessed Dombi Heruka, which enabled him to reach a stage of realisation equal to his own, Virupa sent him on a mission to subdue an evil king. Dombi Heruka is said to have set out on a pregnant tigress,[167] brandishing a snake in his right hand as a whip. Interestingly, this description tallies with drawings and paintings found in the traditional Tibetan Buddhist iconography of the eighty-four Mahasiddhas. The author of the *Seven Instruction Lineages*[168] also shares this view, agreeing with Lamdre sources that Dombi was sent by Virupa to subdue an evil king. However, the preceding story depicts Dombi as himself a deposed king who was invited to be reinstalled by his previous subjects. The confusion seems to be about the identity of the king who was to be subdued. It appears that Dombi Heruka, who was sent by Virupa to subdue an evil king, as explained both in the Lamdre and SIL work was confused with the king it was his mission to subdue. Hence the earlier story about his invitation to be reinstated as a king. It is clear that Dombi Heruka would not have accepted such an invitation, in any case, as he did not wish to become a king. It is unfortunate that the version contained in the explanation of the lives of the eighty-four siddhas only adds to the prevailing confusion.

According to Abhayadatta, it was twelve years before his subjects discovered that Dombi Heruka had taken a low-caste girl as his Tantric consort.[169] He is said to have been succeeded by his son and to have lived for a further twelve years in the forest with his consort after they had both been banished from the palace by his subjects. These stories are not found in the Lamdre or the SIL. If we suppose that he met Virupa after all of these incidents, he must have been at least in his late forties or early fifties. He could not possibly have been a young man. The story further suggests that he was not known as 'Dombi Heruka' until he asked his subjects to throw him and his consort into the fire. If this occurred, it would prove that Dombi had already attained Siddhi prior to that incident. If so, it appears he must have met Virupa at least ten years beforehand if, as Taranatha informs us, Dombi attained Siddhi ten years after Virupa. Neither the Lamdre works nor the SIL make mention of Dombi Heruka having been thrown into the fire at his own request. There is no indication in these works that he attained Siddhi in the fire pit. Of course, Virupa would not have sent Dombi Heruka to subdue the king if he had not yet attained Siddhi.

The discrepancies between the accounts of when and how the two met and developed the Guru disciple relationship cannot be resolved simply by totally accepting one version of the story and totally rejecting the other. If we look again at the two accounts, we may find a way of accommodating both versions. For example, Dombi Heruka may have met another less known teacher while king of Magadha. He may have practised Tantra before meeting Virupa. Of course, there is no evidence to suggest that he met Virupa while still a king. None of the sources give the pre-siddha name of Dombi Heruka to support the theory that he was a king prior to becoming a boatman. He must have attained Siddhi to obtain the name 'Dombi' since the name seems to have come into use as soon as he took a young low-caste girl as a consort. A major problem in verifying the version according to Abhayadatta is that it does not give the name of the king prior to all these incidents. What was Dombi Heruka's name when he was king, if he ever was a king?

It may be fruitful to see whether the recorded political history of Magadha during the period sheds any light on the kingship theory. According to available historical records, the King of Magadha at about that time was Harsa. The most significant information we have about this king is that he established diplomatic relations with China in 641 AD and died around 646-7 AD. Although there were other subordinate kings under his domination such as Purnavarman, Harsa's death nevertheless seems to have brought political disorder to Magadha and its surroundings. This disorder led to intervention and invasion by Tibet. After Harsa, the kingdom was divided into two. Arjuna ruled in Tirabhukti, and Madhavagupta in Magadha. Arjuna suffered defeat at the hands of Tibetan troops (whom he fought at the instigation of the threatened Chinese mission). By contrast B.N. Sinha tells us[170] that Madhavagupta presided over a period of peace and sought to rejuvenate the emaciated, sick and old country of Magadha. This is interesting when we recall that the people of Maghada are said to have invited Dombi Heruka to return when the country was in great trouble. If there is any truth in the theory that Dombi Heruka was a king of Magadha, perhaps he might be identified as Madhavagupta, who was succeeded by his son Adityasena around 650 AD.

Although the author of SIL agrees that Dombi Heruka was a king, he differs from the version above with respect to the location of his kingdom. He, too, fails to actually provide a name for the king. If he was given the name Dombi for taking a low-caste girl as his consort, surely he would have been known by that name before the couple were placed in a burning fire. The incident of the fire must have taken place at least twenty-four years after he took the consort. This is because according to the story, the couple are said to have spent twelve years as king and consort, followed by a further twelve years in the forest, before the king was asked to return by his subjects.[171] Dombi, whether or not he was ever a king, must have been known by another name prior to taking up with this consort.

Another problem with this version is that it does not describe how Dombi spent his twelve years in the forest. If he was a king as this account states, it seems plausible that he may have lived as a boatman for twelve or so years prior to meeting Virupa. After all, and particularly if he was accompanied by his consort, he could not have survived without making a living in the forest. Yet there is no mention of a consort when he met Virupa on the banks of the Ganges. So, the problem remains unresolved even when we try to harmonise the two versions. The twelve years spent in the forest might help to support Taranatha's theory that Dombi Heruka attained Siddhi ten years after Virupa. It might also explain why his subjects invited him to return after the passage of twelve years.[172] This would mean that the meeting between Virupa and Dombi must have taken place soon after Virupa left Nalanda.

If we adhere to the Lamdre sources which make no mention of Dombi having been a king before he became a boatman, we may infer that he was never a king, on the grounds that if he had been, it would have been too important a detail to have simply excluded. We are faced with the question of why a mere boatman would have been given the name Dombi for marrying a low-caste girl. That is, as most sources agree, how he came to receive that name. But if

Dombi Heruka had been a mere boatman, rather than a king, the epithet Dombi makes less sense. Dombi means 'the act of an outcast.' But an ordinary boatman would have been of low caste to begin with. Marrying a low-caste woman would not therefore have been an issue for him. Being of low caste already, he would hardly have been labelled 'Dombi' for doing this, or for any other reason, for that matter.

On the other hand, we might decide that the Lamdre version, merely by omitting mention of Dombi Heruka ever having been a king, does not imply that he never was one. The Lamdre account is brief and to the point. As there is no contradiction between the versions and no positive proof for either of the theories concerning Dombi's early life, the two accounts could co-exist in harmony. However, in order to eradicate confusion and complete the picture, it would be useful to compare and analyse both versions systematically in greater detail than has been attempted so far.

Ngorchen Kunga Sangpo, although he must have been aware of the traditional Lamdre version of the story, gives a very interesting account of Dombi Heruka's life which extends well beyond the bounds of the Lamdre version:

> *Born in Bhangala in Eastern India, this Acharya was*
> *meditating in the forest in that region. In that country there*
> *was a large merchant town called Rada. Its king, named*
> *Dehara, who had become the Acharya's sponsor, used to*
> *invite the Acharya onto the roof of the palace. Revering him*
> *as his Guru, the king prostrated every day and received*
> *instructions. However, having convened a meeting, the king's*
> *ministers passed a motion that: "Since the Acharya's consort*
> *is an outcaste, the king who touched the feet of the Acharya to*
> *his head has become an outcaste. Hence his subjects have*
> *also become outcastes and it is necessary to discover a*
> *method of purification. Since there is no alternative method*
> *that can purify, we must burn the Acharya in the fire." They*

then requested the king to burn the Acharya. Although the king gave no consent, the ministers forcibly flung (the Acharya) into fire. The king wished for the Acharya to demonstrate his skilful means to reverse their disrespectful attitude. The Acharya, who was able to read the king's mind, rode on a man-eating tiger with the outcaste (Dombini) on his back. Adorning his body with many snakes, he passed through the town. Seeing this everyone became faithful. Thereupon the Acharya flew into the sky and the king made the request: "Please accept me." While reciting Amrtaprabha, the Nairatmya Sadhana, the Acharya went higher and higher into the midst of the sky. As soon as the Sadhana was completed he vanished. It is known that the king wrote down Amrtaprabha at that time.

According to another version, as he rode a tiger into the forest, the local inhabitants burned him in fire prepared from acacia and other woods. The Acharya said to the king "Guard the ashes for seven days". Then he was burned to death. Early in the morning when the king saw the burning heap of fire, he cried and circumambulated the pyre. After the fire died out, he circumambulated the ashes for seven days. Early in the morning of the eighth day the Acharya arose in the form of Nine-Deity Hevajra and flew into the sky. When the king requested him to accept him as mentioned above, it is said that he was given Amrtaprabha.'[173]

According to this version, it appears that Dombi Heruka was burned to death but reappeared in the form of Hevajra, whereupon he gave the Sadhana of Vajranairatmya to King Dehara. But this version does not indicate that Dombi Heruka himself was a king as is asserted in other accounts. While it does not explain his presence, it does appear that he was the king's venerated teacher. According to this version, the reason why Dombi Heruka appeared on a tiger was not to frighten the evil king as explained in Lamdre sources. Instead it was in response to King Dehara's wish for him to subdue the ministers and subjects who threw him into the fire. This account goes some way towards bridging the gap between the Lamdre version and others. Judging from Ngorchen's silence, there appears to have been no doubt as to whether Dombi Heruka was ever a boatman or not. This doubt was raised much later by Taranatha. I hope that the present analysis has not added to the doubt and confusion surrounding Dombi Heruka's life story.

At this point I would like to take a step back from the purely historical approach, which although indispensable, has limitations when applied to sacred history. We touched on this earlier on. When it comes to events which transcend the material world, the criteria applied to physical research are not always adequate. In a sense we are entering another realm, with a different set of rules and conventions which are beyond normal human comprehension. After all, this is not the biography of an ordinary man. We are dealing with the hagiography of a 7th century Indian siddha. If a boatman could become a lineage holder of esoteric Tantric teachings, it is possible that the name 'Dombi' may have been conferred with its meaning reversed. The names given to the siddhas were generally very gross and down to earth. They may not be easily comprehensible to beings in the relative world. To the siddhas, this world of ours is crazy, but to us who fail to know the nature of a siddha's enlightenment, they may appear insane. If there were any siddhas around today who were to behave the way those early siddhas did, they would be considered 'outcastes' and might even be locked up. In some circumstances an enlightened being may become an outcaste in the conventional world.

One might question why the account of Dombi Heruka taking a consort and of the two being thrown into a fire at his request is absent from the Lamdre sources. Perhaps these facts were deliberately excluded or suppressed in the traditional hagiography. Perhaps they were thought inappropriate for new students. If these stories had ever been kept as part of the oral history of the lineage, it is unlikely that they would have been altogether lost.

One hypothesis is that these facts were suppressed because of lack of confidence in the authenticity of Dombi Heruka's lineage. This may have resulted from the prevailing criticism of 'the Lamdre without a root.' Sensitivity about the authenticity of Dombi Heruka's lineage may also help to explain the sharp distinction drawn by the Lamdrepa themselves between the two Lamdre lineages originating from Dombi Heruka and Krishnacarin respectively.

3. DATING OF DOMBI HERUKA

We can gain some idea of Dombi Heruka's chronology from the fact that he met Virupa when the latter was in his late seventies or early eighties.[174] If we accept that the meeting between these two took place around 620 AD and the theory that Dombi was a king, Dombi Heruka's birth can be estimated to have occurred between 550 and 570 AD. Readers will recall that according to the kingship theory, he was already a king when he took his consort. He lived in the palace with her for twelve years, and then spent a further twelve years with her in the forest. He therefore must have been at least nearing fifty, although he may have been much older. We have no evidence of how long he lived.

Nagarjuna's disciple in the latter part of his life was Asanga, whose dates have been established as 480-630 AD. He is said to have been Virupa's teacher. Hsüan Tsang, the famous Chinese pilgrim who is said to have reached Nalanda in 635 AD, left no account of the existence of either Virupa or Dombi Heruka although it is known that they were both somewhere in India around that time. Hsüan Tsang was an acute observer and an experienced traveller, but his reports are incomplete in that he has little to say about Vajrayana masters. This is surprising, as his visit coincided with a time of great diffusion of Vajrayana Buddhism throughout India. While dating contemporary masters and their students can help to date other practitioners, it would be a mistake to assume that the disciples were necessarily younger than their teachers, particularly when it comes to Tantric Buddhist masters. Yet this is exactly what Bhattacharyaya does when he allows a standard twelve-year gap between master and disciple.[175] According to his chronological calculations, someone by the name of Nagarjuna was alive around the time Hsüan Tsang was traveling in India. Yet he does not question the fact that Hsüan Tsang did not meet Nagarjuna during his travels. This is one of the contributing factors that has resulted in the late dating of Buddhist Tantras.

4. KRISHNACHARIN, THE FAVOURED SUCCESSOR

Krishnacharin is said to have been born in Karna.[176] According to Jamyang Khyentse Wangchuk (1524-1568),[177] he was also known as Karnapa, and practised mainly near mount Utsayana. The author of SIL[178] does not mention that Virupa was his principal teacher. This fact alone raises questions about his true identity. He names Krishnacharin's main teachers as princess Laksmikara and Jalandharipa, but this account appears not to be comprehensive. On the subject of Krishnacharin, he writes:

> From the time of his youth he was sharp minded. He became
> learned in linguistics and medical studies and skilled in all
> kinds of creative arts. Since his previous residual karma had
> come to fruition, many wisdom-holding Dakinis manifested
> themselves to him. Gradually he reached Glorious Nalanda in
> Magadha where five hundred Panditas lived and where
> monastic colleges had been flourishing. He took Bhiksu
> ordination and stayed there for many years. Through
> studying and contemplating on the Tripitaka and the Four
> Classes of Tantras, he mastered them fully in his mental
> continuum. Accordingly, he became accomplished in Mantra
> and meditation at various levels.
> Once when he was meditating at a secluded place, the fully
> perfected Mahayogini Princess Laksmikara showed her face

directly to him and through her blessings he was able to
attain extraordinary stages of meditative absorption. In that
same place Vajra Dakinis gave him permission from the sky
saying, "In the northern kingdom of Jalandhara is the Guru
known as Jalandharipa. If you adhere to him, then you will
accomplish the siddhis you desire. '[179]

When considering the validity or otherwise of this account, we might ask ourselves what would prompt an intelligent Brahmin to become a Buddhist monk without giving up his Hindu faith. The Lamdre sources confirm that he was a Brahmin, that he was one of five hundred non-Buddhist Brahmin Yogis[180] and that he begged Virupa to accept him as his disciple. The reason he abandoned his faith at this stage is also explained. Unlike the passage quoted above, there is nothing in the Lamdre literature to suggest that he took fully ordained monk's vows from anyone, let alone that he studied either in Nalanda or Magadha.[181] Krishnacharin could not have been ordained by Virupa because he had already given up his monastic vows before leaving Nalanda. If Krishnacharin did become a monk, who ordained him and who taught him how to meditate and practise Mantra? Apart from not mentioning who was his ordination master, the above passage indicates that he had a Tantric Guru other than Princess Laksmikara and Jalandharipa, since he is said to have been practising Mantra even before he met Princess Laksmikara. To my mind the implied Tantric master of Krishnacharin can be no other than Virupa, and it is impossible even to imagine agreeing with Taranatha's assertion that Krishnacharin became a Bhiksu at Nalanda.

Abhayadatta's account of the eighty-four Mahasiddhas also claims that Krishnacharin was a monk and that he lived in Somapuri.[182] This confusion may have developed due to the fact that there were, at that time, many teachers of the same name. Taranatha himself pointed this out. Abhayadatta's account also mentions that Krishnacharin went in search of another teacher who was a weaver.[183] But we know that he did this after meeting Jalandharipa. If he had a Tantric teacher prior to his meeting with Princess Laksmikara and Jalandharipa, who was this teacher if it was not Virupa? We know that Krishnacharin succeeded both Princess Laksmikara and Jalandharipa in two of the succession lineages of the Nine-fold paths.[184] There is no doubt about his discipleship under Princess Laksmikara and Jalandharipa.[185] But these relationships appear to have developed only after he left Virupa, at a later stage of his life.

It is clear from his *History of Buddhism in India* that Taranatha did not know, or at any rate did not mention, that Virupa was a teacher of Krishnacharin. Yet he wrote that Krishnacharin was a practitioner of Mantra before meeting the other two teachers. Taranatha's silence on the subject of Krishnacharin's first Buddhist teacher is probably due to a lack of knowledge. Krishnacharin is said to have had the vision of Vajradakinis before he met Princess Laksmikara and Jalandharipa. Such experiences arise only in realised practitioners of Tantrayana. We do not really know why Taranatha fails to mention Virupa as a teacher of Krishnacharin.

In the work entitled *Seven Instruction Lineage*, which is believed to have been written by Taranatha some ten years before he wrote *History of Buddhism in India* at the age of twenty-six, Taranatha wrote of a person whose name was composed from combined elements of the names of Krishnacharin and Virupa. He calls this person Krishnavirupa.[186] He gives an account of how this Krishnavirupa, after committing four Brahmanic sins, became a disciple of Jalandharipa, and later on a disciple of Virupa under the guidance of Vajrayogini. Although no Lamdre sources mention such Brahmanic offences having being committed by Krishnacharin, we might suggest that these were invented to explain his abandonment of his faith to follow Virupa, a decision which would almost certainly have been criticised by his friends and teachers.

In the account set out below, Taranatha writes as if the so-called 'Krishnavirupa' were the second most important successor to Virupa, the other being Dombi Heruka. However, he seems to regard Krishnavirupa as a person quite distinct from Krishnacharin. In the Lamdre Krishnacharin is regarded as the foremost disciple of Virupa. If we assume that Krishnavirupa is in fact Krishnacharin, Taranatha's account appears to concur with the Lamdre when he asserts that Krishnavirupa was Virupa's second most important disciple. But he makes no mention of there being any relationship between Krishnacharin/Virupa and Dombi Heruka. Since Taranatha would be unlikely to have made such an omission, I believe this casts serious doubt on Taranatha's authorship of the *Seven Instruction Lineage*. Furthermore, as there was no other known disciple of Virupa with a similar name or anyone else of that name who held the Lamdre lineage, I suspect that Krishnavirupa is no other than Krishnacharin:

> *His disciple is Krishnavirupa, who appeared in Uddiyana. It was said that when he was born in the Brahmin caste, the soothsayers prophesied that he would commit four sins. He was thus named Krishna, the black. Around the age of seven, he was sent to wander in other lands so that he might not commit the four sins. After a long time had elapsed his mother, Brahmini Laksmi, whose husband and parents-in-law had since died, also wandered to other lands. Having abandoned her caste, she became a wine seller in the Eastern land of Odivisa. After some time, her son also reached Odivisa, and (unknowingly) entered his mother's tavern. Since they did not recognise each other, they lived together. One day, when he was thirsty and wanted to drink some water, he gulped down a herder's drink which happened to be alcoholic. Being intoxicated he became very angry and flung the pot at the herder, but it missed and killed a cow. Having plotted how to conceal this act, he waited until night then*

flung the corpse of the cow from the roof top for the jackals to
eat. But it hit the head of a wandering Brahmin, who also
died. Because these incidents were so strange, he started to
make various inquiries and, in the process, discovered that
the wine seller was in fact his mother. The previously
predicted four sins, i.e. murdering a Brahmin, cow murder,
co-habitation with one's mother and consumption of alcohol
are the four sins out of the sixteen sins which violate a
Brahmin's authority to expound the Vedas. Realising that he
had committed all four sins at one time, he went to both
Buddhist and non-Buddhist pilgrimage places and inquired
about ways to purify these misdeeds. He could not trust
anybody, but he met Jalandharipa who gave him the
instruction of Vajravarahi and said that it would purify his
sins. "Over many lifetimes you have had a karmic affinity
with Virupa. Go to him, he now lives in Marahata..."[187]

According to this story Krishnavirupa met Virupa after he was
recommended to him by Jalandharipa. This suggests that
Krishnacharin, who becomes Jalandharipa's disciple, is different
from Krishnavirupa. But in his biography of Krishnacharin,
Taranatha does not mention Virupa becoming his teacher. It is also
difficult to understand why Taranatha would fail to know details of
the earlier part of Krishnacharin's life if he himself remembered
Krishnacharin being one of his own many previous incarnations.[188]
There seems to be a parallel between Taranatha's unconvincing
compilation of the histories of both Virupa and Krishnacharin.

Based on our observations about the dating of Dombi Heruka,
we can now suggest that Krishnacharin and Virupa met sometime
in 630-35 AD. Virupa would then have had to be in his late
seventies or early eighties. The meeting would have taken place
after Dombi Heruka became Virupa's disciple. The three would
have met for the first time when Krishnacharin was a Hindu Yogi in
Bhimesara. Strangely, the Lamdre sources not only fail to mention

how long Virupa stayed with the five hundred Hindu Yogis, they also omit mention of how Dombi Heruka spent his time during that period. However, it is clear that Krishnacharin's foremost Buddhist Tantric teacher was Virupa and his encounter with the Princess Laksmikara and Jalandharipa, though important for other practices, was perhaps of less significance to the development of the Lamdre tradition.

The Lamdre sources maintain that even though Krishnacharin met Virupa in the south, he himself was from the East (presumably East Bengal, present day Bangladesh). Hence, he was known as the Krishnacharin, the Easterner (Sharchok Nagpopa).[189] He is said to have been given the name Karna, not only because of his very long ear lobes but also because of his birth-place, Karna. According to the Mahakala lineage, his name is spelled Kanhapa. I have no doubt that his birth-place was called Karna in Karnataka State in South India.[190] But I would like to look into the theory that the name 'Shar-phyogs-nag-po-pa' was associated with his 'native town' or birth-place. The word 'from the East,' [shar-phyogs] seems to refer to his hermitage in Mount Utsayana in East Bengal, where he practised after having travelled and studied with Virupa for some time.[191] Hypothetically speaking, if Krishnacharin had ever taken Bhiksu ordination and studied in Nalanda as has been asserted, this would have happened on his way to or from Mount Utsayana, after he left Virupa. Mount Utsayana is regarded as his hermitage rather than his birth-place. Nalanda lies on the route from Gujarat to Mount Utsayana.

Krishnacharin's reputation as the siddha 'Krishnacharin the Easterner' would not have spread before he left Virupa and had perfected various Mantra and meditation practices. If the name 'From the East' had been associated with him while he was still a practitioner in Utsayana, this would mean that he came from further east than Utsayana. This is not plausible. Therefore, the name 'Shar-phyogs nag-po-pa' must have originated after he met Guru Jalandharipa of Jalandhara,[192] from where Mount Utsayana would be geographically in the distant East. I would say that by then he was already a siddha, but would have gone to meet Jalandharipa because the Vajradakinis encouraged him to do so.

Although Taranatha states that Jalandharipa knew Krishnacharin to be a fortunate being and therefore gave him full and complete empowerments, teachings and follow-up teachings, he does not specify the deity on which he was initiated. Even though Jalandharipa may have given him the empowerment of Hevajra along with other initiations, Jalandharipa is not considered a recipient of Virupa's *Vajra Verses* and he is not canonised among Lamdre lineage masters.

Krishnacharin was a learned Yogi of a non-Buddhist tradition when he met Virupa in the south and afterwards accompanied him to Sovanatha. Thereafter, he stayed with Virupa until he was ordered to achieve the three tasks to which I have previously referred. Pawo Tsuklak Trengwa supports the Lamdre historical view of Krishnacharin when he writes:

> To the less intelligent Yogi, who with his plaited hair had
> followed him, he (Virupa) gave the Margaphala Vajragatha,
> and then sent him to the East.[193]

As one of his three main tasks, he is said to have subdued a king who was attached to his seventy-two queens. When Krishnacharin socialised with the queens, the ministers warned the king who ordered his men to punish the Yogin. When the king's army chased him outside the palace compound he would go into the palace; when the army came inside, he would go outside again. The king's chief army officer deployed many soldiers both inside and outside the palace compound. Krishnacharin multiplied himself from one to ten, ten to one hundred, then from one hundred to one thousand manifestations of armed men. The king came to realise that the Yogin had attained Siddhi. He begged his forgiveness. Subsequently the siddha converted the king and his subjects to the Vajrayana path. His secret name was Padmavajra. As we have already discussed, he was the one out of the five hundred hair-plaited Yogis, who voluntarily gave up his faith to follow Virupa and eventually became the main expounder of Lamdre teachings. Virupa gave the *Vajra Verses* to Krishnacharin. In accordance with Virupa's prophecy, he went to western Uddiyana and brought forth five partial texts of the 500, 000 verses of Hevajra Tantra on the basis of which the *Vajra Verses* were taught. These do not appear to have been translated into Tibetan.

5. WHY DID VIRUPA HAVE TWO SUCCESSORS?

The Lamdre masters in Tibet held a tradition of discriminating sharply between the two successors of Virupa. Through what we know about Dombi Heruka and Krishnacharin, we can analyse the reasons for this. It is not surprising to find differences in their intelligence and aptitude, but how do we explain Dombi Heruka's superiority? The distinction between 'sudden' and 'gradual' schools became well known in Tibet after the famous Samye debate.[194] Presumably the Lamdre masters adopted this distinction to explain the theory of the two types of disciples.

A. Fortunate disciple entering the sudden path

This approach is explained as being relevant to those disciples who are not required to train in the common teachings. They are suitable to enter the path by receiving ripening empowerment.[195] They are eligible to train in the main practices of the path, including the Completion Stage.[196] Dombi Heruka is traditionally regarded as a highly intelligent and sharp-minded disciple who fell into this category. This categorisation of Dombi Heruka raises a number of questions. For example, an intelligent disciple suited to attain Siddhi on the sudden path would not require more than one Guru, nor would it take long for him to attain Siddhi. Yet according to the biographies, Dombi Heruka did not satisfy either of these criteria. However, if we accept that he was a king who abandoned his kingdom, ran away with a low-caste girl, worked as a boatman and finally became a siddha, this would show that he was indeed a courageous and flexible person who was able to live a spontaneous life. This is a criterion for 'an intelligent disciple on the sudden path.' His refusal to accept the ferry-fare which he previously demanded from Virupa and his decision to become a disciple after witnessing the reversal of the Ganges,[197] is further evidence of flexibility and spontaneity. This decision required a speedy change of perception and the ability to transform opposites. The incident at the bank of the River Ganges must have been planned by Virupa in order to find his successor, Dombi Heruka. After this, it was unnecessary for Dombi Heruka to receive preliminary teachings on renunciation and the enlightenment thought. That incident was sufficient for the two to develop the spiritual affinity. This however does not amount to suddenness in attaining enlightenment, although he may have been directly admitted into the Vajrayana path at that time.

B. Less fortunate disciple entering the gradual path

This approach is said to have been for those disciples who are initially not interested in the secret Mantrayana path. Such disciples need to be motivated by hearing the teachings on the difficulties of obtaining the precious human rebirth, the infallibility of the law of Karma, the shortcomings of worldly existence, the law of impermanence and the inevitability of death. It is important that they first be trained in the four teachings of the common path[198] including taking Refuge, and gradually introduced and trained in the secret Mantrayana teachings. Krishnacharin is regarded as less intelligent than Dombi Heruka and is said to fit into this category. For this reason, it is said, he was given the basic teachings in detail. However, when we look at the qualities he displayed, this categorisation may not seem at all clear-cut. The fact that Virupa gave a longer version of Lamdre to him does not of itself prove that he was less intelligent than Dombi Heruka. He showed courage, flexibility and sharpness of mind in courageously abandoning his own faith to follow Virupa. He demonstrated intelligence equal to that of Dombi Heruka in recognising the truthfulness of the teachings.

The striking question which remains to be answered is whether Virupa gave both disciples the same transmission, or whether he gave each a different transmission. Also, did he give them the transmissions separately, or together? According to Lamdre sources, Virupa gave short teachings to Dombi Heruka and elaborate teachings to Krishnacharin. This indicates that each received the teachings individually and that, although the content was the same, the teachings varied in length. It is commonly understood that the detailed teachings contain the brief teachings and that the brief teachings can be elaborated to provide detailed explanations. But some intelligent people may not necessarily believe that they can understand brief teachings more easily than elaborate teachings. Similarly, less intelligent people may not believe that elaborate teachings are easier to understand than brief teachings. Since the difference in the sharpness of the respective mentalities of Dombi Heruka and Krishnacharin does not seem easy to establish historically, the distinction may well have been a convention developed by later Lamdre commentators to legitimise the branching into common and uncommon Lamdre traditions in Tibet.

This division into the two traditions by later Lamdrepas may have been what provoked the accusation from other traditions that there is a so-called 'Lamdre without script' in the Sakyapa tradition. This notion of 'Lamdre without a root' has been misinterpreted by others to mean that the teachings lacked a textual root. But it is said that Virupa wrote down the *Vajra Verses* as notes from his teachings for the sake of Krishnacharin, whose comprehension may have been less sharp than Dombi Heruka's. However, the argument that Virupa prepared notes for

Krishnacharin from instructions he had delivered previously does not of itself prove that one disciple was of high intelligence and the other of low intelligence. Particularly given that the difference in intelligence is not readily provable. If it were true, it would negate the principle that Lamdre teachings are a whispered lineage, which must be transmitted orally from a teacher to one disciple only. However, such an argument does not pose any threat to the authenticity of the *Vajra Verses* teaching because it was transmitted orally and memorised by the disciple. Nevertheless, during the period prior to the lives of Drogmi Lotsawa and Pandita Gayadhara[199] it must have existed in written form because it was translated into Tibetan.

From the textual study point of view, there is a fundamental difference between the two traditions. The 'Commentarial Tradition' ('grel-pa-lugs), also known as the Dombi Heruka lineage, is rather brief on the path of ripening and liberation but has detailed explanations on the Tantric exegesis. The teachings for intelligent disciples are usually said to be detailed and it would be fair to say that it is the scholastic tradition within the Lamdre lineage. The Krishnacharin tradition, otherwise known as the 'Instructional Tradition' (man-ngag-lugs), is mainly concerned with practising the pith instructions rather than relying excessively upon exegetical works. It is a contemplative order with greater emphasis on practice and less on scriptural study. The honorific title of Lamdre teachings has thus become 'The precious words of the pith instructions on the Path, including its Result.' Subsequently most of the Lamdre teachings are said to have remained in a whispered lineage until Sachen Kunga Nyingpo wrote them down for the first time.[200] There were no Indian Lamdre classics other than the *Vajra Verses*. All the thirty-one volumes on Lamdre teachings currently preserved are native Tibetan works written after the twelfth century.

Dombi Heruka[201] and Krishnacharin followed Virupa's instructions strictly. They kept the teachings secret and transmitted the instructions only to their chosen disciples. Krishnacharin was succeeded by Mahasiddha Damarupa or Dharmapa. There are two Dharmapas listed [#36 and #48] amongst the eighty-four Mahasiddhas in the biographical dictionary prepared by Abhayadatta.[202] One could assume that they are in fact one person. In the Lamdre sources it is written that he constantly rattled his Damaru wherever he went and became known as 'Damarupa, the Drummer.' He demonstrated his Carya practices by wandering through all the twenty-four cities and thirty-two sacred shrines.[203] He subdued a Tirthika king named 'Senge Nampar Tsenpa'[204] who abandoned the heretical doctrine of sacrificing animals to the gods. This king eventually renounced his kingdom with the attitude of one who spits on the ground. Thereafter he adopted the behaviour of abandoning the two extremes and spent most of his time playing with the city's children in the streets. Hence, he became known as Avadhutipa[205] and transmitted Lamdre to Gayadhara.

3

THE EARLY DIFFUSION OF LAMDRE IN TIBET

The history of Tibet can be divided into three principal periods. During the pre-Buddhist period, Tibetans practised an indigenous religion known as 'Bon.' The revised Bon or White Bon (bon-dkar) is still practised by a small but devout group of practitioners in Tibetan society to this day. The period from the introduction of Buddhism to Tibet in the early seventh century up to its persecution by King Lang Darma in the mid-ninth century is called 'The Early Diffusion of Buddhism.' The period after the revival of Buddhism in the tenth century until recent times is known as 'The Later Diffusion of Buddhism.' The Lamdre tradition was introduced to Tibet by Pandita Gayadhara and Drogmi Lotsawa during this later period as were all the schools of the New Translation (gsar-ma). Although there were others, Lochen Rinchen Sangpo, Drogmi, Goe Khugpa Lhaytsey Sonam Tsemo and Marpa are regarded as the prominent founding fathers of the new schools in this period.

The history of Lamdre in Tibet is traditionally divided into three stages of development:

    1. The Early Introduction of the Lamdre tradition to
      Tibet by Pandita Gayadhara;

2. The Early Diffusion of Lamdre in Tibet by Drogmi Lotsawa and his successor;

3. The Flourishing of Lamdre in Tibet and beyond brought about by the Great Sakyapas.[206]

In this chapter we will discuss the first two periods and see how Drogmi brought Lamdre to Tibet in collaboration with Gayadhara and other Indian Gurus. Although Drogmi travelled to India twice and studied there for a period of between eighteen and twenty-two years,[207] he met Gayadhara in Tibet. Gayadhara, who outlived Drogmi, was the last Indian lineage holder of Lamdre and visited Tibet on four occasions. He gave Lamdre to Drogmi during his second visit to Tibet. This led to the preliminary introduction of Lamdre to Tibet.

After the persecution of Buddhism in Tibet by King Lang Darma around 978 AD, there was considerable doubt and controversy regarding the authenticity of the kind of Buddhism that had been practised in Tibet. This prompted local Tibetan rulers to select young Tibetans to go to India for study. They brought back many new translations and carried out special revisions of earlier translations. Lochen Rinchen Sangpo (958-1055) was one of the twenty monks sent to India for higher studies in Buddhist teachings by the ruler of Western Tibet, Lha Lama Yeshe O. Special emissaries were sent to invite prominent Indian Panditas to Tibet. Some uninvited Indian Buddhist missionaries also found their way to Tibet. This was the period when the three royal brothers of Lhatse[208] were seeking a spiritual preceptor. Having heard about Loton Dorje Wangchuk[209] and Chetsun Sherab Jungnay of Zhalu, whose activities greatly contributed to the renewal of the doctrine, they requested their assistance with spiritual matters. Loton sent Gya Shakya Shonu, Se Yeshe Tsondru and Nyang Dorje Gyaltshen, accompanied by five Bhikhus, five novices and two Upasakas to establish the grand temple of Drompa Gyang. The number of Sangha members studying in the temple increased rapidly.

1. LIFE OF DROGMI LOTSAWA SHAKYA YESHE (993-1074)

Drogmi was born in the water female snake year (993 AD)[210] to a wealthy nomadic family (as indicated by his family name Drog ['brog]) in Mangkhar Chude region, Tsang province.[211] He was first ordained in the Drompa Gyang temple and received the name 'Shakya Yeshe' derived from the names of Gya Shakya Shonu and Se Yeshe Tsondru from whom he received ordination. Although the temple was firmly established in the practices of Vinaya, both the patrons and the preceptors felt that they should send some young and intelligent monks to India in order to bring the complete teachings of the Dharma to Tibet. One day they offered a special feast to the entire monastic community and announced their plan to send some monks to India. They asked if anyone would volunteer to go on this important project. Drogmi Shakya Yeshe, Leng Shakya Tsondru and Tak Yeshe Shonu[212] volunteered. Everyone praised them for their courage and promised to give all the financial support that was necessary. They were instructed to study Vinaya, the root of the doctrine, Prajñaparamita, the essence of the doctrine, and Vajrayana, the quintessence of the doctrine. Although they planned to travel together, sharing all the gifts they had received, the abbot secretly gave ten gold ounces, the musk[213] of ten musk deer and a donkey load of salt to Leng and had sent him on ahead.[214] Drogmi and Tak could not leave on schedule, as they could not gather enough provisions for the journey in time. Meanwhile, Drogmi learned Sanskrit from a wandering Atsara.[215] This enabled him to have basic conversations in that language so that he did not need to depend entirely on interpreters.[216]

Eventually, the vice-abbot Se Yeshe Tsondru finished organising and collecting the necessary provisions for their departure. He gave them one hundred ounces of gold, the musk of one thousand musk deer, Yaks' tails and many other material goods. Drogmi and Tak, with two attendants were accompanied by the Atsara from whom Drogmi learned Sanskrit. They set out for

India via Mangyul Gungthang (Purang), a convenient border town and the route that all the Lotsawas used to acclimatise themselves to the weather and the food of low altitude countries. They left for India in 1008 when Lotsawa Rinchen Sangpo was fifty years old.[217] On their way to Mangyul, they met Leng and the three stayed there for two months. They journeyed to Nepal together. In Nepal they met Balpo Dza-hung, better known as 'Shantibhadra,' one of the four Phamthingpa brothers.[218] They studied Sanskrit, logic and many Secret Mantrayana teachings with him. When Drogmi was able to understand lectures in Sanskrit, he asked, "Who is the most famous teacher in India that we should go to study with?" To this Shantibhadra replied,

> For the sake of auspiciousness, first go to Vajrasana (modern Bodh Gaya where the Buddha attained enlightenment under the Bodhi tree) and make offerings at the Mahabodhi Temple. After that you should go to the monastery of Vikramasila, where there are the famous six great gate-keeper scholars (Dvarapandita).[219] Go and study with Santipa, the Second Omniscient Being, who is the Pandita of the Eastern Gate-Keeper and is also my own teacher.

Having said this, he sent his younger brother, Balpo Adepa to accompany them to India. The party reached Vajrasana, where they made their offerings, and everything went smoothly. Drogmi studied mainly under Santipa, but also under other Gate-keeper Panditas in Vikramasila[220] for a period of eight years.

Before returning to Tibet, Drogmi visited the shrine of Khasarpani, a sacred shrine in the southern mountains of Devikotta. It is said that if a faithful person fasts there for one week and prays in front of the shrine wholeheartedly, kneeling on the floor with hands folded above his head, all his wishes will be granted. Drogmi performed this practice

*On the way back, you will be received by a siddha, who is a
lineage holder of Virupa. Also, in Tibet, a certain Guru, who
possesses the entire pith instructions of Virupa, will deliver
them to you at your door step. At that time, you should one-
pointedly devote yourself to practising the instructions
without wasting time searching for another Guru and more
instructions.*

One day, when Drogmi was passing through Kuba Grove in South
India, he heard the sound of a monk's staff. Thinking that there
must be a town nearby, he looked carefully into the forest, and
there he saw a vision of an attractive Bhiksu, who was wearing the
three Dharma robes,[221] and carrying his begging bowl and a
monk's staff. The Bhiksu touched his staff to a tree trunk and
suddenly a woman's hand, adorned with jewellery, stretched out
from the tree and poured nectar into the begging bowl of the
Bhiksu.

After seeing this wondrous vision, he developed an uncontrived
faith in the Bhiksu. While remembering the prediction, he
developed confidence that the Bhiksu was the prophesied Siddha.
Drogmi prostrated himself, touched the Bhiksu's feet to his head,
circumambulated him and requested to be accepted as his disciple.
Immediately the Bhiksu accepted his request and gave him some
nectar to taste. Drogmi experienced one hundred flavours from
the nectar and his mind was filled with meditative realisations.
Just as the Bhiksu was about to go, all the leaves of the trees
combined to sprinkle dew drops to rinse the Bhiksu's mouth.
When he saw this other wondrous vision, Drogmi established
unshakeable faith in the Bhiksu. "In order to receive instructions,
you must receive initiation," said the Bhiksu. "I have already
received initiation from Santipa and Nepalese Dza-hung" replied
Drogmi. "In order to receive my instructions, you must receive the
initiation from me." Having said this, the Bhiksu gave him a three-
day Hevajra initiation[222] at a town near Kuba Grove. He also gave

instructions on numerous Tantras. In reply to Drogmi's request for more teachings, he said, "All of my food and necessities are provided by higher, medium and lesser Mimayin.[223] I have no need of wealth. However, since in the Vajrayana path it is extremely important to arouse the auspicious conditions,[224] you must go to your own country and bring wealth if you wish to receive further instructions." "Where will I find you?" asked Drogmi. "I had originally planned to go to Shriparvata,[225] but King Chanakya invited me to stay at his court for at least three years, so I will be there for seven years. You should come directly to me there." This Bhiksu Mahasiddha is identified as Prajñendraruci [shes-rab dbang-pos mdzes-pa], the disciple of Acharya Durjayacandra. His secret name is 'Bhiksu Viravajra' or 'Gelong Pawo Dorje' in Tibetan.

As the three Tibetans were making preparations to return to Tibet, Taklo said, "I will remain in Vajrasana so that I can do more circumambulation to acquire merit." However, at the insistence of Drogmi and Leng, he accompanied them back to Tibet. When they reached Drompa Lhatse, the abbots, monks and devotees gave them a warm reception. Drogmi had become an ultimate scholar, Leng had become a mediocre scholar but Taklo was just able to read the Heart Sutra in Sanskrit. Someone asked: "How is it that they have learned so much, yet you know so little?" "They always seemed to go elsewhere carrying Kapala every day. Since I had great devotion to the Mahabodhi Temple, I spent my time circumambulating there," replied Taklo. However, it is said that Taklo had been sanctified by the blessings of the Mahabodhi Temple. He was pure in keeping his Vinaya vows and was able to establish a great monastery known as 'Takloi Depa.' Leng decided to return to India saying, "Since the Tibetans are stupid like oxen, and make no distinction between learned men and fools, I will return to India." Though he became very learned later on, it appears that he was not very influential in spreading the Dharma. Drogmi, who had become an incomparable scholar and master, was honoured by everyone including the three brothers of Lhatse.

King Palde offered his beautiful princess Lhachik Dzedhen to Drogmi, who married her and received her as his consort.[226]

In the meantime, Drogmi encouraged his patrons and disciples to collect more gold so that he might return to see Viravajra in India and receive further teachings. They offered him the much-needed gold and this time Drogmi went to India with his wife. He met his Guru at King Chanakya's court, where Drogmi offered him gold, musk and other unimaginable offerings. He received Hevajra and thirteen other major initiations and instructions on Mahanuttara-yoga-tantra Mandalas. In addition, he received the entire lineage instructions transmitted by Dombi Heruka, eighty major Tantras, one hundred and sixty minor Tantras as well as fifty Anujña *(rjes gnang)* over a period of four years.[227] As Drogmi was planning to return to Tibet, his Guru said:

> *It has been quite a long time since you came here. You two*
> *should practise Carya for three months and then travel and*
> *have a holiday for three months.*

Drogmi did as advised. While traveling, he witnessed the so-called 'three important spectacles.' At one time, there was a big crowd at a market place. All of a sudden panic gripped the people, who began to disperse hastily. Drogmi asked why, and was told, "Since King Chanakya is famous for having conquered many countries, a war has been declared by king Bhojantahara and fifteen other kings of western countries, whose powerful troops have now reached as close as five days' journey from the palace. It is all due to our king's deceitfulness. Now we will all be killed, and our city will be destroyed and emptied. What shall we do?" Drogmi noticed that every person in the city appeared distressed and frightened. When he asked his Guru about this, the Guru replied, "King Chanakya is faithful to the Triple Gem and is a fortunate man. He will not be defeated at any time." In spite of the omniscient Guru's prediction, Chanakya was saddened. Everybody else predicted his defeat. In the meantime, King Chanakya mounted a strong elephant to ride into battle. On top of the elephant was a Buddhist shrine to the Triple Gem containing beautiful and sumptuous offerings, cared for by ten Bhikhus and ten Brahmins. The king sat on his throne before the shrine, surrounded by many of his attendants. On top of the elephant's head sat a big fighter from Magadha holding a large hammer made of molten thunder-bolt and weighing 20 khals. On the elephant's neck were ten fighters armed with iron hooks. There were other reinforcements behind them. The main fighter elephant was surrounded by twenty-five fighter elephants who in turn were surrounded by fifty ordinary elephants. Each of these elephants was mounted by fifty armies. Outside the elephant troops were horse-carts, cavalry and foot soldiers. These were known as 'the four contingents of force' in ancient military warfare.

There was a tradition in those days that first of all two kings would fight until one of them was defeated. Until that happened, nobody else would engage in battle. But even after fighting for half a day, King Chanakya and his wrathful opponent could reach no conclusion. When his exhausted elephant nearly fell over, Chanakya invoked the name of Mahasiddha Viravajra three times and addressed the big fighter with the following words, "Now is the time that you should display your strength and power. If you are able to win this battle, I shall let you marry my princess and I will give you whatever property you desire." When he heard this, the big fighter hit the forehead of the opponent's elephant with his big thunder-bolt hammer, killing it instantly.

King Chanakya's soldiers then went on to conquer the fifteen kingdoms. However soon after the fighting ended, the king renounced his kingdom and gave it to his eldest son. He sailed away to an island accompanied by five queens, seven ministers and a retinue of two hundred and fifty. He took provisions that would last for fifty years. There he and his retinue lived and practised the instructions which had been received from Viravajra.[228]

The third important spectacle involved an eight-year-old Jñanadakini (wisdom Dakini), who had lost the sense of shame, appeared naked, and acted like one gone mad. She talked nonsense, flew up into the sky then danced upon the floor. A wild elephant lurched into the forest and destroyed all the trees, picking up creatures with his trunk and killing them by throwing them into the distance. As the elephant was about to enter a town to cause destruction, the aforementioned girl appeared, and the elephant suddenly picked her up with its trunk and circumambulating the town three times, placed her on top of a stupa. By the blessings of the girl the elephant's madness was cured and it returned to the forest. The girl vanished into space.

These so-called 'three spectacles' had the special purpose of instilling strong faith in Drogmi towards his Guru Viravajra. Such demonstrations of miracles by teachers to disciples at the conclusion of Lamdre transmission seem to have been practised from the earliest times. After Drogmi returned to Tibet, he built the monastery of Mugulung in Mangkhar region but lived mainly in Lhatse Rocks, where he later met Gayadhara. Marpa, like Goe and many others, came to Mugulung to study with Drogmi and stayed with him for three years.[229]

2. LIFE OF PANDITA GAYADHARA (970-1090)[230]

Gayadhara was the last Indian Lamdre lineage master and the only one to visit Tibet. He brought the Lamdre lineage known as 'Men-ngak Luk' (man-ngag-lugs) which came down through Krishnacharin and was transmitted to Drogmi. The Lamdre lineage known as 'Drelpa Lug' ('grel-pa-lugs) which came down through Dombi Heruka was brought to Tibet by Drogmi Lotsawa himself. He received it from Viravajra, a disciple of Durjayacandra. Gayadhara is also known in Tibet as 'Pandita Marpo' (pan-di-ta dmar-po), the Red Pandita or 'Atsara Marpo'i Shab' (a -tsa-ra dmar-po'i-zhabs), the Venerable Red Acharya. He was well known for his repeated visits to the country. He is not to be confused with the other Astara Marpo in the lineage of Makzorma (dmag-zor-ma).[231] It was during his third visit to Tibet that Gayadhara became known as Gyalbu Tringyi Shukchen (rgyal-bu sprin-gyi shugs-can).[232]

Avadhutipa, who was Gayadhara's teacher, lived and practised near the bank of the river Lohita in central India. Avadhutipa was guided by Arya Avalokitesvara and his Guru Damarupa, who prophesied that he would one day give the instructions to a Bhiksu Vajra Holder,[233] who was a royal preceptor. This person is identified as Gayadhara. Gayadhara was born in Bengal,[234] which was then ruled by king Candarupaksi. He was known as Kayastha because he was the king's scribe. His actual name was Gayadhara. His name means 'Cloud Holder' or 'Serpent Holder' as interpreted by Drogmi and other early masters. He was a renowned scholar of all five sciences,[235] who taught and served in the king's palace. Avadhutipa contacted Gayadhara suggesting that he would be a good disciple and that he should visit him. Gayadhara happily went to see Avadhutipa who bestowed upon him all the four whispered lineage instructions of Lamdre. He is said to have accomplished stability in the stages of generation practice, acquiring the ability to see the numerous manifestations of Nirmanakayas and to suspend his Vajra and bell in the air. He is also said to have possessed the unobstructed ability to go astral traveling and to resurrect dead bodies by transferring his consciousness into them,[236] in addition to numerous other psychic abilities.

In accordance with his teacher's prediction, Gayadhara came to Tibet[237] in search of his future disciple. He first met Shonu Sherab, a Lotsawa from Purang district in south western Tibet, to whom he gave instructions. This Lotsawa, known as 'Purang Lotsawa' (pu hrang lo tsa ba) became a faithful devotee. He requested more teachings, but Gayadhara responded: "I must first go to U-Tsang in central Tibet, where I have some important things to do. After that I shall return here to give you the teachings and instructions you desire." They agreed that the Lotsawa would offer fifty ounces of gold and that Gayadhara would return in three months' time. It is noticeable that from this point forward Gayadhara arranged his time very strictly and made prior agreements with students about the size of the fee they should offer him when he bestowed initiations and instructions. Because he asked set fees for instructions, he received much criticism in Tibet.

When Drogmi was in retreat in Lhatse Rocks,[238] which are known these days as 'Gayadhara Caves' he had some special dreams at night. His prophetic dreams are not discussed anywhere except in the Lamdre history written by Jamyang Khyentse Wangchuk. Jamyang wrote: 'When Drogmi was in retreat in Lhatse Rocks, which are known these days as Gayadhara Caves, he had some rough and special dreams one night.... Sometime after he had these dreams, he heard someone blow an Atsara's trumpet at his door.'[239] The dreams were as follows:

> There was a terrifying giant black man, who came to him flying through the sky saying, "I have come from the south." Having said this, he vomited a conch-lion. From the conch-lion's mouth emerged a golden Vajra. From the centre of the Vajra arose a vase filled with water, which soaked into his [Drogmi's] body, endowing him with an inconceivable transcendental wisdom of great bliss. After that, three balls of light issued from his body. These illuminated three houses which again dissolved into light and were absorbed into his own body. Subsequently his body dissolved into light and was absorbed into his feet. His feet eventually vanished like rainbows into space. With these vivid dreams, Drogmi woke up.[240]

Drogmi had these dreams the night before he met Gayadhara, during Gayadhara's first visit to Tibet. However, it was not until he gave the entire Lamdre to Drogmi that Gayadhara offered the following interpretation of the dreams. This happened some eight years after they first met.[241]

The three houses represent the three realms of existence.[242]
The black man who came from the south represents
Yogeshvara (Virupa). The conch-lion vomited from his mouth
represents Gayadhara, who was Yogeshvara's emanation.[243]
The whiteness of the conch represents Gayadhara's white
garment.[244] His Lion of Speech, which is incomparable to
anyone's (speech), is represented by the lion. The golden
Vajra which emerged from his mouth represents the precious
Lamdre instructions, the essence of the Vajrayana doctrine.
The golden vase filled with water represents the unbroken
four whispered lineages of the undried water of initiation.
The absorption of this into Drogmi's head symbolises that the
aforementioned instruction is appropriately transmitted to
him. The three light rays issuing from his body which
illuminated three houses symbolise the fact that he would
have three accomplished disciples, who would benefit the
three realms of existence by propagating the instructions.
The dissolution of the three realms into him represents the
fact that his mind and the minds of all his disciples would
become indistinguishably merged into one. The dissolution of
his body into his feet symbolises the fact that Drogmi would
have two sons. The vanishing of the feet into space indicates
that his two sons will die young and will become neither his
spiritual nor his hereditary successors"[245]

Having been awakened by the sound of trumpets Drogmi, although he was in strict retreat, sent an attendant to see who was there. It was an Acharya wearing a red gown, who said to the attendant, "I need an audience with Drogmi, since I have come all the way from India to see him. I should also be given some material wealth." To this Drogmi sent a note in Sanskrit saying, "I am observing a strict retreat, I cannot meet you. I have no wealth to give you, but take some food to eat." While he handed over the note, the attendant gave plenty of food to the Acharya. The Acharya would not even look at the food let alone accept it. He remained seated, in an attitude of great unhappiness. When he heard the Acharya's unexpected reaction, Drogmi emerged from his retreat to meet him. He asked what the matter was. "You have insulted me by using abusive words," the Acharya replied. "I said only that I do not have any wealth to give you, but eat some food," Drogmi answered him.

In the meantime, the Acharya touched his right leg to his navel and stretched out the left leg. Resting his two hands on his waist he said, "You did not say that. This is what you have said," When Drogmi's note was carefully rewritten on the ground and translated properly, its correct translation emerged as. "Cover your bottom with your black hands and leave now." Drogmi realised how little Sanskrit grammar he had actually learned even though he had studied in India with eight Panditas for such a long time. He lamented and cried. Seeing this, the Pandita said: "Since the depth of Sanskrit grammar is unfathomable like the ocean, even I do not know exact details. How could you know everything? You already know this much. Compared with other Tibetan Lotsawas[246] you are an exceptional scholar."

Thereupon they discussed the teachings. Drogmi realised that Gayadhara was not only well versed in Vajrayana and Mother Tantra in general, but especially in Hevajra Tantra. He was extremely pleased to discover that Gayadhara also had the whispered lineage transmission of Lamdre. Suddenly Drogmi remembered Khasarpani's prophesy in India. He touched Gayadhara's feet and requested to be accepted as his disciple. "I have come here to look for you according to the prediction by the Great Compassionate One." "Do you have enough gold for the instructions?" asked Gayadhara. "I will make sure I can fulfil your wishes," replied Drogmi. "I came from India with two other Panditas who had gone to China according to their karmic affinities. As for myself, even though I was asked by Purang Lotsawa to stay with him, I came to look for you in accordance with the guidance of my tutelary deity," said Gayadhara. Then they went to a cave and Gayadhara first gave Drogmi the *Gurupancasika*, [247] an elementary teaching, in order to develop the teacher-disciple relationship between them. They were both pleased with the outcome of their meeting. It is said that during this period (approximately three months) they translated this and other texts into Tibetan. These are to be found in the Tibetan canon. Drogmi received the Amoghasiddhi Guru Yoga [248] as the first transmission and some other teachings from Gayadhara. He offered Gayadhara ten ounces (srang) of gold and requested that he bestow the Lamdre upon him. Gayadhara replied:

> In the meantime, I must go to see a Lotsawa in Purang to whom I have already promised to return. With all the offerings I may receive from him, I will go on pilgrimage to India and visit some of my teachers to make offerings of Ganachakra for the accumulation of merits. I will also have to bring back Indian texts[249] for the instructions you have just requested. In three years' time I shall return to give you the complete transmissions. During that period while I am away you have to make the necessary arrangements so that you can give me one hundred ounces of gold for the commentarial teachings on Tantra and approximately four hundred ounces of gold for the pith instructions. If you can provide that, then I will stay for five years. You should come to meet me in Kyirong.

Drogmi requested that Gayadhara accept silver coins, bronze, Yak tails and musk in the event that he could not collect sufficient gold coins. A bargain was concluded and Gayadhara left behind a bibliography of instructions that had been given by Virupa and which he would give to Drogmi on his return from India. At this point, five men with horses arrived from Kyirong to escort Gayadhara. Drogmi made a farewell offering of ten ounces of gold, a complete set of new clothes and two horses loaded with meat and butter. When Gayadhara left Lhatse for Purang with the escorts, Drogmi accompanied the party as far as Parphuk. After reaching Purang Gayadhara gave teachings to Purang Lotsawa and then continued on to India.

Drogmi was invited by a rich nomad family in Padro Namthang Karpo to conduct a religious ceremony and then stayed in retreat in Mangzang Caves. During the period of three years after Gayadhara returned to India, Drogmi received large quantities of gold as offerings for his teachings. Gayadhara returned from India (about five months early) via Dromo (modern Yatung) north of Sikkim. Two Atsaras delivered a message from Gayadhara to Drogmi which said: "Please come to receive me. I am on my way to see you". Drogmi was happy to hear the good news and sent a reply saying: "I will come to receive you in two months time." Drogmi then went to Lhatse to make special preparations for a grand reception welcoming the Pandita. The reception would be sponsored by the three Royal brothers of Lhatse.

Drogmi and his reception party consisted of thirty disciples and his patrons, who carried banners, parasols, a throne and all the appropriate articles for receiving a Pandita. Together with Gayadhara's party, they returned via South Latoe to North Latoe and from there through Gephu pass to Lhatse. As both the Pandita and the Lotsawa were famous, numerous wealthy people in the region came to make offerings of gold. From there the party eventually reached Mugulung in Mangkhar. It is said that Gayadhara chose Mugulung as the appropriate site to give Lamdre after he was inspired by hearing "Mumu," echo of a stream which had its origin in Mangkhar of Mugulung valley in central Tibet. Gayadhara interpreted the echo "Mumu" of the stream as 'mukta,' the Sanskrit word for liberation. He gave the Lamdre transmission of Krishnacarin to Drogmi, who offered three gold ounces as a Mandala offering on the first auspicious day of the Lamdre teachings.[250] Although Gayadhara finished giving the entire Lamdre teachings to Drogmi within three years, he is said to have

125

stayed five years during this his second trip to Tibet. In this time, Gayadhara and Drogmi translated many Tantric texts which are preserved in the Tibetan Buddhist canon.

After having received the entire instructions from Gayadhara, Drogmi realised that he did not have enough gold to make the offerings he had promised. So, he sent a message to his wealthy and famous disciple, Zurpoche Shakya Jungne,[251] saying: "Come with lots of wealth and gold, I shall give you teachings." As Zurpoche was busy conducting a special Vajrakilaya ritual at the behest of Zurchungpa Sherab Drak in Shang region, there was some unexpected delay in receiving the message. However, when he received it, some of Zurpoche's companions, who were afraid that this might interrupt the ritual, tried to dissuade him from going. Zurpoche however, told them: "My main purpose in performing this ritual is to attain Siddhi, and the root cause of attaining Siddhi is Dharma. Drogmi is an excellent repository of instructions on the Dharma and I have heard that he has been receiving more instructions from Gayadhara lately. He must have got some special instructions for me. Since he has invited me, I must go. It cannot be an omen of obstacles, it is in fact an omen about attaining Siddhi."[252]

He appointed Zurchungpa to officiate for the remaining part of the ritual. Before his departure he subdued the serpent of Sampa Wadong and ordered it to bring gold in the shape of various animals. It is said that serpents brought gold either from there or from the sea, and gave it to Zurpoche, who then went to Mugulung and made an offering of one hundred ounces to Drogmi. Drogmi gave him numerous instructions including the Three Tantras, Vajrapañjara[253] and the Hevajra Sadhana by Saroruha. He then made special preparations to thank Gayadhara for having given him the most precious teachings. His offerings included 500 ounces of gold which he arranged on a beautiful tray, the musk of 1000 deer, 200 long white Yak tails, 1000 black Yak tails and many rolls of silks and brocades. Gayadhara found it very difficult to believe the offerings were real, as Drogmi's massive offerings of gold looked like a magical show. So, he took all the offerings to a fair in Mangkhar and asked a crowd of people: "What can you see here?" The crowd replied unanimously: "Here you have the best quality gold." Gayadhara, who was very pleased to confirm that it was real gold, asked Drogmi, "Now, what do you want?" "I request that you give me any remaining Lamdre instructions I have not yet received," Drogmi replied. "There is no part of the Lamdre instructions that have not been revealed to you. Though it is unnecessary for you, this is my way of assuring you that I speak truthfully," saying this Gayadhara covered his back with a thangka of Mahakala Vajra Pañjara, put his prayer beads around his neck, placed the Torma[254] on his head and swore that there were no teachings unrevealed to Drogmi. Again, he said, "What do you want now?" Drogmi insisted that he did not mean to ask for more teachings if he had already been given all of them. Gayadhara also insisted: "What do you want?" Drogmi then requested Gayadhara not to give Lamdre instructions to anyone else. It is said that Gayadhara was very pleased to hear this as he interpreted it to mean that Drogmi had realised the profundity and preciousness of the teachings. According to another version of the story, Gayadhara said, "You made a mistake by making a request to me not to give this Lamdre instruction to anyone else, as it would suggest that you will not have any hereditary successors who will be able to preserve the transmission. But the actual lineage will spread in its purity." This comment is seen as parallel to what Naropa said to Marpa.

Now that he had freed himself from needing to seek other teachers, as Khasarpani had advised, Drogmi concentrated on his practice and on benefiting others by propagating the teachings. One day, after Gayadhara had returned to India, Guru Viravajra came flying through the sky. "For what purpose have you come here?" asked Drogmi. "I came here to visit the land of snowy mountains and also to clarify my son's doubts," replied Viravajra.

He stayed for one month,[255] during which time he composed the Sadhana Rantajvala. One afternoon he flew through the beams of the sunset to a city in the kingdom of Uddiyana where Dakinis were holding a Ganachakra feast. Soon afterwards, it is said that Maitripa came to visit Drogmi and gave him Vajrayogini instructions.

After giving the complete Lamdre instructions, Gayadhara returned to India in order to dedicate his meritorious deeds. He took with him all the offerings he had received from Drogmi. Soon afterwards, Gayadhara made his third[256] visit to Tibet at the invitation of Goe Lotsawa, who was also Drogmi's disciple. In spite of Goe and Drogmi's previous student and teacher relationship, some misunderstanding and discord developed between the two. Drogmi's tight-fistedness or perhaps strictness about giving instructions and his eagerness to obtain gifts failed to impress potential students like Marpa[257]

Incidentally Goe is said to have disparaged Gayadhara by saying: "What kind of Pandita is he? He is a greedy and vagrant Acharya who only wants to collect gold and wealth." Goe decided that he would compete with Drogmi by inviting a more famous and learned Pandita than Gayadhara. After making inquiries, he left for India to invite Mahapandita Maitripa,[258] then the most famous Pandita in all India. He placed all his gold inside a human skull, sealed it, made coloured chalk drawings on it and then he left for India accompanied by Se Sherab Monlam.

They reached Tromo safely. Goe carried the gold on his back, pretending that he was a Tibetan demon. In a frontier province in North India which was inhabited by barbarians, they met a Pandita who was accompanied by two attendants. One of the attendants bore a parasol and fan made from peacock feathers, while the other was carrying his bedding. The mysterious Pandita, who was in fact none other than Gayadhara, knowingly asked, "Where are you two going? Are you looking for anybody?" "We are going to see Maitripa in Magadha, the two replied." "I am Maitripa, what do you want?" replied Gayadhara. Goe was very pleased and replied, "I wish to invite you to Tibet."

After spending a few days discussing Dharma, Goe was impressed with this extremely learned Pandita. Thinking that he was actually Maitripa, Goe invited him to Tibet, offering him seven ounces of gold as an inducement. The Pandita accepted the invitation. However, the Pandita asked about the health of Drogmi several times during their journey. Goe began to be a bit suspicious about this interest in Drogmi's health. By now some former disciples had recognised Gayadhara and began to address him by his true name. Puzzled Goe asked, "Venerable sir, you have told me a lie. You are not Maitripa." Gayadhara replied, "Do you want to receive Dharma teachings or not? I am far more learned than Maitripa. When I was teaching Drogmi in the past you belittled both of us. You kept saying how stupid Drogmi was and how greedy I was. But there is no comparison between you and Drogmi. If you do not wish to accept me as your teacher, I can give back your gold and go to U myself." Goe offered him one ounce of gold as the Mandala offering and replied, "I did not mean to disparage you. Please forgive me and accept my invitation." Gayadhara finally accepted Goe's request and said: "I will come to Tibet as you have asked. You were one of Drogmi's disciples, yet you are jealous of him. How can you behave like this to your own teacher? This is unacceptable."

As Goe and Se were about to go on ahead to prepare an appropriate welcome to the Pandita, they were advised that a gang of Mon bandits were waiting for them up ahead at a point where there was a curve in the road. So they left the gold with a merchant and started out on their journey. Se, however, was very concerned about his teacher's safety. He therefore disguised himself in his teacher's clothes so that the robbers would attack him instead. He became famous for his great dedication to his teacher. They both arrived home unharmed. They gave a grand welcome to the Pandita on his arrival. Goe received the initiation of Guhyasamaja

Arya School[259] and some other commentaries on Tantra from Gayadhara. Together they also made numerous translations of Tantric texts which are preserved in the canon.

At one time both Goe and Pandita Gayadhara were staying in Shang with Zurpoche Shakya Jungnay, who had invited them. One day Drogmi paid a visit to Gayadhara, who was very pleased to meet him again. Gayadhara asked Drogmi to translate the teachings that he was about to give. Goe reacted angrily and became jealous of Drogmi. He asked his teacher to let both of them take turns in translating the teachings. Gayadhara laughed and laughed. He replied, "Here in Tibet, you seem to take what is designed to be helpful as harmful, don't you? I would be happy if you could do the whole translation by yourself, but I am afraid that Drogmi would pick up all of your mistakes. You will be unable to find even one mistake in Drogmi's translation, and yet you are complaining out of jealousy. I was hoping that you would learn by observing how Drogmi translates and improve your ability to translate properly. If you are not nervous and afraid of Drogmi pointing out your mistakes you can do the entire translation from today onwards."

It is said that Goe did not dare to translate after this. One day some time later, Gayadhara secretly gave a Hevajra initiation to Drogmi and others but he did not permit Goe to attend. Next day, Goe was again upset and complained at having been excluded. Gayadhara gave Goe some water from his initiation vase to and said, "Since it is better for you to drink some water from my vase than to receive initiation from evil Gurus, drink this water for your purification." Gayadhara reprimanded Goe for his disrespect to Drogmi, and also asked, "Have you not disparaged me for being greedy? Why did you behave like that?" Goe tried to explain that he had wanted to hurt Drogmi, not to disparage Gayadhara. Goe had to apologise. He made more offerings of gold to Gayadhara.

Lamdre historian Ngawang Kunga Sonam asserts that although Gayadhara gave the Hevajra initiation, the commentary on Hevajra

Tantra, Guhyasamaja and other initiations to Goe Lotsawa, he didn't give him the actual Lamdre instructions. He writes: 'At one time when Drogmi paid another visit to Gayadhara, Drogmi wondered whether Gayadhara had given Lamdre to Goe, and asked, "Have there been any hindrances to your pledge?" Gayadhara replied, "Do not act as if you want to transgress your own pledges. He (Goe) is so contented and involved with his scriptural study that he did not even ask for any instructions."' It is clear from this that Gayadhara did not give Lamdre to Goe.[260]

Gayadhara returned to India once again. When he made his fourth and final visit to Tibet at the invitation of Gyijowa Daway Oser,[261] Drogmi had already passed away. Gyijo Daway Oser received many teachings and made many offerings. One of his disciples named Nyoe also invited Gayadhara and honoured him with great respect. There were many other interested and potential disciples who brought many offerings of gold and begged him to accept them as disciples. The Pandita once said, "Since you have very good fresh water, favourable weather conditions, few creatures, and nutritious food, I must devote my time to intensive practices of virtue here in Tibet. I will not return to India nor do I wish to obtain more gold. I will have no time to give instructions." One day when he was translating a text on Kalacakra, he lamented, "If Drogmi were still alive we, the father and son, would have sat together to do this translation. But now he has already departed to Khechara." Saying this Gayadhara dedicated all the offerings he had received for the beneficial application of virtues. After remaining there for several years, the Pandita experienced signs of his own impending death and said, "I do not wish to stay here. Take me to Thophu where my spiritual descendants live." Nyoe replied, "Nobody lives there except some foolish meditators, including Phakpa Choenang, one of Drogmi's disciples and Serok, one of Drom Depa Tonchung's disciples. In any case, we are also your spiritual descendants." "Though that is true, you will transgress your pledges if you fail to take me there," replied

Gayadhara. Nyoe and his companions took the Pandita to Khareg Thophu[262] in accordance with his wish. As soon as they reached there Gayadhara said: "Now display all the symbols of the Triple Gem and arrange the offerings. Perform the Ganachakra ceremony if you have not broken the pledges." At the conclusion of the ceremony when everyone was satisfied with the feast of Ganachakra, the Pandita held the Vajra and bell in his hands which he crossed at his heart, sat in full meditation posture and said,

All of my sons! You must diligently practise meditation without distraction. Having spent most of my time traveling back and forth between Tibet and India and having become involved in teaching, I did not give myself sufficient time to strive and meditate properly, but this is how a Yogi should die"[263]

After watching the Pandita perform three rounds of breath, the disciples witnessed the following: A pellet-sized ball of light emerged from Gayadhara's crown. Within the light there was crystal-clear image of Heruka which issued bright lights, illuminating the entire space. While hearing the melodious sounds of celestial music and seeing the showers of flowers falling from the sky filled with rainbows, they saw an image of Heruka go towards the South West.

Bodong Panchen[264] makes the important observation that some personal meditational aids of Gayadhara were given to either Se or Rok. They eventually fell into the hands of Sachen some two or three generations after Gayadhara had passed away. The aids are among the most significant relics inherited by the Sakya monastery. According to Bodong[265] sometime after Se and Rok had passed away, Phagpa Choenang, who was their relative and student was given a bronze Stupa, a Thangka of Hevajra, a Sanskrit copy of the Tantra, and a Vajra and a bell (which all belonged to Gayadhara). Later on, Chagthangpa, a student of his, offered the Sanskrit copy of the Tantra and the Thangka to Nagton Lotsawa, who was a disciple of Gyichuwa.[266] It is said that Gyichuwa offered these to Sachen from whom he received the Lamdre teachings. Others say that although Nagton Lotsawa invited Sachen, Lopon Rinpoche Sonam Tsemo[267] came instead. While he hesitated to offer the Sanskrit text himself, it was later offered by his son (probably to Sonam Tsemo).

3. CHRONOLOGY OF DROGMI

No one source contains comprehensive information on Drogmi's life. In order to establish his chronology, it is necessary to review several Lamdre and non-Lamdre sources. Goe Lotsawa Shonu Pal tried to date Drogmi's translation of some Tantras and establish the time when Marpa went to study with Drogmi in the following passage:

> The Tantras belonging to the Yogini class such as the
> Samvara, Hevajra and others were translated by bla-chen
> 'brog mi, when the great lo-tsa-ba was nearing his fiftieth
> year.[268]

The 'great lo-tsa-ba' he refers to is Lochen Rinchen Sangpo, who was born in 958 AD. His fiftieth year occurred in 1008 AD. Drogmi, who was born in 992 or 993 AD, would have been only sixteen years old when Rinchen Sangpo was fifty. Hence the time indicated by Goe Lotsawa is far too early for Drogmi to have translated those texts. Drogmi was only making preparations to go India to study at that time and could not have undertaken those translations. Goe Lotsawa goes on to write:

> At that time, the boy (Marpa) had reached the age of fifteen
> and had a strong desire to learn the profession of a
> translator. With Drogmi he studied assiduously the 'language
> of translations' (Sanskrit) and mastered it thoroughly. Later
> he used to say, 'I studied the interlinear and literary
> translations from Sanskrit under Drogmi Lotsawa at the

*hermitage of My (u)-gu-lung (near Sakya in Tsang). I think
his kindness (towards me) was not little, but great.*[269]

If Marpa, who was born in 1012 AD, came to meet Drogmi when he
was fifteen years old, then Drogmi would be thirty five years old
and Rinchen Sangpo would be sixty nine years old. There is a
discrepancy of nineteen years. Goe Lotsawa also believed that
Drogmi spent thirteen years in India and does not seem to know
about Drogmi's second visit to India. According to his Blue Annals,
Drogmi set out for India in 1008 AD, reached India in 1009 AD and
returned to Tibet in 1022 AD. He does not seem to realise that
Drogmi was only sixteen when Rinchen Sangpo was fifty.

According to Jamyang Khyentse Wangchuk, Drogmi spent eight
years in India[270] during his first visit, but he does not mention how
old Drogmi was at that time. Supposedly Drogmi was sixteen when
he left for India, took one year to arrive and spent only eight years
there. He would have returned in 1017 AD, ten years before the
sexagenary year calendar cycle was introduced to Tibet. He
married after his first return from India. This would have occurred
in 1018 AD or in 1019 AD, when he was twenty-six or twenty-
seven years old. He remained for at least three years before
returning to India. This means he went back to India in 1020 AD.
He stayed four years with Viravajra, returning to Tibet again
around 1024 AD. Jamyang Khyentse Wangchuk does not indicate
that Drogmi had undertaken the translations prior to his meeting
with Gayadhara, who collaborated in the translation works.
Gayadhara did not go to Tibet until Drogmi had returned from
India and the great Lotsawa Rinchen Sangpo would have been in
his late sixties around that time. This contradiction is the result of
Goe Lotsawa's attempt to establish Drogmi's chronology of the
translations in relation to the age of Rinchen Sangpo. It appears
either that Goe had the wrong birth date for Drogmi, or his scribe
made an error. According to Ngawang Kunga Sonam, Drogmi spent
eighteen years[271] in India on his first visit. If this were so, it would

put all the dates Jamyang Khyentse Wangchuk used back by ten years.

A similar contradiction may have been created by Chogyam Trungpa (or the Nalanda Translation Committee), who attempted to date Drogmi's founding of Mugulung monastery in conjunction with Marpa's chronology. Marpa's chronology may help to determine Drogmi's chronology since he was a student of Drogmi. When did Drogmi found his monastery, Mugulung? When did Marpa come to study with him? In attempting to answer these questions, Trungpa appears to create a discrepancy in his introduction and notes to the translation of the *Life of Marpa the Translator*. With regard to the time Marpa met Drogmi, he writes:

> *Drogmi had established his monastery in Nyugu Valley in 1043.[272] He was well versed in Vajrayana Buddhism, but his specialty was the teachings of "path and fruition" (T: lam 'bras), which later became the philosophical foundation for the teachings of the Sakya lineage. Drogmi was also a "lotsawa," a translator, and while in Tibet, he translated a great number of texts now found in the Tibetan Buddhist canon. Marpa came to Nyugu valley to study with Drogmi around 1054 and stayed three years with him, learning Sanskrit and several colloquial languages of India.[273]*

According to Trungpa, Marpa was in his early forties when he first came to study with Drogmi. This is highly unlikely. It would appear to be too late for the meeting between Marpa and Drogmi. Marpa is said to have made three journeys and to have spent eighteen years in India altogether. He was in his early fifties after his last journey. Trungpa's comments then contradict the introduction by saying Marpa was fifteen years when he studied with Drogmi.[274] This means Marpa must have met Drogmi in 1027 (not 1054) and studied with him until 1030. As no mention is made of any relationship between Gayadhara and Marpa, Gayadhara must not have been in Tibet around the time Marpa was with Drogmi. Hence the meeting between Drogmi and Gayadhara must have occurred later by at least three to eight years (1033-38). If Drogmi's monastery was already built when Marpa came to him, Marpa could only have met Drogmi after Gayadhara had given the Lamdre instructions. According to Lamdre sources, the site where Drogmi built his monastery was chosen by Gayadhara to give the Lamdre instruction.

4. Conclusion

A knowledge of the origin of the Lamdre tradition in India is important not only for understanding the history of Tantric Buddhism in India, but also its continuation in Tibet. Since its introduction to Tibet, Lamdre has been a living tradition. This is evidenced by the ten or more volumes of hagiography of the masters and history of the tradition. We hope that this study will motivate others to look closely into the early history of Lamdre in Tibet before it became the central teaching of the Sakyapa tradition. Although neither of Drogmi's sons succeeded him, he had numerous disciples who developed their own traditions, which have been eclipsed by the greater glory of Sakya supremacy. It would be challenging to explore the lives and influence of Drogmi's Lamdre disciples. In this way, we may gain a better understanding of the historical significance of Lamdre within the religious history of Tibet. There must be many Tibetan works beside the Lamdre literature which shed light on how the Lamdre became central to other traditions, whose teachers may themselves never have been to India.

Although based on Lamdre teachings, there may have been various changes in the names of those new traditions before they became established separately. This is a whole field of study in itself, which is yet to be explored. One of the pleasures of research is the freedom to unearth previously undisclosed knowledge from the past. This is a manifestation of the human predisposition for ceaseless activity and boundless curiosity. It will remain until the craving for knowledge finally leads us to our ultimate destination. Then we will discover that the great goal is as it has always been, nothingness. And the seeker himself is found also to be void.

PART TWO

THE ESSENCE OF THE ELEGANT TEACHINGS OF THE THREE TANTRAS

by

Panchen Ngawang Choedak

(1572-1641)

Herein lies

"The Essence of the Elegant Teachings"

The Main Stages of Instructions
of
The Three Tantras

by

Panchen Ngawang Choedak
(1572-1641)

pan chen ngag dbang chos grags kyis gsung
gsung ngag rin po che'i dngos gzhi'i khrid rim rgyud gsum
snying po'i legs bshad bzhugs so

The Essence of the Elegant Teachings of the Three Tantras

"The Essence of the Elegant Teachings"

The Main Stages of Instructions

of

The Three Tantras

HOMAGE

*(1/B) To the Holy Root Gurus,[275] whose kindness is
incomparable
And to the supreme deity Hevajra,
I take refuge and respectfully pay homage. Please bless me!*

*Having been initiated by the immortal nectar of the great
secret
Into the mandala of the fifteen Nairatmayoginis,[276]
You have attained the stage of accomplishment and
destroyed the maras[277] and the tirthikas.[278]
O Holy Virupa, bless me with your protection![279]*

*(You are) the quintessence of good deeds, which
please all sentient beings;
Having perfected the accumulation of merits, (you have)
excelled in peace and happiness;
Your banner of fame extends beyond even the peaks of
existence;
May the excellent Holy Masters[280] remain as a crown on my
head!*

To the great Pandita, the master of the five sciences,[281] who is
a manifestation of Mañjughosa,
To the supreme master of the doctrine of the world
known as 'phags pa,[282]
To the spiritual successors of their hereditary lineage,[283]
And to the assembly of fortunate disciples who came in
succession,
I pay homage.

Especially, O venerable kun dga' bzang po,[284] you
who please all scholars,
And uphold the Dharma with (your) eminent
learning and pure morality;
Who else in this world can be a pillar of the doctrine like you?
To you, who were prophesied by the victorious one, I pay
homage.

(2/A)
The thousand-fold lutes of wisdom and compassion,
the actual Triple Gem;
As you hoist them high up to be the banner of the doctrine
*It is indeed melodious and ambrosial to **those** who*
listen in all directions.
To the Venerable dpal yon bzang po I entrust my faith.

Through the four-fold wheels of a hundred million
magnificent previously accumulated merits
You have been victorious in the battle against the maligners;
You are the lion of speech, matchless in every way.
O venerable omniscient Guru, bless me with your
protection![285]

You are Mañjushri, the great treasure (keeper)
of the jewel of knowledge;
You are the White Lotus Holder, who has compassion
for all sentient beings;
And you are Guhyapati, who excels in spontaneously
fulfilling all activities;
O Evampa, Excellent guide, bless me with your protection![286]

From the stirring of the numerous oceans of learning
Arose klu sgrub's radiant garland of knowledge,
the Eyes of the World[287]
He is the sole friend of the ocean of fortunate disciples;
O omniscient and great teacher, grace me with your
protection!

Crown of all scholars and exponent of logical scriptures
Your glory heightens the majesty of the doctrine
(2/B) And the glory of (your) noble activities radiates
in a hundred directions.
May the lotus feet of the all-encompassing Guru adorn my
crown![288]

Starting with the subject matter of discussion, the stages
of the Triple Tantra,
Being neither too elaborate nor too short, I shall explain
the complete stages
Of the instructions of the main body of the sacred Teachings.
O impartial scholars, please listen joyfully![289]

The Essence of the Elegant Teachings of the Three Tantras

INTRODUCTION

1. CAUSE, THE NATURE OF SAMSARA

In order to explain and practise the instructions of the precious sacred teachings of the path including its result, which possesses numerous aspects of profundities,[290] the preliminary explanation on the Triple Vision has been discussed already[291]. In order to explain the main practices according to the Triple Tantra, Jetsun Rinpoche *(grags pa rgyal mtshan)* states:

> *The Cause is the subjective nature of Samsara*
> *The Path is the (actual) method of meditation*
> *The Result is the ultimate stage of Buddhahood*
> *The first will not be discussed here as it has already been*
> *explained in (the chapter on) Impure Vision.*

2. HOW TO MEDITATE ON THE PATH

There are three divisions:

    A. How to maintain the foundation of the precepts
    B. The method of guiding disciples on the path
    C. Establishing the demarcations of the path and stages by cultivating an exceptional conviction and by recognising Samadhi.[292]

A. How to Maintain the Foundation of the Precepts

There are two divisions:

I. Imparting the initiation in order to bestow the precepts

II. How to maintain the received fundamental precepts
without transgressing them

> I.   *Imparting the Initiation in order to Bestow the
> Precepts*[293]
>
> This refers to those who have already been ripened
> through the eight- or seven-fold clear realisation of the
> initiation.
>
> II.   *How to Maintain the Received Fundamental
> Precepts Without Transgressing Them*
>
> The precepts should be taught here in brief.[294]

B. The Method of Guiding Disciples on the Path

(This) consists of three divisions:

I. Meditating on the View, the Non-Differentiation
between Samsara and Nirvana through the Basis of All
Cause Tantra[295] in order to cut off fabricated views
[Section I]

II. **(3/A)** Meditating on the Body Method Tantra[296] in
conjunction with the Four Initiations in order to
develop experiences of the path [Section II]

III. How to attain the Results of the Five Bodies [Section
III]

I

Meditating on The View the Non-Differentiation of Samsara and Nirvana Through the Basis Of All Cause Tantra In Order To Cut Off Fabricated Views

The first section consists of two divisions:

1. The Preliminary Practices
2. The Actual Practices

The Essence of the Elegant Teachings of the Three Tantras

1

THE PRELIMARY PRACTICES

There are three divisions:[297]

1. The Yoga of the Mandala Offerings in order to accumulate merits
2. The Meditation and Recitation of Vajrasattva in order to purify negative obscurations
3. The Practice of Guru Yoga in order to receive blessings

1. THE YOGA OF MANDALA OFFERINGS IN ORDER TO ACCUMULATE MERITS

Firstly, set up a five-heaped mandala of consecration *(bsgrub-pa'i man-da-la)* surrounded by available offerings at a secluded and conducive place. Having set up a mandala of offering, *(mchod-pa'i man-da-la)* scented water and clean grains in front of you, take a comfortable seat in a sitting posture. Then in the space above and in front of you, clearly visualise the uncommon refuge object, the inseparable nature of your Guru (in the form of) Shri Hevajra Mandala deities, as if it was real. Know that the Guru's mind is the Buddha, his speech the Dharma and his body the Sangha. Thus (Shri Hevajra) embodies all. Feel from the depths of your heart intense desire, hope and determination to request him to be your Refuge until attaining enlightenment, while reciting the refuge prayer from the beginning of the (Hevajra) Sadhana. Repeat the Refuge prayer many times.[298] Once the requesting prayers are completed, dissolve the objects of Refuge into light and absorb them either through the three places[299] or through the crown. Imagine that your body, speech and mind become inseparable from the nature of the Guru's body, speech and mind.

2. THE ENLIGHTENMENT THOUGHT

Think of the tragedy of all those sentient beings of the six realms of existence who for many lifetimes have been your father and mother, who have endless delusions and are experiencing **(3/B)** so much suffering in Samsara. For their benefit one must attain the Two-In-One stage of Vajradharahood. While thinking fervently of practising the profound path of Vajrayana, the fundamental cause (to be able to do this), one recites:

> For the benefit of all sentient beings, I must attain the stage of perfect enlightenment. For that purpose, I shall practise this profound path.

Recite this prayer three times. Then, while focusing (your mind), recite the mantra of svabhava[300] to purify the mandala of consecration into emptiness.

Out of that state of emptiness, from *bhrum* arises a celestial mansion made of various precious jewels. (It is) square; (it) has four doors; (it is) adorned by the four-tiered cornices;[301] (it) is beautified with all the ornaments and complete with all the characteristics (of a celestial mansion). In its centre is a precious throne held aloft by eight great lions. On top of this is a variegated lotus, a sun and moon cushion (one above another) upon which sits one's venerable root Guru, the intrinsic nature of the victorious ones and their (spiritual) sons of the three times.[302] He is in the form of the sixth race[303] great Vajradhara, whose physical colour is clear blue and radiant, like sapphire. He has one face. His two hands are crossed at his heart, holding a vajra and a bell. His face (simultaneously) expresses a smiling, angry, graceful and

152

passionate mood. Some of his hair is tied up in a knot on his crown, while the rest falls loosely in plaits. He is adorned by precious jewels and bone ornaments and is wearing garments made of various silks. His two legs are placed in the diamond sitting posture and he radiates and reabsorbs multi-coloured light rays (from his body). He is surrounded by the lineage gurus[304] also in the form of Vajradhara. They are all facing inwards. To the East is the assembly of the deities of the four classes of Tantra. To the South (the Guru's right) are the Buddhas in Sambhogakaya and Nirmanakaya forms. To the West (behind the Guru) are the Mahayana Dharma Scriptures (wrapped) in silks. To the North are the lay and ordained Arya Sanghas dressed as Viras and Yoginis. Imagine that they are all surrounded by hosts of **(4/A)** immeasurable Dharmapalas and wealth deities like masses of clouds. Light rays issuing from their hearts invoke the Gurus and tutelary deities etc. Think that they have become the embodiment of all the objects of Refuge as the result of absorbing inseparably into them.

With strong devotion and affection, you should pray by chanting the praises of the root and lineage Gurus that you know, such as:

Through your kindness, the great bliss itself etc.[305]

Then imagine the offerings[306] as vast as possible, and offer them with:

om guru buddha bodhisattva saparivara argham etc. ah hum[307]

Then,

One should pray by mixing the (merit) field (the object of offering), (one's) motivation and material into one.[308]

With the splendours of the material offerings untainted by non-virtue, one makes the offerings to the refuge objects appearing in the sky in front of oneself with the motivation of dedicating it for the welfare of all sentient beings. The offerings are made with the understanding that they are by nature one's body, wealth and all virtues accumulated throughout the three times, manifested in the form of Mount Sumeru, the (four) continents, the sun and the moon, embellished with the perfect wealth and multifarious splendour of humans and gods which completely fill the boundless realms of existence. It is said in the *Guhyasamaja (Tantra)*:

> *By completely filling this universe*
> *With the seven precious jewels,*
> *The learned and intelligent beings who wish to attain siddhis*
> *should offer (the mandala offering) every day.*

Thus, perform the 'seven-heap'[309] mandala offering as many hundreds of times as possible, knowing that the three objects of offering etc. (the objects of offering, the substances for offering and the offerer), do not (exist) by their own nature. Then say:

> *Through your compassion please accept (this) for the sake of*
> *sentient beings.*

Every now and then, add (the following):

> *(4/B) May my mental continuum be blessed so that I may*
> *completely accomplish the two accumulations, the*
> *accumulation of merit and the accumulation of wisdom! May*
> *(I be) blessed so that the two obscurations including their*
> *(karmic) propensities be cleansed and purified! May (I be)*
> *blessed so that the extraordinary samadhi of the two stages*
> *be realised in (my) mental continuum! May (I be) blessed so*
> *that (I may) attain the stage of the two kayas!*

154

Thus, pray fervently. Then perform the mandala offering again and pray again. At the conclusion (of the session, perform) the 'thirty-seven heap'[310] mandala offering and also recite *'gang-gi mchod-rdzas-ma'* etc.[311] If you are able and know the prayer *'phyogs-bcu dus-gsum ma'* then also do it (here). Then imagine that the objects of offering dissolve into light, beginning from the outside and absorbing into the root Guru. By dissolving your root Guru into your crown, imagine that your heart appears in the form of an eight petalled lotus with a moon disc, upon which sits (your root Guru), who gives blessings, protection and Refuge at all times. Thinking thus, place the mind in meditative equilibrium for a while with single pointed faith and determination. When you arise from the session, say (the prayer) *'thos-pa rgya-mtshoi' mchod-yon* [312] followed by *'skye-ba kun-tu yang-dak bla-ma dang'* [313] and other appropriate dedication prayers. Even during post-meditation periods, one must strive to be of any service to the Guru by way of using one's three doors (of body, speech and mind) and material wealth.

Indicative signs of the perfection of the accumulations are:

    (1) Increased devotion and respect towards one's Guru.
    (2) Experiencing the pleasantness of one's surroundings and rise of happy moods.
    (3) Seeing one's Guru in happy moods in one's dreams.
    (4) Seeing oneself sitting on thrones in dreams.
    (5) Seeing oneself wearing beautiful clothes and ornaments in dreams.

3. VAJRASATTVA MEDITATION AND RECITATION

Practise four sessions (each day) of Vajrasattva meditation and recitation[314] (from the practice) at the beginning of the sadhana. During the practice when the confession (of non-**(5/A)** virtue) is made, (one should apply the four powers). Firstly, the power of reliance[315] which is taking refuge in the Triple Gem with the Bodhicitta motivation. (Secondly) the power of remorse, which is the development of a strong regret over non-virtue committed previously. (Thirdly) the power of restoration which is the pledge "From now on I shall not commit (such actions) in the future even at the cost of my life" and (lastly) the power of applying the antidote at all times, which is the determination to remedy misdeeds with the powerful antidote of virtuous action in the future. In this manner, the confession should be made in conjunction with the four powers. Imagine (when you conclude the session) that as the result of Vajrasattva dissolving into you, all the impurities including the (karmic) propensities are cleansed and purified, and your `body, speech and mind are blessed and transformed into the nature of Vajrasattva's body, speech and mind. In conclusion, knowing that neither the non-virtues which are to be purified, nor the person who is doing the purification nor the method of the purification itself exist inherently, let (your mind) rest for a short time without any objectification.

Indicative signs of effective purification which may occur are:

(1) The feeling of joyfulness in virtuous deeds
(2) Clarity in visualisation
(3) Dreaming of taking a bath etc.

4. GURU YOGA

Jetsun Rinpoche (*rje btsun*) has said in the instruction manual:

> *In guiding a beginning disciple (on the path), let him (or her) first pray fervently to the Guru for several days in order to cultivate strong devotion.*

It is also said in the Commentary on the Non-Differentiation of Samsara and Nirvana, (*'khor '-das dbyer-med*):

*Those who wish to adopt the practice of the three
simultaneously born Dharmas should firstly meditate until
they establish (Guru) devotion in order to cultivate the
authenticity of the Guru.*

This means: In order to attain enlightenment, one must realise the nature of the existence of the mind. To realise this, one must have accumulated a vast amount of merit, have pleased the Guru and have received initiation and instructions from his mouth. One will be unable to realise the simultaneously born wisdom by any alternative methods, as it is said in the *Root Tantra:*

*The simultaneously born (wisdom) cannot be expounded by
others, etc.*

(5/B) It is said in the *Samputa Tantra:*

*As for the inner distinctions, they will be found (heard) from
the mouth of the Guru.*

It is said in the *Jñanasiddhi:*

He who has the kindness of the Guru will find its nature.

Furthermore, it is said in *rnal-'byor ma kun-spyod:*

*Through your kindness,
The great bliss itself arises in a single instant.
To the Guru with a precious body,
I bow down to your Vajra lotus feet.*

Vajra Ghantipa said:

*By the mere blessings of the Guru
It will arise in an instant.*

The blessings will not arise to those who lack devotion. Devotion is essential. However, the type of devotion cultivated with someone

157

towards whom one is biased or who has provided one with assistance in food and material needs is called "blind faith." How then should one cultivate proper faith? Sakya Pandita has said:

> The notion that the Guru is Buddha
> Comes into effect (only) after having received the (major) initiation.[316]

As said thus, one (the Master) who has bestowed one with the four authentic initiations at the time of the cause[317] which clearly introduced the things to be purified and the purifier together, is in fact the one who enacted the activities of the Buddha. Knowing that he is the embodiment of all the Buddhas, the self-nature of the four Bodies,[318] and the self-nature of the five Families,[319] the sixth race Vajrasattva, one should pray with diligence, cultivating a fervent, loving and respectful devotion. It is said in *Mahamudratilaka*:

> He who has bestowed the initiation should be regarded as Vajrasattva.

And in *Vajrapañjara,* it is said:

> The master who provides guidance
> Is bowed to by all the Buddhas.
> One must keep Him in one's mind
> Together with one's father and mother.

And in the Fifty Verses of Guru Devotion, it is said:

> Making offerings to him (the Guru)
> Becomes offerings to all the Buddhas at all times.
> Making offerings to Him is the accumulation of merit;
> From the accumulation of merit originates the excellent Siddhi.

A. The actual method of the practice

(6/A) Visualise clearly on top of your crown a precious throne held aloft by eight great lions, a variegated lotus and a sun and moon disc upon which sits the Root Guru in the form of Vajradhara, in the same aspect as above. Light rays issuing from his heart in the form of messengers invoke the Root and lineage Gurus, a congregation of tutelary deities, the Triple Gem, Dharma protectors and inconceivable hosts of wealth gods from their natural abode. Imagine that they are absorbed inseparably into the Guru's body.

He is the guru who shows one the path to liberation, (he is) the tutelary deity who bestows siddhis, (he is) the object of refuge who protects from fears, (he is) the Dharma protector who removes hindrances, (he is) the wealth god who fulfils (one's) wishes, (he is) the embodiment of all Gurus, (he is) the master of all the tutelary deities, (he is) the nature of all the Buddhas, (he is) the source of all the sacred Dharma teachings, (he is) the ruler of all the Sanghas, (he is) the master of all the Dharma protectors, and (he is) the self-nature of all the wealth gods. In short, he is the embodiment of all the Refuge objects, the master of all the families and Mandalas, the origin of numerous precious qualities, the sole (master) who when prayed to, bestows both Samsaric and beyond Samsaric siddhis. Thinking thus, while generating a fervent and powerful feeling again and again and an unsullied devotion which cannot be severed, one should pray thus:

> *I pray to the kind Root Guru Vajradhara,*
> *The embodiment of all the objects of Refuge;*
> *(Who is) seated upon my crown on a lotus, sun and moon disc.*
> *Bestow upon me all the initiations and siddhis!*
>
> *Bestow upon my body the Supreme Vase initiation!*
> *Bestow upon my speech the Supreme Secret initiation!*
> *(6/B) Bestow upon my mind the Supreme Third initiation!*

159

*Bestow upon my air (vital energies) the Supreme Fourth
initiative!*

*Through the pure rituals of the initiations, I who have
received the vows of Meditative-Equanimity, Post-Meditation,
Eating, Protection and Non-Separation.*
*May you grace blessings upon me to be able to protect
And maintain these vows through my strong effort and
diligence
Without being tainted by the impurities of non-virtues and
downfalls.*

*Clarity, Emptiness and the Two-In-One are the
Simultaneously born Cause.*
*The Transcendental wisdom of the Generation and
Completion Stage is the great Simultaneously born Path.*
*Nirmanakaya, Dharmakaya, and Sambhogakaya are the
Simultaneously born result.*
*May you bestow blessings upon me to attain the
Simultaneously born Non-duality!*[320]

Thus, with the melody of intense longing one should pray again
and again from the depths of one's heart and inside (the marrow
of) one's bones. Knowing that whether one is happy or unhappy,
since one has no one other than the precious Guru who is
trustworthy and reliable, one resolves to cultivate devotion by
totally surrendering one's lungs, heart and chest, the three
organs,[321] one's crown, the two palms of one's hands and the two
soles of one's feet, (to the Guru) until one develops the experience
of the hairs of the body standing on end or shedding tears from the
eyes. In conclusion, the body of the Guru dissolves into the form of
rainbow light and is absorbed into one's crown. Consequently, as
the blessings of the Guru's (holy) body, (holy) speech, (omniscient)
mind and (enlightened) activities enter into one's body, speech,

160

mind and activities, one receives the four initiations, the four impurities are cleansed, and one's three doors and activities transform into the Vajra body, speech, mind and the nature of the essential Hevajra respectively. While seeing your mind in the nature of the Four-fold form of the Guru, let it remain naturally without grasping at its clarity or emptiness. Conclude with dedication prayers and (other) prayers.[322]

In between sessions, with one's body one should do prostrations and circumambulations to the Guru; with one's speech one should recite his eulogies and praise him; and mentally think that "this Guru is my trustworthy Refuge until I attain Enlightenment." Imagine the Guru on top of your crown during the day and dwelling inside your heart at night. One must take precautions not to lose one's devotion to the Guru by remembering him always.

B. Benefits

(7/A) The superior (benefit) is the attainment of the excellent Mahamudra; the mediocre (benefit) is the eight siddhis[323] and other benefits include the siddhis of peace, increase, power and forceful activities and so forth. The source of all such siddhis is the Guru's blessings. For the person of superior intelligence, Guru Yoga is the main practice, for the mediocre person it (the practice of Guru Yoga) reaps the advantages of the path and for the person of lesser intelligence, it is the preliminary practice of the path. Having developed the awareness that there are limitless explanations as to how it (the practice of Guru Yoga) dispels all hindrances and faults, and how all qualities are dependent on Guru Yoga, it is essential to practise this path of Guru Yoga at all times. All fortunate people should work on this practice with diligence.

THE ESSENCE OF THE ELEGANT TEACHINGS OF THE THREE TANTRAS

2

THE ACTUAL PRACTICES

There are five divisions:

1. The reason why the view has to be taught after bestowing initiation
2. The reason for meditating (on the view) before the two stages
3. The fundamental basis of the meditation
4. The nature of the view of meditation
5. The method of the meditation

1. THE REASON WHY THE VIEW HAS TO BE TAUGHT AFTER BESTOWING INITIATIONS

The view is taught after the initiation to avoid the (possibility of) misapprehending the transcendental wisdom of the initiation as the personal self and (also) to meditate (and maintain) the continuity of the wisdom of the initiation. It is stated in the *Root Tantra*:

> *Thereafter it is taught properly.*
> *The pure transcendental wisdom with form*
> *And the Samsaric concept*
> *Do not have the slightest difference.*

2. THE REASON FOR MEDITATING (ON THE VIEW) BEFORE THE TWO STAGES

(It) is for the purpose of realising that although all the meditation paths of generation and completion (stages) manifest in the forms they are meditated upon, they are not however beyond the transcendental wisdom of the simultaneously born intrinsic nature of the mind itself. *Samputa Tantra (kha sbyor)* states:

> *Firstly, by thinking of its emptiness*
> *Those with a body should cleanse away its impurities.*
> *On the (fertile) soil of the emptiness of the body*
> *The intelligent ones should sow the seeds.*

3. THE FUNDAMENTAL BASIS OF THE MEDITATION

It should be meditated upon the Basis of All Cause Tantra. It is stated in the treatise (*gzhung*):

> *(7/B) It is called "the Fundamental Tantra" since both Samsara and Nirvana are represented in the Basis of All Cause Tantra.*

What is (the meaning of) the basis of all? In so far as the identification of the basis of all (alaya) which is taught in the *Lankavaratara* (sutra) and the *Ghanavyuha* is concerned, it agrees with the Cittamatrin's assertion of a truly existent consciousness which serves as the basis upon which the truly existent propensities are imprinted. However, the past masters have said here according to the school of Yogesvara (Virupa), the mind which is cognitive (of) experience is not segregated by its particulars. It is unbiased and impartial, its methodical seeing is clear and unobstructed, and its intrinsic empty nature is Alaya (Tib. kun-gzhi). What it means is this: since *kun-gzhi* is established from the point of view of clear experiential seeing, the mind is cognitive experience. Since the aspects of the objects have not been demarcated completely, they are not distinguishable by their particulars. On account of its taking the side neither of virtue nor of non-virtue, it is unbiased and impartial. Of the two truths, the relative truth which is method and ultimate truth which arose from method, here, it is method. From a sentient being up to Buddhahood, there is this mere clarity with its uninterrupted continuity, and the unobstructed clarity of its seeing. As its self-nature is devoid of any extremes of activities, its intrinsic nature is emptiness. For these reasons, it is able to execute all the activities of Samsara and Nirvana. As it is said:

> *That which is emptiness,*
> *Can become anything whatsoever.*

Therefore, it (mind) is established into *kun-gzhi* mainly from the point of view of its clarity. It is established into the Dharmadhatu mainly from the point of view of its empty aspect. In so far as their intrinsic nature is the Two-in-One *(zung-'jug),* there is no difference.

Thus, it is said in *bstan-pa rgyas-pa'i nyi-'od.* Since *kun-gzhi* discussed in this context cannot be other than any one of the eight consciousnesses, it is compounded. Dharmadhatu and Tathagatagarbha are uncompounded phenomena. But since Dharmadhatu, which is devoid of activities, is a suitable basis of all Samsara and Nirvana, it fully expresses the etymological meaning of *kun-gzhi* as Kunkhyen Chenpo has said:

> *(8/A) The sphere itself is the basis of all Samsara and*
> *Nirvana.*

According to the pith instructions of Yogeshvara and glorious Candra and others, they also agree with this etymology of *kun-gzhi.*

4. THE NATURE OF THE VIEW OF MEDITATION

(It) is the non-differentiation of Samsara and Nirvana. It is stated in the *Root Tantra:*

> *This, which is called Samsara*
> *Is indeed Nirvana itself.*
> *If Samsara is abandoned, there will be nowhere*
> *Where the realisation of Nirvana can take place.*

As it is said, if all outer objects such as form, etc. the inner senses such, as eye consciousness etc., which are within the realm of relative truth, and especially the three poisonous minds which are the origin of the appearance of Samsara, were to be examined by an undeluded mind, they would all be seen subjectively as Nirvana. The meaning of such "seeing" would confirm that besides the subjective Nirvana there is no other existent objective Samsara. Since there is no notion of such existence, there is also no so-called "existing subjective Nirvana" other than the objective Samsara. Therefore, it is 'the Non-differentiation of Samsara and Nirvana' or 'the Non-Duality of the Two Truths.' The process of bringing about this realisation is known as "the Realisation of the View of the Non-Differentiation of Samsara and Nirvana." The *Root Tantra* states:

> *Due to ignorance, it is in the form of Samsara.*
> *When devoid of ignorance, Samsara will be purified,*
> *And therefore, it becomes Nirvana.*
> *The Bodhicitta is the relative aspect (truth)*
> *Of the ultimate (truth) of Nirvana.*

The Lord Nagarjuna has said:

> *The (concept of) 'Samsara' and 'Nirvana'*
> *Is expounded by those who have not seen reality.*
> *Those who have seen reality*
> *Do not assert the duality of Samsara and Nirvana.*

And Jetsun Rinpoche (*rje btsun rin po che*) has said:

> *The unfound Samsara*
> *Is the intrinsic nature of Nirvana.*
> *The understanding that there is no Samsara and Nirvana*
> *(8/B) Is the view of the Non-Differentiation of Samsara and*
> *Nirvana. Dwell peacefully in the atmosphere of Non-Duality.*

If this is explored carefully in the context of the three simultaneously born Dharmas, it is found that its characteristic of clarity is Samsara; its empty nature is Nirvana and its reality, the Two-In-One, is the Non-Differentiation. In the context of the three essential points of the practice, its objective clarity is Samsara; its subjective emptiness is Nirvana and its reality, the Two-In-One, is the Non-Differentiation. In the context of the Cause Tantra of the Three Tantras, the clarity which is the characteristic of the mind is Samsara; the emptiness which is the nature of the mind is Nirvana and the intrinsic unsullied nature of the mind is the Non-Differentiation. In the context of the Method Tantra the purifying base is Samsara; the purifier is Nirvana and the purifying base which becomes purified into the nature of the purifier is the Non-Differentiation. During the Result, the simultaneous accomplishment is Samsara, its transformation is Nirvana and the Non-Contradiction is the Non-Differentiation. However, this will be elaborated upon later.

5. THE ACTUAL METHOD OF THE MEDITATION

- A Brief Summary through the Three Simultaneously Born Dharmas **[Chapter 3]**
- A Detailed Explanation through the Three Essential points of the practice **[Chapter 4]**
- A Comprehensive Explanation through the Three Tantras **[Chapter 5]**

The Essence of the Elegant Teachings of the Three Tantras

3

A Brief Summary Through the Three Simultaneously Born Dharmas

It is stated in the *Root Tantra*:

> *That which came into existence from simultaneous birth*
> *Is called "Simultaneously Born".*
> *It is its intrinsic nature which is called simultaneously born.*
> *All forms share this one bond.*

There are three divisions to ascertain its meaning:

1. The Three Simultaneously Born Dharmas of the Cause
2. The Three Simultaneously Born Dharmas of the Path
3. The Three Simultaneously Born Dharmas of the Result

1. The Three Simultaneously Born Dharmas of the Cause

Jetsun Rinpoche *(rje btsun rin po che)* said:

> *From its nature of Clarity, Emptiness and the Two-In-One*
> *Arose defilement, winds, letters, veins, elements,*
> *Sicknesses, spirits and gross attributes.*

These also have three-fold divisions in each
Which amounts to twenty-seven Simultaneously Born
Dharmas of the cause.[324]

Let us elaborate upon this further. One's own mind is the
substratum of all outer and inner **(9/A)** phenomena. There is
nothing whatsoever within these phenomena besides the mind.
When the mind is thoroughly examined inwardly, the experience of
its intrinsic nature of mere clarity, knowability and
unobstructability is better known as 'Clarity, the characteristic of
the mind.' Since this mere clarity is devoid of its own birth, it is
unborn from the beginning. (Similarly) it does not remain in
between, nor does it cease at the end. It has neither colour nor
shape and it does not dwell outside the body, inside it or between
these two. That which cannot be found, no matter how one
searches for it, and it is uncreated in whichever way it is looked at,
is empty. This is (called) "the intrinsic nature of the mind." Even
when this empty (nature) is determined, the one who searches the
empty nature is known as the "clarity aspect." Therefore, when the
clarity aspect is determined, it is empty, and when the empty
aspect is determined, it is clarity. This being so, no one will be able
to distinguish between the clarity (aspect) and empty (nature), and
it is (invariably) known as 'non-duality' or 'the Two-In-One' or
'inexpressible' or 'the unsullied intrinsic nature of mind.'

Although all sentient beings have this mode of existence, they
are wandering in the cycle of existence due to their own failure to
identify it and to their erroneous misconceptions. From (due to the
failure to identify) the intrinsic Clear nature (aspect of the mind)
arises the defilement, desire; the wind, inhalation; the letter, Om;
the vein, Lalana; the vein with its opening end pointing downward,
the element; semen, the sicknesses; blood and bile disorders, the
female spirits, and the creation of the gross physical body.

Also due to the misunderstanding of the intrinsic empty nature
(of the mind) arises the defilement, hatred; the wind, exhalation;

170

the letter, Hum; the vein, Rasana, the vein with its opening end pointing upwards; the red element; the sicknesses of wind diseases; the male spirits, and the creation of gross speech.

Also, on account of (misunderstanding) the Two-In-One arises the defilement, ignorance; the wind, retention; the letter, Ah; the vein, Avadhuti; the mixture of the white and red elements; the sicknesses of phlegm; the Naga spirits and the creation of the gross mind. These twenty-seven **(9/B)** factors which are made up of three sets of nine (9x3=27) have to be the realisation of the Simultaneously Born Dharmas of the Cause. Furthermore, one should investigate them carefully and rejoice as Jetsun Rinpoche (*rje btsun rin po che*) has said:

> *If one can thoroughly attain realisation regarding the*
> *spontaneous accomplishment*
> *One will know the characteristics and the (relation of) the*
> *causes and results of Samsara and Nirvana.*
> *With the perfect realisation of auspicious relatedness of the*
> *outer and inner (factors)*
> *One will be able to destroy all the sicknesses and spirits*
> *without exception.*[325]

Let us take delight in discussing its meaning in some depth. There are three divisions:

A. How sicknesses and spirits arise from defilements
B. Examining the relationship between outer and inner factors
C. How to destroy them or recitation of the Essence (mantra)

2. HOW SICKNESS AND SPIRITS ARISE FROM DEFILEMENTS

From the three root defilements arise arrogance and miserliness, which are the qualities of defilement and jealousy, which is the activity of the defilement. Adding these two makes up the five defilements. Similarly, the five basic or root winds arise, namely the life-holding *(Tib. srog -'dzin)*, the downward-pushing *(Tib. thur-sel)*, the upward-flowing *(Tib. gyen-rgyu)*, the pervasive *(Tib. khyab-byed)* and the equally-abiding air *(Tib. mnyam-gnas)*; the five letters *Bhrum, Am, Jrim, Kham, and Hum*; the five hidden veins joined with the central vein; the five elements comprised of the three essences, white, red and their combination and the two coarse elements of excrement and urine; the five sicknesses which are made up of air, bile, phlegm including dual and triple combinations; the five spirits which are made up of male, female, Naga, dual and triple combinations.

The root Two-In-One which developed into clarity and emptiness divided it into three. Remember that just as ignorance develops into desire and hatred, thus becoming the three defilements, all phenomena escalate from one to three, three to five and five to an inconceivable number. Bear this in mind when analysing all the causes and results of Samsara and Nirvana and carefully investigate the auspicious inter-relatedness of all outer and inner factors.

A. Examining the Relationship Between the Outer and Inner Factors

Physical (location)	Defilement	Sickness
Heart, intestine, tongue, right hand	hatred	wind
Lung, stomach, nose, head	ignorance	bile
Liver, bile, eyes, left hand	desire	blood

| Kidneys, testicles, ears, legs | arrogance, miserliness | dual combination |
| Spleen, belly, lips, ribs | jealousy | triple combination |

(10/A) Above and under the throat (and the navel)[326] region(s) are the locations of wind (sicknesses), and above and under *lhan sna'i* are respectively the locations of phlegm and bile (sicknesses). In this manner, defilements, sicknesses and spirit influences have to be investigated in conjunction with their (physical) locations. As said thus, one must thoroughly reflect on their meanings.

3. How to Destroy Them or Recitation of the Essence (Mantra)

Since a wind *(rlung-nad)* disease is caused by the defilement hatred and by the aggravation of male spirits, (it will be destroyed) by sealing emptiness with clarity. It is clarity which is searching for emptiness, and therefore by meditating on emptiness sealed by clarity, wind diseases and male spirits will be eliminated. Since blood and bile diseases are caused by the defilement of desire and by the aggravation of female spirits, (they will be destroyed) by sealing clarity with emptiness. When clarity is searched for it is found not to have any location, race or colour whatsoever. By meditating on the lack of inherent existence of all phenomena, blood and bile diseases and the influence of female spirits will be pacified. Since phlegm diseases are caused by the defilement of ignorance and by the aggravation of nagas, they will be pacified by meditation on sealing the Two-In-One with the Two-In-One. Furthermore, when sicknesses of dual and triple combinations occur, they are provoked by the co-emergence of dual and triple defilements as well as being aggravated by dual and triple spirit influences. They will be remedied by meditating on sealing emptiness with clarity, clarity with emptiness, and the Two-In-One with the Two-In-One respectively.

Similarly, one may recite the essence (mantra) to (pacify) spirits. (For example) the male spirit influence can be pacified by sealing emptiness with clarity which is (done through) the recitation of the mantra while seeing the clarity of the colour of the deity's form and his hand implements, after ascertaining that all phenomena are empty. If one **(10/B)** recites while unobjectifiably knowing that the deity also lacks inherent existence, it will pacify female spirits. If one recites in the knowledge that the deity's appearance is empty of inherent existence just as an image in a mirror, it will pacify spirits belonging to the naga race. If one recites by sealing the three-fold sealings respectively as shown above, the influences of dual and triple combinations of spirits will also be pacified.

In this way, one must study thoroughly under the Guru to learn the original causes of sicknesses and spirits; which defilement causes them to arise; and what are their antidotes. That is to understand the defilement, sicknesses, biological locations of the sicknesses and the spirits etc. as shown above. By doing this one can attain a definite realisation and realise inconceivable reasonings. This is so because all the dependent arisings must be developed within oneself.

4. THE THREE SIMULTANEOUSLY BORN DHARMAS OF THE PATH

Jetsun *(rje btsun)* has said:

> *Having been ripened previously, on the path of acquisition*
> *there are three aspects:*
> *Generation (stage), Completion (stage) and Wisdom.*
> *Each of these is also divided into three,*
> *Comprising the Three Spontaneously Born Dharmas of the*
> *Path.*[327]

The meaning (of the aforesaid) is thus: The Generation stage represents clarity; the Completion stage represents emptiness and the Wisdom (aspect) represents the Two-In-One. Each of these three can be divided into three divisions. (For instance) visualisation of the deity in the Generation Stage is clarity; the dissolution of the deity is emptiness and the lack of self-existence of the appearance of the deity is the two-in-one. The mode of the physical dissolution of the Completion Stage is clarity; the mode of the dissolution of speech is emptiness and the mode of the dissolution of the mind is the Two-In-One. The experience of the multi-characteristics of Wisdom is clarity; the experience of its empty nature is emptiness and the experience of its non-duality is the Two-in-One. In short, one must understand that all the appearances of initiations, paths and wisdom are in fact the non-differentiation of Samsara and Nirvana or the manifestation of the clarity, emptiness and the Two-In-One aspects of the mind. **(11/A)**

5. The Three Simultaneously Born Dharmas of the Result

Clarity is Nirmanakaya, Emptiness is Dharmakaya
And the Two-In-One is Sambhogakaya.
The consideration that each of these three aspects contains
Spontaneous Accomplishment and Transference
Is the Simultaneously Born Dharmas of the Result.[328]

The meaning of (the above) is thus: From clarity, which represents great compassion, arises Nirmanakaya; from emptiness, which represents great wisdom, arises Dharmakaya; and from their non-duality arises Sambhogakaya. This is explained mainly because of their predominance, but in fact each of the three Kayas is inseparable from clarity, emptiness and the Two-In-One. For instance, regarding the great compassionate Nirmanakaya, it is the Two-In-One since it is inseparable from the emptiness which is

175

devoid of natural activities. Regarding the great wisdom
Dharmakaya, it is the Two-in-One since it is not deprived of the
cause of compassion. Also, with regard to Sambhogakaya, the basis
of the manifestation (Nirmanakaya) is clarity, the great
compassion; its non-separation from Dharmakaya is Emptiness,
the great wisdom and their non-duality is the Two-In-One.
Furthermore, with regard to their nature of spontaneous
accomplishment, it is Samsara and with regard to their quality of
transference, it is Nirvana. The non-contradictory nature of
spontaneous accomplishment and transference is the non-
differentiation.

In this way, having developed realisations through listening
and contemplation, in order to actualise these into practice, there
are three divisions:

<blockquote>

A. The three preliminary practices
B. The three actual practices
C. The three concluding practices

</blockquote>

A. The Three Preliminary Practices

<blockquote>

I. Meditation on Bodhicitta
II. Visualising the Guru on the crown
III. Visualising oneself in the form of the deity

</blockquote>

I.   *Meditation on Bodhicitta*

Having first taken refuge, one must meditate on the cultivation of
the Enlightened mind for a long time for the purpose of
accumulating roots of virtues which will be of benefit to others.

II.   Visualising the Guru on the Crown

As before, visualise the guru on (one's) crown and imagine that he dissolves into you as a result of praying to him with strong devotion.   The purpose of this is to enable one **(11/B)** to accumulate the causes of meditation so that the flow of blessings will naturally arise (in one's mind).

III.   Visualising Oneself in the Form of the Deity

While maintaining this (absorption), as one utters Hum, one's place of dwelling (appears) as a protection wheel.[329]   As one (again) utters Hum, inside this (appears) a celestial mansion.   As one (again) utters Hum, in its centre is a lotus seat, a sun-disc and the four maras. Imagine clearly that on top of this is oneself known as "the Blessed One, Shri Hevajra," the embodiment and unification of bliss and voidness, whose body is blue in colour, with eight faces and sixteen arms. One is in union with the consort Vajranairatmya who has one face and two hands. One's appearance is clear, but devoid of self-nature like a reflection in a mirror. If you are unable to do this, visualise yourself in the form of Hevajra with one face and two hands with the right hand holding a Vajra and the left holding a skull-cup and a Khatvanga, resting inside the elbow. On top of one's forehead is a white syllable *Om*, the nature of the diamond body (Kayavajra) of all the Buddhas. On top of one's throat is a red syllable *Ah*, the nature of the diamond speech (Vakavajra) of all the Buddhas. On top of one's heart is a blue syllable *Hum*, the nature of the diamond mind (Cittavajra) of all the Buddhas. Whilst remembering that those (syllables) and one's body, speech and mind are by nature inseparable, one recites:

Om Ah Hum (three times)

This is for the purpose of recollecting how the guru blessed one's body, speech, mind and wisdom into the four kayas[330] during the

initiation (ceremony) and in order to remain uninfluenced by
ordinary conceptions.

B. The Three Actual Practices

> I. Being determined about attaining Clarity
> II. Sealing it with Emptiness
> III. Resolving to attain the Two-In-One

In this case, be decisive about the Clarity *(gsal-bar thag-gcad);* have
it sealed with Emptiness *(stong-pas rgyas-gdab)* and be resolute
with the Two-In-One *(zung-'jug la bzla-ba).* How should one
meditate on them? Cultivate a firm conviction along with a clarity
which remains stable while remembering how the above
mentioned simultaneously born dharmas although groundless,
arose due to the deluded perception of your own mind. While
continuing to exert effort with your three doors (body, speech and
mind) and turning the mind inwards, think thus:

(12/A) All outer and inner phenomena are to be found inside
one's own mind. There are no outer phenomena whatsoever
beside the mind. In any case, the mind does not abandon its clarity
which is called "clarity, the characteristic of the mind." If clarity is
examined carefully, one will be unable to find it in any race,
location, direction, colour or any shape. No matter how one
searches for it, it does not exist. This is known as "emptiness, the
intrinsic nature of the mind". Therefore, the unfound clarity is
called "Emptiness" and the not finding of the Emptiness is called
"Clarity." Under these circumstances, because it is empty when it is
clear, and it is clear when it is empty, the nature of clarity and
emptiness is indivisible. This is what is called "Non-duality," "the
Two-In-One," "Devoid of Expression" or "the unsullied nature of
the mind." Its definite understanding is invoked when it is merely
called "simultaneously born transcendental wisdom". The past
mind has not yet ceased, the future mind has not yet arisen, and
one should strongly watch the bare face of the unobstructed

178

manifestation of "mere clarity" of the present consciousness for a long time. First be determined about the clarity, and then if you experience continuous clarity as the result of watching it, you are seeing the clarity, the characteristic of the mind. One should seal it with Emptiness by knowing how it lacks any sign of existence. Should one experience total Emptiness without seeing anything, one is seeing the emptiness, the nature of the mind, and one should enhance the clarity of its awareness. If it is totally empty when it is clear and totally clear when it is empty, this is the unobstructed manifestation of clarity and emptiness, which is seeing the unsullied nature of the mind. (At this point) one should be resolute on the Two-In-One without grasping at it, without fabricating it and without acceptance or rejection. Beginners may exert strong effort in the beginning and **(12/B)** then relax and in the end maintain stability in this until they develop experiences. Once one develops a minor experience, one must think thus:

Alas! We (sentient beings) have been holding onto the essence of the mind, which is clear, empty, indivisible and unbiased, as an "I" and a "Self," and have fabricated the clarity characteristic of the mind as permanent. (We have) disregarded its intrinsic nature of emptiness as nihilistic and imputed things erroneously upon it and have therefore experienced attachment, hatred, and ignorance on the basis of groundless misunderstanding. It is a terrible misfortune that due to my own negative Karma I have obtained such an unfortunate rebirth and have forced myself to wander in Samsara, just as a worm ties up its body with its own saliva. Now I must understand that the root source of cyclic existence is the ignorant grasping at a self, from which arose the three (poisonous minds) attachment, hatred and ignorance; from which arose the four subtle mandalas; the three gross things; body, speech and mind; the three diseases, (as) the internal hindrances and the three spirits, (as) the external hindrances. Just as one who is awakened from seeing a striped rope to be a snake will (later) come to the realisation that it was nothing but a striped rope, I must be awakened from my grasping at the causes and effects of cyclic existence and realise that they were in fact the manifestations of the clarity, emptiness and the Two-in-One nature of my own mind. In this manner, one must contemplate until one develops a conviction that each of these groups are all in fact (the nature of) clarity, emptiness and the Two-In-One. Moreover, even the Generation Stage, the Completion Stage and Wisdom which are the three actual means to bring about the realisation that the nature of mind is clarity, emptiness and the Two-In-One are also not beyond the manifestations of one's mind. The characteristic of the clarity of the mind is the Generation Stage, the intrinsic nature of emptiness of the mind is the Completion Stage, and the unsullied nature of the mind is Wisdom. Each of these three is also inseparable from clarity, emptiness and the Two-In-One. Likewise, when the clarity, emptiness and the two-in-one nature of one's mind is fully realised into its result, the three Kayas, they are also not beyond the manifestations of one's **(13/A)** own mind. The characteristic of clarity of the mind is Nirmanakaya, its intrinsic nature of emptiness is Dharmakaya, and its unsullied nature is Sambhogakaya. As each of these three is also not separate from the great compassion (which is) the clarity aspect, the great wisdom (which is) its emptiness aspect and the great equanimity (which is) the Two-In-One aspect, they (three Kayas) are also inseparable from clarity, emptiness and the two-in-one. Furthermore, on account of the intrinsic nature of the mind, it is spontaneous accomplishment. On account of its achievable qualities, it is transference. As spontaneous accomplishment and transference are inseparable, they are indivisible. While contemplating these and with unshakeable confidence that the Three Kayas do not exist apart from one's own mind, one must meditate.

In short, decide resolutely that all phenomena that have manifested to you in the form of the cause, path and result have had no creator other than the mere projections of the clear cognition of one's own mind. As a result of not finding even a part of the mere appearances of variable clear cognition after searching with all available means, this should be sealed with emptiness. As soon as the sense of equality of clarity and emptiness eventuates, one should relax to remain in (the realisation of the) Two-In-One without either attempting to bring about any changes or grasping at it. In connection with this, Darika said in his Instructions on Suchness *(Tib. de-kho na nyid-kyi man-ngag):*

> *While knowing the nature of one's mind*
> *The inseparable nature of the two,*
> *And having abandoned all the continuity of the mind*
> *One should dwell on its flavour of equanimity.*

C.   The Three Concluding Practices

> I.   Dedication of merits and prayers
> II.   Meditating on compassion for sentient beings who have not yet obtained the realisation
> III.   Recollecting the continuity of the practice at all times

I.   *Dedication of Merits and Prayers*

If this (meditation on the view) is done in conjunction with the extended generation stage practices, one should (first) practise the concluding parts of the Sadhana. No matter which form of the practice is used, always finish the session with a dedication of merits and recite the prayers, "Due to the roots of this merit, may I attain the stage of Buddhahood in order to benefit sentient beings"[331] or any other prayers (you may wish to add), since there are immeasurable merits deriving from doing this meditation practice.

> *(13/B) To the self-seen mind, which possesses the excellent*
> *victorious ones,*
> *The three seat deities of Dharmadhatu*

*The transcendental wisdom of sensual enjoyment of bliss is
offered.*
May the practice of equanimity be brought to the path.

As it is important not to forget to do this prayer, try to integrate
this into your practice.

II. Meditating on Compassion for Sentient Beings who have not yet Obtained the Realisation

The root of all phenomena is the clear, empty, undivided and
unbiased nature of the mind. However, failing to realise this and
clinging onto the ego, the mind becomes attached to notions of self,
other, environment, inhabitants and all invariable objects. One
should think for a long time about the pitifulness of old mother
sentient beings, who through their own deception have taken
unfavourable rebirths in cyclic existence, and who because of their
negative karma, are tormented by enormous sufferings of
sicknesses, spirits and the like.

III. Recalling the Continuity of the Practice at all times

Even during the post-meditation periods, since all these notions of
self, other, environment, inhabitants and all invariable objects are
not beyond one's own clarity, emptiness and the Two-In-One
nature of the mind, one should develop neither attachment to
friends nor hatred towards opponents. Sicknesses, spirits and
sufferings cannot be abandoned, for there is neither good nor bad
in Samsara or Nirvana. All of this is the great play of the non-
duality of clarity and the empty nature of the mind itself. Thus,
remember this at all times. In connection with this, the Lord of the
Yogis (Yogesvara Virupa) said in his *Doha Sinha*:

182

All sentient beings are the manifestation of Mahamudra
The nature of the manifestation is the primordially unborn
Dharmadhatu.
All the apparent signs of duality such as happiness and
suffering
Are also the play of the primordial Dharmata of Mahamudra.

Thus, it is in accordance with this instruction.

THE ESSENCE OF THE ELEGANT TEACHINGS OF THE THREE TANTRAS

4

_____

A DETAILED EXPLANATION OF THE THREE ESSENTIAL POINTS OF THE PRACTICES

Acharya Aryadeva has said in his Svadhisthana (Tib. *bdag byin rlabs*): [332]

> *(14/A) There is nothing else that exists outside.*
> *One is seeing one's own mind*
> *Which is also an illusion to be meditated on.*
> *Remember this accordingly.*

One must practise according to the aforesaid order suggested by Jetsun Rinpoche (*rje btsun rin po che*):

> *The so-called three essential points of practices*
> *Are (of) Mind, Illusion and (their) lack of Self-Nature.*
> *The thirty-two (or) thirty-seven examples*
> *Are all applied with the preparation, actual (practice) and*
> *the conclusion.[333]*

There are three ways to establish their meaning:

1. The Appearance of Objects is Ascertained as Mind
2. The Visions in the Mind are Ascertained as Illusion
3. The two, Mind and Illusion are (both) Ascertained as lacking Self-Nature

The Essence of the Elegant Teachings of the Three Tantras

1. The Appearance of Objects is Ascertained as Mind

It is said in the *Hevajra Tantra*:

> Self is robbed and made by itself.
> The self-seer is the king, (this is) the primary self.

In the Vajrapañjara (Tantra) it says:

> Neither Enlightened Ones nor ordinary beings
> Exist outside of the precious mind.
> There is not even the slightest existence of
> Consciousness in (any) locality or meaning outside (of the
> mind).

In the *Samputa*, it is said:

> All things, external and internal,
> Are designated to be the mind.
> Apart from the mind itself
> Nothing else exists.

This is shown in the Treatise, where it is said:

> All phenomena are projections of the mind.

The meaning of these is given in the Reply to Traton's (*pra s ston*) Questions:

> First of all, all things are ascertained as mind
> Here there is nothing else apart from the mind itself.
> They are just as the horses and elephants (seen) in dreams
> and as an optical illusion
> Obscured by propensities of the misconceptions of one's
> own mind.

As said thus, (the meaning) is contained in this.

186

How should it be practised?

The mind is obscured by:

> (a) Dreams
> (b) Intoxication by Substances
> (c) Sicknesses
> (d) Spirits
> (e) Eye Movements
> (f) Optical Illusions
> (g) A Fire Brand
> (h) Swift Circular Movement[334]

In order to practise these eight examples, "(a) The Three Preliminary Practices" are the same as stated above **(14/B)** except, when praying to the Guru, insert the following:

> *Just as all the objective appearances in dreams*
> *Do not exist apart from the mind of the dreamer,*
> *The external appearances are deluded Karmic propensities,*
> *May I be blessed to realise that all appearances are nothing*
> *but my own mind.*

A. The Main Meditation[335]

This is divided into three sections:

> I.   *Remembering the examples*
> II. *Mixing the examples with their meanings*
> III. *Setting (the mind) in its (meditative) state*

I. Remembering the Examples:
(Using (a) Example 1: Dreams)

"First one must remember a clear dream." As it is said thus, recollect a clear dream. This dream may be about meeting someone whom one loves or a close friend, or about oneself happily enjoying a sensual experience. One should think that although I have experienced this perception, at that time I did not invite the perceptions of the dream nor did the perceptions of the dream come to me. Since I could not find the source of my perceptions anywhere once I woke up, they cannot be true.

II. Mixing the Examples with their Meanings

Think that there is no difference whatsoever between the perception of the dream that I experienced and the perceptions of invariable objects i.e. environment, inhabitants, as well as the enjoyment of various sensual objects. Think that although the dreams were experienced by myself as 'an experience' they did not exist in fact. Similarly, all these present perceptions of environment, inhabitants and various sensual objects can be experienced, but they (also) do not exist in actuality. Furthermore, the dreamer remembers a dream in which his son dies, for example. There is no difference whatsoever between it and the present perceptions of environment, inhabitants, sufferings etc. Dreams and present perceptions are both equally perceivable and can be experienced. But if (and when they are) examined, neither exist in reality. Thinking thus, one should generate conviction.

The Samadhirajasutra remarks:

> *Just as a young girl, who dreamt of giving birth to a son who later dies, (15/A) will first be happy with his birth and then unhappy with his death, And since neither the birth nor the*

death of the son has occurred (as she dreamt it), realise that
all things are likewise.

Worldly people perceive dreams as false and apparent things[336] as true, because it is easy to regard the perception of a dream as a 'misconception' due to its unstable propensities. Since it is harder to regard the perception of the present moment as a misconception due to its stable propensities, it is conventionally designated as "true". The Mahatma[337] Sakya Pandita has said:

> *Appearances are, in reality, the mind itself*
> *Appearances themselves do not exist externally.*
> *It is the stability and instability of propensities*
> *From which arise the concepts of 'true' and 'false'.338*

III. Setting (the mind) in its (meditative) State

Think thus: Given the circumstances where there is no distinction between my perception of dreams and of apparent things where they are neither 'true' nor 'false,' I must do my best not to allow my mind to be influenced by misconceived perceptions. Think that you will not let the mind be overpowered by conceptions, because all the varied perceptions of Samsara and Nirvana, happiness and suffering, are caused by the sleep of ignorance deluding your mind. There is nothing whatsoever that exists apart from the mind. While in that state, watch the bare perception of the luminous appearance of clear seeing. When you experience its immaculate clarity, let your consciousness relax completely. Remain in this state without developing any clinging to it.

Concerning this also, Jetsun Rinpoche *(rje bstun rin po che)* said:

> *Without searching for the creators, i.e. Phyva and Isvara339*
> *Of all the objects in phenomena which the mind engages*

Nor for (the creators) of the four elements and the like,
Let the mind itself remain in its natural state.

(1) The Three Concluding Practices

1. The first (dedication of the merits and prayers) is the same as stated above

2. The second (meditating on compassion to sentient beings who have not yet obtained the realisation) as far as all phenomena are concerned there is nothing that exists apart from mental (15/B) projections just as appearances in a dream. Alas! Because beings fail to realise this (truth) and because they cling to all external appearances as the truth, the pitiful old mother sentient beings are tormented by the machinery of sufferings

3. The third (recollecting the continuity of the practice):

It is extremely important to forcefully refresh your memory again and again during intermissions between sessions of the fact that all the apparent perceptions of everyday experiences of places, friends, possessions, happiness, sufferings and the like are all in reality (similar to) the perceptions in dreams. Who can be satisfied with the happiness in dreams and who can be troubled by the sufferings in dreams since neither exists in reality? Regarding this, it is said in *gnyis-med rnam-rgyal gyi-rgyud:*[340]

> *All phenomena must be understood*
> *As being one with the nature of dreams.*
> *One must integrate all behaviours*
> *As if they are a part of a dream.*

As said thus, this is an instruction. In this manner in conjunction with the nine techniques, one must meditate on the first example until developing an extraordinary conviction. It has been instructed that even if it takes a long time one should not move on to other objects of meditation (i.e. the second example onwards) until one develops a realisation with unshakeable conviction (on the first example). With regard to the other examples from the second example onwards, the three preparations are exactly the same.[341] Here a detailed explanation of the actual examples will now be provided.

(b) Example 2: Hallucinated by Substances

One should reflect on how due to being intoxicated by beer[342] one can become totally fearless and perceive the earth moving and revolving. Also remember how all of these perceptions such as seeing all appearances as blue by eating Kashokanta[343], or seeing all appearances as yellow by eating Datura[344], occur although they are false. One should mix them with all apparent perceptions of the present moment and generate conviction that in reality appearances do not exist as they are perceived. Likewise, one should know how to integrate the above pattern accordingly i.e. setting (the mind) in its (meditative) state etc.

(c) Example 3: Obscured by Sickness

Remember the various misconceptions that one and others may have had, i.e. how when one suffers **(16/A)** from a severe fever one can see oneself (multiplied) in two or three images. Imagine some friends becoming sick and some experiencing death, and then mix (and integrate) this with the apparent things and generate conviction that in reality appearances did not exist as they were perceived.

(d) Example 4: Possessed by Spirits

Remember instances of misconstrued perceptions, i.e. existing things as non-existent and non-existing things as existent experienced either personally or from the observation of those who were possessed by spirits, and then mix it (and integrate it) with the apparent things and generate conviction that in reality appearances did not exist as they were perceived.

(e) Example 5: Eye Movements

Whether one presses one's eye-ball (from one side) or not, when an eye is made to look in its reverse side or some other ways of looking, one can see an object such as a lamp made into a double image. If you think the first image is true because it was the basis of the misconception and the other (second) image is false because it is a misconception, one should examine which actually is the basis of the misconception. If one thinks that the right eye is the basis of the misconception, then when the right eye is closed the basis of the misconception will dissolve into the misconception. But if one thinks that the left eye is the basis of the misconception, then when the left eye is closed the basis of misconception will dissolve into the misconception. Having made oneself fully understand that both of them are not beyond the manifestation of the mind in the ultimate sense, mix (and integrate this) with all appearances and generate conviction that in reality these appearances did not exist as they were perceived.

(f) Example 6: Optical Illusion

When a person with a cataract[345] or other eye disorder looks into the clear sky, he or she will see strands of hair and swarms of flies.[346] If such things appeared because they really existed then a person with a normal eye should be able to see them too. Since they are invisible for normal eyes and are only visible for people with cataracts, they are false. In the same manner one must generate conviction that all the outside appearances do not exist as they are perceived.

(g) Example 7: A Fire-Brand

If you light the tip of a small stick (or an incense stick) with fire and twirl it with a rapid motion, you will see a glowing red wheel. On examining this, you would find that, since the fiery tip cannot be **(16/A)** in all places when it is only at one place, the wheel cannot be true. Therefore, mix this with the appearances and generate conviction.

(h) Example 8: Swift Circular Movements

If one spins around rapidly and then stands still and looks in all directions, the surrounding mountains and trees seem to be spinning too. However, in reality, this is false. Having mixed this with the apparent things until one generates conviction in this, set the mind in meditation.

In conclusion dedicate the merits. Meditate on compassion to those beings who have not realised that all phenomena are the manifestation of the very mind itself. One must exert one's effort during all actions to renounce clinging to appearances as true, by remembering that all perceptions of forms, sounds and all sensory objects are only projections of the mind as it is said in *Vajrapañjara*:

> *Though the self-nature of objects and sense organs*
> *Does not externally exist except for the mind,*
> *Everything appearing as form and the like*
> *Is the manifestation of that very mind.*

As said thus, this is the instruction. In this way, if one can come to understand that all phenomena are mere projections or manifestations of mind, one will gain realisation that there is no independent Chva or Isvara who is the creator of the atoms of the four elements. One will attain the full understanding that "all these varied manifestations and appearances of the six realms and experiences of happiness and unhappiness arose from the virtuous or non-virtuous conduct of one's own mind".

2. THE APPEARANCES IN THE MIND ARE ASCERTAINED AS ILLUSION

In the *Hevajra Tantra,* it is said:

> By its nature, there is no seer without form;
> There is no hearer without sound.

Furthermore, it adds:

> The self-nature of everything
> Is in agreement with the perfect form of illusion.

In the *Samputa,* it is said:

> Just as the Ghandharva cities
> Illusions, mirages, Harikela
> And also just like the cities in the moon (appear)
> See them just as compassion in dreams.
> *(17/A)* All of them should be regarded
> And be known exactly as the illusion itself.[347]

Concerning the meaning of these, in the Treatise it is said:

> On account of the reflection etc.

Jetsun Rinpoche *(rje btsun rin po che)* has said:

> The mind is not of its own nature
> But it is like an illusion and a mirage,
> The moon in the water and a fire from rubbing together (two pieces of wood)
> Merely appear due to the co-existence of various causes and conditions
> This itself expresses the nature of the mind.

194

As said thus, that which arises from many results of the co-existence of many causes and conditions is regarded as illusory. In the *Bodhicaryavatara,* it is added:

Arising from various causes
Illusion is but itself varied.
Nowhere is there a place
Where one cause can perform everything.

As said thus, that which arose from the co-existence of causes and conditions is called "illusion". In order to establish this, there is a second (set of eight examples):

(a) A Magical Illusion
(b) A Mirage
(c) The reflection of the moon in the water
(d) Lightning
(e) Harikela (Hydro-illusion)
(f) The Illusory City of the Gandharvas
(g) Clouds
(h) A Rainbow[348]

As said thus, first in order to apply it into the practice, (1) The Three Preliminary Practices are the same (as stated above) except when praying (to the Guru) insert this:

Just as the horses and elephants created by a magician
Are void by nature on account of their mere appearances,
May I be blessed so that the various appearances of my
deluded mind
Be realised as the illusory nature of all appearances
which are void!

A. The Three Main Meditations

I. Remembering the examples

II.   Mixing the examples with their meanings

III.   Setting (the mind) in its (meditative) state

I.   *Remembering the Examples*
        (Using (a) Example 1: A Magical Illusion)

When a magician recites formulae of magical mantras and casts
spells on certain insignificant materials such as gravel or a
monkey's tail, he visually deceives the spectators (with his trick)
and makes them see cities, horses, elephants and the like. Although
they have been made to appear, these objects are untrue and
illusory.

II.   *Mixing the Examples with their Meanings*

Similarly, one must think thus: "Since all these various
manifestations of environment, inhabitants, happiness and
unhappiness are in fact illusory appearances of Karma which
(17/B) arise due to the various transformative causes of virtuous
and non-virtuous states of mind, they are not true as they have
appeared".

III.   *Setting (the mind) in its (meditative) State*

Thus, make a firm decision that "both the illusion and the karmic
illusion are the same. They appear the same if each of their various
attributes are brought together. They do not appear the same if
they are not brought together. They are the same as they can
appear without their (true) existence". While turning your mind
inwardly, be assertive (and think thus): 'All of these illusory plays
of appearance and emptiness have appeared due to the causes of
variable manifestations of the very mind itself.' Engage in the bare
perception of the reflective self-awareness and the mere self-
seeing of it. When this bare seeing dawns, deprived of obscuring

196

covers of subjectivity and objectivity, let your consciousness relax for a while without generating any grasping.

In conclusion dedicate the merits. Meditate on compassion towards all old mother sentient beings who are overpowered by the monstrous spirit of grasping to material things because they do not realise that all appearances are illusory. In between sessions one must try to remember the following again and again: 'All perceptions of happiness and unhappiness which arise on account of food, clothing, home, bed, wealth and the like are illusory appearances since they are projected mentally due to causes and conditions. They are similar to the horses and elephants created by a magician'.

Yet again, in *Pañcakrama* it is said thus:

> When a Yogi perceives an object,
> He sees it as an illusion.

All the applicable attributes to the second example and the rest are the same (as stated above). To explain the individual examples:

(b) Example 2: A Mirage

Around midday in springtime, when various causes and conditions such as the sun's rays and vapour from the earth come together, it appears to a person in the distance as the rippling waters of a great river. Thus, it transforms their visual perception. Likewise, one sees various appearances only when all karmic **(18/A)** illusions are present and does not see them when they are not present. It is like seeing a mirage. Thinking thus, one should cultivate conviction in this.

(c) Example 3: The Reflection of the Moon in the Water

Imagine the moon rising in a sky which is free of cloud-cover and that there is water in a clean pot. When these causes and

197

conditions are both present and when a person not suffering from any eye disorder looks (into the pot), the reflection of the moon will appear in the water. If many pots of water were arranged, that many moons would appear and if one pot of water were thrown away, the moon (in that pot) would disappear. Similarly, however many pots of water are thrown away, that same number of moons will disappear. Thus indeed, firstly the moon from space has not been transferred into the pot of water. Secondly (the reflection of) the moon in the water pots is neither one nor many. Lastly, when the water is thrown away the moon in the water did not dissolve into the moon in space. It (the moon) was neither drowned by the water nor did it dissolve into the pot. When the components of the illusion come together, the illusion appears. The illusion does not appear when the components do not come together. In the same manner, since one can see various appearances only when all karmic illusions are present and cannot see them when they are not present, they are analogous to the moon in the pot of water. Thinking thus, one should cultivate conviction in this.

(d) Example 4: Lightning

When clouds and water rays[349] come together, a flash of light manifests in the sky. This is called "lightning". If they do not come together, it (the lightning) does not occur. "In the same manner, one can see in a flash of a moment various appearances when all the karmic illusions are present, and they will instantly vanish away as soon as the various attributes of the illusions are dismantled. Thus indeed, they are not real." Thinking thus, one should cultivate conviction in this.

(e) Example 5: Harikela[350] (Hydro-Illusion)

In the South East (of India), there is a big lake at a place named Harikela. If it rains heavily during the night and if there are clear clouds in the early morning sky, images of cities, horses, elephants and the like appear in the lake. However, when any of the causes or conditions is not present, they do not appear. In the same manner, since one **(18/B)** can see various appearances only when all karmic illusions are present and cannot see when they are not present, they are not real in spite of their manifestation. Thinking thus, one should cultivate conviction in this.

(f) Example 6: Illusory City of the Gandharvas [351]

When some people look into the distance they can see the appearances of cities occupied by non-humans[352] with uncertain visions of (animals that resemble) horses and elephants. When approached, they either appear to recede further into the distance or the appearances vanish all together. In the same manner, since one can see only various appearances when all Karmic illusions are present and cannot see them when they are not present, they are not real. Thinking thus, one should cultivate conviction.

(g) Example 7: Clouds

When a cluster of clouds suddenly appears in a clear sky, firstly one will be unable to find where they have come from and (secondly) when the clouds disappear, one will be unable to find where they have gone. It is merely an adventitious appearance. In the same manner, though they do not exist in reality, due to the force of the accumulations of cloud-like illusions of one's karma, there are various manifestations in the sky-like mind. Since they will not appear if all the Karmic illusions are not present, they are not real. Thinking thus, one should develop conviction in this.

(h) Example 8: A Rainbow

If one gazes from a far distance (into the sky) when it is raining, there (sometimes) appear multi-coloured arched beams of light in between the sun's rays and the shadow of the clouds. This is called a "rainbow." If one approaches it, it disappears. In the same manner, all kinds of appearances do indeed manifest when the causes and conditions such as the sun's rays and rainfall come together. Likewise, Karmic illusions come together in one's sky-like mind in numerous colours and shapes. Since they would not have appeared if the conditions had not come together, they are empty as soon as they have appeared. Also they are appearances because of their emptiness and hence they are non-dually appearance and emptiness. Thinking thus, one should develop conviction in this. Relax and remain in this state for a while.

In conclusion dedicate the merits. Meditate on compassion for the sake of old mother (sentient beings), who are grasping onto appearances as real and are thus ensnared by delusion by not realising that all appearances are illusory. While remembering in **(19/A)** between sessions that all the phenomena of Samsara and Nirvana are just appearances and emptiness and therefore illusory, (one) should enjoy them without discriminating between what is to be practised and what is to be abandoned. Without anything to refute or assert, one will realise every moment as illusion and attain all the ultimate perfection. Concerning this, Acharya Aryadeva wrote in his *Svadhisthanakrama* (*Tib. bdag-byin-rlabs kyis* [353] *rim pa*):

> All things are nothing but the manifestation of illusion.
> This indeed will make Buddhahood possible.
> The Yogi who dwells in illusion
> Is also protected by the Devas.
> It is from within the illusion-like concentration
> That omniscience arises.
> It is in the illusion-like concentration
> One will find all sensual qualities.

As said thus, this is the meaning.

3. Establishing the Lack of Self-Nature within Illusions

There are two divisions:

> A. Establishing (illusions as) Interdependent
> Origination
> B. Establishing (illusions as) Inexpressible

A. Establishing as Interdependent Origination

In the *Hevajra Tantra,* it is said:

> *Once there is the wood to make fire by friction, the base to
> cause friction with and the effort of the person's hand, fire
> will occur instantaneously.*

"Interdependent origination of other powers" etc. has also been mentioned in the Root Treatise.[354] Jetsun Rinpoche *(rje btsun rin po che)* explains its meaning thus:

> *Here the so-called 'Illusion' has no intrinsic nature of its own
> Apart from the arising of interdependent originations.
> Owing to its lack of arising, cessation and abiding
> What is there to think on this which is inexpressible?*

As said thus, Jetsun Rinpoche *(rje btsun rin po che)* added the following examples of how to apply this in practice.

This third has two divisions: The first is Interdependent Origination.[355]

> I.   Oral teaching
> II.   A Butter-lamp
> III. A Mirror
> IV.   A Seal
> V.   A Magnifying Glass

201

VI.   A Seed
VII.   A Sour taste
VIII. An Echo[356]

I.   Example 1: Oral Teaching

The Three Preliminary Practices are the same as the others, except that when praying (to the Guru) insert this:

Just as the impermanent seed does not
transform into a sprout
Even though the sprout seems to have arisen uninterruptedly,
Similarly, all phenomena seem to have arisen
from unborn reality.
(19/B) May I be blessed to realise the profound
interdependent origination!

(a) The (three) Main Meditations

(1) Remembering the examples
(2) Setting (the mind) in its (meditative) state
(3) Mixing the examples with their meanings

(1) Remembering the Examples

When a teacher expounds what is to be taught to his students in his speech, his speech will also appear in the student's mind. Since it is impossible for that speech to appear in the student's mind without depending on the teacher's words, his speech is unceasing. However, since the teacher's oral speech did not transfer into the student's mind, it is unrisen. Thus indeed, while there is no real arising and cessation, its manifestations still seem to appear. Because of its mere appearance, it does not exist independently and hence it is the mere appearance of interdependent origination.

202

(2) Mixing the Examples with their Meanings

Similarly, all (phenomena) are exactly the same whether it is the time of birth and (followed by the time of) death, or the time of death (followed by the time of) birth, or the time of going to sleep and the (time of) actually falling asleep, or the time of the former and latter expression, or at the time of the first and second moment, as well as days, months, years and aeons. Appearances do not arise in the mind without the latter depending on the former; therefore, they are unceasing. Those who have realised this will not hold the nihilistic view. The reason is this: knowing how results arise in dependence on their causes avoids the chances of asserting a causeless result. As the former has not transferred to the latter, this proves it is unborn. Those who have realised this will not hold the eternalistic view. The reason is this: if the former transferred to the latter it would suggest that cause and result exist independently. But since there is no such transference, this avoids the chances of asserting an independent existence of a cause and a result. Thus indeed, since there is nothing whatsoever which can express (the difference) between the teacher's oral speech and the **(20/A)** student's oral repetition, both are devoid of an intrinsic nature. However just as a mere part of the appearance of their dependence on each other is the appearance of interdependent origination. Similarly, the difference between all phenomena which come into existence simply by depending on one another i.e. the mind of death and the mind of birth cannot be expressed. Though they are devoid of an intrinsic nature, since the mere appearance through dependence has not ceased, all phenomena are just the appearance of interdependent origination. Thinking thus, one should develop conviction.

(3) Setting the mind in its (meditative) State

Turn your mind inwards and consider this: All these appearances and thoughts such as birth and destruction, going and coming, beginning and end, centre and circumference, one or many and the like, do not exist ultimately anywhere whatsoever. Notwithstanding their non-existence, they manifest in such appearances due to their mutual inter-dependent origination and the very appearances themselves are suggestive of their lack of inherent existence. Therefore, know of this wondrous condition where the appearance of the interdependent origination has manifested devoid of the entanglement of eternalism and nihilism. One should try to develop the definite conviction that the appearance caused the emptiness and the emptiness caused the appearance. Once definite conviction (on this realisation) has been established, without arising and ceasing, relax and let yourself rest in a state of equanimity, just like water which is poured into water or oil poured into oil. Concerning this, it is said thus in *Dohakosa:*

> *Just as water poured into water*
> *Becomes the equal taste of the water*
> *No one can ever equal the Lord*
> *Whose mind can co-host faults and qualities.*

In conclusion dedicate the merits.

There is nothing whatsoever that suggests that all phenomena within appearances and thoughts such as birth and destruction, going and coming, happiness and suffering, meeting and separation and the like exist independently. But failing to realise this, old mother (sentient beings) who are overpowered by the demon of grasping onto a self of phenomena are instead holding all appearances to be truly existent. I should have compassion for them. One should think thus.

In between sessions, while exerting your effort with determination, be mindful of the unobstructed appearances of happiness and suffering which **(20/B)** portray the appearance of interdependent origination in spite of the primordially unrisen and unceasing nature of all phenomena of appearances and thoughts.

One must carefully adopt what is to be practised and what is to be abandoned without overlooking the interdependently originated difference between the all-encompassing defilements and their thorough purification.

The three attributes of the preparation are the same (as stated above) for the second and the other (examples). What follows is an explanation of the individual examples:

II.   Example 2: A Butter-Lamp

Since the latter butter-lamp cannot be lit without depending on the former butter-lamp, it is unceasing. It is unrisen as the former has not transferred to the latter.

III.   Example 3: A Mirror

The reflection of one's face appears in the mirror because one's face is close to a thoroughly clean and stainless mirror. As the reflection could not have appeared in the mirror without depending on one's face, it is unceasing. It is (also) unrisen since one's face has not transferred into the mirror.

IV.   Example 4: A Seal

A seal which is usually made from horn or wood can leave many imprints of its pattern on wax or clay. As the pattern of the seal could not have been imprinted on the wax or clay without depending on the seal, it is unceasing and yet the pattern on the seal has not transferred on to the wax or clay, therefore it is unrisen.

V.   Example 5: A Magnifying Glass

When all the conditions such as a faultless sun,[357] an uncovered sky,[358] an unbroken or uncracked magnifying glass and some

tinder which is not wet[359] come together, fire can be ignited.
However, the fire cannot be ignited if any of these elements is
missing. Therefore, it is unceasing. If one were to carefully
examine whether the fire came from the sun, or from the
magnifying glass or from the tinder, one would not find it (the
source). Therefore, it is unarising.

VI.   Example 6: A Seed

A seed is considered to be the major example of interdependent
origination according to the *Shalistambaka Sutra*.[360]   Regarding
remembering the example: by depending upon the coming
together of all the conditions such as a fertile soil or field, a warm
and wet season, (other) causes and conditions such as water and
fertiliser, and an unspoiled seed, the seed will grow **(21/A)** from a
sprout to a plant and eventually produce its fruit. Even though the
seed has the causal relation to grow into a sprout, a plant and the
like, it will not grow unless all the conditions are present. Since the
seed grows into a sprout and then into a plant by depending on the
coming together of the aforesaid causes and conditions, it is
unceasing.   However, it is unarising since the seed has not
transferred into the sprout.

(a) Mixing the Examples with their Meanings[361]

Similarly, although the causes of happiness and misery of the six[362]
(beings of the six realms) depend on the karmic propensities of
virtue and non-virtue of their minds, these will not manifest until
such causes and conditions are present.   Although one will
experience various sufferings and happinesses according to the
particular rebirth with all its causes and conditions, the
phenomena are unceasing because the future rebirth depends on
this life's consciousness to arise. However, it is unrisen as this life's
consciousness has not been transferred to the next.

(b) Setting the Mind in its (meditative) State

Ultimately there is neither arising nor ceasing of all the
appearances and thoughts of phenomena, because they do not exist
anywhere. Thinking of their non-existence although they appear in
this manner, one should cultivate conviction in this.

VII. Example 7: A Sour Taste

When someone eats a pomegranate or any fruit with a sour taste in
front of one, one's mouth will water. Since one's mouth did not
water without depending on the water of the fruit, it is unceasing.
It is, however, unrisen as the fruit did not transfer into one's
mouth.

VIII. Example 8: An Echo

If one were to shout loudly either inside a house with a high ceiling
or near a high rocky cliff, one would subsequently hear an echo.
Since the latter voice (the echo) could not have arisen without
depending on the former voice, it is unceasing. However, it is
unrisen since the original voice has not transferred to the echoing
voice.

In a similar manner while applying this with all the former and
latter appearances and thoughts of phenomena such as birth, death
and the like one should try to cultivate conviction (21/B) and relax
one's effort to rest in the nature of this (realisation) for a while.

B. Establishing (Illusions) as Inexpressible

In the *Hevajra Tantra,* it is said:

> *It is either like a baby's laughter*
> *Or a dumb person's dream.*

Furthermore, it adds:

A Yogi presses the two
Waves of enjoyment,[363]
With his thumb and ring finger
Of his right and left hands.

Also, it is said:

The bliss of bola is the great seal etc.

In the *Treatise,* it is said:

Suchness which is inseparable from the meaning of an ocean.

Jetsun Rinpoche interprets its meaning thus:

It is meaningless to express that which is inexpressible
It is unsuitable to think on that which is unthinkable.
What is there to meditate on that which is non-meditation?
If this is understood, one will become free of clinging.

As a result of performing those aforementioned practices, one will know decisively that all objective appearances are mind (only), that all mental appearances are illusions, and that all illusions are interdependent origination. One will experience with conviction that all seemingly contradictory phenomena are in fact non-contradictory. Since the nature of that conviction cannot be identified or expressed, it has been merely called 'inexpressible'. Jetsun Rinpoche has written on how to practice in this:

The second of the third will be explained here:

I.	A baby's laughter
II.	A mute person's dream
III.	Tickling
IV.	Sexual pleasure
V.	The Wisdom of the third (initiation)
VI.	Secret union

VII.   The Wave of enjoyment

VIII.   Mandala Cakra[364]

I.   Example 1: A Baby's Laughter

Regarding the first of the eight examples, the Three Preliminary
Practices are the same as the others except for when praying (to
the Guru) when one inserts the following verse:

> *Just as the bliss of the wave of enjoyment*
> *The non-contradiction of (all appearances as) mind and*
> *illusion, And interdependent origination*
> *can be experienced. They cannot, however*
> *be expressed. May we be blessed to*
> *realise the inexpressible nature of reality!*

(a) The (three) Meditations

(1) Remembering the examples

(2) Mixing the examples with their meanings

(3) Setting the mind in its (meditative) state

(22/A)

(1) Remembering the Examples

When a young baby who is unable to speak laughs, he does that
due to a clear experience he has undergone, but which he is unable
to express.

(2) Mixing the Examples with their Meanings

Similarly, without considering any objective appearance as outside
of one, one should develop the definite conviction that these are

parts of one's own mind according to one's Guru's unbroken lineage of pith instructions. Think 'Without letting the appearances in the mind fall into (the duality of) subject and object I should develop a definite conviction that they are illusion-like Self-Awareness.[365] Without being cynical[366] of the illusion I should develop a conviction that interdependent origination is free of eternalism and nihilism. Although they have been experienced, the experiences cannot be expressed.' Thinking thus one must make every effort to cultivate a definite realisation and a clear view of its meaning without clinging to it.

(3) Setting the Mind in its (meditative) State

By exerting effort with your three doors,[367] look one-pointedly at the naked manifestation of the present consciousness of the self which is devoid of the obscuration of (the duality of) subject and object. When the experience of clarity first dawns, examine it. Ask yourself when this awareness of clarity first arose? Because one cannot find the cause of this first arising, the immaculate voidness of non-arising will manifest. Secondly, when one examines where its intrinsic nature abides, one finds it abides neither outside the body, nor inside nor in between the two. Neither does it exist in any colour or shape. It cannot be found by any means; hence it is in the nature of the immaculate clarity of non-abiding. Lastly, when one examines where it goes, there is no sign of its cessation anywhere. Hence it is in the nature of the immaculate blissfulness of non-cessation. Indeed, since it is devoid of a cause, a result and its intrinsic nature, it naturally does not exist in any way whatsoever. Hence it is in the nature of the immaculate nakedness of emptiness. On account of the non-existence of the self-manifestation of the clarity, the one who has experienced the emptiness is in the nature of the immaculate clarity of self-awareness. When there is clarity it does not exist in any way and when there is emptiness the unobstructed awareness of the clarity is present. Owing to this, maintain a bare piercing gaze without any conceptualisation of 'is' or 'is not' and without a concept of a meditator or meditation. Rest in this unadulterated state itself for it is non-clinging, **(22/B)** clarity and emptiness, devoid of extremes, unbiased, inexpressible and beyond imagination. Free[368] the mind from the notion of "is and is not" without clinging to its mere inexpressibility. Firstly, exert strong effort and rest in this. Secondly loosen and relax (your mind) and again rest in this. Lastly rest in this without hope or fear. In short, let your mind rest in an unsullied and relaxed state without employing any effort, for there is no possibility of being distracted from the non-clinging awareness of clarity and emptiness, neither is there anything to meditate upon. In this way meditate repeatedly on the examples with short but intense sessions. Make sure that you are not bored with the meditations but conclude your sessions properly.[369]

Conclude with the dedication of the merits.

The nature of all phenomena is in actuality devoid of extremes, unbiased, groundless and rootless like space. Meditate on compassion for old mother (sentient beings) who by not realising this are always indulging in their misconceptions and are tightly bound by the notion of 'I' and its clinging to objects. Do not allow your sense consciousness to wander off to sense objects, but realise that all appearances are the manifestation of the immutable sphere and in this way try to benefit sentient beings as much as you are able to even in between sessions.

The three attributes of the preparation are the same (as stated above) for the second and the other (examples). To explain the examples individually:

II.   Example 2: A Mute Person's Dream

Although a mute person experiences clear dreams, he or she is unable to express his experiences. Mixing the examples with their meanings and setting the mind into meditation are the same from here onwards.

III.   Example 3: Tickling

Although when someone touches one's armpit or ticklish places with their hand it causes a tickle and makes one laugh at the ticklish feeling, one will be unable to explain that experience regardless of the experience.

IV.   Example 4: Sexual Pleasure

The blissful experience arising from the joining of two secret organs cannot be expressed regardless of the experience.

(23/A) The Four Uncommon Examples [370]

V.   Example 5. The Wisdom of the Third Initiation

This refers to the wisdom arisen from entering into union with the consort during the Third Initiation. Regardless of the experience, it is inexpressible.

VI.   Example 6: Secret Union

This refers to an induced experience which occurs when an advanced practitioner, after mastering efficiency in controlling vital airs, engages in what is better known as 'meditation on bliss' on the basis of secret union through the lower passage due to the practice of a deliberate search for the 'lost meditation.' Regardless of the experience, it is inexpressible.

212

VII.   Example 7: The Wave of Enjoyment

This refers to an induced blissful experience of meditation on the basis of the wave of enjoyment of the upper doorways.[371] This can be attempted and accomplished by beginners.[372] There are three similar veins at (either) side of the neck. One will be able to experience the cessation of all appearances and conceptualisation if the vein for the vital air passage is carefully pressed, depriving the vein passages of nectar and blood. Those who know how to do this properly must practise it at a secluded place. In spite of the experience one has had, one should cultivate definite conviction about its inexpressibility and mix it with the mode of mental reality without clinging to it.

VIII.   Example 8: The Mandala Cakra

This refers to the experience developed from practising the path of the third initiation. Regardless of the experience, it is inexpressible.

Each of the (above) examples must be applied with the 'Mixing of the Examples with their Meanings' and 'Setting the Mind in its (meditative) State' according to the way it was applied with the first example.

Once again, those who wish to enhance their realisations should take one main example from each of the four sets of eight examples[373] and try to see how each can be established as it is characterised by all the four (aspects of view), mind, illusion, interdependent origination and inexpressibility. With regard to this, the three attributes of the preparation are the same, except when praying (to the Guru) insert thus:

*Without any creator, all phenomena are the manifestation of
the mind itself
(23/B) The mere appearance arising from causes and
conditions is itself empty;
Arising from the unrisen, one experiences it without cessation.*

213

*May I be blessed to realise the inexpressible
experience of voidness!*

C. Synthesis of the 32 Examples

I.   Remembering the Examples

Firstly, remember the dream example which establishes (all
appearances as) the mind. It is mind, because there is nothing
besides the mind of the dreamer. It is illusion, because the result
arose from many causes and conditions such as the karmic
propensities of the daytime. It is interdependent origination,
because concepts such as not going to sleep, falling asleep, the time
of dreaming and the time of awakening could not have arisen
without the latter depending on the former, and it is free of arising
and cessation since the former has not transferred to the latter.
They are inexpressible, because while experiencing them in a non-
contradictory way, they cannot be explained.

(Then) remember the example of the moon's reflection in the
water, which establishes (all appearance as) illusion. It is mind,
because the appearance in the mind occurs without an
independent outside creator. It is illusion, because the appearance
of the moon in many vessels arises from the result of many causes
such as the moon rising in the sky, a lack of any covering in the sky
and clean water in many vessels. Though the moon could not have
been reflected in the water without depending on the moon, it is
interdependent origination and devoid of arising and cessation
since the moon has not transferred into the vessels. They are
inexpressible because whilst one experiences them in a non-
contradictory way, they cannot be explained.

(Then) remember the example of a seed which establishes the
principle of interdependent origination. It is mind, because the
appearance in the mind is occurring to one without an independent

outside creator. It is illusion because the fruits arise from an unspoiled seed etc. and many causes and conditions. The sprout could not have germinated without depending on the seed, so it is interdependent origination and it is devoid of arising and cessation since the seed has not transferred to the sprout. They are inexpressible because whilst one experiences them in a non-contradictory way, they cannot be explained.

(Then) remember the examples of either tickling or sexual bliss which establish their **(24/A)** inexpressibility. It is mind because one experiences it. It is illusion because it arose from mutual touching and many causes and conditions and the resultant experience could not have been developed without depending on these. However, since the cause has not transferred to the result, it is devoid of arising and cessation and so is interdependent origination. They are inexpressible because while one experiences them in a non-contradictory way, they cannot be explained.

Furthermore, remember the examples of an advanced practitioner's experience of simultaneously born transcendental wisdom (which he or she developed) either through the Third Initiation by his or her mastering of the vital airs, or through means of the Mandala Cakra and a mediocre experience of it through the wave of enjoyment. On account of one's experiencing it, it is mind. Since it arose due to various means or causes and conditions, it is illusion. Without depending on the former causes and conditions the experiences could not have been developed. However, since the causes and conditions have not been transferred to the resultant experiences it is devoid of arising and cessation and thus it is interdependent origination. They are inexpressible because, whilst one experiences them in a non-contradictory way, they cannot be explained.

II. Mixing the Examples with their Meanings

In this way, it is mind because the examples with four characteristics and the experiences which have the attributes of the four characteristics do not have an independent creator, yet are still experienced. Since various resultant experiences arise due to various causes such as remembering the examples, it is an illusion. The resultant experiences could not have been developed without depending upon the causes. However, since the cause has not transferred to the resultant experiences it is devoid of arising and cessation and is therefore interdependent origination. Realising that they (mind, illusion and interdependent origination) are inexpressible because whilst one experiences them in a non-contradictory way, they cannot be explained, one should try to intensify the clarity and cultivate a definite conviction on the meaning of this without clinging.

III. Setting the Mind in its (meditative) State

Exert effort with your three doors (and consider the following): Primordially empty, the mind is not truly existent under any circumstances, yet it invariably manifests like an illusion **(24/B)** without obstructing appearances. The illusory appearances which are also primordially free from arising and cessation are interdependent origination. Although this can be experienced in a non-contradictory way, it cannot be explained, so let (the mind) rest in an inexpressible, primordial, uncontrived and relaxed state.

Dedicate the merits at the conclusion.

Meditate on compassion towards old mother sentient beings who have not realised the empty experience of the illusory nature of the mind itself, the manifestation of Mahamudra. In between sessions one should act for the welfare of sentient beings by knowing that

216

all appearances are the manifestation of the mind. Whatever forms of manifestation there are, they are the machinations of the illusions. They are the unobstructed appearances of the interdependent origination and are the intrinsic nature of the Dharmata Mahamudra.

THE ESSENCE OF THE ELEGANT TEACHINGS OF THE THREE TANTRAS

5

———

A COMPREHENSIVE EXPLANATION
OF THE THREE TANTRAS

When praying (to the Guru) insert thus:

> *The Basis of All Cause Tantra comprises Samsara and*
> *Nirvana*
> *The Method Tantra combines the experiences of Ripening and*
> *Liberation.*
> *The Result Tantra nullifies the contradiction of*
> *transformation and spontaneous accomplishment.*
> *May I be blessed to realise the view of Non-Differentiation!*

The Actual Three Tantras consists of:

1. The Basis of All Cause Tantra
2. The Body Method Tantra
3. The Mahamudra Result Tantra

1. THE BASIS OF ALL CAUSE TANTRA

Firstly, the nature of the underlying Cause Tantra is explained
comprehensively.

Its supporting base, how this functions to give support, the
relationship between the cause and root, and by remembering the
three appearances.

These are concerned with how Samsara and Nirvana exist in one's body and mind.[374]

The meaning of 'Basis of All' (kun-gzhi, Alaya) is as follows: The intrinsic nature of Alaya is the experience of clarity and awareness which remains continuously without interruption on a sentient being's path to Buddhahood. Unobscured and indifferent, it is neither virtuous nor non-virtuous. Of the two truths, it is the relative truth as this is the means to realise ultimate truth.

Supporting Base: Its gross supporting base is the physical body, including the sense organs. The subtle body is supported by the four Mandalas. The three realms of existence are its objects and appearances are its wealth.

How is it supported? The supporter and supported exist as if they were of one substance **(25/A)** as in the nature of a flower and its fragrance. On account of itself, it is the Cause Tantra since it creates the cause of Samsara and Nirvana, whether applied with method or not. It (Alaya) is a Root Tantra for it generates all the leaves and branches of Samsara and Nirvana just like a root of a big tree does.

Examining the relationship between the supporting base and the supported: As all phenomena of Samsara and Nirvana are imprinted on the mind, the Basis of All (consciousness), they are ripened as vein letters in the body. All that is ripened in the body is externally projected as 'environment and inhabitants.' Furthermore, whatever is manifested outside is all contained within the body. All that is within the body is also contained in the mind as propensities.

Examining the subsumption of Samsara and Nirvana: All the Samsaric phenomena including those of the six realms of existence are (subsumed) as if they were variable characteristics, clear experiences of the Dharma of the path are subsumed as qualities of Dharmas. All the resultant Dharmas are subsumed as vital strength.

2. The Body Method Tantra

The method deals with the process of ripening,
The path (the process of liberation) and their experiences.[375]

As said thus, its meaning will be elaborated here.

> A. The Non-Differentiation of Samsara and Nirvana
>   of the Ripening Initiation
> B. The Non-Differentiation of Samsara and Nirvana
>   of the Path of Liberation; and
> C. The Non-Differentiation of Samsara and Nirvana
>   of Experiences from Ripening and Liberation.

A. The Non-Differentiable Samsara and Nirvana of the Ripening Initiation

*Firstly, one must receive (hear) from the mouth of the
Glorious Guru
The Non-Differentiation of Samsara and Nirvana of the Three
Seats
For each of the Mandalas, initiations, initiation objects and so
forth.[376]*

This means as follows:

I.   The Vase Initiation

(For example) The five aggregates and the five defilements, (which are the) ground of purification of the Vase initiation are the five Buddhas. The five elements are the five consorts. The six sense organs such as eye etc. are the six Bodhisattvas such as Ksitigarbha, etc. The six **(25/B)** sense objects such as form, etc. are the six goddesses such as Rupavajra, etc. The ten main joints are the intrinsic purity of the ten wrathful ones and likewise the five families, etc. purify their own purifying bases through their individual three seats. Furthermore, the ground of purification is Samsara and the purifier is Nirvana. If one realises that the purifier and the things to be purified are of one taste by sealing the result with its cause and sealing the cause with its result, this is the Non-Differentiation of Samsara and Nirvana.

One has to know that the aggregates, the elements and the sense organs of the disciple contain (represent) the three seats (deities) at the time of bestowing the initiation and by sanctifying the Mandalas of self (generation) and front (visualisation). By generating the initiation objects such as the vase, the crown and the like; and also (by generating) each of the disciples into the nature of the father and mother of the five races by blessing their sense organs and by making them either the complete embodiment of the actual three seats[377] of purity or of enlightened activities. One should realise the Non-Differentiation of Samsara and Nirvana of the three seats of the Vase Initiation by blessing the five elements, the five aggregates and so forth into the five transcendental wisdoms.

II.   The Secret Initiation

At the time of bestowing the Secret initiation on the vein letter mandala of the bhaga,[378] one should know that the disciples' vein letters are the Non-Differentiation of Samsara and Nirvana of the three seats. (For example) *bhrum, am, jrim, kham and hum* (syllables) are the five Buddhas; *lam, mam, pam and tam* are the four mothers. *Mam* at the eyes, *dam* at the ears, etc. are the Bodhisattvas. All objects such as forms which are related to them are the goddesses. The ten long *hums* at the ten big joints are the seat of the wrathful ones and their consorts. Even one sesame seed sized droplet of Bodhicitta nectar of the initiation substance is the refined essence of the five aggregates. The nectar (itself) is the seat of the Buddhas. The refined essence of the senses are the seats of the Bodhisattvas. The refined essence of the four elements are the seats of the goddesses. The refined essence of each of the ten big joints are the seats of the wrathful ones and their consorts. In this way by bestowing and absorbing the nectar of the Non-Differentiation of Samsara and Nirvana, the initiation **(26/A)** substance in its wisdom aspect into the letter of the bhaga of the disciples' continuum and into the pledge holder, the basic Bodhicitta endowed with the three seats, there arises the experiential transcendental wisdom. This is endowed with the three seats. This is the Non-Differentiation of Samsara and Nirvana of the three seats of the Secret Initiation.

III.   The Transcendental Wisdom Initiation

During the Transcendental Wisdom (Initiation), for the purpose of enhancing and increasing the bestowed Secret Initiation, a mudra endowed with the three seats is given to the pledge holder, the disciples' body, letter bhaga and the bodhicitta, which are all endowed with the three seats. From entering into union, the Exemplary Experience of the Transcendental Wisdom is generated through the emission, holding and the like of the disciple's Bodhicitta nectar endowed with the three seats. This is the Non-Differentiation of Samsara and Nirvana of the three seats of the Transcendental Wisdom Initiation.

IV.   The Fourth Initiation

At the time of bestowing the Fourth (Initiation) onto the disciple's essence wisdom air *(sñing po ye shes rlung)* endowed with the three seats by introducing the 'Fourth of the Word' or the Ultimate (wisdom initiation) or the Fourth with the base, there arises the exemplary wisdom which excels the previous (third initiation). This is the Non-Differentiation of Samsara and Nirvana of the three seats of the Fourth Initiation.

Thus, indeed all of the clear ground to be purified is Samsara; the empty purifier is Nirvana; and the introduction of the ground to be purified with the purifier is the Non-Differentiation.

B. The Non-Differentiable Samsara and Nirvana of the Path (of Liberation)

The Non-Differentiable Samsara and Nirvana of the path has three divisions:

    I.   The Non-Differentiable Samsara and Nirvana of the Generation Stage

    II.   The Non-Differentiable Samsara and Nirvana of the Completion Stage

    III.   The Non-Differentiable Samsara and Nirvana of both Stages

I.   *The Non-Differentiable Samsara and Nirvana of the Generation Stage*

In a kindly way, I will explain how each of the practices from the preliminaries to the generation stage relates to the nature of the Non-Differentiation of Samsara and Nirvana. The preliminaries include the ground, the rituals of generation, colour, hand implements, moods, limbs and so forth.[379]

What is meant by the above is as follows. By cultivating the two accumulations (as preliminaries), one purifies (one's) karma and defilements. It fulfils the purposes. It also brings to one's path the merit that the Buddha previously accumulated during three **(26/B)** incalculable aeons. The Protection Wheel protects (the disciple) from obstacles and enables (the disciple) to bring onto the path the ability to conquer Maras at dusk. By meditating on the Dharmodaya it purifies the ether element, the womb of viviparous (beings) as well as any of the four modes of birth.[380] It also brings to the path the three thorough doors of liberation. The four mandalas of the elements purify the four external and environmental elements as well as the four inner physical elements. It also brings to the path the four immeasurables.[381] The celestial mansion purifies the impure environmental world, thus bringing to the path the thirty-seven attributes of enlightenment. The sun, moon and so forth of the five Perfect Enlightenments (Abhisambodhi) purify the four types of birth, thus bringing to the path the five transcendental wisdoms.

With regard to the colours symbolising mirror-like transcendental wisdom, white purifies ignorance. Symbolising the transcendental wisdom of Dharmadhatu, black purifies hatred. Symbolising the transcendental wisdom of discrimination, red purifies desire. Symbolising the transcendental wisdom of equanimity, yellow purifies pride and miserliness. Symbolising the transcendental wisdom of accomplishment, green purifies jealousy. Thus, by increasing familiarisation (with the symbols of different colours), one can use meditation on the ground of purification, the purifier, the colour and hand implements of the deity to transform defilements into wisdom.

Since the attributes of the hand implements have to be abandoned, the wheel, Vajra, jewel, lotus and cross-Vajra are respectively compatible to ignorance and the like. (Each implement also) represents mirror-like wisdom, etc. as results.[382] The hand implements with creatures are (said to be) better symbols since each of them contains all the grounds of purification and purifier such as the five aggregates, five defilements and five transcendental wisdoms. Although the wheel and Vajra, etc. will suffice as hand implements, it should be understood that the hand implements of the sixteen hands and the stamping of the four maras under the feet are more relevant from the point of view of the historical origin of Heruka's manifestation. The outstretching of the hands and legs symbolises the universality of the emptiness of Dharmata and the beneficial activities of compassion for the sake of **(27/A)** sentient beings. The bending (of the arms and legs) symbolises one's endowment with the suchness and great compassion. The crossing of the hands at the heart and legs in the cross-legged posture symbolises the unity of method and wisdom. In this way, the appearance of all the grounds to be purified (and the appearance) of all the things explained earlier is Samsara and their relevant purifiers are Nirvana. The intrinsic nature of the Two-In-One is the non-differentiation.

The secondary (practices) i.e. reciting (Mantras), the Yoga of eating, bathing and other behavioural activities of the path belonging to the method aspect are relevant to the objective Samsara. The wisdom which is not separated from the inexpressible view is more relevant to the subjective Nirvana and the mutual sealing (between the objective Samsara and subjective Nirvana) is the non-differentiation.

II. The Non-Differentiable Samsara and Nirvana of the Completion Stage

There is completion of body, speech and mind in Samsara
Having perfectly completed the result, wisdom and
Buddhahood
With the cause and the result mutually sealed by one another,
The exemplary wisdom of realisation will now be
introduced.[383]

The meaning of the above (verse) is as follows. The ground of purification, which includes the body vein (mandala), vein letter (mandala), element nectar (mandala) and essence wisdom air (mandala), represents Samsara. The purifier, Khandakapali, Candali and other deities situated on one's forehead and on the crown represent Nirvana. The mutual sealing of the two through the sealing of the result with the cause and the sealing of the cause with the result is the non-differentiation of Samsara and Nirvana of the body. Similarly, inhalation, exhalation and retention of air (through breathing), the three letters such as *Om Ah Hum* and the three defilements such as desire, etc. (hatred, ignorance) are the grounds of purification of Samsara. The understanding that the resultant form and wisdom of the Buddha is primordially existent and being able to apply this in one's practice as the purifier is Nirvana. The realisation that the result of the two are indivisible and of one taste is the Non-Differentiation of Samsara and Nirvana **(27/B)** of speech. The mind with its numerous conceptualisations is Samsara. Purifying it through its purifier by meditating on self-blessing and the Mandala Cakra is Nirvana. Cultivating transcendental wisdom by relying on them is the Non-Differentiation of Samsara and Nirvana of the mind. Thus, indeed when one has fully recognised and gained a thorough realisation of the Non-Differentiation of Samsara and Nirvana, that very concept can be introduced as the exemplary transcendental wisdom for it represents the transcendental wisdom of the Path of Seeing.

III. The Non-Differentiable Samsara and Nirvana of both the Generation and Completion Stages

If one wishes to improve one's realisations
One should remember the six common Dharmas of the
Generation and Completion (stages)
And should use the signs of the pledges assiduously,
Investigating (realisations) with a mind free of impurities.[384]

The meaning of the above is as follows. How does the Non-Differentiation of Samsara and Nirvana relate to the six common Dharmas of the two stages? (The six common Dharmas are):

1. The nature of the two stages
2. Distinction

3. Etymology
4. The suitability of the interrelated meditation of the two
5. The reasons (explaining) how the two stages can liberate
6. The method of meditating on the two stages.

The practice which combines the two concepts of the grounds to be purified with the two stages, the purifier, itself inclusively sealed by the inexpressible view is the practice of the common non-differentiation of Samsara and Nirvana of the two stages.

Concerning the Non-Differentiable Samsara and Nirvana of the pledges, the pledge concerning meditative equanimity has already been explained (in the section) on the Non-Differentiation of Samsara and Nirvana. Since the pledge concerning the post meditation deals with the view, there is an earlier explanation at the point where it (the view) was established by listening to and contemplating on (the teachings on the view) and by means of the exemplary transcendental wisdom. With regard to the pledges of eating, protection and non-separation they would appear as Samsara, for they are temporary activities. However, since they can also become contributing factors for generating transcendental wisdom they can manifest as Nirvana, hence they are Non-Differentiable.

With regard to the signs, there is an example of 'five (fingers) clinching' (secret hand gestures) which represents the five grounds to be purified. These are the five aggregates and the five defilements. Given their enumerative **(28/A)** suchness, this totals six. In the process of purifying these, one bestows the initiations of 'the five Vidyas' along with the sixth, (which is) conduct, the purifier. As a result, the five families and the five transcendental wisdoms are accomplished. This is the non-differentiation of Samsara and Nirvana of the Vase Initiation's (secret) sign. Similarly, one should realise the non-differentiation of Samsara and Nirvana of the higher signs for each of the (higher) initiations through the appropriate application, remembering the interplay of the identified grounds of purification with the purifiers etc. This is relevant to the Samsaric appearances of the activities of the Yogas of post-meditation behaviour: sleeping, rising, Torma *(gtor ma)* offering and the like. On account of their intrinsic nature being empty, it is Nirvana. It is important to remember the non-differentiation by sealing appearance and emptiness into the Two-In-One during the time of practice.

C. The Non-Differentiable Samsara and Nirvana of Experiences from Ripening and Liberation[385]

Through the experiences of Samsara, one shuns wrong views
Through the experiences of the path, one adopts (all vehicles) into one vehicle
Through the experiences of the result, there is the joy of excellence
Thus, indeed the Four Authenticities establish all the Dharmas.[386]

The meaning (of the above) is as follows. Using the power of meditating on the path and by primarily merging one's vital air and the mind into the vein letters, one obtains the experiences of different beings of the six realms. By means of this one develops confidence in the Law of Cause and Effect, thereby discarding wrong views. Furthermore, when merging and diffusing air and the mind into the vein letters in practising meditation, the view and the final accomplishment of inside and outside will manifest as if they were different. Because of this one will realise how all views and final accomplishments are experiential visions. Since these will become one Vehicle ultimately, one will have a definite conviction that they are solely non-differentiable Samsara and Nirvana or the Two-In-One. Furthermore, when the air and the mind become increasingly clear they will meet in the vein letters of the five races and their consorts. From this will arise the experiential visions of Dharmakaya and Rupakaya. Subsequently one will **(28/B)** experience exceedingly high devotion and joyfulness by thinking that on the basis of this one will obtain the inconceivable qualities of the result. Thus, indeed the cultivation of the experiences of the ground, the path and the result leads to the authenticity of recalling experiences. Following this the cultivation of an extraordinary devotion to the Guru is the authenticity of the Guru. The faithfulness to the literary quotations of the Buddha is the authenticity of transmission. Its agreement with the Yogesvara's (Virupa's) Vajra Verses is the authenticity of the treatise. Let it be known that this is called "establishing that all Dharmas are endowed with the four authenticities."

3. The Non-Differentiable Samsara and Nirvana of the Result [387]

*Pondering on the cause of its own nature, (one realises that)
it is spontaneous accomplishment,
The boundless collections of the qualities are, however, its
transformation;
Therefore, this very non-contradiction of spontaneous
accomplishment and transformation
Is indeed the Non-Differentiable Samsara and Nirvana of the
result.[388]*

The meaning (of the above) is as follows. The five Kayas namely Nirmanakaya, Sambhogakaya, Dharmakaya, Svabhavakaya and the perfectly pure Svabhavakaya are the natural and spontaneously accomplished Samsara which dwells in the four mandalas. These include the body vein Mandala as the container and the fifth which is the mind as the contained. As the Kayas are endowed with the inconceivable qualities of the Buddha, their transformation is Nirvana. Each of the Kayas is not separate from clarity, emptiness and the Two-In-One. As they are the non-differentiable Samsara and Nirvana of the result of the non-contradiction of spontaneous accomplishment and transformation, one must cultivate definite conviction. If one recognises that the results are (also) clarity, emptiness and the Two-In-One at this time when one is practising on the path, one will traverse the path much more quickly and it becomes the actual practice of the non-differentiation of Samsara and Nirvana of the ground, the path and the result. In relation to this, the Mahatma (Sakya Pandita) has proclaimed thus:

The one who has expounded the meaning of the
Non-Differentiation
Of the ground, the path and the result
And who was born as the excellent Sakya[389] prince in the
holy Khon family,
Is Kunga Gyaltshen Pal Zangpo of the sole diamond race.
Is there anyone other than I who can
teach it so meaningfully?
Here completes the exposition on the view.

The Essence of the Elegant Teachings of the Three Tantras

II

MEDITATING ON THE BODY METHOD TANTRA IN CONJUNCTION WITH THE FOUR INITIATIONS IN ORDER TO DEVELOP EXPERIENCES ON THE PATH

(29/A) It is said thus in the Treatise:

On the path, the Generation stage etc. are explained by the (set of) five fours. Each of the four initiations (I. Vase Initiation, II. Secret Initiation, III. Transcendental Wisdom of the Third Initiation and IV. Fourth Initiation) is to be established with six topics:

The Path
The View
The Final Accomplishment
Dakama ('da'-kha-ma)
The Bardo
The Result

The Essence of the Elegant Teachings of the Three Tantras

6

THE VASE INITIATION

The six topics:

1. The Path: The Generation Stage
2. The View: The Three Intrinsic Natures
3. The Final Accomplishment: The Non-Differentiation of Samsara and Nirvana
4. Dakama: Progressive Transference
5. The Bardo: The Oneness of the Deity and One's Mind
6. The Result: Nirmanakaya, the Self-Nature of Spontaneous Accomplishment

1. THE PATH: THE GENERATION STAGE

There are two sub-sections:[390]

    A. The Outer Generation Stage
    B. The Inner Generation Stage

A. The Outer Generation Stage

There are two parts:

(1) Clearing doubts through listening to and contemplating the subject of meditation

(2) The method of practising the understanding

The first is taught in the explanatory notes.[391] The second (the method of practising the understanding) has two divisions:

(a) The practices of the Generation Stage

(b) The practice of Mind concentration (sems-'dzin)

(a) The Practices of the Generation Stage

Of this, the accumulation, the purification and the conclusion has already been stated above. Regarding the Mandala Offering, there are three types of offerings according to the oral instructions of the Mahatma Sapan:[392]

(1) The Outer Relative Mandala

(2) The Inner Vajra Body Mandala

(3) The Secret Two-In-One Mind Mandala

(1) The Outer Relative Mandala

The first (outer relative Mandala) is to be offered here. Have the Mandala displayed and perform the offering with the following:

In the centre of this celestial and pure realm
Is Mount Sumeru, the king of mountains
Which is adorned by the four continents and the five sensual
qualities
And encircled by a sun and moon.
It contains the perfect splendours of gods and human beings,
The seven precious articles of royalty,[393]
The wish-fulfilling cow, the Kalapatra tree,
An unploughed harvest, gold and silver,

Good quality grains and an inconceivable
abundance of wealth.
As I make offerings to the Guru and the Buddhas
With these richest, plentiful and finest materials
May I attain the state of the perfectly Enlightened One.

(29/B) *om guru buddha bodhisattva saparivara mandala*
puja megha samudra spharana samaye hum

Recite thus. The rest is the same except insert (the following) when praying to the Guru of the Guru Yoga practice:

I pray to the outer Guru who cuts away all doubts;
Who is the Nirmanakaya, the intrinsic nature of Kayavajra
To bestow upon me the Vase Initiation
And bless me to meditate on the sublime practice of the
Generation Stage!

May I realise the view of the three intrinsic suchnesses
And attain the final accomplishment of the Non-
Differentiation of Samsara and Nirvana!
If I am unable to attain the final accomplishment
in this very lifetime
May I be able to actualise the practice of
progressive transference!

If I failed to realise the Yoga of transference
May I attain the Vidyadhara Khechara and the like;
By relying upon the Bardo instruction of the Non-
Differentiation of one's mind and the deity
And bestow the blessings to attain the actual Nirmanakaya!

(b) The Practice of Mind Concentration (sems-'dzin)

There are three Processes:

(1) The Process of Entering into the Practice
(2) The Process of Maintaining the Mind Concentration
(sems 'dzin)
(3) The Process of Arising (from the Practice)

(1) The Process of Entering into the Practice

Starting with going for Refuge, the Enlightenment thought, and the
meditation and recitation on Vajrasattva, one may (first) practise
any of the four-[394] or the six-limbed Sadhanas.[395] Perform up to the
sealing of the master of the race (section) if practising the four-
limbed (Sadhana) or up to the limb of Ratnasambhava if
(practising) the six-limbed Sadhana by recognising the grounds to
be purified and the purifier accordingly. When practising the
Sadhana, go through it in a straightforward manner by making it
explicit, intense and brief. 'Explicit' because it should be read softly
but with precision without the words being slurred. 'Intense'
because one must meditate with a concentrated focus on the words
and their meanings without being interrupted by other discursive
thoughts. If applied with these (qualities), it will naturally make it
'brief' and take less time. It is, therefore, very important that one's
practice not be interrupted by discursive thoughts.

(2) The Process of Maintaining Mind Concentration

There are two sub-divisions:

(i)   Training in the development of the Divine pride
(ii) Training in the visual aspects of the deities

(i) *Training in the Development of Divine Pride*

(30/A) "Adorned with major and minor marks, the indivisible nature of Dharmakaya and Rupakaya, I myself am the glorious Shri Hevajra, the manifestation of the intrinsic emptiness and compassion combined into one form." Thinking thus, one should develop divine pride again and again. Concerning this, *Vajrapañjara* sums up:

> *With the Yoga of the Buddha's pride*
> *One will swiftly accomplish Buddhahood.*

(ii) Training in the Visual Aspects of the Deities

One should clearly understand that the appearance of the complete Mandala Cakra of the container and the contained one has been meditating upon lacks self-nature like an ephemeral illusion or a vision in a dream. Concerning this, *Vajrapañjara* says thus:

> *Those meditating on my image*
> *Must either see it as an ephemeral illusion*
> *Or as if it were like a dream.*

Thereupon, first one should develop concentration of the mind (1) on the middle eye of the main face. As you manifest in the form of Hevajra, focus your mind with concentration on the middle eye, which is dark in the centre, with a whitish colour around it, with its veins reddish in colour, with its eyelashes and eyebrows on its right side. Thus, it is a wrathful eye on the centre of the forehead. If the visualisation lacks precision, then recite the description to yourself "...the middle eye, which is dark in the centre..." and slowly repeat this process again and again to gain clarity. If this also fails to increase clarity, then look onto the reflection of a painting of a middle eye in a mirror. Meditate on this and develop concentration of the mind (sems-'dzin).

In order to avoid the poisons of meditation, one must learn to pause to cut off the remainder of one's focus once clarity develops. If there is no clarity, one must also learn to cut off the focus. If there is clarity, then while there is still some good (experience of clarity) remaining, one rests briefly. If there is no clarity at all, also cut off (your remaining focus) and rest for a while. This is essential so that one does not become discouraged with meditation. If the distinctive appearance still manifests even after cutting off the clarity or if it is not clear when meditating and clear when not meditating, one **(30/B)** has been affected by the poisons of meditation. Then one should allow one's mind to be distracted by objects for a while and take a rest in order to resume meditation later on.

(3) The Process of Arising

Having remembered the purities,[396] the recitation (of the Mantra), and the dissolution of the Mandala, with the divine pride of the main deity one can perform the Yoga of Torma offering. If not, then straight away do the prayer for auspicious conditions and dedication of merits. Thereupon clearly remember the Yoga of conduct. Make actually displayed or mentally imagined offerings which thoroughly please you and transform all appearances into the form of the deities. It is also important to recall that all appearances are the wheel of the deities. Reflect on this again and again. Concerning this, *Guhyasamaja* says thus:

> *While resorting to all the wealth of desires*
> *As much as one wishes to,*
> *Make offerings to oneself and others*
> *By combining with one's supreme deity.*

Once the mind has obtained a stable focus on the middle eye, in addition to this (middle eye), one can meditate on (the following images during different) sessions:

1. One common session on the second and third eyes of the main face
2. One session on the wrathful wrinkles of the nose
3. One session on the high pointedness of the nose
4. As well as all these, one session on the fangs of the mouth, including the rolled tongue
5. One session on the two ears
6. One session on the long ear lobes
7. One session on the entire main face including the neck
8. Two sessions on the white face on the right
9. As well as all these, one session on the red face on the left
10. One session on the two remaining faces on the right
11. Two sessions on the two remaining left faces including the top face, with its protuberance
12. One session on the upraised hairs including the Vishvavajra on top of the crown of the main face
13. One session on the thirty-two spoked wheel on the crown, the five dry skulls on each of the heads, the mini-crowns of bone (on them) including the ear ornaments
14. Two sessions on the necklace(s) with its (their) sixteen circlets and *sku byin*[397] **(31/A)**
15. As well as all these, one session on the eight right hands with ornaments which are holding the hand implements facing inwardly[398]
16. One session on the eight left hands with ornaments and holding the hand implements facing outwardly,[399] the necklace of human heads, *se-ral-kha,* waist (bone) ornaments with sixty-four circlets including the blazing fire (around the whole appearance)
17. One session on the legs with their anklets and stamping on the four Maras [400] and the consort

18. One session on Gauri including the main deity (Hevajra)
19. One session on each of the seven (goddesses)[401] including Cauri
20. One session on the nine deities together with the celestial mansion
21. As well as all these, one session on the cemeteries
22. One session on the protection wheels
23. One session on visualising all the environment and its inhabitants manifested in the Mandala Cakra

In this way, starting from the middle eye up to the last session, there are thirty-two meditation sessions which are actually twenty-nine visualisations *(dmigs-rkang)*. If one is unable to do this then one can do the concentration of mind (practices) on the abridged eight sessions:

1. One session on the middle eye
2. One session on the three eyes
3. One session on the whole head
4. One session on the whole body
5. One session on the consort and the seats
6. One session on the main deity, as well as all the retinue deities
7. One session on the celestial mansion
8. One session on the cemeteries and protection wheels

Practising in this way, when the visualisation of the self-generation (of the deity) becomes clear, one should meditate on any external object in the form of the Mandala and once one has become used to this, meditate on whatever one sees in the form of the Mandala. Having become familiar with this, expand the Mandala you have meditated upon to pervade everywhere in all the realms of existence. Having become familiar with this, reduce the Mandala and the deities to the size of a small sesame seed which pervades as far as the limits of space and meditate with the view that the sesame seed has not become larger nor space become smaller. It is explained in the written works of Drogon Choegyal Phakpa (1235-1280 AD) that this describes the training in the skills of the generation stage. Has the outside appearance which has been meditated in the form of the deity become the deity? It is stated in *Acintya:*

> *(31/B) Pierced by the essence of non-duality*
> *The transformation of stone, wood and clay*
> *Into the form of deities*
> *Has been explained from the mouth of the noble one.*

B. Inner Generation Stage

Clearing doubts through listening and contemplating on the subject of meditation is provided in the explanatory notes.[402] Concerning the method of practising the Body Mandala, the path initiation should have been previously imparted. Then in order to develop the concentration of mind *(sems-'dzin)* there are three stages as above:

I.   *The Process of Entering into the Practice*

When (this is) done in conjunction with the outer Mandala, the body Mandala should be visualised clearly as soon as the wheel of the transcendental wisdom is absorbed into oneself. But when exclusively doing the body Mandala itself, the body Mandala should be clearly visualised as soon as it is absorbed into one's crown after having made offerings to the invoked merit field. After having finished taking the initiation and having sealed the master of the race, one should do the concentration of mind practice.

II.   The Process of Maintaining the Concentration of Mind

One should vigorously cultivate divine pride that one's aggregates, elements, sense organs and sense objects including the four Mandalas are the Mandalas of the contained and container of all the Tathagatas. Then one should develop the visualisation on the (Mandala of) container and the contained separately. If one wishes to do it in detail, there are seven sessions: One (session) for the container body Mandala, one (session) for each of the five palaces,[403] and one (session) for the deities of the limbs. If one wishes to do it in medium length, there are five sessions: one session for the container body Mandala, together with the palace in the heart, one session for each of the three middle palaces, and one session for the palace in the secret (organ) including the deities of the limbs. If one wishes to do it briefly, it is done in three sessions; the first and last sessions are the same as that (of the medium length) and the three middle palaces are done in one session. However, when doing the visualisation on the contained deities, start from the navel as this is the place where the formation of the physical body first started.   But when doing the mind concentration, one should start from the middle eye of the Cittavajra of the heart (Cakra) as this is the location of the mind and the doorway from which the clear light originates.   Then concentrate the mind **(32/A)** on the deity's face, the colour of the body, the hand implements and the surrounding goddesses. After that, concentrate the mind on the deities of the throat, navel and secret organ respectively. This should be done exactly as the outer Generation Stage practices by combining the Nirmanakaya with the veins of the deities' physical body of each of the Cakras, by pausing to cut off the remainder of one's focus if and when clarity develops etc.[404]

III.   The Process of Arising

Should the intrinsic nature of the view arise from inside as the result of doing this meditation, one should maintain its continuity. The remembering of the purities etc. should be done as before if this is a combined practice of the outer and inner generation stages. If the body Mandala is practised exclusively, one should do the following prayers to bring (this practice) into the path and enter into the Yoga of conduct without losing its momentum.

> *The Victorious Ones' bodies are in the wheels*
> *of the physical veins*
> *With the three complete seats (gdan) of the deities of the*
> *Nirmanakaya;*
> *And by the blissful offerings of sensual qualities to the deities,*
> *May I bring forth the path of appearance and emptiness!*

2. THE VIEW: THE THREE INTRINSIC NATURES

It (the realisation, firstly) arises from the efficacy of the veins of the body, (secondly) it arises on the basis of an agent, an external object and (thirdly) one realises the thoughtlessness of one's own intrinsic nature. There are three divisions:

1. The intrinsic nature of the Appearance (Clarity) aspect
2. The intrinsic nature of the Emptiness aspect
3. The intrinsic nature of the Two-In-One aspect

Each of these has three attributes:

1. The relative level which is contrary to the appearances of ignorance
2. The ultimate level which is devoid of mental imputations

3. The two distinguishing aspects of one intrinsic
nature

This is to say that the three attributes are (all found) in one
meditative concentration. The mind that is clearly aware, due to its
focus on either appearance or emptiness, counteracts the
appearances of ignorance at the relative level. Simultaneously the
continual (habitual) ordinary conceptions cease because no other
conceptualisations arise to cause further obstruction. This is the
ultimate level, as the mind now remains immaculately clear and
devoid of any mental constructs. As soon as clear awareness
dawns, the mind remains without thought. While it remains
without thought, the clear **(32/B)** awareness manifests. On the
basis of this, they are of one intrinsic nature. Nevertheless, it still
has two aspects, one from the relative point of view of the
recognition of the clarity, and the other from the ultimate point of
view of the dwelling in non-thought. This principle must be
applied with all meditation practices. There are three methods to
maintain this:

A. How to maintain the intrinsic nature of
meditative absorption
B. How to maintain the intrinsic nature of the post
meditation (period)
C. How to cultivate the uncultivated

A. How to Maintain the Intrinsic Nature of Meditative
Absorption

There are three (divisions):

I. How to maintain the intrinsic nature of the
appearance aspect of meditative absorption
II. How to maintain the intrinsic nature of the
empty aspect of meditative absorption

III. How to maintain the intrinsic nature of the
Two-In-One aspect of meditative absorption

I.   How to Maintain the Intrinsic Nature of the
Appearance Aspect of Meditative Absorption

When the mind remains focused on something like the middle eye
of Cittavajra at the heart (Cakra), it is known as 'a relative contrary
to the ignorance of the middle eye' *(spyan-dbu-mar ma-rig pa-las*
log-pa'i chos-can). Once all conceptualisation other than the mere
appearance of the middle eye ceases and the mind remains
immaculately focused in a state of non-thought, it is known as 'an
ultimate mind devoid of any mental constructs.' The (two)
distinctive aspects of the same intrinsic nature are the same as
explained before. This method should be applied to the face, the
body and all (other) aspects. As this intrinsic nature is free from
the poison of the continuous flow of conceptualisation as well as
being the meditative concentration of the clarity aspect, it is
(called) "the Path of Dispelling Engagements and the Meditative
Concentration of Multi-Characteristics."

II.   How to Maintain the Intrinsic Nature of the
Empty Aspect of Meditative Absorption

Similarly, with regard to the intrinsic nature of the emptiness
aspect and the Two-In-One, whatever the object of the visualisation
might be, it is empty. If the clear awareness is truly cultivated on
the awareness of the emptiness of the visualised object such as the
middle eye, which is appearance but devoid of self-nature, this is a
relative state (of mind) which counteracts the ignorance of
emptiness etc. which believes appearances to be real. Having
ceased all conceptualisation, the mind remains immaculately
focused without any thoughts other than the mere experience of
emptiness and the manifestation of the appearance which is devoid

of self-nature. It is therefore the ultimate mind devoid of any mental constructs. The (two) distinctive aspects of the same intrinsic nature are the same as explained before. As this eliminates (any likely) attachments to the flavour of the meditative concentration of the **(33/A)** empty aspect and the clinging to the objects of visualisation as real, it is (called) "the Path of Detachment and the Meditative Concentration on the Self-Nature of Emptiness".

III.   How to Maintain the Intrinsic Nature of the Two-In-One of Meditative Absorption

With regard to the intrinsic nature of the Two-In-One, the objects manifest both in appearance and emptiness without the fault of contradicting or combining with one another. Therefore, it is the Path of the Great Enlightenment. Its intrinsic nature is the Meditative Concentration of the Two-In-One. Of these three, since the appearance aspect makes one doubt what is real and the empty aspect questions what is not real, they are tainted by faulty meditative concentrations. However, this may lead to the cultivation of flawless meditation if one can steer a middle course by neither accepting nor rejecting them. As the intrinsic nature of the Two-In-One is a flawless experience, if one can steer a middle course and maintain it, it will enable one to quickly give rise to the ultimate transcendental wisdom.

B. How to Maintain the Intrinsic Nature of the Post Meditative Absorption

Once one can focus one's mind to remain one-pointedly as soon as one sees any object during the post meditative absorption through the power of having become familiarised with the appearance aspect etc. of the meditative absorption or if one can anchor the mind on empty space or even if one can remain free of thoughts without clinging to the many manifestations of the appearances of objects as real, one should exert effort to maintain the awareness of the appearances by focusing single-pointedly, instead of letting one's senses become overwhelmed by them.

C. How to Cultivate the Uncultivated

If the (intrinsic nature of the) appearance aspect has not been cultivated, one should go to a secluded place and (first) try to perfect the attributes of meditation such as the seven physical postures of Vairocana [405] etc. Then without being distracted, anchor your gaze with your eyes slightly open at any object such as a mirror and loosen the effort employed for the awareness and remain relaxed. At a certain point in time, when the mind can remain immaculately focused without any thoughts on the clear appearance of the object, that is the time when the intrinsic nature of the appearance aspect is cultivated.

If the (intrinsic nature of the) empty aspect has not been cultivated, perfect the attributes of meditation as before. Then go to a place where neither sun nor the wind can hinder the eyes. Anchor your gaze on the empty sky as an object of meditation without being distracted from it. Then loosen the effort employed for the awareness and **(33/B)** remain relaxed. If the awareness becomes clearly anchored and the mind can remain focused without any thoughts onto empty space, this is when the intrinsic nature of the empty aspect is cultivated.

If the (intrinsic nature of the) Two-In-One has not been cultivated, perfect the attributes of meditation as before. Then keep the eyes moderately open and focus the gaze on a reflection in a mirror during the daytime and the (reflection of the) moon in water at night-time. Then loosen the effort employed for the awareness and remain relaxed. If the awareness becomes clearly focused on the appearance devoid of any self-nature and if the mind remains immaculately focused without any thoughts, then the intrinsic nature of the Two-In-One is cultivated.

Even if one meditates on the generation stage, if the meditative concentration of non-thought is not cultivated it has become what is better known as "the path of accumulation simply gone alone." If meditative concentration of non-thought has been cultivated by practising the generation stage it is reported that the glorious great Sakyapa[406] said that one has arrived at that point of 'heat' on the path of accumulation and has started to tread on the path of the Yogis.

3. FINAL ACCOMPLISHMENT: THE NON-DIFFERENTIATION OF SAMSARA AND NIRVANA

Once one is familiar with the view of the three intrinsic natures of the Samsaric path, one has perfected the generation stage of the path of the vase initiation, 'the gone beyond path' from the first to the sixth Bhumi. Since all appearances of the Samsaric environment and its inhabitants will not manifest in any form other than the Nirvanic mandala of the tutelary deities, there is no environment and inhabitants beside the deities and the mandala. By realising that all of Samsara and Nirvana are inseparable from the non-dual transcendental wisdom of the one's own mind, the appearance and the mind are merged into one taste so that one can penetrate through walls and trees without being obstructed. One will be endowed with inconceivable qualities such as that (the world systems of) the three thousands can fit into a sesame seed without one being (too) big or (the other being too) small. At that point one will no longer need to meditate, as all appearances themselves will manifest as deities, all sounds will be heard as mantras and one realises the actual body mandala. One attains authority in the pure realms of the Nirmanakaya and will enjoy the uninterrupted and uncontaminated bliss through the embrace of the consort in one's lap.

4. DAKAMA: PROGRESSIVE TRANSFERENCE

(34/A) If one is unable to gain the realisation of the final accomplishment in this lifetime, persons of mediocre intelligence must practice Dakama as the way of realising this at the hour of death. However, one must carefully examine whether or not death is approaching. One should actualise Dakama only if death is happening with certainty. Otherwise it becomes equivalent to murdering a god. It is said in *Samvardoya:*

> *One should practice transference only if it is timely.*
> *Otherwise it will kill a god.*

The transference (of consciousness) therefore can only be practised after the time of death has been ascertained. There are three methods:

    A. The examination of the death signs
    B. How to avert it (death)
    C. The transference (of consciousness) if (one has) failed to avert (death)

A. The Examination of the Death Signs

This is divided into three parts:

    I.   Examining the outer death signs
    II.   Examining the inner death signs
    III. Examining the visible perceptions

I.   *Examining the Outer Death Signs*

This includes: dreaming of oneself climbing a mountain of lacquer, plucking red flowers, walking across a red plain, travelling in a foreign land, having sexual intercourse with a black lady wearing a black gown who splits opens one's stomach and removes one's internal organs, riding a monkey or a donkey backwards and also walking backwards. There are death signs which include: becoming extremely depressed with one's body, speech, home and friends, a complete change of behaviour and temperament i.e. where a tolerant person becomes short-tempered and a short-tempered person becomes tolerant, a generous person becomes miserly and a miser becomes generous and abandoning one's meditation practices. These are known as the uncertain death signs.

II.   Examining the Inner Death Signs

Generally breathing more often through the left nostril means one is virtuous and will live long. On the other hand, one who breathes more often through the right nostril is (said to be) non-virtuous and will be short-lived. Notwithstanding this, starting from the dawn session[407] until sun rise most people breath predominantly through their left nostrils on the first, second and third (days of the lunar month) and breathe through their right nostril on the fourth, fifth and sixth. In this manner the breathing pattern changes every three days respectively until the 30th.[408] Breathing several days from one nostril continuously will not bring significant harm but if it is reversed at that point it can be detrimental. For example, if the **(34/B)** reversal occurs after six days, it will bring conflict and one will face deep mental suffering. If the reversal occurs after half a month then one will suffer from terrible diseases. If the reversal occurs after a whole month, disasters will strike one's relatives. If the reversal occurs after a month and a half, then one will definitely die in six normal months.

III.   Examining the Visible Perceptions

One can examine the shape of one's lifespan in the sky above. One will die in six months time if one sees the (following) perceptions.

One's head and limbs are missing. Furthermore, the flower of the sky[409] has diminished. The lustre of the eyes has faded. The sound of the Dakinis is inaudible. The touching point of the horizon of the sky and the earth has been broken. For most people the thin line of a hand placed straight on the nose is almost broken, but if it is totally broken, one will die in six months time. These are among many diversified and uncertain death signs.

B. How to Avert Death

With regard to the outer averting of death, one must enthusiastically perform the ritual of sanctifying one's lifespan,[410] make offerings to the Guru and the Triple Gem with strong devotion, accumulate merits, cast *Tsha-tsha*,[411] make Torma *(gtor-ma)* offerings and protect the lives of living creatures.[412]

I.   *The Inner Averting of Death*

This has two sub-divisions:

     (a) The Common
     (b) The Uncommon

(a) The Common Practice

Having performed the preliminaries of meditative concentration early at dawn, either by doing the recitation of breathing exercises of 'life and effort'[413] one thousand times or by doing the meditation on vase retention it will definitely be averted as said in *Samvardoya:*

> *By the Yoga of the vase*
> *One must be victorious over the lord of the death.*

253

(b) The Uncommon Practice

According to the pith instructions by Yogesvara (Virupa) the 'consuming of the sky' is practised here. Approximately at dawn when one can first see the palm lines of one's hand, sit at a place from where you can clearly see the blue sky. First complete all the nine attributes of meditative concentration and face towards the sky. Imagine that the entire space occupied by the three realms of existence is a bluish colour. Absorb this into your mouth. Inhale through your mouth without making any **(35/A)** sound. As soon as your body is completely filled with this, swallow saliva while pressing your chin onto your adam's apple and imagine that the entire interior of the body is pervaded by the sky-blue light and retain the breath as much as you are able to. If after doing this again and again you belch, then death has been averted. It is said that one will attain the siddhi of immortality if one meditates accordingly. It is said:

> By the practice of consuming the sky for your food
> You will be immortal like the sky.

C. The Progressive Transference (of consciousness) if (one has) Failed to Avert Death

This is divided into three sections:

>   I.   The Dakama Practice of Transforming Appearances
>   II.   The Dakama Practice of the Ball of Light
>   III.   The Dakama Practice of Sound Transference

>   I.   *The Dakama Practice of Transforming*
>   *Appearances*

From now on while doing all activities with a strong sense of mindfulness, one should practice this again and again and think that all appearances are the mandala of the deities. Especially, just before going to sleep, one should think thus: "While not forgetting this recollection I will make sure that all appearances in dreams will also manifest in the form of the deities." By going to sleep with this intention and by habitually using the transformation practice, the deities will manifest. This is as far as the training exercises of the preliminaries is concerned.

Then once all the definite signs of death have occurred, invite your Guru and offer him all your possessions and receive the initiation or otherwise perform the (self) initiation by admitting yourself (into the mandala) and invite the Vajra relatives and friends to take part in the cycle of *tshogs* offering (ganacakra). Confess all downfalls and transgressions of the Samayas. Make sure that all your material possessions are given away to charity for meritorious causes so that you will not grasp and cling to material wealth. Then the light rays at the seed syllable at your heart manifest in the form of the deity, thus invoking the inseparable nature of the deity and the Guru in the space in front of you. Then while making the outer, inner, mentally created as well as any available offerings, perform the seven-fold prayer.[414] Recite fervent prayers longingly and with strong devotion. Consequently, when appearances become invariably hazy and when you are about to die, let go of seeing yourself in the form of the deity but instead remember that all **(35/B)** appearances in front of you are the deity. Finally, as the deity's appearance and your own consciousness merge into one taste, realise the final accomplishment or become a Vidhyadhara[415] and the like without having to experience the manifestation of the Bardo.

II.   The Dakama Practice of the Ball of Light

Perform the invocation of the inseparable nature of the Guru and the deity in the space in front etc. as stated before. Squat down with the two hands supporting the nape. Visualise a thumb sized ball of light inside your heart manifesting in the form of the deity. From there emanates one ball of light which blocks the anal passage, the doorway of taking rebirth in the hells. As well, (the ball of light) blocks the urinary passage, the doorway of the animal rebirth; the navel, the doorway of the desire realm gods; the mouth, the doorway of the hungry ghost rebirth; the two nostrils, the doorway of the Yaksha rebirth; the right and left eyes, the doorway of ordinary human and their ruler's rebirth; the two ears, the doorway of probable human rebirth; the space between the eye brows, the doorway of the form realm god rebirth. Then (the ball of light) blocks the crown, the doorway of the formless realm god rebirth. It is stated in *gdan-bzhi* thus:

> *From the particulars of the doorways*
> *Originate the particulars of Samsara.*

Then inside the navel imagine a half moon shaped blue air Mandala. On top of this lies a moon-disc and upon this a dark blue *Hum*, the basis of the mind in various sizes (as you wish). Then forcefully repeat *Hum* twenty times long and loud. As one does so the air mandala, the moon disc, and the *Hum* gradually rise upwards to the throat. As one repeats the twenty first (*Hum*), the air, the moon-disc and the *Hum* open the doorway of Brahma and all three of them are ejected to the supreme deity's heart. Doing this will enable one to realise the final accomplishment or attain Vidyadhara etc.

III. The Dakama Practice of Transference Through Sound

The invocation of the Guru, deity etc. and the squatting position of the body etc. are all the same as stated before. Block the doorways by syllables similar to the Dakama of the Fourth Initiation. Then at the navel think of the air, the moon-disc and the *Hum* and by repeating **(36/A)** "*Hig*" (twenty times) they rise to the throat. As

256

one repeats the twenty first and if that ejects through the doorway of Brahma as before, one will realise the final accomplishment or attain Vidyadhara etc.

5. THE BARDO: THE ONENESS OF THE DEITY AND ONE'S MIND

If one's Dakama practice has not been as effective as it could have been, in such a case it is necessary to obtain the oral instructions on the Bardo, the path of the inferior person. This has two sections:

> A. The Preliminary Practice
> B. The Main Practice

A. The Preliminary Practice

Firstly, one must at all times cultivate renunciation without being attached to any forms of rebirth in Samsara. With a motivation generated out of a strong sense of sorrow one must develop a pure and deep vision which enables one to realise that all objects of attachment, hatred and ignorance are in fact the mandala wheels of the supreme deity. With such inseparable mindfulness and determination, (firstly) one must remember the (following) three recollections together at specified times (mentioned below):

> 1. The Vajra body of the Nirmanakaya of the Guru Vajra Acharya who totally eradicates all outer doubts
> 2. His teachings which have shown that one's body is the mandala of the supreme deity
> 3. One's Vajra name[416] derived from the deity.

If one recollects these three especially at meal times, in times of great fear and anxiety, just before going to sleep and when waking up with a strong sense of determination, one will naturally be able to recollect these three even in frightful, anxious dreams and so forth. Because of this, one should do this with such vigour that one will pursue it until the deluded perceptions in dreams also manifest in the form of the Guru and the supreme deity. If one is able to do that in dreams because of the power of habit, the accurate application of the practice in the Bardo becomes that much more effective. This is the reason why the Bardo is called 'the time to receive the (ultimate) siddhi'.

B. The Main Practice

As one takes the subtle mental body through the Bardo, once the four fearful sounds and the three dreadful precipices which are called "the seven circumstantial conditions" **(36/B)** occur, there manifests five kinds of odours which is the sustenance of the Bardo being and the pathways of light. Because of these conditions arising and because one is used to it, one will remember the Guru who totally eradicates all outer doubts. One will remember oneself as the supreme deity as shown by him. Simultaneously the odours will also manifest as the supreme deity. Due to this auspicious co-incidence one's secret name will be prophesied. As a result of the appearance and one's own mind merging into one flavour, one will attain Vidyadharahood etc. in the Bardo itself. Since it is possible at that time that the maras may come (in disguise) to prophesy, one should master the signs of the four initiations and should at all costs keep one's secret name undisclosed.

6. THE RESULT: THE NIRMANAKAYA, THE SELF-NATURE OF SPONTANEOUS ACCOMPLISHMENT

This will be explained during the result itself.

258

7

—————

THE CORRESPONDING PRACTICES OF THE SECRET INITIATION

There are six sub-divisions:

1. The Path: The process of Self-Blessing
2. The View: The Four Self-Arisings of Transcendental Wisdom
3. The Final Accomplishment: The Perfect Unmixed Accomplishment
4. Dakama: Clear Light
5. The Bardo: The Clarity of Non-thought in the Transcendental Wisdom of Self- Arising
6. The Result: The Spontaneously Accomplished Sambhogakaya

1. PATH: THE PROCESS OF SELF-BLESSING[417]

There are two parts:

A. The Preliminary Stages of the Teachings
B. The Main Stages of the Teachings

A. The Preliminary Stages of the Teachings

There are two sub-sections:

> I. The preliminary for the teaching: The Yoga of accumulation and purification
> II. The preliminary for the practice session: The limbs of meditative concentration

I.   The Preliminary for the Teaching: The Yoga of Accumulation and Purification

Ideally at this point, one should receive initiation from the Guru again, but (in practice) if only the substitute initiation of the mother has been given, then only the actual teaching on the Secret Initiation can begin. Also, at this point, the signs of the breathing pattern of the Guru and his or her disciples must be examined. If the pith instructions are given at a time when both the Guru and disciple are breathing through their right (nostrils) the experiences will develop faster. However, it will be unstable and vulnerable to obstacles.[418] **(37/A)** The teaching should not be given at such times when 'the air of effort' or 'retention' or 'the generator of misery' or 'the wind-god' or 'the solar air' *(nyi-ma'i-rlung)* flow.

If both (the Guru and his/her disciples) are breathing through their left (nostrils) the experience will develop more slowly, but once generated will remain stable and will face fewer obstacles. Hence the teaching should be given at such times when this 'lunar air' or 'life air' or such 'that holds or generates happiness' or 'the absorbent air' is flowing. If the air flows through both nostrils, this is 'neutral air' which occurs during the transition (of flow of air in the nostrils) then no true meditative concentration can develop. It is possible to transfer the flow to the left nostril by visualising the flow in that nostril, if the air has been flowing too long in the right nostril. Should this fail to actualise transference, one should perform what is better known as 'extracting the breast's essence'. While blocking the left nostril, one should inhale forcibly through the right nostril. Then strongly rub the (right) elbow on your right breast while leaning your palm on your cheek, blocking the right nostril. Then exhale through the left nostril. By doing this several times, transference will occur. Thus, if the teaching can be given when both the Guru and the disciple are breathing through their left nostrils due to such auspicious conditions there will only be slight obstacles.

Then regarding accumulation and purification,[419] these two practices are (to be conducted) as described before, except for the difference that one should offer the inner Vajra body mandala to the Guru dwelling at one's heart after having absorbed (the Guru) into oneself at the conclusion of the Yoga of mandala offering. This has to be performed whilst remembering its meaning:

> *The skin, which is the golden ground*
> *Is anointed by the moisture of Rakta.*
> *The vertebrae, which represent the king of the*
> *mountains, (Mt Sumeru)*
> *Are adorned by four limbs, which are the four continents.*

> *Rasana, Lalana, the white and red Bodhicittas*
> *Which are the sun, the moon, gold and silver etc.*
> *Are the perfect wealth of humans and gods.*
> *The inner organs are the seven precious objects.*

> *The stream falling from the Ham is the wish-fulfilling-cow,*
> *The three spontaneously born bodies are*
> *the unploughed harvest,*
> *And the diverse and minor veins are the wish-granting tree.*
> *One's body, which is indeed full of immeasurable qualities,*

> *(37/B) I offer it together with the immeasurable foods,*
> *clothes and grains*
> *To you, my Guru, the Buddha*

Who is firmly seated at the droplet within (my) heart.
May I attain the perfect Enlightenment!

While reciting "*om guru buddha bodhisattva saparivara ratna mandala puja megha samudra spharana samaye ah hum*" as stated before, perform the offerings as much as you are able to. In this way, count the mandala (offering) and the One Hundred Syllable (Vajrasattva Mantra) and offer it to the Guru, stating the amount you have accumulated. If the number has turned out to be an even number, one will face fierce obstacles and harmful meditation ahead. If it is an odd number, one will face few (or no) obstacles and will develop good meditation.

II.   The Preliminaries for Practice Sessions: The Limbs of Meditative Concentration

There are three sub-sections:

> (a) The three trainings
> (b) The three Essential points
> (c) The three meditations

(a) The Three Trainings

Jetsun Rinpoche has said:

> *With regard to the preliminaries of the profound*
> *Completion Stage*
> *One must master the three trainings and then*
> *the breathing (exercises).*

There are three (divisions):

> (1) The physical training
> (2) The verbal training

262

(3) The mental training

(1) The Physical Training

At a secluded place one should (first) anoint and rub (massage) all parts of one's body with urine and sunbathe for a little while. Press only moderately so that you do not sweat. One should do prostrations and circumambulations. Then,

> Turn around the head and neck
> Wave the two hands separately
> And forcibly shake the two legs,
> This is the training of the five limbs.

Either perform this brief physical training or, if one knows and is able to, one can perform the twenty elaborate physical trainings.[420] In either case, practise until the body is fatigued and then while relaxing physically, maintain the clarity and relaxation of your mind. After a while, one will not experience any fatigue, pain or discomfort and instead one will feel physically light and blissful as a sign of having mastered this training. At this time, it is possible for some people to develop meditative concentration naturally of its own accord. In any case, by doing this physical training for a longer time, one will experience longer periods of meditative concentration and thus one is unlikely to face any obstacles during one's practice.

(2) The Verbal Training

If one has to be in a session where one has to read Sutras and recite mantras, in order not to break (one's **(38/A)** commitment) whisper them. Otherwise abandon all verbal activities such as ordinary conversation.

(3) The Mental Training

If one has virtuous practices with signs,[421] then do them so that you do not break your commitment. Otherwise abandon all virtuous and non-virtuous conceptualisation and place the mind in a saddened and melancholic state as it is said that 'one will develop meditative concentration when the mind is sad'.

(b) The Three Essential Points

There are three sub-sections:

(1) The essential points of the body
(2) The essential points of the speech
(3) The essential points of the mind

(1) The Essential Points of the Body

Sit comfortably either cross-legged or kneeling without leaning one's back on anything while keeping the vertebrae straight. Bend the head forwards slightly, focus the eyes onto the tip of the nose, keep the tongue touching the palate and have the lips and teeth resting naturally. This is similar to the foundation for constructing a building.[422]

(2) The Essential Points of the Speech

Now exhale forcefully through the nostrils three times. This essential point of speech is similar to cleaning and scrubbing the dirt from a house.

(3) The Essential Points of the Mind

After that one must loosely relax the mind. This is the essential point of the mind which is similar to warming up a horse before running a race.

(c) The Three Meditations

    (1) Generating the Enlightenment Thought
    (2) Visualising the Guru on top of one's head
    (3) The Triple *Hum* visualisation practices

(1) Generating the Enlightenment Thought

'I must attain the stage of Buddhahood for the benefit of all sentient beings. For that purpose, I shall practice the path of meditation.' This is the generation of the Enlightenment thought.

(2) Visualizing the Guru on Top of One's Head

With strong devotion one should eulogise with *gang-drin-ma* and the like. During the prayer insert thus:

> *To the Sambhogakaya, the intrinsic nature of Vaka Vajra*
> *The inner Guru, who shows Self-Arising;*
> *I pray to bestow the Secret Initiation upon my speech*
> *And bless me to meditate on the noble path of Candali!*

> *May I realise the four-fold views of Self-Arising*
> *And experience the unmixed perfection of*
> *the final accomplishment!*
> *If I am unable to experience*
> *the final accomplishment*
> *in this life, May I actualise Phowa in*
> *the sphere of the Clear Light!*

> *If I cannot actualise the Yoga of Phowa ('pho-ba) practice,*
> *Having accomplished the knowledge*
> *Holder and Khechara, etc.*
> *By relying upon the Bardo instruction of the*

Clarity of non-thought;
May I be blessed to attain the actual Sambhogakaya!

(38/B)

(3) The Triple *Hum* Visualisation Practices

Say '*Hum*' and visualise the protection wheel. Repeat '*Hum*' again
and visualise yourself in the form of the deity. The nine limbs of
meditative concentration serve as the preliminary to all meditative
concentrations.

B. The Actual Stage of the Teaching [423]

I. The essential oral instructions on the Yoga of Air
II. The essential oral instructions on Candali Practices
III. The essential oral instructions necessary at those
times

I.   *The Essential Oral Instructions on the Yoga of Air*[424]

Although there are many traditions regarding the objects (of
meditation), Yogesvara (Virupa) concentrates mainly on the Yoga
of air (breathing) for it is said that: 'The first merging of the
elements is concerned with the instructions to guide on the path by
means of the signs of Candali air and psychic heat practices'.

The reasons for this should be explained by the Guru in detail.
Although the Fully Enlightened Buddha has taught inconceivable
Yogas of air, they are (all) included in the 21,600 pith instructions.
These are in turn included in the nine hundred and one pith
instructions which are in turn included in the two hundred and
twenty-five (pith instructions). These are also included in ten (pith
instructions) and these are also included in four (namely):

266

(a) Exhalation
(b) Inhalation
(c) Retention
(d) All combined into one

(a) Exhalation (Practices)

In order to actualise all four pith instructions into the path, Yogeshvara has advocated life and effort[425] or Vajra recitation or exhalation (Yoga). This entails the following three pith instructions.

1. Exhale through 'the life' (left nostril) by pressing 'the effort' (right nostril)
2. Exhale forcefully through both (nostrils)
3. Exhale loudly through the mouth

(b) Inhalation (Practices)

The pith instructions on the two inhalation practices are (as follows):

1. Inhale through 'the life' (left nostril) by pressing 'the effort' (right nostril)
2. Inhale silently through one's mouth

(c) Retention (Practices)

Actualising retention into the channel is called 'kissing'. Each of all the practices is divided into four sub-sections:

(i) The method of the practice
(ii) Signs of success
(iii) The Resulting qualities
(iv) The Removal of faults

THE ESSENCE OF THE ELEGANT TEACHINGS OF THE THREE TANTRAS
(1) Vajra Recitation (Life And Effort Practice)

(i) The Method of Practice

If you are practising the Vajra Recitation (i.e. life and effort), once you have completed the nine limbs of meditative concentration, press the right nostril and inhale through the left nostril **(39/A)** for one round and then inhale through bliss as stated above. One should first start from the right nostril (effort) and train with clear awareness i.e. "(I am) exhaling" when exhaling, "(I am) inhaling" when inhaling, and "(I am) retaining" when retaining for a little while.

Once meditative concentration has started to develop one should gradually prolong the practice. Breath in the right nostril (effort) and remember to think "(I am) performing a longer exhalation" when exhaling and remember to think "(I am) performing a short inhalation" when inhaling and "(I am) retaining" when retaining. After developing meditative concentration, one should start from the left nostril (life) thinking "I am inhaling," "I am retaining," and "I am exhaling," thus one should remember.

Strictly speaking with Vajra recitation, it is enough to remember *'Om'* when inhaling, *'Ah'* when retaining and *'Hum'* when exhaling. Once meditative concentration has started to develop, one should gradually prolong the practice of the left nostril (left) and remember "I am performing a long inhalation" when inhaling, "I am retaining" when retaining, and "I am performing a short exhalation" when exhaling. By using this method, it will prolong the retention period and one will experience inconceivable meditative concentration.

(ii) Signs of Success

'A clear breathing pattern' refers to the visibility of the source from where the airs of the four elements flow, their colours, shapes and length. 'Determination of its aspects' refers to the ability to terminate the flow from the right to the left nostril (or vice versa), to exhale through other sense organs or the ability to prevent (breathing).

(iii)   Resulting Qualities

One will accomplish the four activities. (For instance) when the breathing pattern of earth-air element is clear, increasing activities will be accomplished either by merely reciting Mantra or by merely creating the thought. Similarly, one will accomplish peaceful activities through the water-air element, powerful activities through the fire-air element, and forceful activities through the air-air element without facing any obstructions. Or if one injects one's breath through the pathway of another person's life air and looks into the entire interior of that person one will obtain clairvoyance, being able to read his or her mind.

(iv)   Removal of Faults

What kinds of faults will be removed? One will be able to avert all causes of sudden and accidental death caused by (falling into an) abyss, the collapse (of a roof etc.), **(39/B)** being stabbed, a lightning strike or any other causes of sudden death. This is to say one has a minor power over one's life (or causes of death).

(2) Exhaling Through The Left Nostril By Pressing The Right Nostril

(i) The Method of the Practice

Once you complete the limbs of meditative concentration, focus your mind on the tip of the left nostril while pressing the right nostril and inhale then exhale, through the left nostril. During this practice of exhalation, it is extremely important not to let any air come in. Since this exhalation is aimed to expel faulty airs, this will automatically generate the meditative concentration of non-thought.

The Signs of Success

If one can exhale all the air and can cease breathing externally, for as long as one wants to, one will not need to inhale (this is the sign of success).

(ii) Resulting Qualities

As a result, one's body becomes filled with bliss and the meditative concentration of non-thought develops swiftly.

(iii) Removal of Faults

This will remedy the problems of aches and pains in the upper torso and heart problems (diseases). Even when one is not meditating on the path and at times when one has to go to a fearful place or when crossing a river, if one presses the right nostril (effort) and exhales through the left nostril (life) for seven rounds each time, this can remove all obstacles.

(3) Forceful Exhalation Through Both Nostrils

(i) The Method of the Practice

Having completed the limbs of meditative concentration and while focusing one's consciousness at the middle of one's forehead it is essential that one should exhale forcefully through both nostrils and hold it for as long as one is able to. It is equally essential that one does not allow the exhaled air to return in again. Practise this for about three days. After that focus your mind about a cubit (one and half feet approximately) in front of yourself in empty space and then four cubits, and then a spear's length, and then the sky above a valley in the far distance, and then the sky above the horizon of the earth, and finally the sphere of space of the entire universe. Otherwise one should meditate on the state of the mind which is non-thought itself. The essentials of the breathing (practices) are as described above.

(ii) Signs of Success

The signs of success are the same as stated above.

(iii) The Resulting Quality

(40/A) The resulting quality of this practice is the development of the ultimate experience of the clarity.

(iv) Removal of Faults

It removes all the problems of headaches and one's eyes becoming bloodshot etc.

(4) Exhaling Through The Mouth With Sound

(i) The Method of the Practice

Having completed the limbs of meditative concentration, one should anchor one's mind in the sky above the horizon. (Imagine this to be) four cubits around oneself. While focusing on the sound of 'Seeee', one should exhale through the teeth with the sound 'Seeee' and hold it out for as long as one is able to. It is equally essential that one does not allow the exhaled air to return in again.

(ii) Signs of Success

The signs of success are the same as stated above.

(iii) The Resulting Qualities

The resulting qualities include lightness of the body when one rises and the transformation of one's complexion into a blissful form.

(iv) Removal of Faults

It removes all the sicknesses of fever, dead blood cells or the sudden spread of epidemic diseases.

(5) Inhaling Through The Left Nostril By Pressing The Right Nostril

(i) The Method of the Practice

Having completed the limbs of meditative concentration, imagine your breath and your mind are absorbed into an egg shell which is white on the outside and yellow inside, (the egg-shell) located at the navel. Inhale completely through the left by pressing the right and swallow some saliva, using it as the mount of the breath and hold it down.

(ii) Signs of Success

The signs of success are fulfilled if one is able to maintain it for as long as one desires without experiencing any discomfort.

(iii) The Resulting Qualities

The resulting qualities include the generation of inconceivable heat and bliss. It is said that the experiences of the master Yogeshvara (Virupa) developed through this practice.

(iv) Removal of Faults

It cures all the sicknesses of tumours, cold diseases and indigestion.

(6) Inhaling Silently Through The Mouth

(i) The Method of the Practice

Having completed the limbs of meditative concentration, imagine that your breath and your mind are absorbed into a blue triangle Dharmodaya located at the navel, while inhaling soundlessly through the mouth. Swallow some saliva and hold it down for as long as you are able to. One has to hold it down without making any sound since the heat will go off with the slightest sound.

(ii) Signs of Success

If one is able to hold it down irrespective of day and night and does not experience any **(40/B)** discomfort, one has attained the sign of its success.

(iii) Resulting Qualities

Its resulting qualities include the development of heat associated with bliss and clarity.

(iv) Removal of Faults

It remedies many abdominal sicknesses such as dropsy. It especially cures all imbalances and elemental conflicts of one's body if one presses (the air) down, pushing through wherever there are painful parts in one's body.

Furthermore, these two inhalation practices also have a common visualisation object. Either visualise that the air and mind are absorbed into a red syllable *Ah* (finely) drawn like a stroke of vermilion colour inside a white light at the navel, or alternatively visualise the air and mind absorbed into the red (*Ah*) without the white light. This causes the fire to be enlarged to the width of two or four fingers. Or visualise either a red or a yellow Dharmodaya at the navel which is spacious and wide like the earth, deep like the ocean and high and vast like the sky.

When practising the three exhalations, it is essential to exhale gradually for all the three inhalation (practices), the gradual inhalation, the filling (inhalation) and kissing (inhalation). It is most essential not to inhale for exhalation and exhale for inhalation. Furthermore, it is very important that during one application of inhalation one should not inhale again and again. Regardless of how accomplished one may be in the physical Yantra Yoga, one should always kneel for the three exhalations and sit cross-legged for the two inhalations.

(7) Kissing (Vase Retention Practice)

(i)   The Method of the Practice

This is the root of all the paths and is the cause of generating all qualities. With regard to its visualisation, having completed the nine limbs of meditative concentration, it is essential that one must be seated in the cross-legged position and then visualise that all the airs are absorbed into the stroke of an *Ah* at one's navel. As to the stages of its visualisation, firstly contract the air slightly through the lower passage and after that as soon as the upper air has filled up, swallow some saliva and press it to hold it down. After that, contract the lower air as strongly as possible. Through this, if one is able to prevent the loss of upper and lower airs, this is the **(41/A)** unmistaken essence of this practice. It is a mistake if the lower air is not stopped when holding down the upper air and the upper air cannot be held down when the lower air contracts. If by contracting the lower air, the upper air is automatically trapped, and if by holding down the upper air, the lower air exits naturally and (even) if no air is exiting when one exhales, then (the vase is retained). This is the excellent development of precious qualities.

(ii) The Degrees of Mastering the Airs

Those with superior excellence in effort (can maintain) this practice uninterruptedly. Those with excellent effort (can maintain this for) sixty-four (rounds). Those with medium effort (can maintain this for) thirty-two, and those with the least effort (can maintain this) with uncertainty. Speaking in terms of sessions, those with superior excellence in effort can maintain kissing (retention) uninterruptedly for one session whereas those with excellent effort can maintain for sixty-four rounds in one session. Those with medium effort can maintain for thirty-two rounds in one session and those with the least effort can maintain for an uncertain length in one session. However, this is not regarded as the main practice. If we measure this by the actual duration of each kiss, it is the time that it takes to circle once around the knee and to snap (one's finger) thereafter. As to this, those with superior excellence will be able to maintain this practice uninterruptedly. Those with excellent (effort) will be able to maintain the practice for sixty-four rounds. A mediocre person will be able to maintain it for thirty-two rounds and the least will be able to maintain it with uncertainty. If one attempts to prolong the duration in each day or each session, even those with inferior ability will become those with superior excellence. In this way, having become able to maintain this as long as one desires in the cross-legged sitting posture, one should practice this during normal behavioural activities. (First) try to do it while kneeling, then do it while standing, and then do it while walking and then try to integrate it while doing your work and in all activities.

(iii) Signs of Success

With regard to the signs of success, one has succeeded if one can maintain the kiss (vase retention) for many days to the extent that by merely posing in the physical Yantra Yoga, one becomes able to enter into meditative concentration.

(iv) Removal of Faults and Resulting Qualities

It will dispel all faults such as physical discomfort caused by elemental imbalances and will accomplish both Samsaric and Non-Samsaric siddhis as its resulting qualities.

If people have not contracted the lower air properly while doing this Yoga of kissing, those who experience discomfort and pain as if poked with sticks in **(41/B)** their back bones should do the following. First sit cross legged and let the squeezed fists of the two hands press down onto the mattress, first lifting up the rest of the body in the air and then dropping the buttocks onto the floor.

One round of this should remedy the pain. For other obstacles one should consult more comprehensive (texts which contain) methods for removing obstacles.

II. *The Essential Oral Instructions on Candali Practices*

Although there are inconceivable particulars of Candali practices generally taught in the Tantras, all of their quintessential practices are briefly included in nine (practices). These include:

(a) Five practices unrelated to the Cakras
(b) Three (practices) in conjunction (with the Cakras)
(c) One (practice) called 'The Swift One' in conjunction with the essential oral instructions

(a) The Five Practices Unrelated to the Cakras

(1) Rekindling of the Lamp
(2) The Roof of Brahma
(3) The Yoga of the Veins
(4) The Drilling Wheel
(5) The Yoga of the Droplets

(1) Rekindling of the Lamp

How should these (five practices) be practised? From this practice (rekindling of the lamp) onwards, the nine limbs of meditative concentration and several of the 'life' and 'effort' air practices must have already been practised in order to pave the way for the path of meditative concentration. Once this has been done, the actual practices can commence.

First one should kneel as the basic physical posture. One should clearly focus on the essential visualisation object, the inverted dark red syllable *ksa*, using the baseline of four fingers' width below the navel, and a pink *Am* in an upright position at the navel. After that, contract the anal sphincter muscle three times. While contracting for the third time, draw in some air to slightly inflame the syllable ksa which glows a red colour, creating a hot, burning sensation below the navel. Imagine that by its touching the *am* at the navel a thin stream of nectar runs down and rekindles the fire of the syllable ksa as if pouring oil onto the wick of a burning butter **(42/A)** lamp. Thinking thus, one should gradually inhale to trap the air in the upper part of the lung and swallow one's saliva soundlessly as the mount of the breath. While pressing the chin onto your Adam's apple, contract the lower air slightly. Having facilitated the two airs to kiss (vase retention), one should focus the mind on the blazing (of the fire) and dripping (of the nectar). When unable to retain the air, slowly release the breath.

(i) Training in this Path

By practising this visualisation diligently in meditative equilibrium, it becomes the cause of meditative concentration.

(ii) How to Maintain the View

At the conclusion of the session one should relax the mind by freeing it from any effort and let the eyes gaze straight (into the sky) so that one will experience the meditative concentration of non-thought which is devoid of centre and circumference.

(iii) How to Remain Impartial while Maintaining the Heat

When one meditates on the path, one should accept whatever high and low, pleasant and unpleasant experiences one may develop by realising that these experiences arise because of the interdependent origination of the mind and air. Do not develop any sense of hope or doubt, acceptance or rejection.

(iv) How to Avoid Restriction on the Number and Length of the Sessions

Without any certainty one should meditate for three, four or any (number of) sessions and should neither quantify nor identify the session by saying "I shall do such and such a visualisation for such and such a number for each session."

(v) How to Examine the Object of Mental Engagement

This refers to how one should meditate when one is happy and should not meditate when one is unhappy. If one fails to meditate while one is happy, one will not make progress on the path. If one meditates while one is not so happy, and the meditation seems like an unbridled horse, one will be discouraged with meditation and will be unable to meditate in the future.

(vi) How to Moderate it with Health

There is no way that one's meditative concentration can progress if one does not meditate while one is in good health. Since it will deepen the elemental imbalances if one meditates when one is not in sound health, one should restore one's health and meditate in moderation.

(vii) How to Cultivate it through the Whip of (appropriate) Diet and Lifestyle

One should eat light and nutritious food and lead a leisurely and care-free lifestyle. One should avoid sitting in the sun, windy

279

places and (near) fireplaces and one should avoid making the body sweat. One can sit in either of the cross-legged or kneeling postures whichever is the more comfortable.

(2) The Roof of Brahma

In the Treatises it is said: **(42/B)**

> *Mounting an arrow of fire on a bow of air*
> *One should shoot at Ham, the Bodhicitta, the target.*
> *It will swiftly give rise to transcendental wisdom.*

As said before, to practise this path, sit cross-legged and cover the knees with one's two hands. Imagine a blue bow of air at the navel, and a red arrow of fire between the legs. Imagine the arrow and string (where the tip of the arrow is held) touching at the anus. From the crown down to the navel runs the central vein which increasingly widens its lower mouth like a trumpet. Imagine at the crown (i.e. the upper end of the mouth) a white and inverted syllable *Ham*. By strongly pressing back one's stomach to the vertebrae and violently pushing up the lower air by contracting and by gazing upwards with one's eyes, this will automatically prevent the (downward) movement of the upper air. Through the power of the lower air, the bow and arrow upturn with a soaring movement from the back. Imagine that the tip of the arrow is now pointing upwards at the navel. Then as one lifts the upper part of the body, imagine that the bow is filled by the arrow and the tip of the arrow is inserted into the lower mouth of the central vein. As one's shoulders shudder the arrow is released from the bow and ascends through the central vein. When it strikes the *Ham* at the crown, imagine that a continuous thread-like flow of beads of white pearls or a stream of the milk-like nectar drips down, pushing down the fire (arrow) as far as the navel. Thinking thus, while focusing on the blazing and dripping, one should relax physically and mentally. The key to this practice is that this visualisation should not be done more than once in each session. It has been said that since doing this practice once is likely to focus the mind, one should only meditate on the dripping.

(3) The Yoga of Veins

The essential (practice) of the body is that one sits with the knees drawn up. The essential (practice) of the mind is this: While exhaling, imagine that the Rasana, the right (vein) is red in colour and fiery, about the width of a medium sized wheat straw **(43/A)** which goes through the right side of the secret organ to the navel, from the navel to the heart, from the heart to the throat, and from the throat to the crown.

While inhaling, imagine the Lalana the left (vein), white in colour like the nature of a liquid moon, about the width of medium sized wheat straw which goes through the left side of the head to the throat, from the throat to the heart, from the heart to the navel and from the navel to the secret organ.

While retaining the air in between the two (veins), imagine the central vein with the following four characteristics:

1. It is thin like a lotus-(silk) thread which is one thousandth of the width of a hair of a horse's tail
2. It is straight like a plantain tree which is not crooked
3. It is shiny red in colour like the flower of resinous lacquer
4. It is translucent and bright like a sesame seed oil lamp

As you train to focus the mind again and again on the three veins marshalled together from the secret organ to the crown, along with the exhalation, inhalation and retention of the air, let (your mind) rest wherever it desires since there is no certainty as to where the mind will place itself.

In conclusion, the way to maintain the view etc. is the same (as stated above).

(4) The Drilling Wheel

The essential (practice) of the body is to sit with the knees drawn up. The essential (practice) of the mind is this: Imagine from the navel to the crown runs the central vein which is pink in colour and the size of a medium bamboo. To its right is the Rasana and to its left is the Lalana as stated above. At the lower converging point of the three veins is a pea-sized droplet of blood which has the nature of fire. Apply the essential practice of the air, the vase retention (the upper air pushing down and the lower air pushing up) while squeezing and vibrating the right and left veins in order to twist and rotate the central vein just as in drilling. This action pierces through the lower mouth of the central vein thereby inserting the droplet of blood.

In conclusion, the way to maintain the view etc. is the same (as stated above).

(5) The Yoga of the Droplet is divided into four parts:

(i) The kissing of the sun and the moon at the heart
(ii) The sole hero at the navel
(iii) The Blissful droplet at the secret organ **(43/B)**
(iv) The white hair seed at the middle of the forehead

(i) The Kissing of the Sun and the Moon at the Heart

Having completed the nine limbs of meditative concentration, one should (first) be seated in a cross-legged posture while visualising one's heart in the shape of an empty egg (shell). Inside this is a sun disc above a moon disc which are the size of half peas. In between

282

the two (the sun and the moon) imagine a droplet endowed with three characteristics:

1. It is whitish red in colour
2. It is clear in appearance
3. Its intrinsic nature is bliss and void

After that, while focusing the mind slightly on it, imagine that the sound *'Sing'* echoes from the droplet whereupon a hole, through which passes a single hair of a horse's tail, appears in the sun disc at the top. Then imagine that while soundlessly inhaling through the mouth, the air goes through the hole and absorbs into the droplet. By meditating in this way, clear, excellent and ultimate visualisations will be generated in one's meditative concentration. Furthermore, one will quickly master the art of fore-knowledge.

(ii)   The Sole Hero at the Navel

Begin the practice in the same way, while sitting in the cross-legged position. Imagine at the navel a droplet endowed with three characteristics:

1. It is whitish red in colour
2. It is clear in appearance
3. Its intrinsic nature is the non-duality of bliss and void

Blocking the effort (left nostril) upper air, while inhaling either through the life (right nostril) or soundlessly from the mouth, one should push it down and absorb it into the droplet. This will quickly generate the meditative concentration of non-thought.

(iii) The Blissful Droplet at the Secret Organ

The preliminaries are as above. Physically draw up (your knees).
Imagine a droplet endowed with the following three characteristics
at the vase of the Vajra (the secret organ):

1. It is ruby red in colour
2. Its appearance is bliss and void
3. Its intrinsic nature is the Two-In-One

Forcefully draw in the lower air and absorb it (into the droplet). In
case one wishes to release it, do it gently as it is said that if one
releases the air violently the droplet will deteriorate. By
meditating in this way, the bliss will arise as if the jewel were going
to explode. In case an emission of the droplet or thoughts of lust
occur, focus your awareness either on the middle of the forehead
or on the widely spread apart (legs).426 This should remedy (the
difficulty). By shaking the navel area, bliss will permeate all over
the body and one should do the lower air practice at this point.
This will quickly generate blissful meditative concentration.

(iv) The White Hair Seed at the Middle of the Forehead

The preliminaries are as above. The essential (practice) of the
body is to sit in a **(44/A)** cross-legged posture. Imagine an
inverted and crooked *Ham* at the middle of the forehead. Then
when one exhales air through the 'effort,' it passes through the rear
of the uvula and strikes the *Ham* from which a stream of nectar
falls which inundates the uvula. Imagine that from the *Ham* nectar
falls down to satisfy (invigorate) the *Hum* at the heart and maintain
a focused awareness on this. Again, as one inhales, it (the nectar)
flows down and here one should again maintain a focused
awareness on this. While engaging the mind together with the
dripping down of the stream of milk or pearl-like beads, meditate
on it by slightly moving the root of the tongue at times, (and) by

pressing down the chin onto one's Adam's apple and by touching the tip of the tongue to the palate. The breathing (of the air) should correspond with the 'life' (Prana) and 'effort' (Ayama). As a result (one) will not have white hair and wrinkles and revitalisation of the elements will take place.

This way maintains the view etc. the same as the conclusion above.

(b) The Three Practices in Conjunction with the Cakras are:

(1) The sharp practice in conjunction with one Cakra

(2) The quick practice in conjunction with two Cakras

(3) The stable practice in conjunction with four Cakras

(1) The Sharp Practice in Conjunction with One Cakra

The essential (practice) of the body is to sit with the (knees) drawn up. The essential (practice) of the mind is to clearly imagine the Karmic air in the form of a bow at one's anus and a triangle of transcendental wisdom fire between the legs, which dwells there naturally. At the navel is the Cakra of emanation, with sixty-four petals. At the centre of the emanation cakra is an extremely tiny *Am*, (a vein) called Vajranairatmya inside a triangular knot of veins. Imagine on the inner circle of the eight petals are a *ka ca tra ta pa ya sha*, the first eight letters of the vowels and consonantal denominations which are red in colour and surround (the Am) in a clockwise direction. Clearly imagine the sixty-four outer petals without the syllables. As to the essential (practice) of the air, contract the anal sphincter like a ring three time. Pull it in during the last time to inflame the fire between the legs. As this strikes the *Am* at the navel, it emits a burning flame endowed with three characteristics: red in colour, intrinsically hot and soft by its self-nature. Focus the mind on this sharp-tipped fast burning flame which (rises up) at first by one fingers' width, then by two fingers' width, then by three fingers' width and finally by four **(44/B)** finger's width. At this point meditate on it by gradually performing the kissing of the air (vase retention) so that one can recognise the generation of any experience such as the radiation of heat waves under the navel.

The way to maintain the view etc. is the same (as stated above) in the conclusion. Since this is a visualisation device which generates experiences more easily, it is called "Sharp".

(2) The Quick Practice in Conjunction with Two Cakras

The essential (practice) of the body is the same (as stated above). On top of the aforementioned navel Cakra, at the heart is the Cakra of Reality with its eight petals unmarked by syllables. Visualise at its centre a royal blue *Hum*, whose head is inverted like mercury about to drip. Imagine that the *Hum* at the heart and the *Am* at the navel, which are joined by an extremely tiny part of the central vein, are the indwelling intrinsic nature of the Heruka father and the mother. The fire at the conjunction of the legs is rekindled through the contraction of the lower passage striking the *Am* at the navel, from which emits an extremely tiny fire like a light beam through the central vein which touches the *Hum*. From the *Hum* drips down an extremely tiny stream of Bodhicitta which absorbs into the *Am*, causing it to be inflamed more strongly. One now focuses on the process of blazing and dripping of the mixture of the white and red (elements). While attentively meditating with the mind and exerting physical effort, gradually kiss the airs (perform the vase retention).

The way to maintain the view etc. is the same (as stated above) in the conclusion.

286

(3) The Stable Practice in Conjunction with Four Cakras

How are the Cakras generally located? The secret Cakra is just like a gutter. The navel (Cakra) is just like a roll of rope. The heart (Cakra) is just like a blossomed lotus. The throat (Cakra) is just like the palm (of one's hand) held open and the crown (Cakra) is just like an opened umbrella. However, during practice on the path one should visualise the navel and throat Cakras just like fully blossomed lotuses standing up, and the heart and crown Cakras are just like an opened umbrella.

(i) The Method of Practice

As to the method of practice, the essential (practice) of the body is to sit with the (knees) drawn up. The essential (practice) of the mind is to first clearly visualise the **(45/A)** aforementioned two activity Cakras. There is an *Am* at the centre of the sixty-four vein petalled emanation Cakra at the navel. On the inner-most of its eight petals are the eight syllables i.e. *a ka ca tra ta pa ya sha* in a clock-wise direction.

On the front of the outer-most of its sixty-four petals are sixteen vowels[427] repeated twice in an anti-clockwise direction and (from the front) in a clockwise direction are the consonants[428] with the exception of 'Ha' and 'Ksa' repeated once. All of them are red in colour and in an upright position. There is a *Hum* in the centre of the eight petalled heart Cakra of reality. On its four cardinal directions are *Bhrum, Am, Jrim and Kham*, and on its four intermediate directions are the *Lam, Mam, Pam and Tam* syllables which are all black in colour and in an inverted position. There is an *Om* in the centre of the sixteen petalled throat Cakra of enjoyment. On the petals are the sixteen vowels in an anti-clockwise direction and the syllables are all red in colour and are standing in an upright position.

There is a *Ham* in the centre of the thirty-two petalled crown Cakra of great bliss. In the front of the petals are the sixteen

287

vowels in an anti-clockwise direction, and in a clockwise direction are from *ka* to *ta* syllables.[429] These syllables are all white in colour and are in an inverted position.

(Also) clearly visualise the Rasana vein on the right which is red in colour with its open end facing upwards, the Lalana vein on the left which is white in colour with its open end facing downwards and the Avadhuti, the central vein which is white in colour with a reddish tinge. While the three veins merge into one at the four Cakras, visualise that they run vertically from the navel to the crown as a pillar.

After visualising these, contract the anal sphincter, which will vibrate the air at the anus thereby causing the fire at the conjunction of the legs to flare up. By striking the Am at the navel, it is inflamed in a glowing reddish colour emitting a tiny flame just like a light beam rising through the Rasana vein in the right side. Without clinging or obstruction, this consumes all the elements of the syllables at the heart and once again as it passes through to the throat, it consumes all the elements of the syllables there.

(45/B) Then it rises up through to the crown and touches the *Ham*, causing it to melt and the droplet of (the melted) Bodhicitta drips down through the Lalana vein on the left side. While coming back downwards it revives and expands the syllables at the throat and it drips down through the Lalana to the heart and revives and expands the syllables there. Once again, it drips down through the Lalana and absorbs into the *Am* at the navel, reviving and causing the *Am* to blaze even more strongly. This induces a slight opening of the mouth of the central vein, causing an extremely tiny flame to rise through the central vein like a light beam consuming the Hum at the heart and the *Om* at the throat without clinging and obstruction. This (finally) strikes the *Ham* at the crown from which a tiny stream of nectar descends through the central vein and gradually causes the fire to blaze and one should (for a while) focus one's mind on the blazing and dripping taking place at the throat.

Once again it descends gradually, and one should (for a while) focus one's mind on the blazing and dripping taking place at the heart. Again, it descends gradually and one should focus one's mind on the blazing and dripping taking place at about four fingers' width above the navel. If (the problem of) excessive blazing occurs one should push it up. If excessive dripping occurs, one should push it down by intensely focusing the mind on the white and red (elements) which are just like twisted hairs and by meditating on the gradual kissing of the airs (vase retention).

The way to maintain the view etc. is the same (as stated above) in the conclusion.

(c) One (Practice) called 'The Swift One' in Conjunction With the Essential Oral Instructions

For this there are seven visualisation practices:

(1) The Pink Fire
(2) The Blazing Fire
(3) The Fighting Droplets
(4) The Wheel of Fire
(5) The Forceful Blazing of the Fire
(6) The Intense Blazing of the Fire
(7) The Complete Blazing of the Fire

(1) The Pink Fire

If convenient, this practice should be preceded by the Mandala offering and the (recitation) Yoga of the One Hundred Syllable (mantra). At the actual time of practice, all the limbs of meditative concentration are the same as above, with the exception of the essential (practice) of the physical posture. Sit with the knees drawn up and pose in the mudra known as "the eighteen reverse methods". While using the meditation belt, cross the two shin bones and cross one's arms with the hands placed on the shoulders to form six **(46/A)** triangles. The eighteen poses consist of the external postures forming the six reverse methods which have their own corresponding six vein letters as well as six element nectars. If we enumerate them in detail, it is said that even the airs also have the same (eighteen aspects).

As to the essential (practice) of the mind one should visualise that the inside of one's body is hollow. Suddenly from an unknown source, a flaming pink fire appears, completely filling the interior of one's body. The essential (practice) of the air is, while attentively focusing one's mind on this fire, one should slightly pull up the lower air and moderately push down the upper air. One should mentally count it until one is unable to hold it any longer and thereafter release it gently. In this way, one should train in the path uninterruptedly by meditating on the twenty-four air applications (breathing exercises) which consist of the integration of the twelve mentally counted and twelve mentally uncounted practices.

Maintain the view as stated previously. As for the experiences, let them go as they arise. The number of sessions should be four and the duration of the session should be twenty-four air applications. Do not examine the objects of mental engagements. Do not apply restrictions on your health. Whip up your enthusiasm through (appropriate) diet and behavioural conduct. One should also know how to apply these essential instructions to the following six practices.

(2) Training in the Blazing Fire

Continue as above except visualise a dark red syllable *Ram* under both soles (of one's feet). By moving your toes slightly visualise that the natural air at the two soles vibrates, causing each *Ram* to ignite and rise upward through the two ankle bones and main veins of the thighs to converge at the conjunction of the legs. It becomes a "sharp fire" like a point of an Indian needle, swift like the flickering of a butter lamp due to the movements of a breeze, forceful because it issues radiant sparks of fire and rough because it is extremely hot to touch. Thus, it possesses four characteristics. The essential (practice) of the air is the same (as above) with the integration of the twelve mentally counted and twelve mentally uncounted air applications and so forth.

(3) The Fighting Droplets

In addition to the same basic visualisation as before, one should visualise a white pea-sized **(46/B)** droplet on the tip of the fire and a pellet-sized red droplet about four fingers' (width) above that. While holding the air (vase retention) focus the mind on how the top droplet hits the lower droplet. Continue to strike the two droplets to form sparks of fire which illuminate the interior of the body.

(4) The Visualisation on the Wheel of Fire

On top of the aforementioned fire, visualise white and red droplets piled one upon another like a pillar. Above this is either a moving four-spoked wheel of fire or an eight-spoked wheel with short and long vowels on each of the (eight) spokes with their head pointing inside. This should be clearly visualised with the three essential factors:

1. the seed syllables on the outside
2. the wheel(s) in the middle
3. a pillar in the inside

Visualise the wheel circling either in a clockwise or in an anti-clockwise direction without touching the body whereupon it fills the whole interior of the body with sparks of fire. From here onwards one should perform the kissing of the airs (vase retention) practices and the rest is the same (as previously stated).

(5) The Forceful Blazing of the Fire

On top of the wheel of fire, visualise that there is a fire endowed with three characteristics. It is dark red in colour, intrinsically hot and soft by its self-nature. With sparks of fire the blaze rises upwards, reaching to the crown of one's skull.

(6) The Intense Blazing of the Fire

Visualise that this (same) fire blazes with such a great intensity that the blaze turns back downwards, thereby inflaming the entire exterior and interior of the body.

(7) The Complete Blazing of the Fire

Visualise that (same) fire becoming larger and larger and all appearances are inflamed into the Candali fire with its three characteristics.

The way to maintain the view etc. is the same as stated before in the conclusion.

III.   Essential Oral Instructions Necessary at Those Times

It is said in the treatise *jo-lcags-ma:* **(47/A)**

> *It is at these times that the eight kinds of skilful means to improve and reap their benefits and the essential (practice) of the six-fold pith instructions become necessary.*

Furthermore, it adds:

> *This corresponds to the first converging of the element since the thirty protections and the elimination of the hindrances are mainly necessary at these times. As said thus, these are:*

*Alternation between strict and relaxed discipline of the body
and mind*
Alternation between short and long sessions
Alternation between eating (and fasting)
Alternation between a relaxed life-style (or otherwise)

*The essential (practice) of the mind is to transfer the
concentration to various (objects)*
Tasting the nectar of diverse (sensual) objects

(a) The Six Pith Instructions

The removal of the relevant poisons of view and meditations and
the tasting of the nectar and abandoning (applying equanimity) are
the six pith instructions (three instructions on view and three
instructions on meditation) but as for the actual method of practice
one should consult the minor text on the six pith instructions.

(b) The Thirty Protections

It is said in the Compendium of Meanings *(don-bsdus-ma):*

*As for the method there are eight (protections) such as faith
etc.*
*The wisdom (aspect) is protected by the four-fold
awakenings,*
*While the inner Maras are repelled by the (secret) signs of the
four initiations.*
There are fourteen protections common to both of these two.

As said thus, there are eight protective measures such as faith for
those (practitioners) who concentrate on the method (of their
practice), and likewise for those who focus on the wisdom aspect
(of their practice). The eight protective measures consist of four
awakenings and the (secret) signs of the four initiations. For both

there are (fourteen) protective measures for the six pollutions, the six leakings and the two obscurations. These all add up to the thirty protections. One should learn the method of implementing all the instructions so as to eliminate the hindrances as they arise in one's practice.

2. VIEW: THE FOUR SELF-ARISINGS OF TRANSCENDENTAL WISDOM

As for the view, the four Self-Arisings of the Transcendental Wisdom arise from meditating on this path. These (four) arise from the essential actualisation of the vein letters; (they) arise inside the mind and (they) arise in its intrinsic clarity. There are four divisions: **(47/B)**

A. The Transcendental Wisdom of Self-Arising Defilements
B. The Transcendental Wisdom of Self-Arising Thoughts
C. The Transcendental Wisdom of Self-Arising Meditation
D. The Transcendental Wisdom of Self-Arising Clarity, Lightness and Non-Thought

A. The Transcendental Wisdom of Self-Arising Defilements

During the initial converging of the air and the mind into either the syllables of the five races or into the five syllables of the Bhaga Mandala, the five defilements will naturally arise into one's mental continuum. They will appear to arise in other people's mental continuums. One will have visionary perceptions and dream of the annihilation of the five defilements. By letting it be as it arises, it will manifest as faultless clarity and voidness, as it is said in *Guhyasamaja:*

> One will attain the perfect enlightenment
> Of the perfect defilement by defilement.

294

It is thus said.

B. The Transcendental Wisdom of Self-Arising Thoughts

Due to the converging of the air and the mind at the lower mouth of the Rasana and the Lalana, the razor air will increase its force, causing the conceptualisation of the subject and the object to become more gross and causing one's consciousness to be restless so that one cannot remain still even for a single moment. At the very least it can also cause sleeplessness. Just letting it be as it arises, it will itself become faultless clarity and voidness. It is thus said in the *Hevajra Tantra:*

> *It is thoughts which purify thoughts*
> *And existence by existence itself.*

C. The Transcendental Wisdom of Self-Arising Meditation

During the initial converging of the air and the mind around the end of the hollow veins attached to the central vein where the mind has not previously circulated to and fro, there will arise a deep calm abiding which has a stronger abiding aspect but with less clarity. By letting it be as it arises, it will itself become faultless clarity and voidness. It is said in *Samputa:*

> *If one abides in the concentration of non-thought*
> *It will become free of impurities just like the sky.*

Thus indeed, since the first two (transcendental wisdoms) are affected by excitement and the latter by depression it is called "faulty" as it is difficult to distinguish from ordinary depression and excitement. Notwithstanding this, as it is in reality meditative concentration, it will become the direct cause of generating faultless (meditation) if one knows how to maintain it properly.

D. The Transcendental Wisdom of the Self-Arising of Clarity, Lightness and Non-Thought

Through the converging of the air at the *Hum* of the Two-In-One, one will experience **(48/A)** a clear and light awareness which is just like the transcendental wisdom of the Dharmakaya as it is said:

> *This intrinsic nature of the Self-Creation*
> *Is known as "the Dharmakaya".*

Having become used to the perfecting of the final accomplishment of transcendental wisdom beyond worldly existence, it is known as "the state of faultlessness." If the "state of faultlessness" fails to arise, it should be generated in this manner:

At a secluded place, having completed the nine preliminaries of the meditative concentration, one should gaze into the sky without blinking the eyes. While loosely relaxing the awareness and effort one should repeatedly remember the three characteristics which are: 'Secret,'[430] the characteristic of the mind; 'emptiness,' the self-nature of the mind; and 'uncontrived,' the intrinsic nature of the mind. If one lets the mind rest loosely without any deliberate action, it is said that there is no way that the excellent clarity and emptiness will not manifest.

3. FINAL ACCOMPLISHMENT: THE PERFECTION OF THE UNMIXED ACCOMPLISHMENT

In this way, on the basis of having become used to the view of Self-Arising within the worldly path, one would have reached (somewhere) between the seventh and tenth Bhumi (stage) with the knowledge in languages of the six realms, and able to teach the Dharma (to beings) in their own languages. One gains authority in the vowels and consonants, will attain excellence in speech, will be endowed with the power of the four perfect awarenesses,[431] and one will possess numerous qualities in one's mental continuum such as the awakening from the conventional reality which transforms into the melody of Brahma. In short, (it comes with the) ability to teach others completely with one voice through the unmixed discriminatory awareness of diverse conventionalities and their meanings.

4. DAKAMA: THE CLEAR LIGHT

In case one is unable to attain the final accomplishment in this very lifetime, it is necessary to obtain the instructions on Dakama. Due to the (nature of one's last few) breaths before the moment of death, (all) the Karmic airs are primarily reversed inwardly into the all-pervasive air. Subsequently the air and vital Bodhicitta (nectar) of some thirty-five million minor veins are drained by the seventy-two thousand minor veins. The vitality of these veins is also drained **(48/B)** by the one hundred and twenty veins connected with the wheels and their vitality is in turn drained by the thirty-two veins which consist of the veins of the twenty-four sacred places and the eight petalled veins at one's heart. As the airs drop into the limbs, they make each of the toes and fingers of the limbs heavy. As the vitality of the thirty-two veins is also drained by Rasana and Lalana, the breathing becomes extremely heavy. As the vitality of the sun and moon veins, Rasana and Lalana is also drained by Rahula's vein, the middle (vein), the earth dissolves into water making all the doors or sense organs fluid. When the water dissolves into the fire, the mouth and nose become dry. When the fire dissolves into the air, it will cause hiccups and intensify any pain. The pain is eliminated as soon as the air dissolves into consciousness and the eyes roll up and the senses can no longer engage with their objects. All the airs and Bodhicitta nectars enter into the central channel when the consciousness dissolves into the clear light and there will then arise the excellent meditative concentration of clarity and voidness. This is called "the Dharmakaya, the clear light of death" or "the ultimate truth of death" or "the perfection of the wisdom of death." Though this occurs to every sentient being (at the moment of their death) most fail to recognise it. For a Yogi who has experienced the faultless meditative concentration of the Two-In-One, he (or she) will recognise it as if meeting a familiar person. From the merging of the indwelling 'basic mother clear light' and 'the son clear light' into one which is experienced through the power of meditation, one will attain the final accomplishment without having to go through the Bardo, which is called "the ultimate clear light". Even if the practitioner has had some familiarity during the meditation on the path previously but not experienced the faultless meditative concentration, at this point (he or she) will have a glimpse of the exemplary clear light and will attain Vidhyadharahood such as Khechara without having to experience the Bardo.

Hence the actual method of mastering this is as follows: To generate the realisation of the faultless view, one has to exert uninterrupted effort in order to successfully develop and maintain the experiential view. To achieve this, one should adopt an attitude which readily accepts death **(49/A)** (particularly at the final moment) when it comes close just as a son returning to his father's house without even the slightest fear or anxiety of death and (think thus): "I shall resolutely recognise the clear light of death as the clear light itself." Thinking thus, one should aspire resolutely to be mindful again and again. One should ensure that one is not swayed by misconceptions and is capable of setting the mind in a relaxed manner on the experiences of the view.

5. THE BARDO: THE NON-THOUGHT CLARITY OF THE TRANSCENDENTAL WISDOM OF SELF-ARISING

If it is the case that the Dakama has turned out to be ineffective, then the instructions on the Bardo, the path of the inferior, being become necessary. There are two methods to train in this:

A. The Preliminary Practice

One should remember the (following) three interrelated remembrances until they are recalled even in dreams, about the inevitability of the time (of death):

> (1) I shall remember my Guru Vajracarya, the Vakavajra Sambhogakaya who showed me the inner self-arising transcendental wisdom
> (2) I shall remember the path of Candali shown by him
> (3) I shall remember the view of self-arising transcendental wisdom developed from it

B. The Actual Practice

As one becomes familiar with these (the three remembrances) one will be able to remember them when the seven causes of the Bardo manifest. Even the odours manifest in the form of vowels and consonants (ali and kali). By that auspicious co-incidence the perception and one's own mind merge into one taste and one will attain Vidyadharahood etc. while in that very state of the Bardo.

6. RESULT: THE SPONTANEOUSLY ACCOMPLISHED SAMBHOGAKAYA

This will be discussed in the chapter dealing with the very result itself.

The Essence of the Elegant Teachings of the Three Tantras

8

———

THE CORRESPONDING PRACTICES OF THE TRANSCENDENTAL WISDOM INITIATION

There are six divisions:

1. The Path of the Mandala Cakra, the Path of Method
2. The Simultaneously Born View, the Four Descending Joys
3. The Final Accomplishment of Lesser Bliss and Voidness
4. Dakama, the Appearance of Vajrasattva at the time of Death **(49/B)**
5. The Bardo, the Simultaneously Born Bliss
6. The Result, the Self-Accomplished Dharmakaya

The Essence of the Elegant Teachings of the Three Tantras

1. The Path of the Mandala Cakra, the Path of Method

This is divided into two sections:

    A. The Preliminary
    B. The Actual Practice

A. The Preliminary

There are two sub-sections:

    I. The preliminary of the teaching
    II. The preliminary of the practice sessions

I. The Preliminary of the Teaching

The dual accumulation (of merits) and the purification (of negativities) are the same as outlined above. During the Yoga of Mandala offering, one offers it to the Guru absorbed in the centre of one's heart by knowing that the transcendental wisdom, the inseparable nature of one's own mind is the basis of attaining all the common and uncommon siddhis of the unbiased and indivisible clarity and emptiness, the definite and ultimate inseparable nature of the Guru and the deity. The Secret Two-In-One Mandala offering is made to him (with the following) by clearly reflecting on its meanings in one's mind:

> The ground of Dharmadhatu is moistened by
> the water of compassion.
> Mt. Sumeru, the mind is adorned by the continents of
> the four immeasurables.
> The sun & moon, Two-In-One benefits others by means
> of the wish-granting cow,
> The harvest of Dharmakaya and the enlightened

activities of Rupakaya etc.

The wish-fulfilling tree, grains and all the wealth of
gods and human beings,
All of these I respectfully offer to the Guru,
The master who is the manifestation of my own mind.
Bestow the common & uncommon siddhis upon all sentient
beings who equal (the bounds of) space!

While reciting *om guru buddha* etc.[432] as before, make offerings as many times as possible.

II.   The Preliminaries of the Practice Session

Follow either the long or short version of the nine limbs of meditative concentration as before, only with the addition of the following Guru Yoga prayer when praying to the Guru.

To Cittavajra, the intrinsic nature of Dharmakaya
The secret Guru who shows the Simultaneously Born
I pray to bestow upon my mind the third initiation
And bless me to be familiar with the noble path of the
messenger!

May I realise the view of the four Simultaneously Born Joys
And attain the final accomplishment of the lesser
bliss and void!
If I am unable to attain the final accomplishment in
this very lifetime,
May I effectively actualise the Phowa of
Vajrasattva's appearance!

If the Yoga of the Phowa turns out to be ineffective,
By relying upon the Bardo instruction of simultaneously
Born bliss

*(50/A) May I attain the Vidyadharahood in Khechara etc.
And attain the actual Dharmakaya!*

B. The Actual Practice

    I.   The longer path
   II.   The shorter path

I.   *The Longer Path*

There are five parts:

    (a) The Purity of the consort
    (b) The equality of body and speech
    (c) The equality of the blessing
    (d) Mutual desire
    (e) Applicability of the essential pith instruction

(a) The Purity of the Consort

    1. The actual consort
    2. The wisdom consort

The latter (means) one should use a wisdom consort as the object.

(b) The Equality of Body and Speech

Instantly visualising oneself in the form of Hevajra and the consort in the form of Vajranairatmya, is the equality of body. Reciting their individual essence (mantras), is the equality of speech and mantra, as it is said in the *Hevajra Tantra:*

> *The mind (visualising) the physical form of the deity
> And the Samaya's (Sattva) mind are identical.*

304

(Vajra) Pañjara adds:

> *If the lustful one actualises desirous deeds*
> *While visualising himself in the form of Heruka*
> *And meditating on his queen in this form,*
> *I will be pleased with him at all times.*

As said thus, generating (a perception of) one's body in the form of the deity which becomes the perception of the deity is the actual method of bringing Nirmanakaya into the path.

(c) The Equality of the Blessing

This refers to the reciprocal blessing of the "space" and "secret" (organ). The father (deity) unobjectifiably blesses the mother's space (into emptiness) and from its emptiness arises *Om* from which arises an eight petalled red lotus marked by an *Ah* at its anthers. The mother (deity also) unobjectifiably blesses the father's secret organ (into emptiness) and from its emptiness arises *Hum* from which arises a five-pronged blue Vajra marked by a *Hum* at its centre. With its tip (urethra) marked (or protected) by a *Phat* with its head pointing inward, it is circled by a garland of *Om*s as though it was a pearl garland. Think that the tip of the central prong is blessed into a precious pinnacle which arise from (the syllable) *Sva*. The blessing of the space and secret organs performed through the recitation of the mantras[433] is the perception of the mantra which is the actual method of bringing Sambhogakaya into the path.

(d) Mutual Desire

One's desire to attain the perfect enlightenment by **(50/B)** means of realising the experience of the four blisses through the consort, and the same desire by the consort is the actual method of bringing the Dharmakaya into the path.

(e) Applicability of the Essential Pith Instructions

There are five sections:

       (1) The Descent of the Bodhicitta
       (2) Holding it
       (3) Reversing it
       (4) Pervading it
       (5) Protecting it without minimising it

(1) The Descent of the Bodhicitta

Firstly, one should look at the consort's body, listen to her sounds, smell her odours, taste her and while touching various parts of her body one should embrace and kiss her etc. Through the fire of passion, each of these activities will cause the descent of Bodhicitta. Then meditate on the bliss and protect it from the extremity of straddling. First and foremost, of all, it is essential to keep it secret.

The protection through the extremity of straddling is done in the following manner. Cross over the (tight) fisted hands. Squeeze the four muscles (those of the arms and calves of the legs). Stare upwards with the eyes in a fierce gaze. Loosely release the anal muscles, totally eject your mind into the sky and make sure you keep it secret (from anyone knowing this). During this first stage one should not enter into the actual union. Thus indeed, the three stages of increasing the Bodhicitta are inter-related. These are: to cause (the Bodhicitta) to descend, to hold it after increasing it, to make it go up again after holding it. Although the first moment involves many activities, its bliss is comparatively smaller, therefore it is (called) the transcendental wisdom of Joy.

After this, remember the three-fold perceptions,[434] the actual methods of bringing the three Kayas into the path as one joins both the Bola and Kakkola equally in order to make the Bodhicitta

306

descend by igniting the fire of passion. Meditate on the bliss, protect it through the extremity of straddling and make sure you are able to keep it secret but do not engage in the actual intercourse. Although the second moment involves less activity, it produces greater joy, therefore it is (called) the transcendental wisdom of Excellent Joy.

After that, by igniting the fire of passion and by repeatedly engaging in intercourse, one causes the droplet to descend. Meditate on its bliss in a state of non-thought while protecting it by means of the extremity of straddling. Make sure it is kept secret. It is essential that one protects the droplet so that it is not lost (emitted). During the third moment, the bliss itself is devoid of intention, therefore it is (called) Joy beyond Joy.

(51/A) If one faces difficulty in holding the droplet, one can apply what is known as 'the thorough prevention of the upper air' which is done by inhaling through 'the life' while the left ring finger presses 'the effort.' Then one shakes the shoulders in a clockwise direction. If this also fails to hold (the droplets), one should perform the six practices such as 'drying the ocean to the mountain' which are explained below.

Around that time, there will occur signs of holding the droplets. After having searched for the vein whose self-nature is Vajradhatvisvari, one should enter into union through the three-fold perceptions. This will cause the Vajra and lotus to kiss, the two secret veins to kiss, the droplets to kiss and the two airs to kiss. These are known as 'the instructions on the four kisses.'435 The concept of the three preceding joys will cease at the fourth moment and there will arise the meditative concentration which lacks the definite nature to identify with. This is the simultaneously born transcendental wisdom. While maintaining that meditative concentration, one should protect it by means of the extremity of straddling, and one should ensure to keep it secret. It is essential to protect the droplet so that it will not diminish. If the droplet which is the basis of the bliss diminishes, no transcendental wisdom can be generated. Instead it will generate diverse sufferings as a result.

(2) Holding it (the droplets)

As regards how to hold it, 'Dry the ocean onto the mountain' by pulling back your belly and pressing it against the vertebrae. 'Conquer the four continents' by tightening the toes and fingers of one's two feet and two hands. 'Place the taste holder in its own place' by touching the tongue against the upper palate. 'Let the most excellent of senses (eyes) gaze upwards' by staring with one's eyes into space above one's crown.

(3) Reversing it (the droplets)

'Express the power of speech' by chanting *Hum* forcefully at length by crossing one's hands over the heart and by exhaling forcefully with the sound of *Hum*. To reverse it (the droplets) 'shoot the bow and arrow of meditative concentration of *Hum* and *Phat*' by thinking that the *Hum* at the centre of the Vajra causes the *Phat* to rise and the *Phat* reciprocally lifts up the *Hum*.

(4) Pervading it (the droplets)

'Tie up the belt of the airs' by placing both hands around the waist. 'Throw out the lasso' by stretching out and bending in both hands. 'Turn the wheel of the pestle' by resting your **(51/B)** two hands on the waist and by shrugging the shoulders. 'Behave like a small boy' by rocking the body backwards and forwards, and from side to side.

(5) Protecting it Without Diminishing it

To practice this, refer to the treatises for details.

II.   The Shorter Path

(a) Preparation: Controlling the downward pushing air
(b) The Actual practice: Simultaneous emission and holding of the droplet
(c) Conclusion: Stopping it without losing droplets

(a) Preparation: Controlling the Downward Pushing Air

Having concluded the limbs of meditative concentration:

Having perfected the physical behaviours
Crossing one's right hand, the sun, and
one's left hand, the moon
Place them onto the two knees.
(Breath) nine long and short Hums to the front,
Exhale and inhale three times on the right and the left,
And do this one after another (uninterruptedly).
On the third day (after you began)
The genitals will be withdrawn inwardly.

This is the meaning: Revitalise your elements by eating some nutritious food and sit up in a residence which is situated at a high altitude. While imagining the two palms as the sun and the moon, one should cross and cover them onto one's two knees. According to the practice one should exhale to the front, long, short and extremely short breaths continuously. Similarly inhale three times to the right, three in the front, three times to the left and again three times to the front. (In each position) the breaths should begin with a long one, followed by a short one, then by an extremely short (exhalation), one after another. Regarding the essential (practice) of the mind, imagine that your pure elements and all the breaths are imbibed upwards through the central channel just as water is drawn up through a straw. After training in this way for three days, as the sign of having gained control over the downward pushing air, the genitals will either be totally withdrawn inwardly or have become extremely short. If one experiences headache or nausea as a result, loosen the passage of Yakshas (the anal sphincter). If heart-burn and simultaneous defecating and urinating occur, modify the downward (movement) into an upward one.

(b) The Actual Practice: Simultaneous Emission and Holding of the Droplet

(52/A)Having concluded the limbs of meditative concentration:

> *Having concluded the blessing etc.*
> *Slightly tighten the passage (anus) of the Yakshas.*
> *Forcefully draw together the middle fingers*
> *And stare upwards in a fierce gaze,*
> *This will hold the droplet.*
> *Or forcefully recite Ha Hal*
> *And perform other physical Yantras*
> *This will also hold the droplet.*

The meaning (of the above) is as follows: Bless the space and secret organ of oneself and the wisdom consort, etc.' refers to the remembrance of the three-fold perceptions from the equality of body and speech through to the conclusion of the mutual nature of desire. Through entering into union by the kissing (touching) of the Bola and Kakkola, the ignition of the fire of passion causes the descent of the droplet. If it endows the four kisses, then recognise the simultaneously born transcendental wisdom of bliss and void and at that time slightly tighten the door-way of Yakshas (the anus) so that the droplet is not decreased. Insert the middle fingers of the right and left hands into the mouth alternately, suck on the tongue, pull out the hands and gaze upwards (into the sky). By performing all of these simultaneously the droplet will be held or else it will also be held by the forceful chanting of 'Ha Hal'. As to the other physical Yantras, one can apply the practice of the prevention of the upper air as (stated) above.[436]   In this way, without diminishing it, hold it through the three stages of the three physical movements, one verbalisation and prevention of the upper air.

(c) Conclusion: Stopping it without Losing the Droplets

(With) the 'Hing' sound of the elephant and grunting
of the tigress
The vomiting (sound) of the beasts and the
sniffing (sound) of a fox,
Draw it up through to the navel, heart,
Throat and crown respectively and permeate it in the body
By means of the gesture of perfect liberation.

As is said thus, its meaning is as follows:

Stand up with the soles of the feet on the ground and heels raised (but) laden with the body's weight. While crossing the Vajra fists at one's **(52/B)** heart and pulling up one's neck, imagine that as one inhales the air with a 'Hi Hing' sound (like an elephant) the droplet rises up to the navel, with "Hu Hum" (like a tigress) it rises up to the heart, with 'Ha Hag' (like a stag) it rises up to the throat, and with 'Hi Hik' (like a vixen) it rises up to the crown.   While holding the air (vase retention), using the gesture (mudra) of a liberated lion and shaking the head and all parts of the body and while forcefully releasing the air, the droplets will permeate throughout the body.

There are four faults which originate from unskilful practices of these paths:

1. Due to unskilfulness in descending, the droplet will quickly degenerate
2. Due to unskilfulness in holding, the bliss will be short-lived
3. Due to unskilfulness in reversing, simultaneous leakage will occur when urinating
4. Due to the unskilfulness in spreading, it will result in illnesses

There are four skilful antidotes for them:

1. The skilfulness in descending, the gait of a tortoise
2. The skilfulness in holding, the three physical and one verbal movement
3. The skilfulness in reversing, the four movements of animals
4. The skilfulness in spreading, the gesture of perfect liberation or the tying up of the belt of air etc.

The method of arising from sessions is the same as stated above.

2. THE SIMULTANEOUSLY BORN VIEW: THE FOUR DESCENDING JOYS

By meditating on these paths, the simultaneously born view of the four descending joys arises due to the essential emphasis on the element nectar. It arises on both the body and the mind and it arises in bliss, the intrinsic nature of the very self.

1. Joy, the bliss with smaller experience
2. Excellent Joy, the greatly increased bliss
3. Beyond Joy, the bliss of state of non-thought
4. Simultaneous (Joy), the inseparable bliss and emptiness

The first three joys of this and that of the fourth initiation (to be discussed) are relatively faulty since they both fall within Samsara. When one becomes accustomed to the fourth, the transcendental wisdom of 'the simultaneously born,' one will attain the final accomplishment, thus transcending Samsara. This is then called 'the faultless one'.

The method of generating the uncultivated faultless transcendental wisdom of 'the simultaneously born' is as follows:

(53/A) First go through the nine limbs of meditative concentration. If the person is a mediocre practitioner who has excelled in air (practices), (he or she) should meditate on bliss on the basis of the secret union of the lower door. If the person is a beginner, he or she should meditate on bliss on the basis of the wave of enjoyment of the upper door. Either of these two can be put into practice.

3. The Final Accomplishment of Lesser Bliss and Voidness

In this way, on the basis of having become accustomed to the transcendental wisdom of the simultaneously born view on the Samsaric path, there exists the condition in which one can realise numerous Dharmas of Nirvanic bliss and voidness on the eleventh and twelfth Bhumi, which has transcended Samsara.

4. Dakama: The Appearance of Vajrasattva at the Time of Death

If one has failed to attain the final accomplishment in this lifetime and if there is the likelihood that the time of death is already approaching while one is still meditating on the view, then the instruction on Dakama becomes necessary. As stated above in the chapter on Dakama of the Secret Initiation,[437] the air of death causes the Karmic airs to return inward, intensifying the flow of the pervasive air and causing the gross and subtle vein knots to be released in sequence. The vitality of the former (veins) being robbed by the latter (veins), the droplets which are the support of the mind also gradually merge together to be dominated by the power of the Rasana and Lalana. (Finally) the vitality of all the veins, airs and droplets is robbed by the central channel inducing the *Ham*, dwelling in its intrinsic nature of the white aspect at the crown, to descend and the short *A*, dwelling in its intrinsic nature of the red aspect at the navel, to ascend. From the re-uniting and kissing of the refined essence of all the airs, mind and droplets at the heart there then will arise the meditative concentration endowed with supreme bliss and voidness. Since 'Vajra' is empty, and 'Sattva' is bliss, it is this which is called the 'very fundamental Vajrasattva.' Although this occurs to every sentient being with a physical body, most of them fail to recognise this.

However, in the case of a Yogi who has (previously) experienced the meditative concentration of the transcendental wisdom of the simultaneously born bliss and void, the fundamentally existent (Vajrasattva) and the five refined essences of bliss **(53/B)** and void merge into one taste which has manifested due to the power of meditation. He or she will attain the final accomplishment without (having to go through the) Bardo just like meeting a person with whom one has previously been acquainted. He or she will directly perceive the ultimate transcendental wisdom equalling the excellent, immutable, great bliss and the voidness which is universal excellence.

Even though one may have had a slight familiarity with the view of bliss and voidness when one previously meditated on the path, if one has not actually developed the faultless transcendental wisdom, at this point one will depart either to Vidyadharahood or to Khechara etc. without (having to go through the) Bardo by directly realising the faultless exemplary transcendental wisdom.

The method of training in this instruction on Dakama is as follows:

314

When one assiduously practises this method of generating the faultless view and diligently maintains the transcendental wisdom generated from this (view) and because of familiarising with this, one should think, "I must recognise Vajrasattva myself, the ultimate truth of death" with a resolute mind and strong determination instead of being frightened of death. Here it is emphasised that one should persevere to remain in the view of bliss and void so that one is not controlled by deluded appearances, as it is said in the *Hevajra Tantra:*

> *That bliss which caused this death*
> *Its bliss is called 'meditative concentration.'*

As is said, this implies its practice. If one questions "What is the difference between this and the Dakama of Secret Initiation?" In the former, it is recognition of the meditative concentration on clarity and emptiness of solar and lunar eclipse airs mainly according to the stages of air dissolution. As for this, it is recognition of the meditative concentration of bliss and void of the solar and the lunar eclipse nectars since there also occurs the dissolution of the droplets during the dissolution of air. They are indeed different aspects.

5. THE BARDO: THE SIMULTANEOUSLY BORN BLISS

If it is likely that the Dakama has been ineffective, the instructions on Bardo, the path of people with inferior intelligence, become necessary. To train in this there are two divisions:

(54/A)

    A. The Preliminary (Practice)

    B. The Actual (Practice)

A. The Preliminary Practice

One should remember the three interrelated remembrances at specified times until they are recalled even in dreams:

1. *I shall remember my Guru Vajracarya, the Cittavajra Dharmakaya who showed me the secret simultaneously born transcendental wisdom*
2. *I shall remember the path of the Mandala Cakra shown by him*
3. *I shall remember the view of the simultaneously born transcendental wisdom of the descending joys developed from it*

B. The Actual Practice

Through the power of familiarisation (with the remembrances), one will be able to experience the three previous remembrances when the seven circumstantial causes of Bardo come into manifestation and the five odours manifest in the form of white and red Bodhicittas. By means of that auspicious coincidence, appearances and one's own mind will be merged into one taste enabling one to attain Vidyadharahood, etc. within that very Bardo.

6. RESULT: THE SELF-ACCOMPLISHED DHARMAKAYA

This will be discussed in the chapter on the result itself.

9

THE CORRESPONDING PRACTICES OF THE FOURTH INITIATION

There are six divisions:

1. The Path of Vajra Waves
2. The View: The Four Ascending Joys of the Suchness and Perfect Purity of all Phenomena
3. The Final Accomplishment of Extensive Bliss and Void
4. Dakama: The Transference from Mahamudra
5. The Bardo: The Transcendental Wisdom of the Excellent Bliss and Void
6. The Result: The Spontaneously born Svabhavakaya

1. THE PATH OF VAJRA WAVES

There are two sections:

A. The Preliminary Practice
B. The Actual Practice

A. The Preliminary Practice

Do either the long or short versions of the nine limbs of meditative concentration as before with the exception of the following insertion when doing the prayers in the Guru Yoga:

To the Essence Vajra, the intrinsic nature of Svabhavakaya
The ultimate Guru who has shown this (to me)
I pray to bestow upon my air the fourth initiation
And bless me to meditate on the noble path of waves!

May I realise the view of the perfect purity
And attain the final accomplishment of the
extensive bliss and void!
If I am unable to attain the final accomplishment in
this very lifetime,
(54/B)
May I effectively actualise the Phowa through the path of
Mahamudra!

If the Yoga of the Phowa becomes ineffective
By relying upon the Bardo instruction of excellent
bliss and voidness
Having attained the Vidyadharahood, Khechara etc.
May I be blessed to attain the actual Blissful body!

B. The Actual Practice

    I. The Physical Waves of the Movement of Lower Air
    II. The Peaceful and Wrathful Waves of Verbalisation
    III. The Mental Waves of Meditative Concentration

I.   *The Physical Waves of the Movement of Lower Air*

Once one has completed the six air (breathing) Yogas such as 'life' and 'effort,' one should vigorously practice the vase retention. Sit up cross legged and press the hands down to cover both your knees. Lift up the waist and pull back the belly to the vertebrae. By the means of the three exhalations and the three inhalations, inhale the upper air. Having pressed down the right and left buttocks alternately, one should gently draw in the lower air and inhale forcefully to let them (the lower and upper airs) kiss one another. When you have to release it, do it first from the lower air. This has to be practised with and without counting them in sessions. This is known as 'The Precious Vase' or 'The Bottomless Vase Retention.'

II.   *The Peaceful and Wrathful Waves of Verbalisation*

Having gone to a secluded place one should do the limbs on meditative concentration. Then sit up in a cross-legged position and cross the Vajra (fists of the hands) at one's heart. While bowing one's head to the front, do the first verbalisation pertaining to peace by softly drawing in the melody of "*E*." Later increase the volume (a little) and (gradually) make this sound louder. After that, draw in the wrathful one with the melody of "*Hum*" and (again) gradually increase the sound. This will exercise the air in the throat making one's voice as loud as the sound of a brass trumpet.

III.   *The Mental Waves of Meditative Concentration*

There are three sub-sections:

    (a) The Purification of the mental continuum of the 'Method'

(b) The Purification of the mental continuum of the
'Wisdom'

(c) The Separate Purification of the mental
continuums of both

(a) The Purification of the Continuum of the 'Method'

Complete the limbs of meditative concentration and the
visualisation of a wisdom (consort) of the lotus family[438] in front of
oneself by remembering the three-fold perceptions as before.
Then enter into union causing the refined essence of all the
elements of both the **(55/A)** father and the mother to gather into
(the syllable) *Ham* at the crown. Through the pathway of the
central channel (while generating) the four descending joys, a
droplet the size of a sesame-seed gradually becomes a whitish
illuminating light at the precious excellence of the vein situated at
the lower mouth of the father and mother's central channel. As it
transforms into light, its own colour becomes (both) invisible and
diversified either like the sun's rays (reflected) in the ocean or like
a shining dew drop (on a bright varnished surface) or like a
Kokalika[439] bird's neck. It goes up through the Rasana, the right
(channel), and endows the navel Cakra with three characteristics:

1. It becomes yal-yal (illuminated) as at day-break
2. Clear as at sun-rise
3. Tang-tang (reflexes) as coughing from the lungs

Again, it rises up through the Rasana, the right (channel), and
reaches the heart endowing it with the three characteristics. Again,
it rises up through Rasana, the right (channel), and reaches the
throat endowing it with the three characteristics. Again, it rises up
through Rasana, the right (channel). Going out through the right
ear it radiates light rays which become manifestations of Mandalas
of deities who bestow the four initiations into the mental

continuums of sentient beings who are transformed into deities. After that, these two, the manifestation and manifestor, merge into one, becoming what is known as 'the quintessence of the nectar' which is capable of transforming and empowering one's mental continuum into the five Kayas. As it reabsorbs into itself, it enters through the Door of Brahma, endowing it with the three characteristics. Reaching the throat, it becomes reddish in colour and as bright as the glorious rays of one thousand suns. As it reaches the heart it transforms into five colours as an indication of transforming one's mental continuum into the five Kayas. Having originated from the navel, the path of the pure vein, it resides at the mother's space in the form of a droplet as before, causing the waves of the right's object to become stiff thereby controlling the Rasana, the right channel and mastering exhalation. This causes the direct manifestation of the 'signlessness' of **(55/B)** the thorough door of liberation. This is the first result.

Similarly repeat this on the left. The wave of the left's subject becomes stiff, thereby controlling the Lalana, the left channel, and mastering inhalation. This causes the direct manifestation of "wishlessness" of the thorough door of liberation. This is the second result.

Similarly, repeat this on the central channel. The waves of both subject and object become stiff, thereby controlling Avadhuti, the central channel and mastering retention. The 'emptiness' of the thorough door of liberation is the third result.

(b) The Purification of the Mental Continuum of the Wisdom

Similarly, do this to the mental continuum of wisdom, except that the vein reaches to the doorway of the crown of one's central channel as well as to the right and left. It is unnecessary to radiate out because wisdom is emptiness and thus it is deprived of many activities. One should know how to apply the stiffening of the three waves, the controlling of the three veins, mastering of the three (breathing exercises) airs and direct manifestation of the three thorough doors of liberation as stated before.

(c) The Separate Purification of the Mental Continuums of Both Method and Wisdom

The refined essence situated at 'the precious excellence' shoots up like a star in the form of light rays through the central channel of both the father and the mother. As they separately absorb into the excellence of the crown of both the father and the mother, one should merely remember that both of them spontaneously accomplish the five Kayas.

During these seven moments, which consist of three moments of purifying the mental continuum of the method, three moments of purifying the mental continuum of the wisdom and one moment of purifying the individual mental continuum (of both), it is not necessary for these to correspond with the exhalation and inhalation of the airs. Nor is it required to have four definite sessions. Since it is uncertain as to where (and when) experiences will manifest, one should let whatever experiences are generated just be. When concluding the individual sessions and when it is done in conjunction with the Sadhana, one should do the concluding parts such as 'remembering of the purities' etc. accordingly.

2. VIEW: THE FOUR ASCENDING JOYS OF THE SUCHNESS AND THE PERFECT PURITY OF ALL PHENOMENA

(56/A) From meditating on that path, they (the four ascending joys) are generated through penetrating the essential points of the airs. They are generated by the body, speech and mind. They generate blissful voidness, their intrinsic nature. There are three sections:

    A.   The Advantages to the body
    B.   The Advantages to the mind
    C.   The Advantages to both the body and the mind

A. The Advantages to the Body

The congenial causes destroy the white hairs
And perfect maturation bestows powerful strength.
It develops through the person's activities
And he or she will become immortal because he or she is free
from impurities.

The meaning of this is as follows: As the refined essence remains firm at the navel, one's navel will become smooth and soft like the surface of a mirror and all the white hair and wrinkles will disappear. As the refined essence becomes firm at the heart, one will not even be defeated by the power of Narayana and (his) elephant. As it becomes firm at the throat the tongue will extensively enlarge and reach the middle of the eye-brows and when it becomes firm at the crown one will live for a thousand years or even more.

B. The Advantages to the Mind

When the refined essence becomes firm at the navel, the initial dawning of realisation of the meditative concentration of bliss and void will occur in one's mental continuum. When it remains firm at the heart, the appearance of material objects will manifest in bliss and voidness and when it is firm at the throat the Dharmas of Nirvana will manifest in bliss and voidness. When it remains firm at the crown, all the Dharmas of Samsara and Nirvana will manifest in bliss and voidness.

C. The Advantages to Both the Body and the Mind

Furthermore, when the Bodhicitta remains firm at the navel all sentient beings will appear attractive and dear to one's heart. When it is firm at the heart, one will become slightly clairvoyant. When it remains at the throat, one is able to enjoy all the tastes in the universe and when it remains firm at one's crown, one can show some minor miracles.

3. THE FINAL ACCOMPLISHMENT OF EXTENSIVE BLISS AND VOIDNESS

Thus indeed, once one is familiar with this view, i.e. the suchness of perfect purity on the Samsaric path of the twelfth and a half Bhumi, and once one has realised the 'one flavour' of the one transcendental wisdom of bliss and voidness of all the Dharmas of Samsara and Nirvana, no difference will appear between things to accept and reject, things to refrain from, and things to renounce and accomplish.

(56/B)

4. DAKAMA: THE TRANSFERENCE FROM THE MAHAMUDRA PATH

If one has failed to attain the final accomplishment in this lifetime, knowing the likelihood of imminent death while still meditating on the view, then the instructions on Dakama become necessary. There are (two) parts:

> A. The Training
> B. Familiarisation

A. The Training

It is said that generally the perfection of the seven air (breathing) practices will enable one to (properly) employ the mind to destroy old sicknesses, prevent new diseases from developing, live long (if that is desirable) and execute the Phowa effectively without any difficulties. Hence here follows the training in the breathing practices. On the first day of any of the (lunar) months and definitely in four sessions, one should practise seventeen rounds of the breathing exercises of 'life' and 'effort.' Similarly, one should increase one round for each day for twenty-one days resulting in thirty-seven rounds. Again, one should decrease one round for each day for twenty-one days to bring it down to the former scale. In this way, one should train in this until there is clarity of the flow and establishment of a definite form.

B. Familiarisation

There are two sections:

> I.   Familiarising oneself with sounds
> II. Familiarising oneself with syllables

I.   Familiarising Oneself with Sounds

The essential practice of the body is to sit up (in a kneeling position). Having concluded the limbs of meditative concentration, one should concentrate on the throat while saying "Hik" twenty times, and after the twentieth time, say 'Kahik' and take a rest. Do these two alternately. The twenty first is to be done only during its actual application. It is said that if one actualises this during training, it will shorten one's lifespan. Thus, one should train in this in association with the four definite sessions until the essential point has been detected. The signs of its detection are as follows:

1. One's hair stands on end as soon as one remembers it
2. One experiences repeated heart-burn
3. One experiences it as if one's head has been cracked

II. Familiarising Oneself with the Syllables

There are two divisions:

      (a) Familiarising with the outer syllables
      (b) Familiarising with the inner syllables

(a) Familiarising with the Outer Syllables

The doors have to be sealed with the syllables as follows:
(57/A)

1. At the anus are *'ham-ma-ra-yu'* which are all white in colour in an upright position
2. At the urethra are *'sam-ma-ra-yu'* which are all yellow in colour in an upright position
3. At the navel is *'ksum'* which is red in colour with its head in a parallel position
4. At the root of the uvula is *'sum'* which is white in colour with its head in a parallel position
5. At each of the two nostrils are blue *'yums'* with their heads in a parallel position
6. At each of the eyes are curled blue *'hums'*
7. At each of two ears are red *'yums'*
8. At the middle of the eyebrows are *'yam-ma-ra-yu'* which are yellow in colour in an inverted position
9. At the aperture of the Brahma are *'ham-ma-ra-yu'* which are white in colour in an inverted position.

All of them have moon discs and the two that are parallel are partitioned by a moon disc. If they are not clear, they will not be able to seal the doors. It is said that by meditating on them naturally, they will be able to protect one.

(b) Familiarisation with the Inner Syllables

This is somewhat similar to the Candali practice in association with the four Cakras[440] with the following differences: In between each of the two syllables, with the exception of Ha and Ksa of the white and inverted thirty-two Kalis, (the consonants) at Rasana and Lalana, one inserts one syllable of the red and upright sixteen Alis, (the vowels) alternatively and seals the doorways of the conceptualisation of subject and object. While visualising them in ascending order when breathing through the 'effort' and visualising them in descending order when breathing through the 'life' one should meditate on the syllables until they manifest as clearly as if looking at the lines on the palm of one's hand. This way of sealing the doors through the inner syllables is required 'only for this uncommon fourth' (initiation of application) but is not applicable to the other Phowas. After having detected the (near) death signs and having failed to avert death, this (Phowa) may be executed in its application. There are four kinds (of Phowa):

1. Applying it for a happier rebirth
2. Applying it (for rebirth) into another family
3. Applying it (for rebirth) into another continent or other ways of birth
4. Applying it into the path of Mahamudra

Since the first three are common to all the four initiations one should learn how to practise them elsewhere. The sole uncommon practice of the fourth is as follows:

(57/B) Having concluded the limbs of meditative concentration and having placed the body in a cross-legged position, firstly seal all the outer and then inner doors with the syllables as mentioned before. Moreover, when exhaling, imagine that from the outer form of the '*A*' up to the '*Ham*' at the crown, the air is absorbed into the central channel. When inhaling from the crown's '*Ham*' up to the outer form of '*A*' the air goes out from the central channel. One is actually breathing through the mouth and nose, although one is imagining one's air naturally penetrating into the central channel. When this actually occurs at the time of death, one's meditation becomes compatible with this practice when the airs of life and effort subsequently become exhausted at the central channel. They will be absorbed into that very perfect path. Through the power of this process and the pace of the gradual dissolution of the air, the vitality of the veins, the syllables and the element nectars will also penetrate inside the central channel. One will thereby attain direct realisation of the suchness of the perfect purity of bliss and voidness of Mahamudra, either by attaining the final accomplishment or by attaining Vidyadharahood due to familiarisation with the former meditative experiences.

5. THE BARDO: THE TRANSCENDENTAL WISDOM OF THE EXCELLENT BLISS AND VOID

If there is a likelihood that the Dakama practice is going to be ineffective then the instructions on the Bardo, the path of the inferior person, become necessary. There are two divisions in its training:

  A. The Preliminary Practice
  B. The Actual Practice

A. The Preliminary Practice

One should train to remember the three interrelated remembrances at specified times until they are recalled even in dreams:

> One should remember my Guru Vajracarya, the Hrdyavajra
> Svabhavakaya who showed me the ultimate suchness of the
> perfect purity of all Dharmas
> One should remember the path of Vajra Waves shown by him
> One should remember the view of perfect purity of suchness of
> the ascending joys of 'firm bottom' developed from it

B. The Actual Practice

Through the power of such familiarisation one will be able to remember the three **(58/A)** remembrances when the seven circumstantial causes of Bardo manifest and also the five odours will also appear as (the breathing process) of exhalation, inhalation and retention. Finally, the two veins become of the same flavour as the central channel. The two airs become the same flavour as the retention. Their auspicious coinciding causes one's mind and all appearances to become one flavour. One will attain Vidyadharahood in the Bardo itself.

6. RESULT: THE SPONTANEOUSLY BORN SVABHAVAKAYA

This will be discussed in the chapter on the result itself.

The Essence of the Elegant Teachings of the Three Tantras

How to Directly Attain the
Results of The Five Bodies
(Kayas)

The ultimate result will be attained by succeeding in the body method Tantra. When the four supporting Mandalas are transformed, the supported basis of all *(kun-gzhi)* itself is also transformed by having all of its impurities and propensities purified. The four bodies which are free from their obscurations become the directly manifested Svabhavakaya, the intrinsic nature of their perfect purity. This causes the actual direct realisation of the five bodies. At that time while not moving from the sphere of equanimity and transcendental wisdom, the blind will obtain eyes, the deaf will hear sounds as the greatness of (benefiting) other beings. Through one's body and speech one will open inconceivable doors of Dharma, which will assist sentient beings to subdue themselves according to their temperament, intention and predispositions. Subsequently one will preach the Dharma at all times uninterruptedly so that the auspicious blessings gather to fulfil all the wishes of sentient beings effortlessly.

COLOPHON

Filled with the quintessence of the nectar of the ultimate
And boundless secret Tantras of the Great Secret,
The vase of the noble mouth of Mahasiddha Virupa
Is indeed the noble path leading all fortunate beings to the
excellence of immortality.

(58/B) From the successive Sakya masters came
this transmission of
The downpouring of the elegant teachings
into Evampa's mouth
Causing its currents of waves to spread in
one hundred directions
And permeating the world with glorious
enlightened activities.

Other than those of The Beautiful Ornament
of the Three Tantras,[441]
Here in the language and its meaning there is nothing
arising from my own effort;
However, in order to simplify the practice and
to teach (others)
The practical meditational exercises have been
compiled exclusively.

Whatever errors there may have been from compiling this
I shall confess them with all the misdeeds (accumulated) since
beginningless time.
Having undertaken this with exceedingly pure sincerity
To benefit myself and others who share a similar fortune,

Whatever collection of virtuous deeds there may
have been accrued
I shall always offer it to the hosts of the Gurus
Imagining them as the offering clouds of Samantabhadra.
Please bestow upon me and sentient beings all of our wishes!

Thus 'The Essence of the Elegant Teachings of the Main Stages of
Instructions of the Three Tantras' of the Sacred and Precious Path
and (including its) Result Teachings was compiled carefully at *spu-*
dkar bla-brang rdzong) near *dpal-bzang ldan* in the year of the
water female pig (1623) by Bhiksu, the holder of the pitakas,
Ngawang Choedak. I had the good fortune to possess the Four
Whispered Lineages such as the undried stream of the initiation
etc. since I first received the complete teachings of this path
including its subsidiaries due to the kindness of the omniscient
holder of everything, Mangtho Ludrup Gyatsho and later again
received the complete teachings due to the kindness of the great
and precious abbot whose name if I may (be permitted to) disclose
here for this purpose is Khenchen Rinpoche Wangchuk Palzang.
The scribing work was respectfully undertaken by Jampa Choedak.

(59/A) May this also help to prosper and spread the teachings of
the Three Tantras together with its pith instructions, the father
teachings of the glorious Sakyapas!

Subhamstusarvajagatam

DEDICATION

I thank the following people who have made generous donations towards this translation:

Malaysian Donors:
Kuantan Dzongsar Manjushri Centre, Tan How Chee, Joseph K. Ling, Lim Chan Kwang, Mdm. Thong Lee Thor, Chan Chun Weng, Mr. and Mrs. Wong, Miss Au Mun Yin, Mr. Mrs. S. K. Yaui and Tan Chin Hua.

Australian Donors:
Daryl Dorje, Brian and Megan, Atisha Center, Jenny Chen, Mark Thomann, Ken Gardiner, Merril Cook, Vajrayogini Retreatants at Vajradhara Gompa, Tony Pratt, George Roubis, David Cheah, Rod Woolley, Sakya Losal Choe-Dzong, Rongton Buddhist Training College and the late Venerable Gyalsay Tulku Rinpoche.

Hong Kong Donors:
Tan Chin Hor, David Tsang, Lau Mo Hung, Lam Bik Ling, Leung Mo Man, Yeung Chun Poh, Fung Man Ki, Mandy, Chan Oi Chu, Yeow Yow Kit, So How, Le Kwai Kiu, Lau Yui Keung, Wong KareWai, Ho Pink Kee, Chan Ying Sze, Lai Shuk Yee, Chan Kit Chun, Wong Siu Kee, Lai Lit Ki, Lau Yui Keung, Lee Shing Hing, Lee Kok Choi, Ching Wai Ling, Leung Kar Shin, Anthony Ng Po Yee, Tsui Pui Fong, Gem Stone Jewellery, Tse Siu Fu, Peter Lee, Shiu Cheong Wong Kok Wah, Lam Shau Lan., Chun Pak Kong, Lam Tin Wai, Artorient Company, C. H. Tan, Yan Mei Lee, Lau Fook Hing and Hong Kong Dharma Friends.

May the blessings of the Triple Gem
And the Dharma protectors bestow

Upon them with good health, happiness, prosperity
And attain enlightenment for the benefit of all sentient beings.

May their deceased relatives
Be freed from the fears of the Bardo
And be reborn in the pure land of Sukhavati!
May the blessings of the Triple Gem be always with them!

BIBLIOGRAPHY OF SA SKYA LAM 'BRAS LITERATURE SERIES (SLLS)

Published by Secretary General
Sakya Centre, 187 Rajpur Road, Dehra Dun, U. P. India 1983

Note: The title number and Tibetan alphabetical notation are according to the order of thirty one volumes and works contained therein.

Vol. 1 Ka [slob bshad]

SLLS (LS) Ka. 1, ff. 1 - 13
Hagiography of Virupa
bla ma 'phags bod kyi lo rgyus las rnal 'byor dbang phyugs bir va pa'i lo rgyus
Author: rJe btsun grags pa rgyal mtshan (1147-1216)

SLLS Ka. 2, ff. 14 - 17
Hagiography of Drogmi Lotsawa
bla ma bod kyi lo rgyus bla chen 'brog mi lo tsa ba'i lo rgyus
Author: rJe btsun grags pa rgyal mtshan (1147-1216)

SLLS Ka. 3, ff. 18 - 31
Hagiography of Sachen Kunga Nyingpo
sa chen kun dga' snying po'i rnam thar
Author: rJe btsun grags pa rgyal mtshan (1147-1216)

SLLS Ka. 4, ff. 32 - 34
Hagiography of Sonam Tsemo
bSod nams rtse mo'i rnam thar
Author: rJe btsun grags pa rgyal mtshan (1147-1216)

SLLS Ka. 5, A ff. 35 - 56

Hagiography of Drakpa Gyaltshan
rJe btsun rin po che'i rnam par thar pa
Author: sBal ston seng ge rgyal mtshan

SLLS Ka. 6, (A) ff. 57 - 63, (B) ff. 64 - 75
Versified Hagiography of Sakya Pandita
Chos rje sa pan gyi rnam thar
Author: yar klung pa grags pa rgyal mtshan

SLLS Ka. 7, ff. 77 - 112
Hagiography of Sakya Pandita
sa pan gyi rnam thar
Author: rin chen dpal

SLLS Ka. 8, ff. 113 - 133
Hagiography of Sakya Pandita
rnam thar gsung sgros ma
Author: 'phags pa blo gros rgal mtshan (1235-1280)

SLLS Ka. 9, ff. 134 - 289
Path of the Fortunate Aeon: A Hagiography of Sakya Pandita
rnam thar skal pa bzang po'i legs lam
Author: rin spung ngag dbang 'jig rten dbang phyug grags pa (in 1255)

SLLS Ka. 10, ff. 290 - 338
Hagiography of Dharma King Choegyal Phakpa (1235-1280)
bla ma dam pa chos kyi rgyal po rin po che'i rnam par thar pa
Author: ye shes rgyal mtshan (in 1283)

SLLS Ka. 11, ff. 338 - 340
Hagiography of Tshog Gom Kunga Pal (-1307)
bLa ma tshogs sgom rin po che'i rnam thar
Author: ?

SLLS Ka. 12, ff. 341 - 344
Hagiography of Nyenchen Sonam Tenpa (lived 96years)
Nyen chen bsod nam bstan pa'i rnam thar

Author: ?

SLLS Ka. 13, ff. 345 - 361
Auto-Hagiography of Rinchen Senge
shangs kyi bla ma chos rje rin chen seng ge'i rnam thar rang gis mdzad pa

SLLS Ka. 14, ff. 362 - 367
Hagiography of Zhang Konchok Pal (1240-1302)
zhang dkon mchog dpal ba'i rnam thar
Author: dGe slong dpal ldan tshul khrims (1333-1389)

SLLS Ka. 15, ff. 367 - 374
Hagiography of Gyalwa Drakphukpa Sonam Pal (1277-1350)
rgyal ba brag phug pa'i rnam thar
Author: dpal ldan blo gros brtan pa (1315-1358)

SLLS Ka. 16, ff. 374 - 385
Hagiography of Hermit Lodro Tenpa (1315-1358)
ri khrod pa blo gros brtan pa'i rnam thar
Author: dge slong dpal ldan tshul khrims (1333-1389)

SLLS Ka. 17, ff. 386 - 406
Hagiography of Lama Dampa Sonam Gyaltshan (1312-1375)
bla ma dam pa bsod nams rgyal mtshan gyi rnam thar
Author: dge slong dpal ldan tshul khrims (1333-1389)

SLLS Ka. 18, ff. 406 - 412
Hagiography of Lama Dampa Paldhen Tshultrim
bla ma dam pa dpal ldan tshul khrims gyi rnam thar
Author: mus chen dkon mchog rgyal mtshan (1388-1469)

SLLS Ka. 19, ff. 413 - 431
Hagiography of Mahasiddha Buddha Shri (1339-1419)
grub chen bu dddha shri'i rnam thar
Author: ngor chen kun dga' bzang po (1382-1456)

SLLS Ka. 20, ff. 432 - 473
A short Hagiography of Ngorchen Kunga Sangpo

339

ngor chen gyi rnam thar mdor bsdus
Author: mus chen dkon mchog rgyal mtshan (1388-1469)

SLLS Ka. 21, ff. 475 - 585
Ocean of Collected Elegant Sayings: A Hagiography of Ngorchen
Kunga Sangpo
rnam thar legs bshad chu bo 'dus pa'i rgya mtsho
Author: dge slong dpal ldan don grub (1563-1636)

SLLS Ka. 22, ff. 586 - 627
Wondrous Ocean: A Hagiography of Muchen Konchok Gyaltshen
(1388-1469)
mus chen gyi rnam thar ngo mtshar rgya mtsho
Author: go ram pa bsod nams seng ge (1429-1489)

Vol. 2 Kha [slob bshad]

SLLS (LS) Kha. 23, ff. 1 - 33
Wondrous Garland: A Hagiography of Muchen
mus chen gyi rnam thar ngo mtshar phreng ba
Author: bDag chen blo gros rgyal mtshan (1444-1479)

SLLS Kha. 24, ff. 35 - 151
Garland of Utpala Flowers:
A Hagiography of Dagchen Lodro Gyaltshen (1444-1479)
bdag chen blo gros rgyal mtshan gyi rnam thar ut pa la'i do shal
Author: Tshar chen blo gsal rgya mtsho (1502-1567)

SLLS Kha. 25, ff. 153 - 247
A Hagiography of Doringpa Kun-pangpa Chenpo (1449-1524)
rje btsun kun spang pa chen po'i rnam thar ngo mtshar dad pa'i spu long
Author: Tshar chen blo gsal rgya mtsho (1502-1567)

SLLS Kha. 26, ff. 249 - 397
A Treasure of Jewel: A Hagiography of Gorum Kunga Lekpa (1477-
1544 ?)
rje btsun sgo rum pa'i ram thar yid bzhin chu gter

Author: 'jam dbyangs mkhyen brtse dbang phyug (1524-1568)

SLLS Kha. 27, ff. 399 - 638
Solar Radiance of of the Dharma: A Hagiography of Tsharchen
(1502-1567)
tshar chen rdo rje 'chang gi rnam thar bstan pa'i nyi 'od
Author: Vth Dalai Lama (1617-1682)

Vol. 3 Ga (slob bshad)

SLLS (LS) Ga. 28, ff. 1 - 250
Wondrous Kernel: An Auto-Hagiography of the Great Abbot (1524-
1568)
bla ma rin po che mkhan chen pa'i rnam thar ngo mtshar snye ma

SLLS Ga. 29, ff. 251 - 394
A Hagiography of Great Abbot Zhonu Lodro (1527-1599)
mkhan chen gzhon nu blo gros rnam thar
Author: bDag chen blo gros rgyal mtshan (1444-1479)

SLLS Ga. 30, ff. 395 - 625
Auto-Hagiography of Dagchen Lodro Gyaltshen (1444-1479)
rang gi rnam thar yul sna tshogs kyi bdud rtsi myong ba'i gtam du
byas pa zol zog rdzun gyis ma bslad pa sgeg ma'i me long

Vol. 4 Nga (slob bshad)

SLLS (LS) Nga. 31, ff. 1 - 123
A Hagiography of Maitri Dondrup Gyaltshen (1527-1587)
rje btsun rdo rje 'chang mai tri don grub rgyal mtshan
Author: mi pham chos rgya mtsho

SLLS Nga. 32, ff. 125 - 151
Reservoir of Faith: A Hagiography of Jetsun Dingmapa Chenpo
(1526-1577)
rje btsun sdings ma chen po'i rnam thar byin brlab kyi chu gter
Author: dBang phyug rab brtan (1559-1636)

SLLS Nga. 33, ff. 153 - 335

A Hagiography of Great Abbot Sonam Choephel (1527-1603)
mkhan chen bsod nams chos 'phel gyi rnam thar
Author: dkon mchog rdo rje

SLLS Nga. 34, ff. 337 - 387
A Hagiography of Panchen Ngawang Choedak (1572-1641)
mkhan chen ngag dbang chos grags kyi rnam thar
Author: dgon gsar ba bsod nams rgyal mtshan

SLLS Nga. 35, ff. 389 - 497
A Hagiography of Wangchuk Rabten (1559-1636)
dbang phyug rab brtan gyi rnam thar
Author: Vth Dalai Lama (1617-1682)

SLLS Nga. 36, ff. 499 - 701
A Hagiography of Kagyurwa Gonpo Sonam Chogdhen (1603-1659)
mgon po bsod nams mchod ldan gyi rnam thar
Author: Vth Dalai Lama (1617-1682)

Vol. 5 Ca (slob bshad)

SLLS (LS) Ca. 37, ff. 1 - 109
A Hagiography of Shalu Rinchen Sonam Chogdrup (1602-1681)
rin chen bsod nams mchog grub kyi rnam thar
Author: Vth Dalai Lama (1617-1682)

SLLS Ca. 38, ff. 111 - 449
An Auto-Hagiography (1633-1703)
lce btsun ngag gi dbang phyug mkhyen rab byams pa'i rang rnam
Author: lCe btsun mkhyen rab byams pa (1633-1703)

SLLS Ca. 39, ff. 451 - 626
An Auto-Hagiography (1654-1728)
rmor chen kun dga' lhun grub kyi rnam thar
Author: rMor chen kun dga' lhun grub (1654-1728)

Vol. 6 Cha (slob bshad)

SLLS (LS) Cha. 40, ff. 1 - 300

Hagiography of Nesarpa (1704-1760)
gnas gsar pa chen po 'jam mgon bla ma thams cad mkhyen pa legs pa'i rgyal mtshan gyi rnam thar ngo mtshar rab 'byams
Author:

Vol. 7 Ja (slob bshad)

SLLS (LS) Ja. 41, ff. 1 - 147
A Hagiography of Thartse Khuwon Jampa Namkha Chime (1765-1820)
thar rtse khu dbon byams pa nam mkha' 'chi med kyi rnam thar
Author: byams pa kun dga' bstan pa'i rgyal mtshan (1829-1870)

SLLS Ja. 42, ff. 148 - 345
A Hagiography of Jampa Kunga Tenzin (1776-1862)
byams pa kun dga' btsan 'dzin gyi rnam thar
Author: byams pa kun dga' bstan pa'i rgyal mtshan (1829-1870)

SLLS Ja. 43, ff. 346 -523
A Hagiography of Naljor Jampal Sangpo (1789-1864)
rnal 'byor 'jam dpal bzang po'i rnam thar
Author: byams pa kun dga' bstan pa'i rgyal mtshan (1829-1870)

SLLS Ja. 44, ff. 524 - 678
A Hagiography of Jampa Kunga Tenpay Gyaltshen (1829-1870)
byams pa kun dga' bstan pa'i rgal mtshan gyi rnam thar
Author: 'jam dbyangs blo gter dbang po (1847-1914)

Vol. 8 Nya (slob bshad)

SLLS (LS) Nya. 45, ff. 1 -235
A Hagiography of Jamyang Khyentse Wangpo (1820-1892)
'jam dbyangs mkhyen brtse dbang po kun dga' bstan pa'i rgyal mtshan dpal bzang po'i rnam thar mdor bsdus
Author: kong sprul ngag dbang yon tan rgya mtsho (1813-1899)

SLLS Nya. 46, ff. 237 - 335
A Hagiography of Jamyang Loter Wangpo (1847-1914)
'jam dbyangs blo gter dbang po'i rnam par thar pa

Author: mkhan chen bsam gtan blo gros (1868-1931)

SLLS Nya. 47, ff. 337 - 387
A Hagiography of Ga Ngawang Lekpa (1864-1941)
bla ma rdo rje 'chang sga ston ngag dbang kun dga' legs pa'i 'byung gnas kyi rnam thar
Author: sDe gzhung sprul sku kun dga' bstan pa'i rgyal mtshan (1885-1952)

SLLS Nya. 48, ff. 389 - 414
A Hagiography of Khangsar Khenchen Dampa Rinpoche Ngawang Lodro Shenphen Nyingpo (1876-1952)
rje btsun bla ma dpal e wam khang gsar mkhan chen ngag dbang blo gros gzhan phan snying po'i rnam thar
Author: tre hor gdong thog sprul sku btsan pa'i rgyal mtshan

SLLS Nya. 49, ff. 415 - 465
A Commentary on Fifty Verses of Guru Devotion
bshes gnyen dam pa bsten par byed pa'i thabs shloka lnga bcu pa'i 'grel pa
Author: Tshar chen blo gsal rgya mtsho (1502-1567)

Vol. 9 Ta (slob bshad)

SLLS (LS) Ta. 50, ff. 1 - 760
Solar Radiance: An Extensive Commentary on Hevajra Tantra
rgyud kyi rgyal po dpal kye rdo rje'i rgya cher 'grel pa nyi ma'i 'od zer
Author: bLa ma dam pa bsod nams rgyal mtshan (1312-1375)

Vol. 10 Tha (slob bshad)

SLLS (LS) Tha. 51, ff. 1 - 325
Garland of Precious Diamond: A Commentary on the Root Tantra
rtsa rgyud tshig 'grel dag ldan bsrubs skyes rdo rje rin po che'i phreng ba
Authors: pan chen ngag dbang chos grags (1572-1641) and 'jam dbyangs blo gter dbang po (1847-1914)

SLLS (LS) Tha. 52, ff. 327 - 581
Sun's Rays: An Exposition on Hevajra (Sadhana)
dpal kye rdo rje'i rnam bshad nyi ma'i 'od zer
Author: tshar chen blo gsal rgya mtsho (1502-1567)

Vol. 11 Da (slob bshad)

SLLS (LS) Da. 53, ff. 1 - 8
Bibliography of Lamdre Works
gsung ngag rin po che lam 'bras bu dang bcas pa'i don gsal bar byed
pa glegs bam gyi dkar chag
Author: rJe btsun grags pa rgyal mtshan (1147-1216)

SLLS Da. 54, ff. 9 345
The Yellow Annals: An Exposition on Root Vajra Verses
rtsa ba rdo rje tshig rkang gtsos pod ser gzhung bshad
Author: rje btsun grags pa rgyal mtshan (1147-1216)

SLLS Da. 55, ff. 348 - 386
The Instruction on Inconceivable According to Kotalipa
tog rtse pa'i bsam mi khyab pa'i gdams ngag
Author: Kotalipa

SLLS Da. 56, ff. 387 - 399
Simultaneously Born Accomplishment of Dombi Heruka
dom bhi he ru kas mdzad pa'i lhan cig skyes grub
Author: Dombi Heruka

SLLS Da. 57, ff. 399 - 406
Received In Front of a Stupa of Nagarjuna
slob dpon klu sgrub kyi mdzad pa'i mchod rten drung thob
Compiled by rJe btsun grags pa rgyal mtshan (1147-1216)

SLLS Da. 58, ff. 406 - 419
Mahamudra Without Letters According to Vagendrakirti
slob dpon ngag dbang grags pas mdzad pa'i phyag rgya chen po yi
ge med pa
Compiled by rJe btsun grags pa rgyal mtshan (1147-1216)

SLLS Da. 59, ff. 419 - 443
The Nine Profound Methods by Saroruha
slob dpon pad ma ba dzras mdzad pa'i bskyed rim zab pa'i tshul dgus bryan pa
Compiled by rJe btsun grags pa rgyal mtshan (1147-1216)

SLLS Da. 60, ff. 445 - 456
The Complete Path of Psychic Fire by Krishnacarin
slob dpon nag po spyod pas mdzad pa'i gtum mo lam rdzogs
Compiled by rJe btsun grags pa rgay mtshan (1147-1216)

SLLS Da. 61, ff. 457 - 460
The Instruction on Straightening the Crooked by Utsita Amara
nag po u tsi ta 'chi ba med pas mdzad pa yon po srong ba'i gdams ngag Compiled by rJe btsun grags pa rgyal mtshan (1147-1216)

SLLS Da. 62, ff. 461 - 479
Complete Path of Mudra by Indrabhuti
slob dpon in da bhu tis mdzad pa'i phyag rgya'i lam skor
Compiled by rJe btsun grags pa rgyal mtshan (1147-1216)

SLLS Da. 63, ff. 481 - 580
A Brief Book of the Citations
lung 'di nyid dang mdor bsdus su sbyar ba
Author: rJe btsun grags pa rgyal mtshan (1147-1216)

SLLS Da. 64, ff. 581 - 593 (See Ka. 1)
Hagioraphy of Indian Gurus
bla ma brgyud pa rgya gar ba'i lo rgyus
Author: rJe btsun grags pa rgyal mtshan (1147-1216)

SLLS Da. 65, ff. 594 - 599 (See Ka. 2)
Hagiography of Tibetan Gurus
bla ma brgyud pa bod kyi lo rgyus
Author: rJe btsun grags pa rgyal mtshan (1147-1216)

Vol. 12 Na (slob bshad)

SLLS (LS) Na. 66, ff. 1 - 446

For the Sons: An Exposition on Lamdre
lam 'bras gzhung bshad sras don ma
Edited by phul chung ba

SLLS Na. 67, ff. 447 - 476
An Outlined Synthesis of Vajragatha
rdo rje tshig rkang gi bsdus don dang sa bcad kyis bkral ba

SLLS Na. 68, ff. 477 - 615
Technical Key:
A Manual to Teach the Uncommon Ngor Lamdre Lobshe Tradition
gsung ngag rin po che lam 'bras bu bcas pa ngor lugs thun mong ma
yin pa slob bshad kyi 'chad thabs gsang chen mdzod brgya 'byed pa'i
legs dshad 'phrul gyi lde'u mig
Author: 'jam dbyangs blo gter dbang po (1847-1914)

Vol. 13 Pa (slob bshad)

SLLS (LS) Pa. 69, ff. 1 - 469
Miscelleneous Lamdre Works
According to the Bibliography of Minor Red Annals
lam 'bras pu sti dmar chung dkar chag ltar gsung thor bu tshar du
dngar ba tshangs 'grigs
Author: mus chen dkon mchog rgyal mtshan (1388-1469)

SLLS Pa. 70, ff. 471 - 609
Initiation Rites on the Six-Limbed of Body Mandala Path Initiation
According to Hevajra Instruction Lineage, Clear Mirror of Initiating
Rites, Blessing of Path of the Profound Guru Yoga
dpal kye rdo rje man ngag lugs kyi mngon rtogs yan lag drug pa lus
dkyil lam dus kyi dbang chog, dbang bskur ba'i cho ga gsal ba'i me
long, lam zab mo rnal 'byor gyi byin rlabs nyams len
Author: mus chen dkon mchog rgyal mtshan (1388-1469)

Vol. 14 Pha (slob bshad)

SLLS (LS) Pha. 71, ff. 1 - 225
Flourish of the Great Secret Doctrine: A Lamdre History

*gsung ngag rin po che lam 'bras bu dang bcas pa'i khog phub kyi
rnam bshad las gdams ngag byung tshul gyi zin bris gsang chen
btsan pa rgyas byed (lam 'bras slob bshad khog phub)*
Author: 'jam dbyangs mkhyen brtse dbang phyug (1524 -1568)

SLLS Pha. 72, ff. 227 - 234
Nejar ma: A Lineage Guru Prayer of Lamdre
*gsung ngag rin po che lam 'bras bu dang bcas pa'i bla ma brgyud pa
la gsol ba 'debs pa gnas sbyar ma*
Author: rGyal ba brag phug pa (1277-1350)

SLLS Pha. 73, ff. 235 - 247
Kunzang Wangshi ma: A Prayer to the Gurus of the Three
Combined Lineages of Lamdre with Prayer to Realize the
Graduated Path of Lamdre
*gsung ngag rin po che brgyud pa gsum 'dus kyi bla ma la gsol ba
'debs a lam rim smon lam dang bcas pa*
Author: 'jam dbyangs mkhyen brtse dbang phyug (1524-1568)

SLLS Pha. 74, ff. 248 - 251
Namdak ma: A Prayer to The Lineage Gurus of Lamdre
gsung ngag rin po che'i brgyud 'debs
Author: ngor chen kun dga' bzang po (1382-1456)

SLLS Pha. 75, ff. 253 - 344
The Unmistaken Tradition of Khau Drak Dzongpa:
The Path of The Three Visions
*snang ba gsum du bstan pa'i lam gyi zin bris kha'u brag rdzong pa'i
bzhed pa ma nor ba*
Author: 'jam dbyangs mkhyen brtse dbang phyug (1524-1568)

SLLS Pha. 76, ff. 345 - 433
The Path of The Three Tantras: The Practice of Old Monk Khyentse
*rgyud gsum du bstan pa'i lam gyi zin bris kha'u brag rdzong pa'i
khyad chos ban rgan mkhyen brtse'i nyams len*
Author: 'jam dbyangs mkhyen brtse dbang phyug (1524-1568)

SLLS Pha. 77, ff. 435 - 503

The Unmistaken Tradition of Khau Drak Dzongpa:
Notes on Outer Generation Stage Practice
phyi bskyed rim gyi zin bris kha'u brag rdzong pa'i bzhed pa ma nor ba
Author: 'jam dbyangs mkhyen brtse dbang phyug (1524-1568)

SLLS Pha. 78, ff. 505 - 517
The Unmistaken Tradition of Khau Drak Dzongpa:
Notes on Inner Generation Stage Practice
nang bskyed rim gyi zin bris kha'u brag rdzong pa'i bzhed pa ma nor ba
Author: 'jam dbyangs mkhyen brtse dbang phyug (1524-1568)

SLLS Pha. 79, ff. 519 - 553
The Unmistaken Tradition of Khau Drak Dzongpa: Notes on Dream
Yoga etc.
rmi lam man gyi zin bris kha'u brag rdzong pa'i bzhed pa ma nor ba
Author: 'jam dbyangs mkhyen brtse dbang phyug (1524-1568)

SLLS Pha. 80, ff. 555 - 619
Lamdre Annals of Three Practical Rituals
bsnyen pa gsum gyi lag len gsung ngag be'u bum
Author: mang thos klu sgrub rgya mtsho (1523 - 1594)

Vol. 15 Ba (slob bshad)

SLLS (LS) Ba. 81, ff. 1 - 12
Prayer to the Lineage Gurus of Lobshe Tradition
slob bshad brgyud 'debs lam rim dang bcas pa
Author: mang thos klu sgrub rgya mtsho (1523-1594)

SLLS Ba. 82, ff. 13 - 29
Prayer to the Lineage Gurus of The Three Tantras
dges mdzad rgyud gsum brgyud 'debs
Author: mang thos klu sgrub rgya mtsho (1523-1594)

SLLS Ba. 83, ff. 31 - 151
The Three Visions

snang gsum khrid yig zla ba bdud rtsi'i thig phreng
Author: mang thos klu sgrub rgya mtsho (1523-1594)

SLLS Ba. 84, ff. 153 - 240
The Instruction on Path of Mantra
sngags lam gyi khrid yig nyi gzhon gsar pa'i thig phreng
Author: mang thos klu sgrub rgya mtsho (1523-1594)

SLLS Ba. 85, ff. 241 - 255
Outer Generation Stage
phyi bsked rim
Author: mang thos klu sgrub rgya mtsho (1523-1594)

SLLS Ba. 86, ff. 257 - 274
Inner Generation Stage
nang bskyed rim
Author: mang thos klu sgrub rgya mtsho (1523-1594

SLLS Ba. 87, ff. 275 - 315
Vase Initiation
bum dbang
Author: mang thos klu sgrub rgya mtsho (1523-1594)

SLLS Ba. 88, ff. 317 - 359
Secret Initiation
gsang dbang gi khrid yig
Author: mang thos klu sgrub rgya mtsho (1523-1594)

SLLS Ba. 89, ff. 361 - 378
Transcendental Wisdom Initiation
shes rab ye shes kyi dbang
Author: mang thos klu sgrub rgya mtsho (1523-1594)

SLLS Ba. 90, ff. 379 - 404
The Fourth Initiation
dbang bzhi pa'i 'khrid
Author: mang thos klu sgrub rgya mtsho (1523-1594)

SLLS Ba. 91, ff. 405 - 646

Dispelling Doubts of Darkness: A Synthesis of Two Instruction Manuals
khrid kyi zung bcud bsdus log rtog som nyi mun sel
Author: 'jam dbyangs blo gter dbang po (1847-1914)

SLLS Ba. 92, ff. 647 - 648
Supplementary to Prayer to Lineage Gurus
rgyud bshad brgyud 'debs kyi kha skong

Vol. 16 Ma (slob bshad)

SLLS (LS) Ba. 93, ff. 1 - 121
Wondrous Vision: Black Annals of the Lineage Gurus
lam 'bras pod nag bla ma brgyud pa'i rnam thar ngo mtshar snang ba
Author: bLa ma dam pa bsod nams rgyal mtshan (1312-1375)

SLLS Ba. 94, ff. 123 - 449
An Exposition of Treasure of Instructions
gzhung bshad man ngag gter mdzod
Author: bLa ma dam pa bsod nams rgyal mtshan (1312-1375)

SLLS Ba. 95, ff. 451 - 543
Illucidating the Hidden Meanings
sbas don kun gsal
Author: bLa ma dam pa bsod nams rgyal mtshan (1312-1375)

SLLS Ba. 96, ff. 545 - 597
Clear Realisation (Abhisamaya) of the Glorious Hevajra
kye rdor mngon rtogs
Author: bLa ma dam pa bsod nams rgyal mtshan (1312-1375)

SLLS Ba. 97, ff. 598 - 605
Initiation Rites of the Body Mandala
lus dkyil dbang chog
Author: bLa ma dam pa bsod nams rgyal mtshan (1312-1375)

SLLS Ba. 98, ff. 606 - 614
Guru Yoga

bla ma'i rnal 'byor zhal shes
Author: bLa ma dam pa bsod nams rgyal mtshan (1312-1375)

Vol. 17 Tsa (slob bshad)

SLLS (LS) Tsa. 99, ff. 1 - 417
The Essential Moon's Rays of Generation Stage: An Exegesis of Hevajra Sadhana
dpal kye rdo rje'i sgrub thabs rgya cher bshad pa bkyed rim gnad kyi zla zer
Author: ngor chen kun dga' bzang po (1382-1456)

SLLS Tsa. 100, ff. 419 - 640
Illucidating the Pith Instructions: An Exegesis of Hevajra Sadhana
kye rdor man ngag lugs kyi bskyed rim rnam bshad man ngag gsal byed
Author: go ram pa bsod nam seng ge (1429-1489)

Vol 18 Tsha (slob bshad)

SLLS (LS) Tsha. 101, ff. 1 - 27
Illucidating the Meaning of Signs
brda don gsal ba
Author: bDag chen blo gros rgyal mtshan (1444-1495)

SLLS Tsha. 102, ff. 27 - 32
Explanation of the Hidden Path
lam sbas bshad
Author: bDag chen blo gros rgyal mtshan (1444-1495)

SLLS Tsha. 103, ff. 32 - 58
Non-Differentiation of Samsara and Nirvana
'khor 'das dbyer med
Author: bDag chen blo gros rgyal mtshan (1444-1495)

SLLS Tsha. 104, ff. 58 - 65
Essential Visualization
dmigs gnad
Author: pan chen ngag dbang chos grags (1572-1651)

SLLS Tsha. 105, ff. 65 - 92
Explanation of Vajra and Bell
rdor dril rnam bshad
Author: bDag chen blo gros rgyal mtshan (1444-1495)

SLLS Tsha. 106, ff. 92 - 113
Method of Blessing Nectar Pills
bdud rtsi ril bu sgrub pa
Author: bDag chen blo gros rgyal mtshan (1444-1495)

SLLS Tsha. 107, ff. 113 - 115
Method of Repelling Malediction Through Asta (Mantra)
asta'i byad zlog
Author: bDag chen blo gros rgyal mtshan (1444-1495)

SLLS Tsha. 108, ff. 115 - 242
Essential Notes From Shalu Khenchen and Ludrub Gyatsho
nyer mkho'i zin bris zhwa lu mkhan chen gsung dang klu sgrub gsung skor
Edited by mGon po bsod nams mchog ldan (1603-1659)

SLLS Tsha. 109, ff. 243 - 274
Beautiful Ornament of Six-Limbed Clear Realisation (Abhisamaya)
mngon rtogs yan lag drug pa'i mdzes rgyan
Author: ngor chen dkon mchog lhun grub (1497-1557)

SLLS Tsha. 110, ff. 275 - 292
Beautiful Ornament of Body Mandala
lus dkyil mdzes rgyan
Author: ngor chen dkon mchog lhun grub (1497-1557)

SLLS Tsha. 111, ff. 293 - 364
Beautiful Ornament of Great River of Initiation
dbang chu chen mo mdzes rgyan
Author: ngor chen dkon mchog lhun grub (1497-1557)

SLLS Tsha. 112, ff. 365 - 374
Praise and Benediction Verses

bstod pa bkra shis
Author: Saroruha

SLLS Tsha. 113, ff. 375 - 398
Beautiful Ornament of Torma Rites
gtor chog mdzes rgyan
Author: ngor chen dkon mchog lhun grub (1497-1557)

SLLS Tsha. 114, ff. 399 - 476
A Synthesis of Instructions on Initiation Rites
dbang chog man ngag gi snying po
Author: 'jam dbyangs blo gter dbang po (1847-1914)

SLLS Tsha. 115, ff. 477 - 536
Initiation Rites of Path Initiation
lam dbang bskur chog
Author: bDag chen blo gros rgyal mtshan (1444-1495)

SLLS Tsha. 116, ff. 537 - 626
A Guide Illucidating the River of Hevajra Initiation
dpal kye rdo rje'i dbang gi chu bo'i gsal byed kyi lhan thabs
Author: Tshar chen blo gsal rgya mtsho (1502-1567)

Vol. 19 Dza (slob bshad)

SLLS (LS) Dza. 117, ff. 1 - 39
Clear Unmistaken Path: A Sadhana of Vajranairatmya
rje btsun rdo rje bdag med ma'i sgrub thabs ma nor lam gsal
Author: ngag dbang kun dga' bsod nams (1537-1601)

SLLS Dza. 118, ff. 41 - 117
A Mandala Ritual of Vajranairatmya
rje btsun rdo rje bdag med ma'i dkyil chog gsal byed phrin las kun khyab
Author: ngag dbang kun dga' bsod nams (1537-1601)

SLLS Dza. 119, ff. 119 - 135
A Bibliography of Sadhanas
sgrub thabs kyi tho yig

Author: ngor chen dkon mchog lhun grub (1497-1557)

SLLS Dza. 120, ff. 137 - 223
Rites of Imparting Initiation in the Vajranairatmya Mandala
bdag med ma'i dkyil 'khor du dbang bskur ba'i cho ga
Author: 'jam dbyangs blo gter dbang po (1847-1914)

SLLS Dza. 121, ff. 225 - 415
Rites of Imparting Bodhisattva Vows According to Two Exceptional
Lineages
*brgyud pa'i khyad par gnyis ldan sems bskyed kyi cho ga dam pa'i
bzhed srol sems nyid ngal bso*
Author: pan chen ngag dbang chos grags (1572-1641)

SLLS Dza. 122, ff. 417 - 445
Blessings of Protecting Interdependent Origination
rten 'grel bsrung ba'i byin rlabs
Author: 'jam dbyangs mkhyen brtse dbang po (1820-1892)

SLLS Dza. 123, ff. 447 - 481
Blessing and Dharani of Vajravidarani
rnam 'joms gzungs dang byin rlabs
Author: dGe slong brang ti nam mkha' dpal bzang (1535-1602)

SLLS Dza. 124, ff. 483 - 529
The Shower of Siddhis: A Guru Puja
bla mchod dngos grub char 'bebs
Author: byams pa kun dga' bstan pa'i rgyal mtshan (1829-1870)

SLLS Dza. 125, ff. 531 - 567
A Brief Practice of Outer Profound Guru Yoga
*lam zab mo phyi ma'i nyams len shin tu bsdus pa byin rlabs mchog
rtsol*

SLLS Dza. 126, ff. 569 - 619
Annals on Guru Ratnasambhava
bla ma rin 'byung be'u bum

Vol. 20 Va

SLLS (LS) Va. 127, ff. 1 - 17
Profound Guru Yoga
lam zab mo bla ma'i rnal 'byor
Author: bDag chen blo gros rgyal mtshan (1444-1495)

SLLS Va. 128, ff. 18 - 35
The Melody of Essential Meditative Experiences:
A Commentary on Prayer of Graduated Path
lam rim smon lam rnam bshad thugs dam gnad bskul rol mo
Author: byam pa bstan 'dzin snyan grags (1816-1884)

SLLS Va. 129, ff. 37 - 60
A Short Guru Puja on Profound Guru Yoga
lam zab bla mchod nyung bsdus
Author: 'jam dbyangs blo gter dbang po (1847-1914)

SLLS Va. 130, ff. 61 - 103
Jewel Mirror: A Synthesis of the View
lta snying nor bu'i me long
Author: byam pa bstan 'dzin snyan grags (1816-1884)

SLLS Va. 131, ff. 105 - 191
Refutation of Errors: A Commentary Illucidating the Meanings of
Tantric Pledges
*dam tshig gi rnam bshad 'grel pa 'khrul spong gi dgong pa rab tu
gsal ba*
Author: bDag chen blo gros rgyal mtshan (1444-1495)

SLLS Va. 132, ff. 193 - 225
The Profound Stages of the Path of Enlightenment of Vein,
Channels, Yantra and Blazing and Blissful Heat of Candali Yoga
*rtsa rlung 'phrul 'khor zab lam byang chub sgrub pa'i rim pa bklags
chog ma dang gtum mo'i bde drod rab 'bar ma*
Author: shar bla ma mkhas dbang kun dga' dpal ldan

SLLS Va. 133, ff. 257 - 262
Prayer to the Lineage Gurus of Last Eight-fold Paths
lam skor phyi ma brgyad kyi brgyud pa'i gsol 'debs

Author: ngor chen kun dga' bzang po (1382-1456)

SLLS va. 134, ff. 263 - 287
Clear And Auspicious Crystal Mirror:
The Instruction on Inconceivable by Kotalipa
tog rtse pa'i bsam mi khyab pa'i khrid yig bkra shis dwangs shel me long
Author: kong sprul blo gros mtha' yas (1833-1899)

SLLS Va. 135, ff. 287 - 301
Auspicious Medicinal Extract:
The Instruction on Simultaneously Born Accomplishment by Dombi Heruka
dom bhi he ru ka'i lhan cig skyes grub kyi khrid yig bkra shis gi vam sman bcud
Author: kong sprul blo gros mtha' yas (1833-1899)

SLLS Va. 136, ff. 301 - 333
Auspicious Heap of White Mustard:
The Instruction on Nine Profound Methods by Saroruha
pad ma ba dzra'i zab pa'i tshul dgu'i khrid yig bkra shis yungs dkar gong bu
Author: kong sprul blo gros mtha' yas (1833-1899)

SLLS Va. 137, ff. 333 - 350
Auspicious White Conch Swirling in the Right:
The Instruction on Path of Mudra by Indrabhuti
in dra bhu ti'i phyag rgya'i lam gyi khrid yig bkra shis dung dkar g.yas 'khyil
Author: kong sprul blo gros mtha' yas (1833-1899)

SLLS Va. 138, ff. 350 - 367
Heap of Auspicious Vermillion:
The Instruction on Complete Path of Candali by Krishnacarin
nag po pa'i gtum mo lam rdzogs kyi khrid yig bkra shis li khri'i thig le
Author: kong sprul blo gros mtha' yas (1813-1899)

SLLS Va. 139, ff. 367 - 374
The Instruction on Straightening the Crooked by Utsita Amara
nag po utsi ta 'chi ba med pa'i yon po srong ba'i khrid yig
Author: kong sprul blo gros mtha' yas (1833-1899)

SLLS Va. 140, ff. 374 - 397
The Instruction Received in front of a Stupa by Nagarjuna
'phags pa klu sgrub kyi mchod rten drung thob kyi khrid yig
Author: kong sprul blo gros mtha' yas (1833-1899)

SLLS Va. 141, ff. 398 - 415
The Instruction on Mahamudra Without Letters by Vagendrakirti
ngag dbang grags pa'i phyag rgya chen po yi ge med pa'i khrid yig
Author: kong sprul blo gros mtha' yas (1833-1899)

SLLS Va. 142, ff. 417 - 512
The Golden Garland of Lineage Chronicles of Common and Uncommon Lamdre
gsung ngag rin po che lam 'bras bu dang bcas pa ngor lugs thun min slob bshad dang thun mong tshogs bshad tha dad kyi smin grol yan lad dang bcas pa'i rgyud yig gser gyi phreng ba byin zab 'od brgya 'bar ba
Author: 'jam dbyangs blo gter dbang po (1847-1914)

Vol. Zha 21 (lam 'bras tshogs bshad)

SLLS (TS) Zha. 143, ff. 1 - 314
Ocean of Collected Elegant Sayings: A Lamdre History
gsung ngag rin po che'i byon thsul khog phub dang bcas pa rgyas par bshad pa legs bshad 'dus pa'i rgya mtsho
Author: 'jam mgon a mes zhabs ngag dbang kun dga' bsod nams (1537-1601)

SLLS Zha. 144, ff. 315 - 350
The Precious Ornament of Illucidating the First Three Modes
tshul dang po gsum gyi don nyung ngu'i ngag gis ston par byed pa'i legs par bshad pa tshul gsum gsal bar byed pa'i rin po che'i rgyan
Author: ngor chen dkon mchog lhun grub (1497-1547)

SLLS Zha. 145, ff. 351 - 427
Beautiful Ornament of Sublime Tree of Tantric Shastra
rgyud kyi mngon par rtogs pa'i don nyung ngu'i ngag gis gtan la
'bebs par byed pa'i rin po che'i rgyan
Author: ngor chen dkon mchog lhun grub (1497-1547)

SLLS Zha. 146, ff. 429 - 575
Fundamentals of General Classes of Tantra
rgyud sde spyi'i rnam par gzhag pa
Author: sLob dpon bsod nam rtse mo (1142-1182)

Vol. Za 22

SLLS (TS) Za. 147, ff. 1 - 227
The Tree of Abhisamaya
mngon rtogs ljon shing
Author: rJe btsun grags pa rgyal mtshan (1147-1216)

SLLS Za. 148, ff. 279 - 625
Ornament of the Superior Master's Thought:
Elegant Saying Which Illucidates the Abhisamaya of The Tantra
rgyud kyi mngon par rtogs pa'i gsal byed legs par bshad pa gong
ma'i dgong rgyan
Author: ngor chen dkon mchog lhun grub (1497-1547)

Vol. 'A 23

SLLS (TS) 'a. 149, ff. 1 - 8
Prayers to the Lineage Gurus of Lamdre
gsung ngag rin po che'i brgyud 'debs
Authors: ngor chen kun dga' bzang po (1382-1456) and dkon
mchog lhun grub (1487-1547)

SLLS 'a. 150, ff. 9 - 79
Shri Hevajra, The King of Tantras
dpal kye rdo rje zhes bya ba'i rgyud kyi rgyal po
Translators: 'Brogmi lo tsa ba sha kya ye shes (992-1074) and
Gayadhara (970-1090)

SLLS 'a. 151, ff. 81 - 553

Ornament of the Secret Vajradhara's Thought :

A Sub-Commentary on the Commentary "dag ldan" on The Two Part Hevajra Tantra

dpal kye rdo rje'i rtsa ba'i rgyud brtag pa gnyis pa'i rnam par bshad pa ma dag par 'joms pa'i 'grel pa dag ldan zhes bya ba'i mchan gyi tikka gsang bdag rdo rje 'dzin pa'i dgong rgyan

Author: 'jam dbyangs blo gter dbang po (1847-1914)

SLLS 'a. 152, ff. 555 - 588

The Gratifier of the Readers:

A Versified Eulogical Hagiography of Lamdre Masters

gsung ngag lam 'bras bu dang bcas pa'i gdams ngag zab mo byung tshul gyi yi ge don gnyer dga' ba bskyed byed

Author: 'jam mgon a mes zhabs ngag dbang kun dga' bsod nams (1537-1601)

Vol. Ya 24

SLLS (TS) 'a. 153, ff. 1 - 52

Garland Of Jewels: Abbatial Succession of The Glorious Ngor Evam Monastery

dpal e vam chos ldan gyi gdan rabs nor bu'i phreng ba

Author: dge slong sangs rgyas phun tshogs (1493-   )

SLLS 'a. 154, ff. 35 - 73

Pleasant Grove of The Intelligent:

An Easy Guide to Understand the Meaning of All the Commentaries (11) on Root Vajra Verses

gsung ngag rin po che lam 'bras bu dang bcas pa'i rtsa ba rdo rje tshig rkang gi don 'grel khog phub rnam 'grel ma lus pa bde lag tu rtogs par byed pa blo gsal yid bde 'byu_ ba'i dga' tshal

Author: 'jam mgon a mes zhabs ngag dbang kun dga' bsod nams (1537-1601)

SLLS 'a. 155, ff. 75 - 269

Beautiful Ornament of Three Visions:

Instructions on the Preliminaries of Lamdre
lam 'bras bu dang bcas pa'i gdams ngag gi gzhung shing rgyas pa
gzhung ji lta ba bzhin bkri ba'i lam gyi sngon 'gro'i khrid yig snang
gsum mdzes par byed pa'i rgyan
Author: ngor chen dkon mchog lhun grub (1487-1547)

SLLS 'a. 156, ff. 271 - 493
Beautiful Ornament of Three Tantras: Instuctions on the Actual
Path of Lamdre
lam 'bras bu dang bcas pa'i gdams ngag gi gzhung shing rgyas pa
gzhung ji lta ba bzhin bkri ba'i lam gyi dngos gzhi'i khrid yig rgyud
gsum mdzes par byed pa'i rgyan
Author: ngor chen dkon mchog lhun grub (1487-1547)

SLLS 'a. 157, ff. 495 - 651
Bestower of the Wish-Fufilling Blessings:
Supplement of the Abbatial Succession of Ngor Evam Monastery
e vam pa'i gdan rabs rin chen phreng mdzes kyi kha skong rtogs
brjod byin brlab 'dod dgu'i dpal ster
Author:

Vol. Ra 25

SLLS (TS) Ra. 158, ff. 1 - 149
Treasure of Siddhis: Instructions on Lamdre
gsung ngag rin po che'i khrid yig dngos grub 'byung ba'i gter
Author: dge slong sangs rgyas rin chen (1453-1523)

SLLS Ra. 159, ff. 151 - 196
Blossoming of the Lotus Grove: A Lamdre History
gsung ngag rin po che'i byung tshul dang khog phub kyi zin bris
gsung ngag bstan pa'i pad tshal bzhad pa
Author: pan chen ngag dbang chos grags (1572-1641)

SLLS Ra. 160, ff. 197 - 217
Nectar of The Heedful Talks: A Commentary on the Vajrayana
Pledges

rdo rje theg pa'i bslab bya dam tshig gi tshogs rnam par bshad pa'i
zin bris lam gyi rtsa ba bag yod gtam gyi bdud rtsi
Author: pan chen ngag dbang chos grags (1572-1641)

SLLS Ra. 161, ff. 219 - 281
Essential Elegant Sayings of the Three Visions:
Instructions on the Preliminaries of Lamdre
gsung ngag sngon 'gro'i khrid rim snang gsum snying po'i legs
bshad
Author: pan chen ngag dbang chos grags (1572-1641)

SLLS Ra. 162, ff. 289 - 399
Essential Elegant Sayings of Three Tantras:
Instructions on the Actual Path of Lamdre
gsung ngag dngos gzhi'i khrid rim rgyud gsum snying po'i legs
bshad
Author: pan chen ngag dbang chos grags (1572-1641)

SLLS Ra. 163, ff. 401 - 483
Essential Elegant Sayings on Outer Generation stage
phyi bskyed rim rnam par bshad pa blo gsal bde 'jug mkhas la nye
bar mkho ba snying po'i legs bshad
Author: pan chen ngag dbang chos grags (1572-1641)

SLLS Ra. 164, ff. 485 - 545
Light Beams of the Great Secret Doctrine:
An Exposition on Outer Generation Stage of Hevajra
dpal kye rdo rje man ngag lugs kyi phyi bskyed pa'i rim pa'i rnam
par bshad pa'i zin bris gsang chen bstan pa'i 'od phreng
Author: pan chen ngag dbang chos grags (1572-1641)

SLLS Ra. 165, ff. 547 - 569
A Concise Exposition (I) on the Profound Body Mandala
zab mo lus dkyil gyi rnam bshad zin bris nyung ngus rnam gsal
Author: pan chen ngag dbang chos grags (1572-1641)

SLLS Ra. 166, ff. 571 - 577
A Concise Exposition (II) on the Profound Body Mandala

zab mo lus dkyil gyi rnam bshad zin bris nyung ngus rnam gsal
Author: pan chen ngag dbang chos grags (1572-1641)

Vol. 26 La

SLLS (TS) La. 167, ff. 1 - 65
Accomplishment of Secret Path:
Rites of Initiating Disciples in the Profound Body Mandala of Shri
Hevajra
*dpal kye rdo rje'i zab mo lus kyi dkyil 'khor du slob ma dbang bskur
ba'i cho ga grub pa'i gsang lam*
Author: 'jam dbyangs blo gter dbang po (1847-1914)

SLLS La. 168, ff. 67 - 68
A Supplement to Path Initiation
lam dbang zur bkol

SLLS La. 169, ff. 69 - 144
Melody of Pleasing the Victorious Ones: A Commentary on the
Versified Prayer of Graduated Path of Lamdre by Tsharchen, The
Great King of Dharma
*tshar chen chos kyi rgyal pos mdzad pa'i gsung ngag lam rim smon
lam gyi rnam bshad rgyal ba dgyes pa'i rol mo*
Author: gzim 'og bstan 'dzin snyan grags (1816-1884)

SLLS La. 170, ff. 145 - 203
Drops of Nectar: Testament of Guru Manjunatha
'jam mgon bla ma'i zhal lung bdud rtsi thig pa
Author: sde gzhung sprul sku kun dga' rgyal mtshan (1885-1952)

SLLS La. 171, ff. 205 - 286
Great Melodious Drum of the Devas: A Dissertation on
Identification of Alaya and Differentiation Between Consciousness
and Wisdom
*kun gzhi ngos 'dzin dang rnam shes ye shes 'byed tshul bstan pa legs
bshad lha yi rnga chen*
Author: sde gzhung sprul sku kun dga' rgyal mtshan (1885-1952)

SLLS La. 172, ff. 287 - 323
Nectar For the Beginners: A Guide to Conduct Basic Hevajra Retreat
kye'i rdo rje'i gzhi bsnyen bya tshul gsar bu'i bdud rtsi
Author: (ngor dpon slob) ngag dbang legs grub

SLLS La. 173, ff. 325 - 393
Destroyer of Evil Troops: Land Taming Rites of Shri Hevajra Yoga
dpal kye rdo rje'i rnal 'byor la brten pa'i sa chog bdud dpung tshar gcod
Author: ngor chen dkon mchog lhun grub (1487-1547)

SLLS La. 174, ff. 395 - 433
Clear Mirror:
Practical Rites of Burnt Offerings of the Four-fold Activities of Shri Hevajra
dpal kye rdo rje'i sbyin sreg gi cho ga lag len gsal ba'i me long dang las bzhi'i sbyin sreg
Author: thar rtse nam mkha' dpal bzang (1535-1602)

SLLS La 175, ff. 425 - 431
A Prayer to Realize the Graduated Path of Lamdre
lam rim rgyud la skye ba'i smon lam
Author: thar rtse nam mkha' dpal bzang (1535-1602)

SLLS La. 176, ff. 433 - 467
Chariot of Bringing the Sun of Siddhis: A Prayer of the Graduated Path of Lamdre
gsung ngag lam rim gyi smon lam dngos grub nyin byed 'dren pa'i shing rta

SLLS La. 177, ff. 469 - 482
Kernel of Siddhis: Rite of Offering Ganacakra of Shri Hevajra
dpal kye rdo rje'i tshogs 'khor gyi cho ga dngos grub snye ma
Author: mkhyen rab bstan 'dzin lhun grub

SLLS La. 178, ff. 483 - 521

Ocean of Wealth: A Brief Rituals of Consecration According to Shri Hevajra
dpal kye rdo rje'i rnal 'byor la brten pa'i rab gnas mdor bsdus pa dpal 'byor rgya mtsho grub skyes lja'i bcud len
Author: ngag dbang legs grub

SLLS La. 179, ff. 523 - 619
Liturgical Texts According to the Consecration Ritual of Ocean of Wealth
rab gnas dpal 'byor rgya mtsho mar grags pa'i lag len dang ngag 'don gyi rim pa mtho ris legs byas kyi rdzing ring
Author: ngag dbang blo gros snying po gzhan phan mtha' yas (1876-1952)

SLLS La. 180, ff. 621 - 624
Supplement to the Two Texts
de gnyis la mkho ba'i zin bris

Vol. Sha 27

SLLS (TS) Sha. 181, ff. 1 - 189
Commentary on Vajra Verses Requested by
Shujay Ngodrup to Sachen Kunga Nyingpo
gzhung rdo rje'i tshig rkang gi 'grel pa rnal 'byor gyi dbang phyug dpal sa skya pa chen po la zhu byas dngos grub kyis zhus pa
Author: sa chen kun dga' snying po (1092-1158)

SLLS Sha. 182, ff. 191 - 395
Commentary on Vajra Verses Requested by
Lokya Wangchuk Drak to Sachen Kunga Nyingpo
gzhung rdo rje'i tshig rkang gi 'grel pa rnal 'byor gyi dbang phyug dpal sa skya pa chen po la klog skya dbang phyug grags kyis zhus pa
Author: sa chen kun dga' snying po (1092-1158)

SLLS Sha. 183, ff. 397 - 529
Commentary on Vajra Verses Requested by
Changchub Sempa Dawa Gyaltshan to Sachen Kunga Nyingpo

gzhung rdo rje'i tshig rkang gi 'grel pa rnal 'byor gyi dbang phyug dpal sa skya pa chen po la byang chub sems dpa' zla ba rgyal mtshan gyis zhus pa
Author: sa chen kun dga' snying po (1092-1158)

Vol. Sa 28

SLLS (TS) Sa. 184, ff. 1 - 148
Commentary on Vajra Verses Requested by
Bende Shinjema to Sachen Kunga Nyingpo
gzhung rdo rje'i tshig rkang gi 'grel pa rnal 'byor gyi dbang phyug dpal sa skya pa chen po la ben de gzhin rje mas zhus pa
Author: sa chen kun dga' snying po (1092-1158)

SLLS Sa. 187, ff. 149 - 491
Commentary on Vajra Verses Requested by
Khampa Gatheng to Sachen Kunga Nyingpo
gzhung rdo rje'i tshig rkang gi 'grel pa rnal 'byor gyi dbang phyug dpal sa skya pa chen po la kham pa sga theng gis zhus pa
Author: sa chen kun dga' snying po (1092-1158)

Vol. Ha 29

SLLS (TS) Ha. 188, ff. 1 - 159
Commentary on Vajra Verses Written by
Sachen Kunga Nyingpo for Machik Shangmo
gzhung rdo rje'i tshig rkang gi 'grel pa rnal 'byor gyi dbang phyug dpal sa skya pa chen pos yum ma gcig zhang mos don du mdzad pa
Author: sa chen kun dga' snying po (1092-1158)

SLLS Ha. 189, ff. 161 - 295
Commentary on Vajra Verses
Requested by Jomo Hahuma to Sachen Kunga Nyingpo
gzhung rdo rje'i tshig rkang gi 'grel pa rnal 'byor gyi dbang phyug dpal sa skya pa chen po la jo mo 'a 'u mas zhus pa
Author: sa chen kun dga' snying po (1092-1158)

SLLS Ha. 190, ff. 297 - 496

Commentary on Vajra Verses Requested by
Jodhen Denbuma to Sachen Kunga Nyingpo
*gzhung rdo rje'i tshig rkang gi 'grel pa rnal 'byor gyi dbang phyug
dpal sa skya pa chen po la jo gdan ldan bu mas zhus pa*
Author: sa chen kun dga' snying po (1092-1158)

Vol. A 30 (Pod dmar)

SLLS (PM) A. 191, ff. 1 - 295
Commentary on Vajra Verses on the Basis of the Teachings of Guru
Manjunatha
*gzhung rdo rje tshig rkang gi 'grel pa 'jam mgon bla ma'i gsung
sgros ma*
Author: dmar chos kyi rgyal po (Sakya Pandita's Disciple)

SLLS A. 192, ff. 297 - 303
Essence of the Profound Meanings: A Synopsis of Lamdre
Teachings
*gsung ngag rin po che'i khrid yig bsdus pa gsol 'debs zab don snying
po*
Author: ngor chen dkon mchog lhun grub (1497-1557)

SLLS A. 193, ff. 305 - 314
Essence of Nectar: The Essential Meanings of the View
"Non-Differentiation of Samsara and Nirvana"
*'khor 'das dbyer med kyi lta ba'i gnad rnams legs par bshad pa bdud
rsti'i nying khu*
Author:

SLLS A. 194, ff. 315 - 430
Jewel Mirror of Profound Meanings:
A Manual to Teach Uncommon Lamdre Tradition
*gsung ngag rin po che slob bshad 'chad thabs mdor bsdus zab don
nor bu'i me long*
Author: bco brgyad khri chen legs bshad rgya mtsho (His Eminence
Chogye Trichen Rinpoche) (1932- 2007)

SLLS A. 195, ff. 431 - 446

Wondrous Technical Key: A Complete Bibliography of the Profound Dharma Articles of Common and Uncommon Lamdre Teachings

thun mong ba tshogs bshad dang thun min slob bshad zab mo'i chos skor cha lag dang bcas pa'i dkar chag ngo mtshar 'phrul gyi lde'u mig

Editor: skyabs mgon ngag dbang kun dga' (His Holiness sakya Trizin) (1945-   )

Vol. Evam 31 (Pod sngon)

SLLS (PN) Evam. 196, ff. 1 - 14
Illuminating Torch of Lamdre: Synopsis of Lamdre
gsung ngag rin po che lam 'bras bu dang bcas pa'i khrid yig gsung ngag bstan pa gsal ba'i nyi ma'i 'od zer zhes bya ba las bsdus don gsung ngag gsal byed sgron me
Author: (stong ra) kun dga' legs grub

SLLS Evam. 197, ff. 15 - 95
Illuminating Torch of Enlightenment Thought:
Instructions on Preliminary Three Visions
snang gsum gyi khrid yig byang chub sems nyd gsal ba'i sgron me
Author: (stong ra) kun dga' legs grub

SLLS Evam. 198, ff. 97 - 151
Illuminating Torch of the Wisdom of Initiation: Instructions on Non-Differentiation of Samsara and Nirvana of Three Tantras
rgyud gsum 'khor 'das dbyer med kyi khrid yig dbang gi ye shes gsal ba'i sgron me
Author: (stong ra) kun dga' legs grub

SLLS Evam. 199, ff. 153 - 179
Illuminating Torch of Pure Vision:

Instructions on Outer and Inner Generation Stage
phyi nang bskyed rim gyi khrid yig dag snang gsal ba'i sgron me
Author: (stong ra) kun dga' legs grub

SLLS Evam. 200, ff. 181 - 204
Illuminating Torch of Blissful Heat: Instructions on Self-Blessings
rang byin rlabs kyi khrid yig bde drod gsal ba'i sgron me
Author: (stong ra) kun dga' legs grub

SLLS Evam. 201, ff. 205 - 223
Illuminating Torch of the Supreme Path of Messenger
pho nya lam mchog gsal ba'i sgron me]
Author: (stong ra) kun dga' legs grub

SLLS Evam. 202 ff. 225 - 233
Illuminating Torch of Bliss-Void: Instructions on Mandala Cakra
dkyil 'khor 'khor lo'i khrid yig bde stong gsal ba'i sgron me
Author: (stong ra) kun dga' legs grub

SLLS Evam. 203, ff. 235 - 240
Illuminating Torch of Becoming rainbow Body: Instructions on
Vajra Waves
rdo rje'i rba rlabs kyi khrid yig 'ja' lus mngon gyur gsal ba'i sgron me
Author: (stong ra) kun dga' legs grub

SLLS Evam. 204, ff. 241 - 249
Illuminating Torch of Textual Sources
bstan bcos dang lung gi skabs gsal ba 'brel bsgrigs gsal ba'i sgron me
Author: (stong ra) kun dga' legs grub

SLLS Evam. 205, ff. 251 - 335
Vital Essence of Great Bliss: Instructions on Precious Lamdre
gsung ngag rin po che'i khrid yig bde chen bcud kyi snying po
Author: (stong ra) kun dga' legs grub

SLLS Evam. 206, ff. 337 - 463
Mine of Siddhis: Instructions on Precious Lamdre
gsung ngag rin po che'i khrid yig dngos grub 'byung ba'i gter
Author: dge slong sangs rgyas rin chen (1453-1524)

SLLS Evam. 207, ff. 465-659
Moon's Rays:

An Exposition on Generation and Completion Stage of Shri Hevajra
*dpal kye rdo rje'i bskyed rdzogs kyi rnam bshad nges don gsal byed
zla ba'i 'od zer*
Author: dge slong dkon mchog dpal ldan (1526-1590)

SLLS Evam. 208, ff. 661-673
Refuting the Evil Talks: Clear Answers to the Questions of
Brahmacakra
*dri ba tshangs pa'i 'khor lo'i lan gsal bar bstan pa smra ba ngan
'joms*
Author:

OUTLINE OF THE TRIPLE TANTRA

PART ONE

THE ORIGIN OF THE LAMDRE TRADITION IN INDIA 57

PART TWO

THE ESSENCE OF THE ELEGANT TEACHINGS OF THE THREE TANTRAS 139

NOTES ON PREFACE

1   He is the root Guru of both His Holiness Sakya Trizin and His Eminence Chogye Trichen Rinpoche. He belongs to the Khangsar Labdrang of Ngor monastery in Tsang Province. There is a brief biography of his written by Dhongthog Tulku. See SLLS (LS) Nya. 48, ff. 389-414.

2   Situated some fifty meters east of the actual birth-place of the Buddha in Lumbini, Tashi Rabten Ling (bkra-shis rab-brtan gling) monastery is built on the plot of land given by the Nepalese government. I was privileged to study there for twelve years including the three and half years experiential retreat on Lamdre Lobshe (1976-1980) with His Eminence Chogye Trichen Rinpoche.

3   The revised edition of that outline appears as the contents on this translation.

4   Alex Wayman, Introduction to the Buddhist Tantric Systems, New York, 1980.

5   The Dalai Lama, *Tantra in Tibet*, Snow Lion Publication, 1977, p. 17.

6   He was a direct disciple of Padmasambhava. The renowned Vajrakilaya tradition presently preserved in the Sakyapa lineage came down through him. See Dudjom Rinpoche, *The Nyingmapa School of Tibetan Buddhism*, tr. by Gyurme Dorje and Matthew Kapstein, Vol. I, Wisdom Publications, 1991, p. 712.

7   Mahasiddha (grub chen) is a title given to greatly accomplished Tantric masters who attained both the common [thun mong] and uncommon [mchog] attainments or "siddhis." Generally it is an honorific title for the eighty-four Buddhist saints

[siddhas] of India, but it is also used for later accomplished masters in Tibet. Virupa is transliterated as "bi ru pa" in all the Tibetan *bstan 'gyur* editions of Narthang, Derge and Peking. Tibetan prayer books also render the word as "bir va pa". The etymological rendering is "lus ngan can" and means 'deformed', 'ill-mannered' or 'one with ugly form." *See* Dorje, Acharya Sempa, *The Biography of Eighty-four Saints,* Bibliotheca-Indo-Tibetica [4], Central Institute of Higher Tibetan Studies, Varanasi, 1979, p. 35.

8 *Lam 'bras bu dang bcas pa'i rtsa ba rdo rje'i tshig rkang* See Prof. Hakaju Ui and Co., *A Complete Catalogue of the Tibetan Buddhist Canons* [sde dge bka' 'gyur and bstan 'gyur], Published by Tohoku Imperial University, Japan 1934, Vol. Shi, T. 2284, p. 355. In the Peking Edition it is entitled *"Marga-phalanvitavavadaka" [lam 'bras bu dang bcas pa'i gdams ngag].* See Suzuki, Dr. Daisetz T., *The Tibetan Tripitaka, Catalogue and Index,* Tokyo, 1962, Vol. 156, rgyud 'grel, XLVII [Tsi], P. 3131, ff. 150a -155b.

9 Snellgrove, David, *Indo-Tibetan Buddhism,* Serindia Publications, London, 1987, p. 491. Also *see* Roerich, George, N., *Blue Annals,* Part I, Royal Asiatic Society of Bengal, Calcutta, 1949, p. 208.

10 See Tsepon W. D. Shakabpa, *Tibet: a Political History,* Yale University Press, 1967, p. 71.

11 This is indicated by the impressive collection of *bka' brgyud gdams ngag mdzod* in which most essential Lamdre works are also preserved. See Jamgon Kongtrul Lodro Thaye, *gdams ngag mdzod, a Treasury on Instructions and Techniques for Spiritual Realization,* Delhi, 1971, Vol. IV. Phagmo Drupa [1110-1170] studied under Sachen for 12 years and became the founding father of Phagdru Kagyu. He received Lamdre and wrote a commentary known as

"mdzod mar." See Chogay Trichen, *History of the Sakya Tradition*, Ganesha Press, Bristol, 1983, p. 25.

12 The Fifth Dalai Lama [1617-1682] wrote four comprehensive hagiographies of Lamdre Lobshe lineage teachers including one of Gonpo Sonam Chogden, who is known as "Kagyurwa Chenpo" [1603-1659]. These hagiographies are to be found in his collected works as well as in the *Sa-skya Lam 'bras Literature Series*, Published by Sakya Center, 187, Rajpur Road, Dehra Dun, U.P. India, 1982, Vol. IV, ff. 389-701, Vol. V, ff. 1- 109, and Vol. XI, ff. 399-638.

13 Lama Dampa Sonam Gyaltshen and Tishi Kunga Lodro are half-brothers. They are two of the eight sons of Dagnyi Chenpo Zangpo Pal who had six wives.

14 Dudjom Rinpoche, NSTB, p. 578.

15 Prior to Ngorchen Kunga Zangpo [1382-1456], there were no common and uncommon Lamdre traditions. It is said to have been a practice of Muchen Konchog Gyaltshen [1388-1468], the most remarkable disciple of Ngorchen, but it was not known until Dagchen Lodro Gyaltshen [1444-1495], who first introduced and practised the tradition of giving the common teachings in public and the uncommon to selected disciples in private. One can clearly see the development of these two traditions when one examines the arrangement of the Lamdre literature.

16 Both common (Tshogshe) and uncommon (Lobshe) Lamdre teachings are taught within the three sub-traditions. In Ngor monastery Tshogshe used to be given annually until 1959. Lobshe is given less frequently.

17 See *gzhung bshad man ngag gter mdzod*, in SLLS., Vol. XVI, ff. 125-126. This is the main Lamdre Poenag (Lamdre Black Annal) teaching manual.

18 A number of Lamdre scholars have refuted the idea that Sakyapa School propounds the Yogachara viewpoint. For instance *see* Ngorchen's (1382-1456) *rgyud dsum gnod 'joms*, The *Complete Works of the Great Masters of the Sa-skya sect of Tibetan Buddhism* SKB, Vol. 9. Toyo Bunko, 1968.

19 This of course contradicts the rest of the Tibetan chronological traditions, including the Sakyapa chronology.

20 For instance on the 23rd of 4th Lunar month, according to the Tibetan Calendar, all the Sakya monasteries perform a special ceremony to commemorate Virupa's enlightenment.

21 For instance, Marpa is regarded as the reincarnation of Dombi Heruka. *See* gtsang smyon he ru ka, *The Life of Marpa the Translator,* Prajña Press, Boulder, 1982, p. 4.

22 *See* Snellgrove, David, *Buddhist Himalaya,* Bruno Cassirer, Oxford, 1957, p. 85.

23 Grags pa rgyal mtshen, *Hagiography of Indian Gurus* [HIG] Also *see* SKB, Vol. 3, ff. 342-350 and pp.170-173. Also see SLLS, Vol. I, ff. 1-13 and Vol. XI, ff. 581-593. He has also written "*Chronicles of the Tibetan Masters*" which briefly covers the story of Drogmi and his successors. Ibid., ff. 348-350 and pp. 173-174 Ibid.,Vol. l, ff. 14-17 and Vol. Xl, ff. 594-599.

24 SLLS, Vol. XVI, ff. 1-122. He is also the author of the famous "*The Clear Mirror of the Royal Genealogies*" [rgyal rabs gsal ba'i me long]. B. I.Kuznetsov translated the eighth chapter into Russian in 1961 and a few years later published the transliteration of the Tibetan text without any translation. He says that this work has two translations in Chinese. *See* "*The Clear Mirror of Royal Genealogies,*" Leiden, 1966, p. XVIII. My friend, McComas Taylor

and I have published an English translation of this work.

25 He is probably better known for his work: *Sa skya'i gdung rabs rin chen bang mdzod, A History of the 'khon Lineage of the Prince-abbots of Sa-skya,* Tibetan Bonpo Monastic Centre, Dolanji, P O. Ochghat, H. P., 1975.

26 See SLLS., Vol. I, ff. 1-314. Hereafter this text is abbreviated as OCES. He cites many sources of his work and some of them may not even be extant. *bla ma rgya bod kyi lo rgyus* [HIG] by Jetsun Drakpa Gyaltshen, *zhib mo rdo rje* by Marton Chokyi Lodro, *zhib mo rnam dag* by Barton, *ngo mtshar snang ba* [W. V.] by Lama Dampa Sonam Gyaltshen, *de'i gsal byed* by Mue-saypa, *chos 'byung bstan pa rgyas pa'i ñi 'od* by Ngorchen, *de'i kha skong* by Gorampa Sonam Senge, *zha ma'i lo rgyus chen mo* by Zhama, *dpang rje'i chos 'byung* by Pangje, *'brom lugs kyi chos 'byung* [probabaly by Drom Depa Tonchung, a disciple of Drogmi], *cha rgan gyi bla ma rgya bod kyi lo rgyus* by Chagen, and *rje klu sgrub rgya mtsho'i chos 'byung khog phub zin bris* by Mangthoe Ludrup Gyatsho. See SLLS, Vol. III, ff. 555-589.

27 See SLLS, Vol. XIV, ff. 1 - 225. Hereafter this text is abbreviated as FGSD.

28 *Caturashiti-siddha-pravrtti [grub thob brgyad bcu rtsa bzhi'i lo rgyus* was written by Abhayadatta and translated by Minyak Lotsawa Monlam Sherab. Two English translations have appeared: J. R. Robinson's *Buddha's Lions, the Lives of the Eighty-four Siddhas,* Dharma Publishing, 1979 and Keith Dowman's *Masters of Enchantment: the Lives and Legends of the Mahasiddhas,* Inner Traditions International, Vermont, 1988. There is also a Hindi translation by Acharya Sempa Dorje, *The Biography of Eighty-four Saints,* Central Institute of Higher Tibetan Studies, Sarnath, 1979.

387

29 See Roerich, George, N., *The Blue Annals*, Part I, Published by Royal Asiatic Society of Bengal, Calcutta, 1949, pp. 204-240.

30 See *chos 'byung mkhas pa'i dga' ston smad cha, The Feast of the Scholars*, [FS] Part II, Published by National Minorities Publishing House [mi rigs dpe skrun kha_], Peking, 1986, pp. 1362-1369.

31 See Prof. Dr. Chandra, Lokesh, *Pad ma dkar po's Tibetan Chronicle*, [PT], New Delhi 1968. ff.393-408.

32 It was first translated into Russian by V. P. Vasil'ev in 1866 and was subsequently translated into German by A. Schiefner in 1869. *See* Chattopadhyaya, A., *Taranatha's History of Buddhism in India*, [THB] Indian Institute of Advanced Study, Simla, 1970.

33 *Taranatha, Five Historical Works of Taranatha*, [FHWT], Tibetan Nyingmapa Monastery, P.O. Tezu, Distt. Lohit, Arunachal Pradesh, 1974. Taranatha's *bka' babs bdun ldan, the Seven Instruction Lineages* was first translated into German by Albert Grünwedel in 1914. Bhupendranatha Datta translated it from German into English in 1944. David Templeman, an Australian Tibetologist provided its English translation from the Tibetan in 1983. *See* jo nang Taranatha, *bka' babs bdun ldan, The Seven Instruction Lineages*, tr. by David Templeman, Library of Tibetan Works and Archives, Dharamsala, 1983.

34 Ananda was Buddha's cousin, son of Amrtodana, paternal uncle of the Buddha. He was a celebrated disciple who became the second of the seven early Buddhist patriarchs. Ananda and Rahula, the Buddha's son were, both born on the night of Vaishakha full-moon when the Buddha attained enlightenment under the bodhi tree in Bodh Gaya, outside modern Gaya in Bihar state, India.

35 As the most senior of all the Arhats and the Lord's disciple, Mahakashyapa was the regent of the Lord and thus became the first patriarch. After over forty years of compiling the teachings and propagating the doctrine and benefitting many living beings, he entrusted the teaching to Ananda before passing into Nirvana.

36 Upali, the barber.

37 Manjushri, Vajrapani and Avalokiteshvara.

38 It is said that Tripitaka was first written down when the first council was held under the patronage of King Kanishka. They had earlier been formalised during the first council sponsored by King Ajatasatru. *See* Dudjom Rinpoche, NSTB, Vol. I, Wisdom Publication, 1991, p. 430.

39 See below the section on *The Hevajra Tantra* and its commentarial traditions.

40 The best Tibetan translation of this text is that by Drogmi and Gayadhara. Revised by Shonu Pal. Peking ed., bka' 'gyur, Vol. 1, P. 10, 210 - 2 - 3 to 222 - 5 - 7, 230a - 261b. Sde dge ed., bka' 'gyur, Vol. nga, T. 417, 1b - 13b. For its English translation, *see* Snellgrove, David, L., *The Hevajra Tantra, A Critical Study*, Part I, Introduction and Translation, Oxford University Press, London, 1959.

41 *Hevajrapindartha-tika [Kye'i rdo rje bsdus pa'i don gyi rgya cher 'grel pa]*, sde dge bstan 'gyur, Vol. rgyud Ka, T. 1180, ff. 1b - 126a. Peking ed., rgyud 'grel Ba, Vol. 53, P. 2310, ff. 1 -139b.

42 *Vajrapadasara-samgraha-pañjika [Rdo rje'i tshig gi sñing po bsdus pa'i dka' 'grel]*, Vol. rgyud Ga, T. 1186, ff. 58b - 146b. In the Tohoku Catalogue this title is ascribed to sñan grags bzang po instead of *Naropa*. Some say it is Naropa's name. Peking ed., rgyud 'grel Tsa, Vol. 54, P. 2316, ff. 69a - 169b.

43 *Yoga-ratnamala-nama-hevajra-pañjika* *[Dgyes pa rdo rje'i dka' 'grel rnal 'byor rin po che'i phreng ba zhes bya ba],* Vol. rgyud Kha, T. 1183, ff. 1b - 61a. Peking ed., rgyud 'grel Ma, Vol. 53, P. 2313, ff. 1 - 72b.

44 *Shrihevajravyakhyavivarana-nama* *[Dpal dgyes pa rdo rje'i rnam bzhad rnam par 'grel pa zhes bya ba],* Vol. rgyud Ka, T. 1182, ff. 173b - 275a. Peking ed., rgyud 'grel Ba, Vol. 53, P. 2312, ff. 190b - 307a. The name of the author appears in several different spellings: Bapabhata zhabs (Bhavabhattapada) and Bhavabhadra.

45 *Shrihevajratantrarajatika-suvishadasamputa-nama* *[rgyud kyi rgyal po dpal kye'i rdo rje'i 'grel bshad kha sbyor shin tu dri ma med pa zhes bya ba],* Vol. rgyud Kha, T. 1184, ff. 61a - 294a. Peking ed., rgyud 'grel Ma, Vol. 53, P. 2314, ff. 73a - 351a. The author's name is spelled in different forms: Dhamkadasha, Dhamkadasa.

46 *Hevajratantrapañjikapadmin-nama [Kye'i rdo rje'i rgyud kyi dka' 'grel pad ma can zhes bya ba],* Vol. rgyud Ka, T. 1181, ff. 126b - 173a. Peking ed., rgyud 'grel Ba, Vol. No. 53, ff. 139b - 190b.

47 *Kaumudi-nama-pañjika [Kau mu di zhes bya ba'i dka' 'grel],* Vol. rgyud Ga, T. 1185, ff. 1b - 58b. Peking ed., rgyud 'grel Tsa, Vol. 53, P. .2315, ff. 1 - 69a. *Durjayacandra* is translated as mi thub zla ba and sbyang dka' ba'i zla ba in Tibetan.

48 *Shrihevajrapañjika-nama-muktikavali [Dpal dgyes pa rdo rje'i dka' 'grel mu tig phreng ba zhes bya ba],* Vol. rgyud Ga, T. 1189, ff. 221a - 297a. Peking ed., rgyud 'grel Tsa, Vol. 54, P. 2319, ff. 262a - 349a. His full name is *Shriratnakarashanti* [dpal rin chen 'byung gnas zhi ba].

49 *Hevajra-nama-mahatantrarajadvikalpa-mayapañjikasmrtinipada-nama [Rgyud kyi rgyal po chen po dgyes*

pa'i rdo rje zhes bya ba sgyu ma brtag pa gñis pa'i dka' 'grel dren pa'i 'byung gnas zhes bya ba], Vol. rgyud Ga, T. 1187, 146b - 194a. Peking ed., rgyud 'grel Tsa, Vol. 54, P. 2317, ff. 169b - 228b. In both catalogues the author's name is given as *Krishna* [nag po pa] but his full name is *Krishna Samayavajra* [nag po dam tshig rdo rje].

50 *Hevajra-nama-tantraraja-tika [Kye'i rdo rje zhes bya ba'i rgyud kyi rgyal po'i 'grel pa],* Vol. rgyud Ga, T. 1188, ff. 194b - 220 b. Peking ed., rgyud 'grel Tsa, Vol. 54, P. 2318, ff. 228b - 262a. His full name is pad ma'i myu gu rdo rje.

51 *Shrihevajravajrapadoddharaja-nama-pañjika [Dpal dgyes pa rdo rje'i dka' 'grel rdo rje'i tshig btu ba zhes bya ba],* Vol. rgyud Ca, T. 1192, ff. 1b - 12a. Peking ed., rgyud 'grel Tsha, Vol. 54, P. 2322, ff. 1 -13b.

52 *Shrihevajra-mahatantrarajasya-pañjika-netravibha ga-nama [Rgyud kyi rgyal po chen po dpal dges pa rdo rje'i dka' 'grel spyan 'byed ces bya ba],* Vol. rgyud 'a, T. 1191, ff. 236b - 321a. Peking ed., rgyud 'grel Tsa, Vol. 54, P. 2320, ff. 349a - 444a. With regard to the twelve commentaries, Jetsun Drakpa Gyaltshen said: "Dpal ldan brtag pa gñis pa yi / rgyud kyi tshig don 'grel byed pa'i / rdo rje sñing po na ro pa / nag po spyod pa bha wa pa / tam ka da sha pad ma pa / mi thub zla ba shan ti pa / dam tshig rdo rje pad myug dang / ka ma dhe nu chos grags ste / 'phags yul 'grel pa bcu gñis mtho_ng"// See *Illuminating Sun's Rays of the Doctrine,* [ISRD] in SLLS, Vol. X, f. 332.

53 snying po'i don gyi kye rdor ni / bir wa'i rjes 'brang dom bi'i skor / yan lag med rjes pad ma'i skor / dam tshig rdo rje nag po'i skor / gtso che'i chos sna sum cu dgu / lam skor dgu ni khyad par ro //

54 A disciple of Krishna Samayavajra (nag po dam tshig rdo

rje).

55 This is popularly known as Naropa's tradition.

56 See ISRD in SLLS, Vol. 10, f. 334.

57 Ibid.

58 Although his real name is Sonam Tsemo, he is often referred to as "Goe Lotsawa" in the Lamdre texts, not to be confused with the author of Blue Annals. "Goe Khugpa ('gos khug pa)" is perhaps his family name and "Lhaytse" (lhas btsas) means "one born in a cattle-shed". Whether Goe received Lamdre or not is a controversial topic. Even if he did receive, it is very likely that he did not maintain the lineage. There are also reports that he criticised Lamdre, Drogmi and Gayadhara. *See* Dudjom Rinpoche, NSTB, p. 930.

59 See SKB., Vol . 1, ff. 27 - 131a. Ngaripa Salway Nyingpo also was one of the main disciples of Drogmi.

60 Ibid. Vol. 3, ff. 194 - 326a.

61 Tib. *rgyud sde spyi rnam*, See SLLS, Vol. 21, ff. 429 - 575.

62 Ibid. Vol. 3, ff. 1 - 139a.

63 *dpal kye rdo rje'i rtsa rgyud brtag gnyis kyi rnam par bshad pa ñi ma'i 'od zer*, SKB, Vol. 2, 41 - 3 - 1 - 109 - 3 - 6.

64 Ibid. Vol. 1, ff. 158 - 246a. It is also cited in ISRD in SLLS, Vol. 10, f. 333.

65 His master Shangton Choebar instructed: "Do not write anything about the instructions and do not even divulge the existence of the name of this teaching for eighteen years. After the passage of that time, you are the owner of the teaching, it is entirely up to you whether you wish to teach or write about it." See FGSD in

SLLS, Vol. 14, p. 124.

66 SLLS, Vol. 27, [sha], ff. 1-189.

67 Ibid., ff. 191-395.

68 Machik Tshetsha was the mother of Kunga Bar, the elder step brother of Drakpa Gyaltshen and Sonam Tsemo. Ibid., Vol. 29 [ha], ff. 1-159.

69 Ibid., Vol. 12 [na], ff. 1-446.

70 Ibid., Vol. 27 [sha], ff. 397-529.

71 Ibid., 28 [sa], ff. 149-491.

72 Ibid., 29 [ha], ff. 161-295.

73 Suzuki. D. T., _The Lankavatara Sutra_, Routledge & Kegan Paul, London, 1932, verse 252, p. 246.

74 For details _see_ Appendix for a traditional format of _Lamdre Tshogshe_ Teachings based on the writings of Jamyang Loter Wangpo (1847-1914].

75 Ideally the disciples should have already taken refuge vows during the teachings on the topic in _The Three Visions_ as well as Bodhisattva vows during the Bodisattva vow ceremony. This repetition simply restores these vows. The Vajrayana vows will be received the day after.

76 The disciples throw the flower onto the Mandala. The Guru will tell which Tathagata family each belongs to on the basis of where their flower had landed.

Centre	East	South	West	North
Akshobhya	Vairocana	Ratnasambhava	Amitabha	Amoghasiddhi

[77] "Dakama ('da' kha ma)" is an exclusive Lamdre term for transference of consciousness practice otherwise known as Phowa in the mainstream Tibetan Buddhist practices.

[78] *See* C. W. G. M. S., Vol. IX, p. 120 - 3 - 4.

[79] Tsharchen Losal Gyatsho is the founder of the Tsharpa sub-tradition Formerly a monk at Tashi Lhunpo monastery, Tsharchen truly became the inspiration behind the whispered lineage teachings in general and Lamdre Lobshe instructions and Vajrayogini practices in particular. Tsharchen was also the teacher of Mangtho Ludrup Gyatsho whose manuals on *Lamdre Lobshe* are said to be written on the basis of his notes on Tsharchen's teachings.

[80] He was a pupil of both Tsharchen and Jamyang Khyentse Wangchuk [1524-1568]. He is regarded as an emanation of Yamantaka.

[81] *'phags pa she rab kyi pha rol tu phyin pa sdud pa tshig su bcad pa*, bka' 'gyur, [Ka . 1b-19b] T. 13.

[82] The Five Treatises by Maitreya (byams chos sde lnga) are: *Mahayanottaratantra* [T. 4024], *Ahbisamyalankara* [Toh. 3786], *Madhyantavibhaga* [T. 4021], *Mahayansutralankara* [T. 4020] and *Dharmatuvibhanga* [T. 4022].

[83] Ganapati, Takkiraja and Kurukulle. These three red deities belong to the thirteen golden Dharmas of Sakya.

[84] He belonged to the Shithog Labdrang, one of the four Labdrangs.

[85] He was a disciple of Wangchuk Rabten. He became popularly known as "Kagyurwa Chenpo" after he re-established the lineage of the oral transmission of Kagyur. The lineage of oral transmission of Kagyur which is a living lineage today is largely attributable to his

dedication. It is from him that the Vth Dalai Lama received the *Lamdre Lobshe* and many Sakyapa instructions.

86 See the catalogue of SLLS.

NOTES ON PART ONE

THE ORIGIN OF THE LAMDRE TRADITION IN INDIA

The Life of Mahasiddha Virupa

87 See SLLS, Vol. XIV, f. 10. But in the biography of the eighty-four siddhas known to be written by Acharya Abhayadatta [slob-dpon mi-'jigs-sbyin], he is said to have been born in Tripura, the kingdom of king Devapala in east India. See BL, p. 27.

88 He is famous for his six commentaries on Dharmakirti's works on Buddhist logic.

89 His Eminence Chogay Trichen says Acharya Dharmakirti, the logician. See HST, p. 8.

90 Taranatha says that it is worse than a grave mistake to say that this Dharmamitra, the direct disciple of Gunaprabha, was the same as the Dharmamitra who composed the commentary called the *Prasphutapada*. THB, p. 254.

91 He also ordained Shantideva at Nalanda Monastery.

92 Abhayadatta does not seem to know of Virupa studying in Nalanda, or even going there. He writes as if Virupa took the Bhikhu ordination and did his study in Somapura.

93 It is a name which is identified with many teachers and with

the fourth Pala Dynasty king Dharmapala (765-879), who is referred to either as the founder or a restorer of Vikramashila. According to Pawo Tsuklak Trengwa, King Dharmapala was contemporary with the Tibetan King Senalek. Drogmi and other Lamdre masters have repeatedly claimed that Dharmapala is not only Virupa's pre-siddha name but was also predicted in Mañjushrimulatantra: yi ge dha zhes sdom brtson 'gyur / lho yi phyogs su rnam par grags / sdom brtson de bzhin sngags kyang 'grub // The letter 'Dha' [indicates that he] will apply himself to his vows and will become very famous in the South. The one who has applied himself to his vows will also accomplish Mantra. This is cited in in SLLS, Vol. XIV, f. 28.

94 See HST, p. 8.

95 Tib. Gnod sbyin, Skt. Yaksa. In Tibetan, it literally means that which provokes harm. It is identified with a harmful spirit which nevertheless can be very generous if not disturbed. For instance, there was a famous Yakshi with five hundred offspring [gnod-sbyin 'phrog-ma ma-bu lnga-brgya] said to have been bound by oath by the Buddha that she and her children would not harm Dharma practitioners if they dedicated part of their food during meal times. Jambhala is a kind of Yaksha, too.

96 See SLLS, Vol. XIV, f. 12. This dream is not mentioned or explained in other Lamdre texts.

97 Tib. tshogs-lam [Skt. sambhara marga].

98 Tib. sbyor-lam [Skt. prayoga marga].

99 Tib. mthong-lam [Skt. darshana marga].

100 Tib. lte-ba'i 'khor-lo [Skt. nabhimandala].

101 See SLLS, Vol. XIV, f. 13.

102 Tib. Sa-dang-po mthong-lam.

103 Tib. Khams-'dus-pa dang-po.

104 Tib. Gtum-mo. Taranatha honours Virupa as the transmitter of the Candali practices, the second Instruction Lineage [bka'-bab gnyis-pa gtum-mo] in his *Seven Instruction Lineages.* He assumes the existence of the Candali practices prior to Virupa but does not mention from which Guru Virupa heard them.

105 Tib. Khams 'dus-pa bar-pa.

106 Tib. Khams 'dus-pa mtha'-ma.

107 1]The Vase Initiation [bum-dbang], 2] The Secret Initiation [gsang-dbang], 3] The transcendental Wisdom Initiation [shes-rab ye-shes kyi-dbang] and 4] The Fourth Initiation [dbang-bzhi-pa].

108 There are ten stages of enlightenment on the Bodhisattva path and thirteen in the Vajrayana path. Bhumi literally means ground, earth or stage of enlightenment. The sixth Bhumi is called 'sa-drug-pa mngon-du phyogs -pa' [abhimukha].

109 See SLLS, Vol. XIV, ff. 15 - 16.

110 Taranatha seems to know that Virupa was known by that name but he raises doubts by saying: "Although this Acharya is known as Shri Dharmapala, he is not the same person, Sthavira Dharmapala who was an abbot of Nalanda." See *The Collected Works of Jo nang Taranatha* [CWJT] Vol., XVI, f. 572. But he also refers to Virupa as a former Bhikshu Pandita of Nalanda which implies a difference between a Pandita and upadhyaya [mkhan-po] of Nalanda. Ibid., f. 569.

111 Taranatha's account of Virupa's encounter with the boatman at the bank of River Ganges is a brief version: "Then, on the banks of the Ganges he asked the boatman to ferry him. When he was asked to pay the ferry fare, he made the threatening gesture to the Ganges which reversed its flow uphill and thus he went across it."

See SIL, f. 569. Templeman translates the above passage as follows: "Then, on the banks of the Ganges he told the ferryman that he needed a ferryboat. The ferryman told him that he had to pay for such a trip, but Virupa could not find any money and, pointing his forefinger at the River Ganges it reversed its flow uphill and thus he went across it." See SIL, Tr. p.15.

[112] Tib. Bsdigs-mdzub. Templeman's translation of "pointing forefinger" is a partial description of the gesture and does not explain the full meaning of word 'bsdigs-mdzub'. It is a standard phrase for 'threatening gesture,' which is posed by pointing the forefinger and the little finger while clenching the thumb under the middle and ring fingers of the left hand.

[113] Tib. Skal-ldan cig-car ba'i-lam. See Chapter II, pp. 53-66.

[114] Taranatha says it was in Oddivisa, but Templeman has translated it as Odisa, unless this is a misprint. See CWJT, Vol. XVI, f. 569 and SIL, tr., p. 15.

[115] See Yuthok, 1990, p. 82 which has an illustration depicting the brewing of the intoxicants.

[116] Interestingly, this is the second time Virupa says he will give whatever is wanted, the first being to the boatman.

[117] Taranatha says it was in the land of Trilinga. See SIL in CWJT, Vol. XVI, f. 569.

[118] Tib. Ral-pa-can lnga-brgya.

[119] Templeman misreads the passage: lha'i gtso bo ni vi shva na tha bya ba 'jigs sdes bzhengs pa'i ling ga gdong bzhis mtshan pa gcig yod pa de bzhi tshal du gas yod gsung / and translates it as "The principal god Visvanatha had an effigy (Linga) which had been erected by the workers' guild in the form of a phallus with four faces, and it is said that it too broke into four pieces". I would

translate: "The main god, a Linga with four faces named "Vishvanatha" which had been erected by Bhayasena is said to have broken into four pieces".

120 Tib. 'dod-khams, [Skt. kamadhatu].

121 See SLLS, Vol XIV, f. 20.

122 Tib. Thugs-rje chen-po spyan-ras-gzigs [Skt. Mahakarunika Avalokitesvara].

123 See Chapter Two for details.

124 See SLLS, Vol. XIV, ff. 23-24.

125 Tib. zag-bcas-kyi mngon-shes.

126 Tib. shar-lus 'phags-po.

127 See SLLS, XIV, ff. 24-25.

128 Although Lamdre historical texts have variant spellings i.e. dgu-ca-ra, ghu-ca-ra and gu-ca-ra, it is the modern state of Gujarat in West India where Buddhapalita is said to have been born. There is a district named Saurastra in the state. The Chinese pilgrim Hsüan Tsang calls "ku-che-lo" country in his travel records [629-645] which is his attempt to transcribe Gujarat. *See* Watters, Thomas, *On Yuan Chwang's Travels in India* [YCTI] Edited by T.W. Rhys Davids and S.W. Bushell, Peking 1941 p. 250.

129 See SLLS, Vol. XIV, ff 25-26.

130 Tib. gser-bsgyur gyi-rtsi.

131 Skt. Haritaki [myrobalan, universal medicine].

132 See SLLS, Vol. XIV, ff. 25 - 26.

133 Sometime later, a king of Jonaghata begged and received 20,000 [srang] ounces of gold from the statue. When he thought "I will ask for more," the stone image clenched its fist. *See* SIL in CWJT

Vol. XVI, f. 570.

134 See SLLS, Vol. XIV, f. 26.

135 Taranatha says that the king became mad and also died. See SIL in CWJT, Vol. XVI, f. 570.

136 Tib. bsod-nams 'phrog-byed.

137 Tib. dpal-stobs-kyi mgon-po.

138 Tib. gzhon-nu kar-tti-ka. It is not clear whether Kumara Karttika is a divine being or a historical ruler since Kathika era is also mentioned as contemporary to Rudrasena III [348-378]. See Moray, M. S., _History of Buddhism in Gujarat,_ [HBG] Saraswati Pustak Bhandar, Ahmedabad, 1985, p. 65.

139 Templeman identifies this as Somanatha temple in Saurastra which was destroyed by Mahmad of Ghazni in 1025 AD. SIL, tr. p. 108.

140 It is not found in the Tibetan Buddhist Canon but his commentary on chapters nine to sixteen is extant in the _Chinese Buddhist Canon:_ Taisho ed. Vol. 30, No. 1571, pp. 187-250.

141 Sumpa Khenpo Yeshe Paljor makes an interesting comment in his _dpag bsam ljon bzang_ about the elephant and its mysterious relationship with the Yogi Sira's [second manifestation of Virupa] dirty water of his leg and the elephant, who was known as"Bhanada" during the reign of the king Ramapala. If the elephant drinks the dirty water of Sira's leg, it could conquer the troop of one hundred barbarian kings. _See_ Das, Sarat Chandra, _History of the Rise, Progress and Downfall of Buddhism in India_, Edited with a list of comments and an _Analytical Index in English_, Calcutta, 1908, p. 104.

142   A khal is a weight or measurement equal to thirty pounds or about twenty eight rgya ma- s. One rgya-ma is slightly over one pound. The difference between a 'degs-khal [an average

weight of a load] and a ru- khal [an average measurement] is that the latter is 10 rgya-ma more than the former. See Das, S.C., _Tibetan English Dictionary_, Kyoto, 1983, p.143. Also see _bod rgya tshig mdzod chen mo stod cha_, mi rigs dpe skrun khang, 1981 p. 227.

143   After the British rule, it became known as "Bengal", but Bhangala was the original name.

144   See SIL in CWJT, Vol. XVI, f. 571.

145 See HST, p. 12.

146 Tib. _grub thob brgyad cu rtsa bzhi'i lo rgyus_ No. 5091, _The Tibetan Tipitaka_, Peking Edition, Catalogue and Index, Tokyo, 1962, Vol. [195] rgyud 'grel LXXXVI [Lu], 173 - 1 - 1, [1 - 69a]. See f. no 29.

147 See SKB, Vol. IX, 177 - 2 - 3 and also in SLLS, Vol. XVII, f. 15.

148 See Vidyabhusana, S.C., _History of the Medieval School of Indian Logic_, Oriental Books Reprint Corporation, New Delhi, Second Edition, 1977, p. 302-303.

149 Born in Bhangala in the east, he was a disciple of Asanga and his brother. He went to the countries all around and built in each direction a temple of Arya Mañjushri. He is said to have written a commentary on the entire Yogacarabhumi. See THB, p.186.

150 See HMSIL, p. 102.

151 See Das, S.C., _Indian Pandits in the Land of the Snow_, Calcutta , 1965, p. 41.

152 See SIL in CWJT, Vol. XVI, f. 672.

153 THB, p.197.

154 See SIL in CWJT, Vol. XVI, f. 569 and SIL, tr. p. 15.

155 The Seven Instruction Lineages listed in the work which covers about some fifty Indian Mahasiddhas does not confirm all

the traditions and lineages which have become the mainstream of Tibetan Buddhist traditions. The names of the Lineages neither distinguish between different classes of Tantra and their lineages, nor does it explain why and how such lineages came into existence. It requires careful investigation.

[156] See THB, p. 214.

[157] Sankalia, H.D., _The Nalanda University_, Oriental Publishers, Delhi, 1972, p. 130.

[158] He is not to be confused with Rahulabhadra's sponsor Jayadeva mentioned by chag lo tsa ba chos rje dpal.

[159] See THB, p. 213.

[160] See SKB, Vol. IX, 179 - 1 - 3, and also LL., Vol. XVII, f. 22 [13b].

The Successors of Virupa in India

[161] However generally there are several types of disciple: An individual of highest intelligence [dbang-po yang-rab], like King Indrabhuti, who can be liberated at the time of initiation, does not require to train in the gradual stages of the path. On account of receiving the valid ripening initiation [smin-byed kyi-dbang] from a Guru, such a disciple, free of doubts, with great confidence takes the Guru as the embodiment of Four Kayas and Five Transcendental Wisdoms, and prays day and night without discrimination, being classed as a person of highest intelligence [dbang-po-rab]. It is said that such a disciple will be self-liberated by the Profound Guru Yoga practice [lam-zab-mo bla-ma'i rnal-'byor]. Since he will guard the Root and Branch pledges [rtsa-ba-dang yan-lag-gi dam-tshig] voluntarily, he or she will gain final enlightenment effortlessly on the Generation and Completion stage practices. On the other hand, the path of the mediocre [dbang-po-'bring] is known as liberation through the means of guarding the Samayas. Unable to avoid the transgression of minor Samayas, the practitioner has to practice the

Yogas of Generation and Completion stage accordingly through the path of Five Interdependent Originations [rten-'brel-lnga] to attain enlightenment, what is known as the"inferior" [dbang-po mtha'-ma]. Either within one or at least in sixteen lifetimes, it is said that a practitioner on the Vajrayana path will attain the ultimate result of perfect Enlightenment.

162 See Chapter I.

163 See BL, pp. 33-36 and pp. 316-317.

164 See FHWT, f. 385. David Templeman translates the word "ko-mkhan" as "leather worker" without knowing what Taranatha was referring to. Another reason for this confusion may have been caused by the fact that in Tibetan, both leather and boat are called "ko-ba". Furthermore most of the boats in Tibet are made out of Yak [gyag] hide or some other animal skin. In India, the boats were mainly made of wood. However the preferred Tibetan word for a leather worker or a tanner would be "mnyed-mkhan". In the Indian caste system, a leather worker or a shoe maker is closely associated with "Camaripa", which is the name of the 14th of the eighty four Mahasiddhas. A shoe maker is termed *"lham mkhan"* in Tibetan but not "ko-mkhan". The Tibetan word "ko-ba", for a boat, when compounded with the agent suffix mkhan (equivalent to 'er' in English), becomes "ko-mkhan" and drops its nominal suffix 'ba' in the process. Although Taranatha (or whoever is the author) does not specify the exact Tibetan sources of his reference, this indicates that he was aware of the lam -'bras version of the story that Dombi Heruka was a boatman. Also see SIL, p. 19.

165 See THB, p. 222.

166 See FS, Vol. II, p. 1363.

167 But in OCES it does not say that it was a pregnant tigress but a tiger who eats humans [stag-mi-zan]. See SLLS,Vol. I, f. 99.

[168] Bka'-babs bdun-ldan-gyi rnam-thar, ff. 576-577.

[169] See EFS, p.136, and also BL, p. 34.

[170] Sinha, Bindeshwari Prasad, _Dynastic History of Magadha_, cir. 450-1200 A.D., Abhinav Publications, New Delhi, 1977, pp. 156-157.

[171] Thereupon the king gave his kingdom to his son and he, with his low-caste mistress, went into the forest to practice for twelve years. _See_ EFS, p. 136.

[172] Ibid., p.137.

[173] See SKB, Vol. IX, 281 - 4 - 6, ff. 219b - 220b.

[174] See Chapter I.

[175] See IBE, p. 64.

[176] It is not certain whether there were any places in Bengal with this name. Sachen confirms the identity of Karna with the modern state of Karnataka in the south, which is associated with his birth-place, name and eventually where he met Virupa.

[177] See SLLS, Vol XIV, f. 29.

[178] David Templeman, who translated the _Seven Instruction Lineage_ has also translated his biography into English. See _Taranatha's Life of KrishnAcharya_ [TLK], Library of Tibetan Works and Archives, Dharamsala, India. 1987.

[179] See FHWT, ff. 267-268. _Also see_ TLK, pp. 6-7.

[180] Other sources say that he was of the scribe's caste [rigs-yi-ge-pa]. See BL, pp. 81 and also 333.

[181] In the story of the Eighty-four Mahasiddhas, he is said to have been a monk of the Vihara of Somapuri, which was built by King Devapala [rgyal-po lha-skyong]. Ibid., p. 81.

[182] See Robinson, JBEFS, p. 175.

183 Ibid., p.176.

184 See the Lineage Tree of the Nine-fold paths in Yuthok, 1990, pp. 80-81.

185 Ibid.

186 Tib. Nag-po vi-ru-pa. There is no one with this name associated with Virupa mentioned in the Lamdre texts as his disciple. It is quite likely that outstanding disciples of famous masters could have been given the name of the master and respected as "Junior so and so". But I haven't seen this name elsewhere.

187 SILS, ff. 572-573. Also see SIL, tr. pp. 17-18.

188 He wrote an invocation in which he listed all the names of his previous incarnations which includes Krishnacarin as the first one in the list. See CWT, Vol. XVI, ff. 1011-1012. Also Kong-sprul blo-gros mtha' -yas [1813-1899] is said to have described himself as an incarnation of the lineage that passed from Krishnacharin through to Taranatha in his autobiography compiled and edited by Gnas-gsar bkra-'phel.

189 See OCLS, f. 100.

190 Taranatha says that Acharya Krishnacharin is said to have born in Kamboja, and Templeman assumes this is somewhere in North Western frontier of Pakistan. See TLK, p. 83 and footnote 182. Also see OCLS, f. 100.

191 In one of the famous lam-'bras Lineage Guru Prayers, "gnas-sbyar-ma" written by Brag-phug-pa bSod nams dpal (1277-1350), the prayer to Krishnacharin reads: gnas ri bo u tsa ya na'i dur khrod du / brtun bzhugs nag po spyod pa la gsol ba 'debs / I pray to Caryapa Krishnacarin, who dwells at the cemetery of Mount Ucayana, in the East. See Chogay Trichen Rinpoche, _Liturgical Texts_

of the Lam 'bras Tradition, New Delhi, 1977, p. 1.

[192] The modern city of Jullunder in Haryana State. It is also recognised as one of the twenty four sacred shrines of Cakrasamvara practice.

[193] See FS, Vol. II, p. 1363.

[194] See PHT, pp. 37-39. Also see Bell, Charles, *The Religion of Tibet*, Clarendon Press, Oxford, 1931, pp. 40-41.

[195] Tib. Smin-byed kyi-dbang.

[196] Skt. Sampannakrama, Tib. rdzogs-rim.

[197] See Chapter II p. 20.

[198] Tib. Thun mong ba'i sngon 'gro bzhi ni 'khor ba'i nyes dmigs, dal 'byor rnyed dka', 'chi ba mi rtag pa, las rgyu 'bras.

[199] See *Early Diffusion of Lamdre Tradition in Tibet*, Chapter III.

[200] See Introduction, pp. 20-21.

[201] See Yuthok, p. 72.

[202] See BL, pp. 134-135 and also pp. 166-167.

[203] Tib. gnas-nyi-shu rtsa-bzhi yul-sum-bcu so-gnyis.

[204] Skt. Vikramaditta.

[205] See Yuthok, p. 56. His secret name is: Tib. Mi-mnyam rdo-rje, Skt. Atulyavajra.

The Early Diffusion of Lamdre in Tibet

[206] See SLLS, Vol. XV, ff. 42-43.

[207] See Chronology of Drogmi in this chapter.

[208] Palde [dpal-lde], Ode ['od-lde], Kyide [skyid-lde] were known as "lha-rtse'i mched-gsum," the three royal brothers, as they

were the princes of Tri Tashi Tsekpa pal [khri-bkra-shis brtsegs-pa-dpal], who was the prince of King Palkhor Tsan [dpal-'khor-btsan]. They were all descendants of king Lang Darma's legitimate son, O Sung ('od srungs). The three royal brothers are also known as "smad-kyi lde-gsum", the three "ldes" of lower region in Tsang province.

209 Loton Dorje Wangchuk (lo-ston rdo-rje dbang-phyug) was the eldest of ten men from U-Tsang who were ordained by Lachen Gongpa Rabsal (bla-chen dgong-pa rab-gsal) at the beginning of revival of Buddhism which started in Kham. He found zhwa-lu rgyan-gong byang chub dge-gnas at the behest of Lce-btsun shes-rab 'byung-gnas. According to available sources, he was born in 975 A.D. See BA, p. 405.

210 See Lo-tshig re'u-mig in the *Collected Works of Sum-pa mkhan-po ye-shes dpal-'byor*, Vol. l, f. 546 in Sata-Pitaka Series, International Academy of Indian Culture, New Delhi, 1975, Vol. 214.

211 The Mangkhar valley is situated south of Lhatse and is famous for its caves where the pioneers of Tibetan translators and Indian Panditas did their first translation works. Many of the caves i.e. Dragyur Lotsaphuk [sgra-bsgyur lo-tsa-phug] and Sungak Lamdre Phuk [gsung-ngag lam-'bras-phug] have been used as meditation caves by many great masters including Sakya Pandita, Jetsun Drakpa Gyaltshen etc. according to Khyentse's *Guide to the Holy Places of Central Tibet*. *See* Dowman, K., *Power-Places of Central Tibet*, Routledge And Kegan Paul, London, !988, p. 279.

212 The author of the *Blue Annals* does not mention Leng Shakya Tsondru and has thus misconstrued the name of Stag ye-shes gzhon-nu as "Stag-lo-gzhon-nu brtson-'grus," a clear indication of his limited knowledge of Leng's involvement. See BA, p. 205.

213 Tib. Gla-rtsi, Skt. kasturi. See Das, Sarat, Chandra, *Tibetan*

English Dictionary, Compact Edition, 1983, p. 254.

[214] Possibly as a protest against the abbot for nepotism, not many scholars include the name of Leng in the group including Ngawang Choedak. See his _Blossoming of Lotus Grove,_ [BLG] in SLLS, Vol. XXV, p. 163.

[215] This appears to be the corrupt version of 'Acharya.'

[216] The word 'Atsara' is a corrupted form of the Sanskrit word 'Acharya'. Tibetans who do not know that an Atsara actually means "slob-dpon" in Tibetan call all Indian Yogins 'Atsara', and paint an image of an old man with a long beard, who knows black magic. Mothers tell white lies to children about an Atsara's presence at the door if they cannot put their children to bed.

[217] See BA, p. 205.

[218] The Phamthingpa brothers are also held in high esteem in the Vajrayogini teachings of the Naropa lineage (Na-ro mkha'-spyod]. The sacred Vajrayogini shrine under the care of Newari Buddhist in Pharphing, situated outside Kathmandu, is the place where they attained Khecara.

[219] The Six Great Scholars [mkhas-pa sgo-drug] are: 1) Shantipa, the Pandita of the Eastern Gate, who specialised in Linguistics and Logic, 2) Vagendrakirti [pan-grub ngag-dbang grags-pa], the Pandita of the Southern Gate, who received direct guidance from Tara, 3) Shes-rab 'byung-gnas, the Pandita of the Western Gate, who specialised in the Doctrines of Tirthikas, 4) Naropa, the Pandita of Northern Gate, who specialised mainly in Vajrayana, 5) Ratnavajra [rin-chen rdo-rje] and 6) JñanaShri, were known as the two pillars of centre. Ratnavajra collaborated with Drogmi on a number of translations. See FGSD in SLLS, Vol. 14 f. 53.

[220] See SLLS, Vol. XIV, f.

408

221 The three Dharma robes, Tib. chos-gos rnams-gsum [Skt. tricivara] are: 1. chos-gos, an upper robe worn by ordained monks and nuns; 2. rnam-sbyar, an upper robe worn by only a Bhiksu and 3. thang-gos, the lower robe.

222 Tib. kye'-rdo-rje'i-dbang nub-gsum-pa.

223 Skt. Amanusha, lit. one that is not a human being, a spirit. See Das, Sarat, Chandra, _Tibetan English Dictionary_, Compact Edition, 1983, p. 959.

224 Tib. Gsang-sngags rten-'grel gnad-du che-bas.

225 It is a sacred mountain in Southern India where Nagarjuna is said to have spent his last days absorbed in deep meditation.

226 The sources do not point out the exact conditions under which the transition of Drogmi's monkhood into married life occurred or was allowed. It appears that the ruler Palde married his princess to Drogmi as a reward for the latter's achievement in his studies in India. However the above remark on how Taklo became successful in keeping his Vinaya vows pure implies a comparison with either Drogmi or Leng's monastic life. We know that all three were ordained at least as novices before their departure to India in 1008. In Drogmi's case, he could not have been a Bhiksu when he left for India as he was only sixteen years old. Leng returned to India and there is no mention of his disrobing. We do not know whether they took Bhiksu ordination in India or not.

227 Goe Lotsawa Shonu Pal ('Gos-lo-tsa-ba gzhon-nu-dpal) does not seem to know of Drogmi's second visit to India and thus asserts that Drogmi spent three years with Bhiksu Viravajra after he spent eight years with Shantibhadra. This is incorrect, as shown above, according to the Lamdre sources. The same miscalculation is also shared by modern scholars such as Snellgrove and others who have relied on the _Blue Annals_. See BA, p, 206 , ITB, p. 491 and also

chronology of Drogmi in this chapter.

[228] It would not be wrong to assume that king Chanakya and his ministers sailed to some island in the east of India and propagated the lineage there. Perhaps Indonesia. No question was raised by early Lamdre historians as to the possible survival of the lineage through king Chanakya and his followers. Was it because it was a lineage transmitted from Dombi Heruka?

[229] See Chronology of Drogmi in this chapter.

[230] Gayadhara's name is not listed in the names of the eighty-four Mahasiddhas according to Abhayadatta's biographical dictionary of the Mahasiddhas. The Sakyapa tradition has canonized him as the prominent Indian master who brought Lamdre to the door-step of Drogmi. But it should be pointed out that not all Indian Panditas necessarily earned the title of Mahasiddha. Regarding the chronology of Gayadhara, we know that he definitely outlived Drogmi who died in 1074. His first visit to Tibet occurred before Atisha visited Tibet in 1042. He made three subsequent visits and died there. His birth date 970 is tentative.

[231] Dudjom Rinpoche makes some scathing attacks on a certain red Pandita.

[232] Ngawang Kunga Sonam's vagueness about this name's association with Gayadhara's third visit to Tibet is briefly discussed by Ngorchen, who seems to regard this as one version of the story asserted by Goe and his followers but he also does not analyse far enough to support or refute it when he says: "gsang 'dus 'gos lugs pa rnams slob dpon 'di dang rgyal po sprin gyi shugs can gnyis gcig pas bzhed la..."Those who follow the Guhyasamaja Goe tradition assert that this master and king Sprin-gyi shugs-can are the same person." This is plausible since it was at Goe's invitation that

Gayadhara made his third visit to Tibet. See SKB, Vol. lX, p.111. 2. 2. Lamdre historians regard Gayadhara as having been a prince and quote the following verse from the _Praises to the Eighty-four Mahasiddhas_ by Vajrasanapada: rgyal rigs rig pa'i gnas la mkhas / nam mkha'i lha la the tshom gcod / sprin gyi shugs can zhes bya ba'i / bla ma de la phyag 'tshal lo // The royal prince who is learned in sciences, Clarifies his doubts with the gods in the sky; To the Guru who is known as Gayadhara, I pay my homage!

233 Tib. Dge-slong rdo-rje 'dzin-pa.

234 Dowman erroneously calls Gayadhara, "the Kashmiri Pandita Gayadhara" which is groundless. This way of giving random names to past scholars can be very misleading as most Tibetan Buddhist historians familiar with Indo-Tibetan scholars will identify Kashmiri Pandita with Kashmiri Pandita Shakyashri, from whom Sakya Pandita [sa-kya pan-di-ta] received his Bhikhu ordination. Gayadhara is neither a Kasmirian nor was he known with this name. See PPCT, p. 278.

235 Generally there are eighteen fields of study, but the five sciences referred to here are the five major fields of study "rig gnas che ba lnga", [pañcamahavidyasthana] : 1. bzo-rig-pa [silpavidya], Fine Arts, 2. gso-ba rig-pa [cikitsa], Medicine, 3. sgra-rig-pa [sabdavidya], Linguistics, 4. gtan-tshigs-rig-pa [nyayavidya], Logic, and 5. nang-don rig-pa [adhyatmavidya], Philosophy. See _bod rgya tshig mdzod chen mo smad cha_, mi rigs dpe sprun khang, 1981, p. 2682 and TED, p. 1178.

236 Tib. Grong-'jug.

237 There is no indication how soon after Drogmi returned from India Gayadhara came to Tibet. Whether Drogmi had built his monastery or not, he had become very famous when the two met for the first time. There are some sarcastic remarks made by the

associates of Atisa about Indian Panditas going to Tibet to collect gold. Gayadhara and others have been criticized for their desire to obtain gold in return for instructions. It must have been before 1042 when Atisa came to Tibet, hence I would estimate 1038 as the year when Gayadhara first came to Tibet and met Drogmi.

238 This cave is situated in Lhatse about 151 kilometres west of Shigatse [gzhis-ka-rtse].

239 See SLLS, Vol. XIV, f. 44.

240 Ibid., ff. 43-44.

241 Ibid., f. 63.

242 According to the Buddhist teachings, the cyclic existence known as 'Samsara' consists of the three realms: Skt. Kamadhatu, Tib. 'dod-khams; Skt. Rupadhatu, Tib. gzugs-khams; Skt. Arupadhatu, Tib. gzugs-med khams.

243 This is confirmed in the biography of Buton by Dratsepa Rinchen Senge (sgra-tshad pa rin-chen seng-ge) who lists among others both Gayadhara and Virupa as previous incarnations of Buton. See _zha lu dgon gyi lo rgyus mdor bsdus_, Published by bod ljongs mi rigs dpe sprun khang, p. 30.

244 Even though 'red Pandita' is the nickname of Gayadhara and he may have occasionally worn a red garment, he is traditionally painted wearing a white garment.

245 See SLLS, Vol. XIV, f. 64.

246 Ibid., ff. 44-45.

247 This text known as _'bla ma lnga bcu pa'_ Fifty Verses on Guru Devotion, (Toh. 3721) in Tibetan, is one of the first works that Drogmi and Gayadhara translated together. It is included in the Lamdre teachings. See Tsharchen's commentary _bshes gnyen dam_

pa bsten par byed pa'i thabs shloka lnga bcu pa'i igrel pa, SLLS, Nya.
49, ff. 415-465.

248   Tib. Don-yod grub-pa'i bla-ma'i rnal-'byor.

249 Ngawang Kunga Sonam makes an interesting comment
regarding where Gayadhara was going to get his Indian texts from.
He says: "I have to go to Nepal to get the texts etc. ...' which suggests
that Gayadhara could have left his texts in Nepal. See SLLS, Vol. XXI,
f. 131. Although it is difficult to know which texts he was referring
to, it is possible that this is the same Sanskrit text on Tantra [rgyud-
kyi rgya-dpe] said to have reached Sachen's hand later on.   This
indicates that there was some form of written text which
Gayadhara had to resort to even though he should know everything
by heart as far as the Lamdre instructions were concerned. He
could have also said that as an excuse for not disclosing why he was
going to India or Nepal as we know that Gayadhara purposely did
not always tell the truth to his disciples.   Similar comments were
made by later Lamdre masters such as Shangton Choebar [zhang-
ston chos-'bar], who told Sachen that he had to first consult some
texts before he could give Lamdre instructions. It appears to me
that these teachers were deliberately using such techniques as a
way of examining the genuineness and patience of their disciples
[snod-brtag-pa]. There is also a tradition within Lamdre that the
instructions should not be given to disciples who have not made at
least three formal requests to test their suitability and devotion.
During the formal teaching of Lamdre instructions, disciples have to
make at least three mandala offerings to request the instructions at
the beginning of the session and one at the end.

250 This tradition of making special offerings on the first day of
Lamdre is still practised as explained in the lam-'bras 'chad-thabs,
the procedures of preaching Lamdre. Sponsoring a whole Lamdre
teaching is considered a very meritorious deed as it requires a

strong financial commitment to make it happen.

251 Dudjom Rinpoche's history has a comprehensive chapter on Zur Family and Zurpoche's discipleship under Drogmi Lotsawa. See NSTB, p. 633.

252 See SLLS, Vol. XIV, f. 61.

253 See NSTB, p. 633.

254 A Torma is sacrificial cake used as a medium through which the deity is invoked in order to bestow initiations. There are many types of Tormas including those which are used as effigies of evil demons and obstacles.

255 Some say that he stayed in Tibet three years or more.

256 Jamyang Khyentse Wangchuk correctly asserts that Pandita Gayadhara visited Tibet four times. All the other Lamdre historians as well as all Tibetan historians believe that Gayadhara visited Tibet only three times. The first visit took place at the prediction and guidance of his teacher and Khasarpani during which he met Drogmi, but did not give Lamdre. It was hosted mainly by Purang Lotsawa but Drogmi and Gayadhara first met during this visit. He made preliminary arrangements to bestow Lamdre after three years' time. During the second visit, he gave gsung-ngag lam-'bras to Drogmi and stayed five years in Tibet. In spite of his detailed account of all the four visits which agrees with other accounts, Ngawang Kunga Sonam and others seem to treat the first and second visit as one. It is important to differentiate between the first and second visits. Notwithstanding the maturity of Drogmi, it is unlikely that Gayadhara would have given Lamdre during his first visit. We have to accommodate Gayadhara's explanation that he had to collect his Indian texts [rgya-dpe] from India. Drogmi also would not have managed to collect sufficient gold if Lamdre had been given during the first visit. Gayadhara told Drogmi that he

was going to India to visit his teachers to offer the gold to accumulate merits and to bring back his texts. Though he may have left his texts in Nepal, there is no mention of his teachers living in Nepal. Even if he went only as far as Nepal, his return from there to Tibet would still be treated as his second visit. See Ngawang Kunga Sonam's OCES in SLLS, Vol. zha, f. 135. The third and fourth visits were respectively invited by Goe Lotsawa Sonam Tsemo ('Gos-lo-tsa-ba bsod-nams rtse-mo) and Gyijo Daway Oser (Gyi-jo zla-ba'i 'od-zer).

257 A phrase which Drogmi often used with his potential students was: "If you wish to receive teachings, go and bring some wealth from your home" [chos dgos na yul du song la na nor 'khyer la shog]. It is this effective approach of Drogmi, undoubtedly taught by Gayadhara which has been interpreted unfavourably by scholars such as Tsang Nyon Heruka who reports what Marpa thought when he faced Drogmi's strict approach: "Even if I stayed a long time with this guru [Drogmi] in order to complete the four abhisekas of Nairatmya, I would have had to give fifteen female Yaks [Dri]. To receive the permission-blessing of the devi Ekajati, I would surely have had to give at least one yak or dri. Without offerings, it is impossible to fill one's mind completely with the dharma. Even if I had such offerings and completely received the dharma in this way, I couldn't say that I had received the teachings from a great pandita. In particular, I have asked again and again to borrow the _Dakini-vajrapañjara-tantra_ to look at briefly, but Drogmi would not give it to me. I should give this guru as many offerings as will please him, and exchange the rest of my provisions for gold. Then I should take my share of the inheritance from my parents and go to India to study the dharma." See LMT, pp. 6-7. Although Marpa may have thought that in the beginning, it was the skilful means of Drogmi which actually led him to go to India and become what he is renowned for. Marpa himself appears to have used this approach

415

later to his students. This is the same with Goe Lotsawa.

[258] He does not seem to be included among Abhayadatta's eighty-four siddhas. Maitripa was one of the main teachers of Marpa and Khyungpo Naljor (Khyung-po rnal-'byor). Since he is not only known as Avadhutipa but also "mNga'-bdag mai-tri-pa", he appears to have been a king previously. This raises the question whether he is to be identified as Gayadhara's teacher Avadhutipa or someone else.

[259] There are two main schools in the Guhyasamaja Tantric lineage in India. They are Arya School (gsang-bsdus 'phags-lugs) headed by Arya Nagarjuna and Jñanapada school, headed by BuddhaShrijñana.

[260] See SLLS, Vol. XXI, f. 138.

[261] There are also a number of texts translated by him with the collaboration of Gayadhara and many other Indian Panditas.

[262] Khareg Thophu is Gayadhara's hermitage situated in Tsang province. See LLT, p. 1.

[263] See SLLS, Vol. XXI, f. 139 and also Vol. XIV, f. 49.

[264] He was born in 1306 and died in 1386. See BA, pp. 778-779.

[265] See _Lam 'bras bla ma tshad ma'i lo rgyus_, Encyclopaedia Tibetica, _The Collected Works of Bodong Panchen Choklay Namgyal_ [Bo-dong pan-chen phyogs-las rnam-rgyal], Tibet House, New Delhi, 1973, Vol. 106, ff. 439-440.

[266] Gyichuwa Dala Bar (Sgyi-chu ba dgra-lha-'bar) was also a teacher of Sachen Kunga Nyingpo.

[267] Slob-dpon rin-po che bsod-nams rtse-mo was one the five founding masters of Sakyapa tradition and elder son of Sachen.

[268] See BA, Pt. I, p. 205.

269 Ibid., Pt. II, p. 399.

270 Panchen Ngawang Choedak says Drogmi studied in India 12 years with the six scholars including Shantipa, but does not mention about the second visit. See SLLS, Vol. XXV, f. 163.

271 See SLLS, Vol. XXI, p. 124. But Ngawang Kunga Sonam contradicts his earlier work written in 1616 where he says: rgya che'i dam chos lo brgyad bar du bslabs / de nas dpa' bo rdo rje'i zhabs dru_ du / dba_ khrid rgyud gsum bshad pa mang po gsan / mdor na rgya gar bal yul dang bcas par / mi lo bcu gsum bzhugs nas mkhas par gyur / Its translation is: He (Drogmi) studied extensive sublime Dharma during eight years. After that he listened to many initiations, instructions, explanations on Tantra etc. from Viravajra. In short, he became learned after having spent thirteen years in India and Nepal. See *Gratifier of the Readers* in SLLS, Vol. XXIII, f. 563. We find that the same author is quoting conflicting facts in between different works or even paragraphs of the same work. Khetsun Sangpo, a modern Nyingma scholar repeats the same mistake regarding the number of years Drogmi spent in India. He copies a large passage from Ngawang Choedak's work and says Drogmi spent eight years in India. See *Biographical Dictionary of Tibet and Tibetans*, Vol. XI, pp. 34-44. In his earlier volume he copies Ngawang Kunga Sonam's OCES and says Drogmi studied with Shantipa for eighteen years. See BDTT, Vol. X, p. 44. Although it is evident from where Khetsun Zangpo copied them, he does not cite his sources and thus contradicts himself.

272 Even though he does not cite his sources, he must have based this on the chronological table by Sumpa Khenpo Yeshe Paljor's (Sum-pa mkhan-po ye-shes dpal-'byor) history. See SPS, Vol. 214, f. 547.

273 See LMT, p. xxvi.

274 Ibid., p. 199.

275 A Root Guru referred to as rtsa-ba'i bla-ma in Tibetan is from whom a Vajrayana disciple has at least received a major initiation and therefore entered into a qualified mandala. One can have more than one Root Guru as the author here pays homage to the Holy Root Gurus; he is most probably referring to Mang-thos klu-sgrub rgya-mtsho (1523-1594) and Dbang-phyug dpal-bzang who are mentioned in his colophon.

276 Tib. ri-dvags mig-can is a poetic synonym for excellent and beautiful women, hence here it refers to the fifteen goddesses (Nairatmayoginis) who bestowed initiation to Virupa the night before he attained the first Bhumi.

277 In the Buddhist teachings mention of the four Maras are made repeatedly as a person will not attain enlightenment until he or she overcomes them. They personify factors of negativity in one's mind and thus the entire cycle of rebirth and death. They are: 1) Tib. phung-po'i bdud, Skt. skandamara, the mara of aggregate, 2) Tib. nyon-mongs pa'i-bdud, Skt. kleshamara, the mara of defilements, 3) Tib. 'chi-bdag gi-bdud, Skt. mrtyupatimara, the mara of death, 4) Tib. lha'i-bu'i bdud, Skt. devaputramara, the mara of the son of the god.

278 Mu-stegs pa refers to all proponents of extreme or wrong views, a common term used for all non-Buddhist schools of philosophy. Virupa is known for his use of spiritual and magical powers when subjugating the Tirthikas. For details see Part I, Chapter One.

279 In this verse the author is seeking the blessing of Mahasiddha Virupa, the founding father of the lam 'bras teachings in order to fulfil the wishes of the past great masters.

280 Here the author is paying his salutation to the first three

masters of the Sakyapa tradition, namely to Sa- chen kun-dga' snying-po [1092-1158], Slob-dpon bsod-nams rtse-mo [1142-1182] and Rje-btsun grags-pa rgyal -mtshan [1147-1216], the former being the father of the latter two. The meanings of their names are intertwined in the Tibetan stanza.

281 The five major sciences are : Art (Tib. bzo, Skt. silpa), medicine (Tib. gso ba, Skt. cikitsa), linguistics (Tib. sgra, Skt. sabdavidya), logic (Tib. tshad ma, Skt. hetu) and inner philosophy (Tib. nang don rig pa, Skt. adhyatma). Lnga-rig pan-chen is a title given to a master who is well versed in all major fields of studies and Sa-skya Pan-di-ta [1182-1251] was the first Tibetan to receive this title.

282 This refers to Sa-skya Pan-di-ta's famous nephew 'Gro-mgon chos-rgyal 'phags-pa [1235-1280] who gave Hevajra initiation to the Mongol emperor, Kublai Khan in 1253 and subsequently became the first Tibetan Lama to become the spiritual and temporal leader of Tibet. It is through Sa-skya Pan-di-ta's influence that Tibetan Buddhism was first introduced and established in Mongolia. The first Mongol script was also invented by 'Phags pa.

283 The hereditary lineage referred to here is the 'Khon lineage which has had a special influence on the Tibetan civilisation since the early days of the diffusion of Buddhism in the 7th century. For instance 'Khon klu'i dbang-po, one of the first seven Tibetans to be ordained as a Buddhist monk came from this family. The throne holders of the Sa-skya-pa tradition have all been descendants of this family and are therefore regarded to be the emanations of many Bodhisattvas. The present throne holder of Sakya tradition, His Holiness Sakya Trizin (1944-   ) is the 41st patriarch of the lineage.

284 Believed to be prophesied by the Buddha himself, Ngor-chen kun-dga' bzang-po was the founder of the Ngorpa sub-tradition and

was probably the most influential master in the Sakyapa tradition after the five great masters. Historically he transmitted the Lamdre teachings the most number of times (out of all the masters in the Lamdre lineage). Regarded as one of the greatest Vinaya holders in Tibet, his contribution to the lam-'bras tradition includes the famous commentary on four commentarial traditions of the Hevajra lineages known as zla- zer "the Moon's Rays". See SLLS, Vol. XVII (Tsa), Title No. 100, ff. 1- 417.

285 This refers to Go-bo rab-'byams pa bsod-nams seng-ge) [1429-1489] who is commonly known as Gorampa. He was the 6th abbot of Ngor monastery and his scholarly works are considered highly stimulating and controversial. Having studied under highly reputed Sakya teachers such as Ngor-chen, Rong-ston and Mus-chen, his sharp and fearless approach in teaching and debating on Buddhist philosophy earned him coveted respect within the Tibetan scholars of his time. The mainstream of the Sa-skya-pa school holds his interpretation of Madhyamika philosophy in accordance with the correct doctrine of Nagarjuna and the commentaries written by renowned Indian and Tibetan scholars. Although there are numerous works which belong to the lam-'bras teachings in his fourteen volumes of collected writings, strangely only two of his works (a commentary on the Generation Stage of Hevajra Sadhana and a biography of Mus-chen) are included in the SLLS. See SLLS, Vol. I (Ka), Title No. 22 and Vol. XVII (Tsa), Title No. 101.

286 This refers to Ngor-chen dkon-mchog lhun-'grub [1497- 1557], a prolific Sa-skya master and 9th abbot of Ngor monastery, who our author venerates as one of his inspirations. Although Dkon-mchog lhun-'grub had long passed away before the time of the author, his collected works (believed to be four volumes) became a source of inspiration to many rising scholars and a remarkable contribution to the Sakyapa liturgy. Among others it

was Dkon-mchog lhun-'grub's numerous works on the lam 'bras and particularly his *Three Tantras, the Beautiful Ornament of Liberation* which our author used as the model to compose this particular work which is in fact a concise version of the former. The author modestly admits in his colophon that he in fact has done very little except making Dkon-mchog lhun-'grub's work more concise. Many of the annotations found in this translation are extracted from his works. See SLLS, Vol. XXIV (Ya), ff. 271 - 493.

287 Here the author pays his respect to Mang-thos klu-sgrub rgya-mstho (1523-1594) who was one of the main masters from whom he received the lam-'bras slob-bshad teachings. Mang-thos klu sgrub rgya-mtsho is also a renowned translator and this is the reason why the author calls him the Eyes of the World. The Tibetan word for translator "lo tsa ba", is not only an abbreviated form of the Sanskrit word lokacaksu (Tib. 'jig-rten mig), "the Eyes of the World" but it is also Tibetanised to a degree that non-Tibetan scholars without Sanskrit knowledge are unlikely to be able to trace its root. Etymologically in ancient times one who could understand and translate other languages appears to have been regarded as equivalent to having the eyes or knowledge of the other cultures at least. Of the eleven volumes of his writings there is at least one volume on the lam-'bras slob-bshad alone making him an important figure in the lam-'bras hierarchy. His scholastic and rational interpretation on kun-gzhi, alayavijnana has made numerous later Sa-skya scholars apprehensive about using his work except for references. Blo-getr dbang-po was perhaps the only teacher who so skilfully defended Mang-thos klu-sgrub rgya-mtsho's view without widening the gap of misunderstanding that existed between the different schools of thoughts within the lam-'bras traditions. See SLLS, Vol. XV (Ba), ff. 1 - 648.

288 Here the author pays his homage to Rje-dbang-phyug dpal-bzang who is his second most important master. There is no work

by him to be found in the lam-'bras. All these verses are technically called 'mchod-par brjod-pa' paying homage to past masters and calling upon their blessings to succeed in the composition. It is a common practice in composing all religious works which can be compared to the few lines of acknowledgements traditionally found in modern works.

[289] This last verse expresses the promise to compose the work rtsom-par dam-bca' ba and nyan-par skul-ba, exhorting the readers to reap the benefit of reading it joyfully. It is because of the conciseness of this work that his writings are widely used during hastily given lam-'bras teachings.

[290] This is to be found in his *gsung ngag sngon 'gro'i khrid rim snang gum snying po'i legs bshad, Essential Elegant Sayings of the Three Visions: Instructions on the Preliminaries of Lam-'bras*, SLLS, Vol. No. XXV (Ra), Title No. 162, ff. 219-281. Unfortunately this work has not been translated into English but *Konchok Lhundrup's Three Visions, the Beautiful Ornament of Liberation* has been translated into English and published in Singapore by Golden Vase Publications.

[291] Here the word "great" [rnam grangs du ma] refers to the eleven profundities or great qualities of the lam- 'bras teachings: (i) The instructions of the "Path Including Its Results", the jewel of the holy teachings, the only way traversed by all the Tathagatas of the three times; the extracted essence of the meaning of all collections of Sutras and Tantras containing the Enlightened One's profound discourses; the precepts taught by the fearless Sri Dharmapala (Virupa), the great and reverent lord of Yogis; the instructions found worthy to be traversed by the wise; the true nature of the transic absorption of emptiness, excellent in every way; a lamp that illuminates all Sutras and Tantras; and that which is difficult to understand by those who have no merit, but a stairway for those

who set out for the city of liberation. (ii) The instruction on the result that includes the path. (iii) The instruction that through knowing one thing, one will know many. (iv) The instruction on transforming faults into virtues. (v) The instruction on accepting obstacles as spiritual attainments. (vi) The instruction on removing the obstacles of concentrative meditation by recognising the meditative absorptions. (vii) The instruction on removing the Mara's hindrances through recognising these obstacles for what they are. (viii) The instruction on knowing how to transform faults into virtues and accept obstacles as spiritual attainments. (ix) The instructions on unerringly knowing the true essence of the Three Collections of the teachings (Tripitaka). (x) The instruction that is like a philosopher's stone (which changes all that it touches into gold). (xi) The instruction of the Root Treatise, The Vajra Verses, which is like a wish-fulfilling gem. For the Root Treatise See *lam 'bras bu dang bcas pa'i rtsa ba rdo rje'i tshig rkang* by Virupa, rgyud Shi, 139a- 143b, sde dge bstan 'gyur, Toh. 2284.

292 There is no content under this heading in the original text.

293 Before receiving the Hevajra Cause initiation, one must receive the Bodhisattva vow in the traditional lam-'bras teachings. See Introduction. Although there are several transmissions on the ceremony of the Bodhisattva vow, according to Mahasiddha Virupa's tradition it is one which is a combination of two exceptional Lineages. See SLLS, Vol. XIX (Dza.), Title No. 122, ff. 137 - 223 for the text on the Bodhisattva vow ceremony by the author.

294 It must be pointed here that after receiving a major Vajrayana initiation such as the Hevajra Cause initiation (rgyu-dbang) the disciples have already received the twenty complete Vajrayana vows which consist of five vows for each of the four initiations. There are different schools of views as to at what point

in time of the initiation ceremony one receives the complete Vajrayana vows. The five vows are: 1. The vow of meditative equanimity (mnyam-bzhag gi dam-tshig), 2. the vow of post meditational behaviour (rjes-spyod kyi dam-tshig), 3. the vow of eating (bza'-ba'i dam-tshig), 4. the vow of protection (bsrung-ba'i dam-tshig) and 5. the vow of non-separation (mi-'bral ba'i dam-tshig). There are considerable differences between the five vows of the four initiations. For instance, the commonly known fourteen root and eight branch downfalls (rdo rje theg pa'i rtsa ba'i ltung ba bcu bzhi dang yan lag gi ltung ba brgyad) of Vajrayana are in fact the protective vows of the Vase Initiation alone. See _Refutation of Errors: A Commentary: Ellucidating the Meaning of the Tantric Pledges (dam tshig gi rnam bshad 'grel pa 'khrul spong gi dgong pa rab tu gsal ba)_ by Bdag-chen blo-gros rgyal-mtshan [1444 - 1495], SLLS, Vol. XX (Wa), Title No. 132, ff. 105 - 191.

295 Tib. kun-gzhi rgyu-rgyud, Skt. Alayahetutantra

NOTES ON PART TWO
THE TRIPLE TANTRA

MEDITATION ON THE VIEW THROUGH THE CAUSE TANTRA

296 Tib. lus thabs-rgyud, Skt. Kayopayatantra.

297 Generally there are two types of preliminary practices in all Tibetan Buddhist practices. 1. The common preliminary practices [Tib. thun mong ba'i sngon 'gro] consists of the understanding of the difficulty of obtaining a precious human rebirth, death and impermanence, the Law of cause of effect and the shortcomings of worldly existence. The number of uncommon preliminary practices [Tib. thun-mong ma-yin pa'i sngon-'gro] varies from tradition to tradition. Although only three preliminary practices are mentioned in this and most lam -'bras manuals, the practice of Refuge including prostration and Bodhicitta are implied as all of the three preliminaries have to be practised with Refuge and Bodhicitta. Due to the commonness of Refuge and Bodhicitta in all causal Mahayana practices, here they are not treated as a new preliminary in spite of the introduction of the uncommon visualisation of the Refuge object in the Tantric path, the resultant Mahayana. Despite different numbers or sets of practices (usually 100,000 times each), all of the uncommon preliminary practices, whatever they may be, are included in the basic idea of the need to accumulate merits and the purification of karmic obscurations.

298 **The refuge prayers:** In the most holy Guru who is the quintessence of the qualities and the deeds of the body, voice and mind of all the Tathagatas abiding in the ten directions and three times, the source of the eighty four thousand articles of the

Doctrine and Master of the Noble Assemblies -- I and all living beings, equal to the bounds of space, from this time forth until the essence of Enlightenment is reached steadfastly take Refuge in the venerable root Guru and in the holy masters of the lineage; take Refuge in the blessed Accomplished Buddhas; take Refuge in the Holy teachings; take Refuge in the Noble Assemblies.

(Thus recite as many times as possible and then with folded hands say:)

In the Guru and Three Precious Gems I bow down and take refuge; may you bless me in all my lifetimes.

[299] Forehead, throat and heart.

[300] *om svabhava suddha sarva dharma svabhava suddho 'ham* (All phenomena is naturally pure, so I am (also) naturally pure). The svabhava mantra as it is conveniently called here, is recited before most creations of visualisations in the Vajrayana practices. Here when the mantra is read, the practitioner reflects on the emptiness of the conventional ritual and shrine objects which are then regenerated in the form of manifestations of pure divine substances.

[301] Tib. rta babs bzhi symbolise the four immeasurables and purification of the four elements.

[302] Past, present and future.

[303] Vajradhara is the sixth race, the first five being the five Tathagatas Akshobhya, Vairocana, Ratnasambhava, Amitabha and Amoghasiddhi respectively.

[304] LINEAGE A: The following is according to the Lam-'bras slob-bshad lineage of Ngor tradition: Vajradhara, Vajranairatmya, Virupa, Krishnacarin, Damarupa, Avadhutipa, Gayadhara, Drogmi Lotsawa, Seton Kunrig, Shangton Choebar, Sachen Kunga Nyingpo,

426

Lopon Sonam Tsemo, Jetsun Drakpa Gyaltshen, Sakyapa Pandita Kunga Gyaltshen, Choegyal Phakpa, Shang Konchok Pal, Sonam Pal, Lama Dampa Sonam Gyaltshen, Choje Paldhen Tsultrim, Drubchen Buddha Shri, Ngorchen Kunga Zangpo, Muchen Konchok Gyaltshen, Dagchen Dorje Chang, Doring Kunpangpa Chenpo, Tsharchen Losal Gyatsho, Jamyang Khyentse Wangchuk, Khenchen Labsum Gyaltshen, Dorje Chang Wangchuk Rabten, Gonpo Sonam Chogdhen, Rinchen Sonam Chogdrup, Khyenrab Jampa, Morchen Kunga Lhundrup, Nesarpa Kunga Lekpe Jungne, Kunga Lodro, Thartse Namkha Chime, Kunga Tenzin, Tenpe Gyaltshen, Sonam Gyaltshen, Lodro Nyingpo, Kunga Jamyang, Jamyang Loter Wangpo, Chokyi Nyima and Khenchen Dampa Rinpoche Zhenphen Nyingpo. LINEAGE B: The following is according to the Lam-'bras slob-bshad lineage of Na-len-dra Tshar-pa tradition: Vajradhara, Vajranairatmya, Virupa, Krishnacarin, Damarupa, Avadhutipa, Gayadhara, Drogmi Lotsawa, Seton Kunrig, Shangton Choebar, Sachen Kunga Nyingpo, Lopon Sonam Tsemo, Jetsun Drakpa Gyaltshen, Sakyapa Pandita Kunga Gyaltshen, Choegyal Phakpa, Shang Konchok Pal, Tshogom Kunga Pal, Nyenchen Sonam Tenpa, Drag Phukpa, Lama Dampa Sonam Gyaltshen, Paldhen Tshultrim, Buddha Shri, Ngorchen Kunga Zangpo, Muchen Konchok Gyaltshen, Dagchen Dorje Chang, Doring Kunpangpa Chenpo, Gorum Kunga Lekpa, Tsharchen Losal Gyatsho, Jamyang Khyentse Wangchuk, Khenchen Labsum Gyaltshen, Dorje Chang Wangchuk Rabten, Gonpo Sonam Chogdhen, Rinchen Sonam Chogdrup, Khyenrab Jampa, Morchen Kunga Lhundrup, Nesarpa Kunga Lekpe Jungne, Khyenrab Tenzin Lhundrup, Ngawang Losal Phuntshok, Lhatsun Khorloi Gonpo, Gendun Tashi Pajor, Zimok Tenzin Nyendrak, Chogye Rinchen Khyentse Wangpo, Zimok Kunga Tenzin and Chogye Khyenrab Lekshe Gyatsho. LINEAGE C: The following is according to the Lam-'bras tsgogs-bshad lineage of uncommon Ngor tradition: Vajradhara, Vajranairatmya, Virupa, Krisnacarin,

Damarupa, Avadhutipa, Gayadhara, Drogmi Lotsawa, Seton Kunrig, Shangton Choebar, Sachen Kunga Nyingpo, Lopon Sonam Tsemo, Jetsun Drakpa Gyaltshen, Sakyapa Pandita Kunga Gyaltshen, Choegyal Phakpa, Shang Konchok Pal, Sonam Pal, Lama Dampa Sonam Gyaltshen, Choje Paldhen Tsultrim, Drubchen Buddha Shri, Ngorchen Kunga Zangpo, Muchen Konchok Gyaltshen, Dagchen Dorje Chang, Doring Kunpangpa Chenpo, Tsharchen Losal Gyatsho, Jamyang Khyentse Wangchuk, Khenchen Labsum Gyaltshen, Dorje Chang Wangchuk Rabten, Gonpo Sonam Chogdhen, Rinchen Sonam Chogdrup, Morchen Kunga Lhundrup, Nesarpa Kunga Lekpe Jungne, Kunga Lodro, Thartse Namkha Chime, Kunga Tenzin, Tenpe Gyaltshen, Khyentse Wangpo, Namkha Gyaltshen, Sherab Gyatsho, Sonam Gyaltshen, Lodro Gyaltshen, Chokyi Nyima and Khenchen Dampa Rinpoche Zhenphen Nyingpo.

[305] Through your kindness, the great bliss itself arises in a single instant. To the Guru with a precious body, I bow down to your Vajra lotus feet. *Tib. gang gi drin gyis bde chen nyid / skad cig nyid la 'char ba gang / bla ma rin chen lta bu'i sku / rdo rje cen zhab pad la 'dud //*

[306] Although here the author only mentions the mentally imagined offerings one should have arranged the physically displayed offerings [Tib. dngos-su gshams-pa'i mchod-pa] which consists of drinking water, water for washing the feet, flowers, incense, lamps, perfume and food around the mandala of sanctity in the correct order according to the witnessed rituals of the lineage (mthong-ba brgyud-pa'i phyag-len).

[307] *om guru buddha bodhisattva saparivara argham ah hum*
om guru buddha bodhisattva saparivara padyam ah hum
om guru buddha bodhisattva saparivara puspe ah hum
om guru buddha bodhisattva saparivara dhupe ah hum
om guru buddha bodhisattva saparivara aloke ah hum

om guru buddha bodhisattva saparivara ghandhe ah hum
om guru buddha bodhisattva saparivara naividyam ah hum
om guru buddha bodhisattva saparivara shabda ah hum

308 Mixing the merit field with one's motivation and the material of offering refers to the importance of reflecting on their dependent origination.

309 Om vajra bhumi ah hum! The golden earth, the base is extremely powerful and totally pure. Om vajra rekhe ah hum! Surrounded by an iron fence in its outermost limit, in the centre is the (syllable) Hum, the king of mountains, Mount Sumeru. (In the) east is Purva videha, (in the) south is Jambudvipa, (in the) west is Aparagodaniya, (in the) north is Uttarakuru. The sun, moon and all the perfect collections of the wealth and splendour of humans and gods without exception, I offer these to the holy, kind and glorious root and lineage Gurus, to the hosts of tutelary Deities of the mandalas, to the Buddhas and the Bodhisattvas, to the protectors who guard the holy Dharma, to the Yaksas and to the wealth deities. Through your compassion, please accept this for the sake of all sentient beings. Having accepted it please bestow your blessings.

310 Om vajra bhumi ah hum! The golden earth, the base is extremely powerful and totally pure. Om vajra rekhe ah hum! Surrounded by an iron fence in its outermost limit, in the centre is the (syllable) Hum, the king of mountains, Mount Sumeru. (In the) east is Videha, (in the) south is Jambudvipa, (in the) west is Aparagodaniya, (in the) north is Uttarakuru. Deha and Videha, Camara and Aparacamara, Satha and Uttaramantrina, Kurava and Kaurava, the precious mountain, the wish-fulfilling tree, the wish-fulfilling cow, the unploughed crops, the precious wheel, the precious queen, the excellent and precious horse, the precious general, the great treasure vase, the goddess of beauty, the goddess of garlands, the goddess of songs, the goddess of dance, the goddess

of incense, the goddess of flowers, the goddess of light, the goddess of perfume, the sun, the moon and all the perfect collection of the wealth and splendour of humans and gods without exception, I offer (all of) these to the holy, kind and glorious root and lineage Gurus, to the hosts of tutelary Deities of the mandalas, to the Buddhas and the Bodhisattvas, to the protectors who guard the holy Dharma, to the Yakshas and to the wealth deities. Through your compassion, please accept this for the sake of all sentient beings. "May my mental continuum be blessed so that I will completely accomplish the two accumulations, the accumulation of merit and the accumulation of wisdom! May (I be) blessed so that the two obscurations including their (Karmic) propensities be cleansed and purified! May (I be) blessed so that extraordinary Samadhi of the two stages be realized in (my) mental continuum! May (I be) blessed so that (I will) attain the stage of the two kayas!"

[311] One's own offering substances are an ocean of pure realms adorned by a cloud of various offerings equal to the atoms of an ocean from which ornamental light rays issue in the ten directions, and at the tips of the rays are (pure realms) equal in number to the atoms of an ocean. (At the tip of) each ray is a precious lotus which gives precious radiant light. In the corolla of these (precious lotuses) are the excellent sense desire objects of gods and human beings from which arise whatever one wishes abiding in the millions. Just like the miraculous offerings of Samantabhadra, this cloud of offering which is created by one's virtuous mind fills the space just like the all-pervasive Dharmadhatu and remains as long as sentient beings and the sphere of existence abide. I always offer (this) to the King of Dharma, the Conqueror, who is surrounded by a circle of Conqueror's Sons, Pratyekabuddhas and Arhats -- may you always be pleased by all these offerings.

From this time forth until the essence of Enlightenment is reached, I respectfully offer to you my body, wealth and virtues of

430

the three times for the sake of all sentient beings. May you, the Holy ones, who possess the eye of omniscience and who are most worthy of receiving offerings, through compassion for me, partake of these, my offerings; having accepted these, may you bless me. *Om guru buddha bodhisattva saparivara ratna mandala puja megha samudra sapharana samaya hum.*

₃₁₂ An ocean of the pure drinking-water offerings of learning circles all around; excellent flowers are qualities; morality, a cloud of incense. Wisdom is a lamp; faith, a lake of scented water. Meditative concentration is the noble food of ambrosia; the music of melodious eulogies is sounded. With universal compassion, discernment and confidence, the parasols, victory banners and streamers exquisitely adorn the celestial mansion, my body. The Master of Dharma who is the Teacher of all living beings firmly dwells on the full-moon lotus of my heart. As I offer these to you with sincere devotion, may you always be pleased!

₃₁₃ In every lifetime, may I never be parted from perfect teachers but ever enjoy the wealth of the Holy Dharma. Fully perfecting the spiritual virtues of the stages and Path of enlightenment, may I quickly attain the stage of Vajradhara.

₃₁₄ In an instant, on the top of one's head is a lotus and moon disc upon which is seated the blessed one, Vajrasattva Shri Heruka whose body is white in colour, with one face and two hands holding a Vajra and bell and embracing his consort. Adorned with the six ornaments of bone, he sits cross-legged in the Vajra position. On his head like a crown is his master the same in appearance as himself. He is in union with his consort, Vajragarvi, white in colour and holding a curved knife and a skull-cup and adorned with the five bone ornaments. In his heart, upon a moon-disc is a white Hum. Rays of light issue from the Hum invoking the essence of mind of all the Tathagatas in the form of the nectar of transcendental knowledge which is absorbed back into the Hum.

"O Blessed One, cleanse and purify, I pray all the accumulations of negative deeds and mental obscurations, non-virtues, failures, and impurities which I and all sentient beings have accumulated since beginningless Samsara."

Nectar flows from the Hum filling all the body of Heruka. Then from his body it fills the body of his consort. Nectar descends through the bodies of both the father and the consort, entering through the crown of one's head, and washing away all illnesses, evil spirits, negative deeds and mental obscurations which pass through the two lower passages as faeces and urine, and through the two soles of the feet as smoky liquid or as pus and blood. The body is then completely filled with nectar.

Om sri vajra heruka samayam anupalaya heruka tvenopa tishta drdho mebhava sutosyo mebhava anurakto mebhava suposyo mebhava sarva siddhim meprayaccha sarva karma sucame cittam sriya kuru hum ha ha ha ha hoh bhagavan vajra heruka mame muñca heruko bhava mahasamaya sattva ah hum phat

I, deluded by ignorance, have broken the samaya vows. Guru and protector be my refuge. To the highest Vajradhara, possessed of the essence of great compassion, the chief of beings, I go for Refuge. I confess all my transgressions of the root and branch vows of body, speech and mind. Cleanse and purify, I pray, all the obscurations of negative deeds, mental obscurations, faults, downfalls and impurities.

From the mouth of Vajrasattva, who is inseparable from one's Guru, come the words:

"O one of the noble lineage, you are cleansed and purified of all negative deeds and mental obscurations, faults, downfalls and impurities. From this time forth you should not perform any

432

negative deeds."

Vajrasattva and consort dissolve into light which is absorbed into oneself through the top of one's head and one's own body becomes like a rainbow.

315 Here it should be pointed out that the four powers listed above do not agree with the traditional listing. While the author admits (in the colophon) that he had written this work mainly on the basis of Dkon-mchog lhun-'grub's Three Tantras, he does not fully explain his version of the four powers which is rather different. Dkon-mchog lhun-'grub lists the four powers (stobs-bzhi) in this manner: One should perform the confession in its conclusion with the inclusion of the four powers: 1. The Blessed father and mother are the power of reliance; 2. The development of strong regret over non-virtue committed previously is the power of remorse; 3. "From now on I shall not commit (such actions) in the future even at the cost of my life" is the power of applying the antidote at all times and 4. "Through practising (skilful) methods such as this, I would certainly have purified the misdeeds (imprinted) on my mental continuum", is the power of restoration. See SLLS, Vol. XXIV (Ya), Title No. 157, f. 12/A 5-6.

316 _Sdom-gsum rab-dbye_, Classification of the Three Vows.

317 rgyu-dus kyi-dbang.

318 The four Bodies are: The Emanation Body, Nirmanakaya (sprul-sku); the True Body, Dharmakaya (chos-sku); the Enjoyment Body, Sambhogakaya (long-spyod rdzogs-pa'i sku) and the Body of Intrinsic Nature, Svabhavakaya (ngo-bo nyid-sku).

319 The five Families refer to the five main Tathagatas. Some modern writers have used the term the "Five Dhyana Buddhas" but it is not found in the Buddhist Tantric literature. The Sanskrit terms used for the five Families are: Five Jinas or more commonly

Pancakula (rigs-lnga). They are:

Buddha	Family	Body	Wisdom
Vairocana	Tathagata	Dharma	Dharmadhatu
Ratnasambhava	Ratna	Vipaka	Samata
Amitabha	Padma	Sambhoga	Pratyaveksana
Amoghasiddhi	Karma	Nirmana	Krtyanusthana
Akshobhya	Vajra	Svabhavika	Adarsa

[320] This version and other Guru Yoga prayers also appear in other Lam-'bras tshogs-bshad manuals. See SLLS, Vol. XXIV, Title 157.

[321] Blo-snying brang-gsum is a traditional Tibetan expression which conveys the notion of total submission out of faith and devotion.

[322] The prayer here refers to one given below which is for the purpose of integrating the practice into the Path of everyday activities. Dkon-mchog lhun-grub fittingly gives as follows:

O Venerable *Guru,* you are the embodiment of all the victorious ones' form, complete with the deities of the three Seats. Through (experiencing) the blissful devotion, I offer (all) the sensory qualities; may I be able to integrate the *Samayas* into the path!

rje bstun bla ma rgyal ba'i sku / kun 'dus gdan gsum tshang ba'i lha / 'dod yon mos gus bde bas mchod / dam tshig lam du longs bar shog // See SLLS, Vol. XXIV (Ya), f. 13/A-1-2.

[323] The eight siddhis refer to the eight common mystical attainments (thun-mong gi dngos-grub) gained through meditation

practices but not necessarily realising emptiness. They are: 1. the mystical power of sustaining life by chewing a pill (ril-bu) without eating gross food; 2. the mystical power of gaining extraordinary sight by the anointing of one's eyes with a lotion (mig-sman); 3. the mystical power to frequent the underworlds (analogous to the chthonic realms of Greek mythology) (sa-'og); 4. the mystical power to mount a flying sword (ral-gri); 5. the mystical power to fly ('phur-ba); 6. the mystical power to become invisible (mi -snang ba); 7. the mystical power of immortality and 8. the mystical power to heal sicknesses (nad-'joms-pa).

324 *lam 'bras pod ser, 'khor 'das dbyer med kyi lta ba'i rtsa ba rin chen snang ba*, SLLS, Vol. XI, ff. 191- 192.

325 Ibid., f. 192.

326 Of the phrase "mgrin-lhan yan-man" lhan definitely is a printing error which appears to have escaped the attention of the careful editors of the Sakya Centre. It should instead read "mgrin-lte yan-man" which means 'above and under the throat and the navel'. The scriber wrote 'lh' instead of 'lt' and subsequently suffixed 'n' which was an eminent suffix for the two following syllables and thus missed altogether to put the vowel 'e'. One is simply required to double check what is in the *rgud gsum mdzes rgyan* where the scriber fortunately didn't make the same mistake. Ibid f. 23/A-4.

327 *lam 'bras pod ser, 'khor 'das dbyer med kyi lta ba'i rtsa ba rin chen snang ba*, SLLS, Vol. XI, f. 192.

328 Ibid.

329 The practice of the Protection Wheel (bsrung-'khor) is used as one of the uncommon preliminary practices of Hevajra Sadhana in addition to those which have already been discussed above. Generally there are two types of Protection Wheels: common and

uncommon protection wheels. Here it refers to the common protection wheel.

[330] Nirmanakaya, Sambhogakaya, Dharmakaya and Svabhavakaya.

[331] Tib. dge ba'i rtsa ba 'di la brten nas 'gro la phan phyir sang rgyas 'grub par shog See f. 13/A-6.

[332] The full title is: *Skt. Svadhisthanakramaprabheda, Tib. bdag byin gyis brlab pa'i rim pa rnam par dbye ba.* See sde dge bstan 'gyur, Vol. (ngi. 112a - 114b), T. 1805.

[333] *lam 'bras pod ser, 'khor 'das dbyer med kyi lta ba'i rtsa ba rin chen snang ba*, SLLS, Vol. XI, f. 192.

[334] Ibid.

[335] This sub-heading actually refers to "The Three Main Meditations" as explained above.

[336] da-ltar-gyi which literally means 'that of now' actually implies da-ltar gyi snang-ba, the apparent things of the present moment. For instance what is apparent now is one's reading of this line and all other sensory perceptions which oneself and others commonly share as the same perceptions.

[337] Tib. Bdag-nyid chen-po is a title reserved for highly respected persons such as Sakya Pandita. In the present century it appears that only Mahatma Gandhi is conferred with this title. Bla-ma dam-pa bsod-nams rgyal-mtshan's father is also known as Bdag-nyid chen-po bzang-po dpal (1262-1324).

[338] Sakya Pandita's famous work on Buddhist logic (Pramana) "*tshad ma rig pai gter*".

[339] Phyva is a term referred to the creator of the universe by Bonpos as Isvara is by Hindus.

436

340   The full title is:

Skt. Shri
Sarvatathagataguhyatantrayogamaharajadvayasamatavijaya-
nama-vajra-shrivaramahakapai, Tib. dpal de bzhin gshegs pa thams
cad kyi gsang ba rnal 'byor chen po rnam par rgyal ba zhes bya ba
mnyam pa nyid gnyis su med pa'i rgyud kyi rgyal po rdo rje dpal
mchog chen po brtag pa dang po, See *sde dge bstan 'gyur,* Vol. (Cha.
103a - 331a), Toh. 453.

341 Since this is the same case with all the other examples,
remember to include all the nine stages as given here: (A) The
Three Preliminary Practices: 1) Developing the Enlightenment
Thought, 2) Visualising the *Guru* on the top of one's head and
praying to the *Guru* and 3) Visualising oneself as the deity. (B) The
three Main Meditations: 1) Remembering the examples, 2) Mixing
the examples with their meanings and 3) Setting the mind in itself.
(C) The Three Concluding Practices: 1) Dedication of merits, 2)
Meditation on compassion for the sake of sentient beings who have
not realised and 3) Pray to maintain the practice resolutely at all
times.

342 Tibetan word chang actually refers to homemade beer from
wheat, rice or any grain.   But in this context it refers to
consumption of any alcoholic drink which has the effect of changing
the perception and the behaviour of the consumer.

343 By consuming Kashokanta drug, all appearances change into
blue.

344 By consuming Datura (Skt. Dhattura), a poisonous plant, all
appearances change into gold. Monier Williams renders it into
white thorn-apple. See Williams, Sir Monier, Monier, *A Sanskrit*
English Dictionary, Reprinted by Motilal Banarasidass 1984, p. 508.

345 The Lankavatara Sutra says: As a man whose eye is affected

with a cataract perceives a hair-circle because of his delusion, so the ignorant perceives an objective world rising with its various aspects. See Suzuki, D. T., _The Lankavatara Sutra_, p. 236.

346 Regarding this, His Holiness Sakya Trizin told a story at the lam 'bras teaching He gave at Sakya College, Rajpur in mid-1987. It was about a lady with an eye disorder whose son had to work away. During his absence she refused food served by her daughter-in-law, maintaining that the food contained hairs from home which made her sick. But her stomach problem only came about because she believed that her food was deliberately contaminated by her daughter-in-law. Later when her eyes were treated, her stomach problems also disappeared. It seems that her misconception could project what she believed in whether or not her-daughter-in-law put hairs in her food.

347 _The Lankavatara_ p. 240 concurs: (Individual existences are) appearances, images, like Maya, like a mirage, a dream, a wheel made by a revolving fire-brand, the Gandharva's (castle), an echo -- they are all born in the same manner.

348 _lam 'bras pod ser, 'khor 'das dbyer med kyi lta ba'i rtsa ba rin chen snang ba_, SLLS, Vol. XI, f. 192.

349 Chu'i-'od-zer refers to droplets of water or even water bubbles in the air which by its associating with the sun's rays becomes a thin sparkling streamline of water. Lightning in the conventional sense is said to be caused by a discharge of atmospheric electricity.

350 'Phrog-pa literally means to embezzle, to rob or to snatch forcefully. A commonly used phrase in this relation is yid 'phrog pa 'to fall in love' and 'to loose one's heart to'. 'phrog byed is also synonymous with many nouns i.e. sun, wind god, brave person, Vishnu, Hari, lord of death, mercury etc. It is said that this example

refers to the reflection of a king named "Sinhacandra" going into Khechara along with his retinues reflected in the lake. This is extremely fitting as the equivalent of the word 'phrog-pa, Hari is also translated into seng-ge, 'lion'. See SLLS, Vol. XXIV, [Ya], ff. 35 - 36.

351 Gandharvas are often mentioned as a class of spirits in the Buddhist literature who are believed to survive mainly on smells and are particularly fond of flowers and fragrant objects as well as not so fragrant objects such as dung-hills. At the same time they seem to have a place in the heavens where they are highly respected celestial musicians. Beings in the intermediate state (bar srid) dwell in a similar experience of the Gandharvas prior to the finding of a new rebirth. In this context dri za'i grong is regarded as a perception of cities due to hallucination. It is also synonymous with bzang po'i grong (City of the nobles) and zla-ba'i-grong (city in the moon). Thus indeed the chances of making the moon inhabitable look like mere imagination.

352 Mi-ma-yin in Sanskrit is called amanusa, a type of ghost. They may look like humans but they are ghosts who some people can see and hear in the night. Often they are seen lighting fires and running up and down with fire.

353 It should read byin-rlabs kyi rim-pa without the instrumental suffix sa. Spelling errors are a major problem in working with unedited and unrevised Tibetan texts although this edition is said to have received a careful spelling check before it went to the press.

354 The Root Treatise refers to *lam 'bras bu dang bcas pa'i rtsa ba rdo rje'i tshig rkang* written by Virupa. Toh. 2284.

355 This sentence repeats the orientation of the reader to the structure of the current section; it does not indicate new

subheadings.

356 SLLS, Vol. XI, f. 192.

357 Nyi-ma skyon-med pa actually refers to a bright sun without being hindered by unfavourable weather conditions such as clouds, rainfall, mist or storm. Even if any of these conditions were present it is not regarded as the fault of the sun. Therefore 'nyi-ma skyon-med pa' can be loosely translated as an unhindered sun rather than a faultless sun though this is what it means literally.

358 Technically and generally bar-snang sgrib-gyogs med-pa refers to a cloudless sky. But I prefer to translate it as 'uncovered sky' since the sky does not have to be necessarily covered by clouds alone. One cannot ignite fire with a magnifying glass under an umbrella or indoors where there is no direct sunlight.

359 Tib. spra-ba rlan-med-pa refers to any combustible material used to light fire with a flint or any primitive fire making technique.

360 Tib. _Sa lu ljang pa'i mdo [Salistambaka sutra]_ was written by Nagarjuna. He later wrote his own commentary on it. There is another longer commentary by Kamalashila. See _sde dge bstan 'gyur_, Vol. (ngi. 18a - 20b), Toh. 3985, Vol. [ngi. 20b - 55b], Toh. 3986 and Vol. [Ji. 145b - 163b], Toh. 4001.

361 The author invariably inserts the 'Mixing the Examples with their Meanings' and 'Setting the Mind in its (meditative) State' only after the example of a seed (6) instead of at the end of the example of an echo (8) although they should be applied after each example. Dkon-mchog lhun-'grub explains them after each example except after the examples of a mirror (3), seal (4), and a magnifying glass (5). See SLLS, Vol. XXIV, ff. 36 - 41, f. 40/A-5 and ff. 40/A-3-40/B-4.

362 Tib. Rigs-drug refers to the six realms of existence which consist of the realm of the transient gods [Tib. lha, Skt. deva], realm

440

of the demi-gods [Tib. lha-ma-yin, Skt. asura], realm of human beings [Tib. mi, Skt. manusa], realm of animals [Tib. dud-'gro, Skt. pasu], realm of hungry ghosts [Tib. yi-dvags, Skt. preta] and the realm of the hell beings [Tib. dmyal-ba, Skt. naraka].

363 Tib. *Longs-spyod kyi-rlabs* refers to a certain vein situated on either side of one's neck which when pressed gently with one's thumb and ring finger can stop one's normal flow of thoughts.

364 SLLS, Vol. XI, f. 192.

365 Tib. Rang-rig-pa refers to cognition of the true nature of the self. Unlike intellectual knowledge and cognition which depends on the explanation of views and ideas on an issue, Self-Awareness is a deep intuitive experience within oneself which does not require any reference point to legitimize its realisation. Rang-rig pa'i ye-shes or the transcendental wisdom of the self-awareness is the all-encompassing wisdom at which point the meditator need not differentiate between the meditation and meditator, let alone the quality of his meditation. All the dualities and opposites disappear without becoming one or the other.

366 Tib. Sgro-skur is the abbreviated form of yod-pa la sgro-'dogs dang med-pa la skur-ba 'debs-pa. 'Sgro 'dogs-pa' means 'attaching a feather' which actually refers to an act of fabrication or exaggeration and 'skur-pa 'debs-pa ' refers to 'an act of blasphemy or deprecation'.

367 'Three doors' is a commonly used Tibetan phrase to express the interplay of body, speech and mind. They are the doorways through which one performs any karma, virtuous or otherwise. All deeds are committed through these three doors either singularly i.e. the mind - or two together, mind and speech or mind and body, or all three together. Where all three doors are employed together to fulfil a deed it is naturally much more powerful than one or two

doors performing a deed.

368 Chad-de refers to a link that has been totally severed.

369 This is an important instruction on how to develop the practice of meditation. The emphasis here is on how to develop the quality of one's meditation through frequency rather than duration. Many people meditate with some kind of expectation and make sessions so long that at the conclusion of their practice they are left with a sense of disappointment and may feel discouraged to continue. Shorter, frequent and intense sessions can make a vast difference to understanding the mind and this leads to a positive conclusion of one's practice with a sense of earnestness to resume again. The idea of 'sgom-bzang-gyes-byas' is analagous to two friends who separate on very good terms and who are more likely to see each other sooner than two friends who separate with negative feelings.

370 They are referred to as the four uncommon examples (thun-mong ma-yin-pa'i dpe) as they are only known within the Anuttarayoga Tantra of the Vajrayana teachings. Dkon-mchog lhun-'grub also refers to them as uncommon examples. See SLLS, Vol. XXIV, Title No. 157, ff. 45/B-3 and 47/B-5. What about the other sets of the examples? In earlier works of Jetsun Rinpoche Drakpa Gyaltshen the examples were simply referred to as the four former and latter examples (dpe dang po bzhi dang dpe phyi ma bzhi). According to 'Jam-dbyangs mkhyen-brtse dbang-phyug, the idea of major and minor examples (rtsa-ba dang yan-lag gi-dpe) was introduced by Bla-ma dam-pa bsod-nams rgyal-mtshan. See Ibid., Vol. XIV, Title No. 77, f. 22/B - 4-5. In the earlier sets of examples the distinction between major and minor examples were mainly associated with mental sensory consciousness. This does not apply with all the sets of examples. Nevertheless when one examines them carefully, in order to fathom the implied meaning,

all the latter examples of each of the sets of the examples warrant subtle interpretations in contrast to the former examples.

371 'Upper doorways' in this case refers to the upper openings of the three veins, the central (Avadhuti), right (Rasana) and left (Lalana) veins. The right amount of pressure on the vein can fluctuate the flow of the vital airs and create extraordinary floating and wave-like enjoyment.

372 In spite of this encouragement of the possibility of anyone developing the experience of inexpressibility by pressing the said veins, it can be very dangerous if one presses the wrong veins. Do not attempt to do this without the guidance of an experienced practitioner and without the requirement of this induction.

373 This is called the synthesisation of the (4 x 8 = 32) thirty two examples.

374 SLLS, Vol. XI, f. 193.

375 Ibid.

376 Ibid.

377 The concept of three-fold seats of the initiation deities 'dbang-lha gdan-gsum tshang-ba' refers to the congregation of the five Tathagatas, eight Bodhisattvas and ten wrathful deities along with their consorts who take up their respective seats which are arranged in three platforms.

378 The secret organ of the consort.

379 SLLS, Vol. XI, f. 193.

380 The four types of birth are explained as follows in the _dpal bde mchog 'byung ba zhes bya ba'i rgyud kyi rgyal po chen po, Sri mahasamvarodaya tantrarajanama_, Toh. 373, rgyud 'bum, Kha, ff. 265a-311a. In accordance with the nature of various deeds, there

are four types of births: oviparous (sgong skyes, andaja), viviparous (mngal skyes, jarajuja), (beings born from) moisture (drod sher skyes, samsvedaja) and (beings) born miraculously (rdzus rkyes, upa-padukaja). Geese, cranes, peacocks, parrots, thrushes and so on are oviparous; elephants, buffaloes, oxen, horses, donkeys and human beings are viviparous. Insects, worms, butterflies, fish and so on are born from moisture. Devas and hell-realm beings, as well as Bardo (the intermediate state between death and rebirth) beings and beings of the first kalpa and so forth, are born miraculously.

[381] The four immeasurables are: 1. Immeasurable loving-kindness [byams-pa tshad-med, maitriapramana], 2. Immeasurable compassion [snying-rje tshad-med, karunapramana], 3. Immeasurable joyfulness [dga'-ba tshad -med, muditapramana] and 4. Immeasurable equanimity [btang-snyoms tshad-med, upeksapramana].

[382]

Defilement	Colour	Hand Symbol	Wisdom
ignorance	white	wheel	dharmadhatu
hatred	blue	vajra	mirror-like wisdom
desire	red	lotus	discrimination
pride	yellow	jewel	equanimity
jealousy	green	cross-vajra	accomplishment

[383] SLLS, Vol. XI, f. 193.

[384] Ibid.

[385] Although the author does not give the complete sub-heading as he listed above, I have provided the full translation to avoid confusion.

[386] SLLS, Vol. XI, f. 193.

[387] This sub-heading is confusing in the sense that it is listed as

"The Mahamudra Result Tantra".

388 SLLS, Vol. XI, f. 193.

389 All ordained Tibetan Buddhist monks (dge-tshul and dge-slong) and also some Brahmacaryopasakas (tshangs-spyod dge-bsnyen) who have a reputation of being great upholders of the Vinaya lineage often prefix their name with 'Shakya' which is derived from the name of the Buddha's clan. Hence here Sa-skya Pan-dita calls himself *'sha-kya'i sras-po'*, a Sakya prince.

MEDITATING ON THE BODY METHOD TANTRA IN CONJUNCTION WITH THE FOUR INITIATIONS

390 Here the author is providing some sub-headings which are apparently not found in Dkon-mchog lhun-grub's work. See SLLS, Vol. XXIV, f. 58-A-3.

391 The explanatory notes refers to the author's work entitled *phyi bsked rim rnam par bshad pa blo gsal bde 'jug mkhas la nye bar mkho ba snying po'i legs bshad* or those by other scholars. See SLLS, Vol. XXV, Title No. 164, ff. 401 - 483.

392 Tib. bdag nyid chen po sa pan. Sapan is the abbreviation of Sa-skya Pan-di-ta.

393 The seven precious articles of royalty are: 1. The Precious Wheel, 2. The Precious Gem, 3. The Precious Queen, 4. The Precious Minister, 5. The Precious Elephant, 6. The Precious Horse 7. The Precious General. See footnote 34.

394 The four-limbed model is one of the several ways of describing the generation of the deities as found in Tshar-chen's commentary (nyi-zer): 1. The visualisation of the pledge being is the limb of approaching (the deity), 2. The blessing of the sense organs, the body, speech and mind is the limb of near acquisition, 3.

the invocation and absorption of the wisdom being is the limb of acquisition 4. The conferring of initiation and the application of the seal of the master of the family is the limb of the great acquisition. See SLLS, Vol. X, (tha), Title No. 53, f. 39/B-4-5.

[395] The six-limbed model Sadhana consists of: 1. gzhal-yas khang bskyed-pa rnam-par snang-mdzad kyi yan -lag [The Creation of the Celestial mansion, the Limb of Vairocana], 2. rjes-su chags-pa rdo-rje sems-dpa'i yan -lag [The Entering into Union, the Limb of Vajrasattva], 3. mi-skyod pa dbang-gi yan-lag [Initiation, the limb of Akshobhya], 4. bdud-rtsi myang-ba 'od-dpag med-pa'i yan-lag (The Tasting of Nectar, the Limb of Amitabha], 5. mchod-pa don-yod grub-pa'i yan-lag, [Offering, the Limb of Amoghasiddhi] and 6. bstod-pa rin-chen 'byung -ldan [Praising, the Limb of Ratnasambhava].

[396] Remembering the purities (dag-pa dran-pa) reflects on the symbolic meaning of the mandala and the deities included in the visualisation.

[397] Sku-byin is the honorific expression of byin pa (calf), the fleshy part behind the knee.

[398] This refers to the eight animals (creatures) held in Hevajra's right hands: a white elephant, a blue horse, an ass with a white patch on its forehead, a yellow bull, an ash-coloured camel, a red man, a blue Sharabha (cross-breed between a lion and garuda bird), and a rat with a white patch on its forehead.

[399] This refers to the eight gods held in Hevajra's left hands: a yellow god of earth, a white god of water, a red god of fire, a green god of air, a white god of moon, a red god of sun, a blue lord of death and a yellow holder of wealth.

[400] 1. Yellow Brahma representing "the mara of the son of the gods" (lha'i-bu'i bdud tshangs-pa ser-po), 2. white Indra

representing "the mara of the aggregates" [phung-po'i bdud dbang-po dkar-po], 3. blue Upendra representing "the mara of defilements" [nyon-mongs pa'i-bdud nye-dbang sngon-po] and 4. black Siva representing "the mara of death" ['chi-bdag gi-bdud drag-po nag-po].

401 The seven goddesses are: 1. red Cauri [chom-rkun ma dmar-mo], 2. yellow Vetali [be-ta li ser-mo], 3. green Ghasmari [ghas-ma ri ljang-khu], 4. blue Pukkasi [pu-kka si sngon-mo], 5. white Savari [ri-khrod ma dkar -mo], 6. sky-blue Candali [gdol-pa mo sngon-mo] and 7. multi-coloured Dombini [gyung-mo kha-mdog sna -tshogs pa].

402 The explanatory notes refers to the author's work entitled _zab mo lus dkyil gyi rnam bshad zin bris nyung ngus rnam gsal_ and works on the same topic by other scholars. See SLLS, Vol. XXV, Title No. 166, ff. 547- 569.

403 The five palaces (pho brang lnga) are situated at the crown, throat, heart, navel and secret organ. For details see the Hevajra Sadhana.

404 See the passage "In order to learn how to avoid the poisons of meditation..." under the sub-section 'Training in the visual aspects of the deities' on page 60.

405 This is discussed in the section on The Essential Points of the Body. See p. 75.

406 The great Sa-skya-pa refers to Sa-chen kun-dga' snying-po (1092-1158). The word "sa-chen" being the abbreviation of Sa-skya-pa chen-po is however used as a title for exceptional teachers who have held the throne of Sa-skya monastery or are in many ways regarded as a second Sa-chen. But in such cases the word 'Sa-chen' is simply prefixed to the actual name of the teacher i.e. Sa-chen kun-dga' blo-gros. Where the word 'Sa-chen' occurs by itself,

it refers to Sa-chen kun-dga' snying-po.

[407] A Vajrayana practitioner who is in a proper retreat which involves the practices of generation and completion stages has to follow a regulated number of sessions scheduled according to the time of sun rise and sun set. It is said that one should avoid being in session at the four periods when harmful spirits congregate to interfere with practitioners. The number of sessions vary according to different schools. Generally thun-bzhi'i rnal-'byor, the Yoga of four sessions, consists of 'tho-rangs kyi thun' referring to the early morning session which should conclude before sun rise;'snga thun' referring to the morning session which should conclude before midday; 'dgong-thun' referring to the afternoon session which should conclude before sun set and 'srod-thun' referring to the late evening session which should conclude before midnight. When referring to the Yoga of six sessions, [thun-drug rnal-'byor] one adds one session before midnight [mtshan-gyi cha-stod] and one session after midnight [mtshan -gyi cha-smad]. The difference between the numbers of sessions reflects the emphasis on frequency rather than duration or vice versa. A beginner would find it easier to do short but more frequent sessions whereas an advanced practitioner may prefer to do longer sessions. For instance, monks of certain schools who have to be qualified to preside over a major Tantric ceremony must have completed certain serviceable retreats [las-rung bsnyen-pa] doing three sessions in most retreats so as to finish the number of mantras as quickly as possible.

[408] In this context "30th" only refers to the 30th of the lunar month which means the new moon, Tib. gnam-gang.

[409] The flower of the sky [nam-mkha'i me-tog] is generally used as an example of something non-existent or impossible in the Buddhist terminology. In this context it is referring to the aura or

halo of light reflected in the sky around one's head.

410 Of the three main long-life deities [tshe-lha rnams-gsum] in the Vajrayana pantheon, life prolonging rituals are mainly performed through the medium of White Tara or Amitayus. One can either receive the same number of the initiations of Amitayus as one's own age from a qualified Lama or have rituals of long life deities performed on one's behalf. If one is initiated and familiar with the practices, it is better still for oneself to do the Sadhana in a short retreat format. Most Tibetan practitioners do an annual long life retreat whether or not there are any signs of death approaching to avert untimely death.

411 Tsha-tshas are clay votive miniature stupas representing the reliquary of the enlightened mind of the Buddha. They are made by using a metal cast while reciting prayers and are later placed near bigger stupas or monasteries so that many devotees can pay homage and circumambulate them in order to accumulate virtue. A few consecrated grains are also placed inside each of the tsha-tshas as they are made even though all of them could be consecrated together during the installation ceremony.

412 This includes releasing caged animals who are suffering from torture and lack of freedom by purchasing them from fishermen, hunters or duck shooters. This has to be done with the motivation to reduce the pain of the animals rather than for one's own quick recovery from sickness alone. While these are some of the prescribed practices to avert death, the real benefit does not accrue from the acts but from the quality of the motivation.

413 For details on srog-rtsol or Pranayama breathing exercises, see the Chapter on the Corresponding Practices of the Secret Initiation.

414 The seven-fold prayer can be considered like the backbone of

Buddhist practices and ceremonies. They are: paying homage, making offerings, confession of mis-deeds, rejoicing in the virtue of others, requesting to turn the wheel of the Dharma, requesting not to pass away into Nirvana and dedication of the merits. This is according to the Sutra tradition stated in bzang-spyod smon-lam.

[415] An accomplished Tantric practitioner.

[416] Given during the Vairocana name initiation (rnam-par snang-mdzad ming-gi dbang), the 'secret name' (gsang-ming) is supposedly named after the Tathagata family upon whom one's flower fell during the inner admission to the Mandala. Each disciple is given a secret name which they should not disclose to anybody but must remember at the specified times. Beside the specified times, disciples should also remember it during their daily Sadhana practice. However, in certain traditions, only one name is given to all the participants which does not appear to serve the purpose of the secret name.

[417] Dkon-mchog lhun-'grup explains its meaning as follows: The blessing of oneself done through the transcendental wisdom of self-arising on the basis of one's own physical Candali and by not relying upon an external consort is called "the process of self-blessing". See SLLS, Vol XXIV, Title No. 157, f. 72/B 2-3.

[418] Dkon-mchog lhun-'grup explains the obstacles associated with sickness, old-age and even death. Ibid f. 73/A 2.

[419] This refers to the Yoga of Mandala offering in order to accumulate merit and the Yoga of the One Hundred syllable Mantra (of Vajrasattva) in order to purify negativities.

[420] The twenty physical trainings (Yantra Yogas) are the medium length of physical trainings. See lam -'bras pod-ser for the elaborate Yantra Yoga practices known as the Thirty Two Enlightened Activities [phrin -las so-gnyis].

421 *Mtshan-bcas kyi dge-sbyor* refers to ritual orientated practices which have distinctive signs or symbols associated with the way in which the ritual has to be performed.

422 Sit in a tight cross-legged Vajrasana posture so that the essential point of the downward pushing (air) will enter into the central vein. Place the hands together in the meditative posture of equilibrium below the navel so that the essential point of the equally abiding (air) will enter into the central vein. Keep one's vertebrae straight just like silver coins placed one above another so that the essential point of the life-holding (air) will enter into the central vein. Bend one's neck just as the bend of a crane's neck so that the essential point of the upward flowing air will enter into the central vein. Focus one's eyes onto the tip of the nose so that the essential point of the all-pervasive (air) will enter into the central vein. Touch one's tongue onto the palate so that all of their essential points will have the vibrant strength of the central vein. Without touching the teeth and parting the lips, breathe gently while raising one's upper torso. Their significance can be elaborated further.

The significance of the 'Vajrasana', the cross-legged posture: It is the sitting posture of the conquest of the four external maras; it is the sitting posture of the lack of inner obstacles; it is the sitting posture of the entering of the four secret Samsaric veins into the central vein; it is the sitting posture of the ultimate non-duality of subjectivity and objectivity and it is the sitting posture of ultimate Enlightenment.

The significance of placing the hands together in the meditative posture of equilibrium below the navel: signifies the blossoming of the youthful utpala of the central vein; the resounding of the sound of Hum of rgod ma kha (a vein) and also igniting the fire of Brahma. The significance of the touching of the tips of the thumbs is for the purpose of focusing single-pointed concentration, signifies conquering the three realms of existence and dominating other people's perceptions.

The significance of keeping the vertebrae straight: Through the straightening of the body, the veins become straight; through the straightening of the veins, the elements become straight and through the straightening of the elements, the airs become straight. With the instructions of these four straight things, it is the essential point of guiding the vital airs into their natural locations; it is the essential point of dispelling the faulty and dead airs and it is the essential point of remedying exhaustion and conflicting merging.

The significance of bending one's neck just like a crane's is for the purpose of cutting the doorway and precipices of air; for the purpose of the pressing down of the Adam's apple with one's chin; for the purpose of perfect suppression of upper air and for the significance of developing the meditative concentration of non-thought.

The significance of focusing the eyes on the tip of the nose is for the purpose of abandoning depression and discursive thoughts concerning the objects of meditation; for the purpose of enhancing the clarity of awareness; for the purpose of equalising the inner elements and for the significance of inducing the proper creativity of the mind.

The significance of touching the tongue to the palate is for the purpose of milking the cow of the upper palate; for the purpose of restoring the elements of the Yogi; for the purpose of sanctifying and extracting the essence of both the physical body and its life-span and for the significance of comforting the tongue by suppressing its air.

If one wishes to squat, then place one's buttocks and the two legs equally on the ground just as one places a tripod. It is improper to place the (entire) weight (of the body) on one of them. Embrace one's two hands outside the legs in the manner of using them as a meditation belt. All the other essential points of the body are as stated before. These also have to be adapted according to the season, age and health (of the practitioner). In autumn and spring, when the weather is mainly warm, humid or hot, those who are aged and have illnesses of blood and bile should mainly sit cross-legged. In summer and winter, those who are young and mainly have illnesses of cold and phlegm should squat whenever it is cold. In this way, one's physical posture is similar to the foundation for constructing a building as it is from the essential point of a comfortable body that there will be sound breathing which in turn will enable to focus the mind. This will automatically generate meditative concentration. See SLLS, Vol. XXIV, Title No. 157, ff., 74/A- 4 - 75/A- 2.

423 The text gives 'The main meditative concentration' (bsam-gtan gyi dngos-gzhi) but here I have included 'The Actual Stages of the Teaching' (dngos-gzhi'i khrid-kyi rim-pa) to be consistent with the listing shown above.

424 As the author does not enlist the above three important sub-sections and does not provide this sub-heading but gives the two sub-headings below, we have included them here according to Dkon-mchog lhun-'grub's text. See SLLS, Vol. XXIV, Title No. 157, f. 75/B-3 & 4.

425 "Srog-rtsol" generally refers to Pranayama but it will be a mistake to render here into Pranayama as in this tradition "srog" (Prana), life, refers to the left nostril and "rtsol-ba" (Ayama), effort, refers to the right nostril.

426 A standing Yoga position doing the splits.

427 The sixteen vowels are: *a a i i u u r r l l e ai o au am a*

428 The consonants are: *ka kha ga gha na ca cha ja jha ña ta tha da dha na ta tha da dha na pa pha ba bha ma ya ra la va sa sa*

429 These are: *ka kha ga gha nga ca cha ja jha ña ta tha da dha na ta*

430 This is an obvious printing error. It should read 'Clarity' the characteristic of the mind, *[gsal-ba sems kyi mtshan-nyid]* instead of 'Secret', the characteristic of the mind, [gsang-ba sems-kyi mtshan-nyid]. I have confirmed this correction by verifying Dkon-mchog lhun-'gr*up's* work. See SLLS, Vol. XXIV, Title 157, f. 90/A- 3.

431 The four perfect awarenesses (Tib. so-so yang-dag par rig-pa bzhi, Skt. catvari pratisamvid) are: (1) The Perfect awareness of Dharma (Tib. cho so-sor yang-dag par rig-pa, Skt. dharmapratisamvid), (2) The Perfect awareness of meaning (Tib. don sos-sor yang-dag par rig-pa, Skt. arthapratisamvid), (3) The Perfect awareness of definitions (Tib. nges-tshig so-sor yang-dag par rig-pa, Skt. niruktipratisamvid) and (4) The Perfect Awareness of courage (Tib. spobs-pa so-sor yang dag-par rig-pa, Skt. pratibhanapratisamvid).

432 *om guru buddha bodhisattva saparivara ratna mandala puja megha samudra spharana samaye ah hum*

433 The blessing of the space and secret organs together with their mantras are given in the medium length Hevajra Sadhana as follows: The consort's space vanishes, and from the state of emptiness (arises) an Ah. From the Ah (arises) a red lotus with eight petals and the centre marked with Ah. *om padma sukhadhara maharaga sukhananda caturananda bhaga visva hum hum hum karyam kurusvame*

The father's secret organ vanishes and from the state of emptiness (arises) a Hum. From the Hum (arises) a blue Vajra with five prongs, and the centre marked with Hum. *om vajra mahadvesa caturananda dayakah khagamukha ekarasonatha hum hum hum karyam kurusvame*

434 The application of three-fold perceptions are: (1) perception

of the deity, (2) perception of the mantra and (3) perception of the Dharma. See SLLS, Vol. X, (Tha), Title No. 53, f. 60/B-3.

435 Tib. kha-sbyor bzhi'i gdams-ngag.

436 See f. 51/A.

437 See ff. 48/A - 49/A.

438 Although the wisdom consort is concerned here rather than action consort, *Dge-'dun chos-'phel* gives a detailed description on the lotus family, Tib. pad-ma-can, Skt. padmavati (padmini) which is highly praised as the action consort.

The lotus family is the excellent type of woman. She is beautiful, smiling, slim and has a radiant white form with a colour of swans devoid of any moles and marks. She is endowed with dark, bright and extremely long hairs and has the blinking eyes of a frightened deer. She has small nostrils but thick eye-brows. She is fond of clean garments and simple foods and wears simple ornaments such as flowers. Full of love, she is indeed devoted to all deeds that are virtuous. She desires no man other than her own husband. She has soft and big breasts and the depth of her womb is about six fingers width. Since the aroma of a lotus permeates from her menses she is known as 'lotus family'. See dge-'dun chos-'phel, *'dod pa'i bstan bcos*, p. 10. Published by Tibetan Cultural Printing Press, Dharamsala, Distt. Kangra, H. P. India, 1983.

439 This refers to the Indian cuckoo frequently alluded to in Hindu and Buddhist poetry for its musical cry.

440 See the above section on 'The stable practice in conjunction with four cakras'.

441 This work which I have quoted throughout this book was written in 1552, the Year of Water Male Mouse (*chu-pho byi-ba'i lo*).

Made in the USA
Lexington, KY
08 July 2019